THE
SPA
BOOK

THE SPA BOOK

A Guide to
The Top 101 Resorts
in America

Judith Brode Hirsch

A Perigee Book

Perigee Books
are published by
The Putnam Publishing Group
200 Madison Avenue
New York, NY 10016

Since they did not personally visit each one of the spas, health resorts, and
facilities included in this book, the author and publisher do not necessarily en-
dorse these establishments nor do they accept responsibility for errors in description, although they have done their best to provide the most complete and
up-to-date information. Please be aware that the phone numbers of these spas
change frequently, so you should be prepared to double-check them.

Library of Congress Cataloging-in-Publication Data

Hirsch, Judith B.
    The spa book: a guide to the top 101 resorts in America / Judith
  Brode Hirsch.

        p. cm.
      Includes indexes.
      ISBN 0-399-51491-0 (pbk.)
      1. Health resorts, watering places, etc.—United States—
Directories. I. Title.
RA805.H57   1988
613'.122'0973—dc19   88-25518

Printed in the United States of America

1 2 3 4 5 6 7 8 9 10

Acknowledgments

First and foremost, I want to thank my husband, Howard, whose generous support and encouragement have seen me through this writing endeavor. I'm also grateful to my children, Laurie and Ronald, whom I love "in spite and despite," who unwittingly served as guinea pigs, and who will never eat chicken again. And to my Dad, George Brode, Sr., who, busy as he is, always finds time to clip out and send me the latest research articles.

I am particularly indebted to Jean Sander, Mary Kay Rosteck, Mary Ann Zierak, and Nancy Tieszen, my researchers, who became dear friends as we explored together the fascinating world of publishing. And to Ruth Duskin Feldman, whose assistance in producing the narrative was invaluable.

Special thanks to my editor, Lindley Boegehold, whose enthusiasm and superior editorial skills were essential ingredients in the shaping of this book. And thanks, too, to Gene and Erika DeRoin, editors of Bookcrafters, Inc., whose gentle guidance and expertise made this seemingly impossible dream a reality.

Thanks are also due to those supportive women, all authors in their own rights: Annie Moldafsky, Sandra Pesman, and Susan Hirsch Schwartz. Thanks, too, to the following individuals whose generosity and professional support was most appreciated: Dominick Abel, my literary agent, Lionel Corbett, Carol DeChant, Steve Durchslag, Howard Dubin, Lucianne Goldberg, Sheldon Liebman, David Moscow, Ernest Rosemont, and Nancy Silberman.

Finally, I want to acknowledge some dear friends who have been so understanding during this artistic retreat period: George Brode, Jr., Robert Fuchs, Antonieta Lino, Alfred London, Nancy and Jim Lurie, Celia Rice, Josephine Sloan, Ms. Henry Sun, and Lois Weissman.

Without the encouragement and support of these people this book would not have been born.

To all the diet health facilities
that help keep us slim, fit,
and feeling good about ourselves!

Contents

1
INTRODUCTION TO THE SPA EXPERIENCE

Perhaps you want to take a vacation and lose weight at the same time. Or you are looking for a peaceful escape to a totally stress-free environment. Maybe you've just come through a nerve-racking period—a career change, perhaps, or graduate exams—and your figure has collapsed along with your spirits. An upcoming "significant birthday" has made you newly aware of the importance to your career of looking attractive and vigorous. You may even need cold-turkey withdrawal from whatever's ailing you: food, smoking, or a bad marriage.

Maybe you've heard that the coed spa scene is a great place to meet opposite-sex friends who share your interest in fitness. On the other hand, women-only spas can help you work on looking your best without being observed by men.

Once upon a time, and not long ago, a spa was marked by a cluster of elegant hotels surrounding a natural "watering place." Ladies weary of riding to hounds and waltzing all night would come to take the mineral waters and listen to the rippling springs and harp strings.

European spas still center around the concept of a watering place. But trust American ingenuity to come up with the notion that fresh air, sunshine, diet programs, health maintenance—even upscale entertainment—can be had with or without gushing spring waters. Add the American mania for slimming down and shaping up, and presto! a new hybrid, the American spa. (The word "spa" in this chapter covers all four categories of health resorts we have established for the directory listings: Spas Proper, Natural Health Retreats, Mineral Springs, and Medical Weight-Control Centers.) Today, you'll find the word "spa" attached to practically any resort that boasts an exercise room and a whirlpool. Business is booming, even if the only gushing comes from satisfied guests.

Whether you're primarily interested in weight or inch loss, a bit of pampering, or even fighting off a weight-related disease, there's a health getaway to fill the bill. It can be luxurious or spartan, frenetic or relaxed, urban or rural. It can be located in a desert, on a mountain, at the seaside, or even shipboard.

So where will you go? This book tells you. In the course of pursuing my mania for shedding pounds and inches, I've visited scores of health establishments in the last twenty years. What began as a means to personal fitness and fulfillment has evolved into a career of investigating and reporting on every conceivable type of weight-loss and fitness facility in North America. The Directory that has grown out of my work and play includes more than one hundred diet and health establishments—more than half of them affordably priced for working women and men. In the course of this pleasurable investigation, I spent many hours interviewing managers, directors, and satisfied or dissatisfied guests to determine the pleasures—and occasional pitfalls—each health resort has to offer.

WHAT TO TAKE ALONG

You can look the part of a fitness expert the very first time out if you loosen up and heed these few tips. Number one, be adventurous in your choice of outfits. Red leotards with purple tights are wonderful. Wear colors you normally wouldn't go near—electric hues you don't have anywhere else in your closet. Lighter colored or pastel tights are more "in" now, soft pink with wine or beige or gray leotards. Two-color outfits are more trendy than single-color. As for leotards, sleeveless are best because they don't chafe your arms. If the room is air conditioned, you can start with a top over it, then strip down as you warm up.

Leg-warmers are a must. Apart from looking great, they keep your leg muscles warm and help prevent cramps. Shorts and T-shirts are great for warm climates. Shorts are definitely more convenient when necessity calls.

Headbands brighten your outfit, and they keep perspiration from trickling down your forehead. Bring along a peaked tennis hat for sunning by the pool or jogging in the hot sun. Try to color coordinate it with your bathing suit for a dashing look. Tennis sweatbands on your wrists are handy for wiping your brow, as is a wild-colored towel worn around the neck.

Your wardrobe needs will be mostly determined by the type of facility you're visiting, its location, and the time of year you go. At the Golden Door all you need is underwear and a toothbrush! They provide everything else. If you're headed for La Costa with its swinging bar, tuck in a pair of wool gabardine pants and a silk shirt. For early morning walks in the fall, winter, or spring, bring a pair of gloves and a stocking cap that covers your ears. In most cases you can let your own good judgment and the Directory information be your guide.

Now for a few specifics. I have classified the following items in two categories: Absolute Essentials and Nice to Have.

ABSOLUTE ESSENTIALS

A jogging outfit. The best is one with zippered pockets to carry change for phone calls or Perrier, your schedule, or your watch. If you can't find a woman's suit with zippered pockets, consider buying a man's in a small size or whatever fits you.

Good shoes for jogging or walking.

Supportive bra for those who need one.

Wool or double-thick tennis socks can save your feet some pain.

Liquid detergent for laundry items.

Large, soft tote bag with shoulder straps. Use it to carry around clothing changes. Get one with an inside zippered compartment to hold your watch and loose change while you're massaging or swimming. (You shouldn't have to run around a health haven with a pocketbook!) Dark colors are most practical for dragging around at the pool or tennis court. (At one spa my room was in a beautiful, private area far from the activity centers. Luckily, I'd brought my tote bag so I could stay out the whole day without running back to my room.)

Heavy, warm sweater if headed for mountain areas that are cool in the mornings and at night (such as Ixtapan, Canyon Ranch, and The Golden Door). Be advised that all California spas fall into the cool mornings and evenings category.

Safety pins are a necessity for pinning your schedule to warm-up jacket or leotard.

NICE TO HAVE

See-through plastic change purse to house your safety pins, lip balm, Band-Aids, and other frequently used items.

Pony-tail holders if you have long hair. Pull your hair all the way into a topknot so your bun won't dig into your head when you're exercising on your back!

Facial moisturizer.

Aspercreme®, a nonsmelly cream containing aspirin that is a wonder for arthritis as well as exercise aches.

Your own electric hot pot, herbal tea, and Hauser broth (chock full of vitamins). Most spas provide early morning coffee or tea in the rooms where you assemble for your morning walk, but I can't wait that long.

Sturdy, slip-on scuffs. (Better be sure they're sturdy at places like Rancho La Puerta, where the roads are dusty and rough.) You'll always be slipping in and out of your slippers—between classes, at the tennis courts, in and out of treatment area. Some spas provide white plastic scuffs, but your own will always be more comfy.

Reading material. Most establishments have meager libraries, so bring your own.

Travel alarm clock. It's nice not to have to depend on anyone else for a morning wake-up call or the dinner gong.

Hooded nylon parkas and plastic/rubber tote boots to wear over jogging shoes in case of rain.

HOW TO USE THIS BOOK

Embarking on your own health happening is as simple as 1, 2, 3:

1. Select the place, using the Directory listings.
2. Get ready.
3. Go!

The key step is the first one: choosing the health facility that's best for you.

To illustrate the importance of making the right selection, let me tell you about a woman who put on some weight after giving up smoking and wanted to take it off fast. She chose the expensive and notoriously tough Ashram vegetarian retreat in Calabasas, California. (Barbra Streisand refers to it as "the boot camp"; Jane Fonda calls it "special.")

After a week of daily three-mile hikes, plunges into an ice-cold pond, rigorous calisthenics, shared bathrooms, and a spartan diet, this lady was climbing the walls. She longed for a taste of salt; she was angry at herself for biting off more than she cared to chew; she was dying for a cigarette! She left Ashram in a negative frame of mind and regained her lost weight quickly.

The lesson is that not every health spot is ideal for every health seeker. With the help of this guide, you will find out enough about the establishments you're considering to decide realistically on the best place to spend your time and money based on your specific needs.

The establishments you'll find in the Directory sections are for basically healthy people who wish to lose weight, keep fit, and prevent major health problems from occurring by trying to change their daily life-style. I have also included medical weight-control centers because most (not all) offer preventive programs as well as treatment. Those listed require patients to be self-sufficient and ambulatory.

The book is broken down into four main categories of health establishments—Spas Proper, Natural Health Retreats, Mineral Springs, and Medical Weight-Control Centers. Although they're all aiming at the same goals—good health, fitness, and weight control—each category attracts a particular kind of clientele. The majority of guests at most spas are women; natural health retreats appeal to both men and women, young and old. I've found that health-trekking usually works best for couples when it's the husband who wants to lose weight and the wife goes along for the ride. (The good old double standard.)

Because prices change so rapidly, I found it simpler to classify facilities as "affordable," "moderate," and "expensive." Costs, in general, are quoted for a 7-day stay, double occupancy, in high season, meals included. "Affordable" ranges up to $1,000 weekly. "Moderate" means $1,000 to $1,700; "expensive," $1,700 to sky's-the-limit.

Directory entries also cover important indicators of whether you'll be happy and "fit in" at particular spots. Indicators include: the physical environment (are you an outdoor or indoor type?); guest population (are you happier exercising in mixed or singlesex spas?); dinner dress code (do you prefer diamonds or sweatsuits at dinner?); meal service (is there a hostess to help you "mix" during those first meals?); accommodations (do you mind sharing a bath?); house rules (is it all right with you if smoking is permitted only in the solarium?). All these and other elements will make a difference in your comfort level during a visit, and it's important to consider them before you make reservations.

Accommodations are important emotional-comfort indicators. They tend to vary widely. Many natural health retreats have small rooms, and four or five guests share a bath. Rancho La Puerta in Mexico has no telephones in the rooms, and the three main house phones are usually on the fritz. So if you have children or need to be reached in an emergency, that may not be the place for you. (Then again, inaccessibility may be your heart's desire!) Lack of air conditioning may not matter in some climes, but on a hot, dry summer day in Mexico, when the sun rises early and sets late, you might have to tumble out of bed at dawn and stay away from your room until 7:00 P.M.

For women traveling alone, it's often pleasant to find hostesses at meal service times. They seat you so you don't have to face that first evening by yourself. You may also want to know whether room service is available so you can be completely private, which can be very relaxing.

Women-only spas tend to be more expensive, but they allow you more freedom in terms of makeup and dress. With no men around the pool, you needn't care if your tank suit shows your nipples—or ripples.

Not to ignore male readers, there are men-only weeks at some of the posh spas while other spas offer men a segregated male environment during the day.

The places listed in the Directory are suitable for people with a fairly high modesty quotient. You won't find coed skinny-dipping, and you won't need to worry about exposing too much too soon. Of course, you can always take two towels into the solarium instead of one!

I hope this book will prepare you for your adventure. It will tell you how to select the place that's right for you and what to expect when you get there. Guidelines have been included to help you de-cide whether the atmosphere, approach, and ambience suit your needs, taste, purse, and emotional comfort zone.

I'll also reveal my personal take-it-off secrets, inside stories of health-hoppers, favorite recipes, spa menus, activity schedules, and much more. My own trips have been a journey inward as well. Along with the excess fat, I've lost self-consciousness, gained many friends, and gotten in touch with myself. May your experiences be equally rewarding.

ONE

SPAS PROPER

2
FIRST THINGS FIRST

My first day at any spa, I take a familiarization tour to get acquainted with my surroundings and fellow spa-goers. The women's nude-bathing areas in the solarium can be an easy place to strike up a conversation with a stranger; it's harder to wear a mask when you've got nothing else on. Even if you've never sunbathed *au naturel*, you'll soon get used to the idea and love it. Start out wrapped in as many towels as you like. Then, as you begin feeling overheated from the baking sun, gradually uncover as much of yourself as you wish. You'd be surprised at how quickly you'll begin to take for granted the sight of other nude bodies and feel comfortable joining them.

The whirlpool is another friendly place, where the warm jets relax your body and your defenses. Here, the dress code (or the "no-dress" code) is flexible. Some women prefer wearing leotards while others, like me, who are no longer shy in a "women-only" environment, blithely take off their robes and march in.

Cozy saunas are also natural conversation dens. Or try the steam room, where an attendant will give you ice to apply to your forehead or to chew on. When both you and your neighbor have your mouths full, it's easy to break the ice.

SCHEDULING HINTS

Your first few days at any spa can be hectic. Scheduling can be especially complicated at the large, "permissive" resorts. Keep your schedule with you at all times. The smaller women's spas provide an individual counselor to help you.

For a first-timer, it's probably simplest to take the package plan of exercise classes, massages, herbal wraps, etc. Spa veterans might be better off going à la carte, paying only for treatments and classes they want, plus the entry fee to the spa building. I've saved as much as $126 on a four-night stay.

For example, most of the large resorts allow only three or four exercise classes daily. I prefer more. Some give you half-hour massages. To me, that's just a tickle. (The posh women's spas give you forty-five minutes.) Some spa packages offer daily facials. If you're allergic, as I am, and on a package plan, see if a substitute treatment is available (manicure or hair-set, for instance). If you're on a package plan, you'll meet with a staff member at the outset to review the items included and discuss your schedule. Ask for an orientation tour to acquaint yourself with the facilities, and feel free to ask any questions.

At the large resorts, all spa facilities must be reserved through the appointment desk. In a busy spa it's important to think ahead (unless you're a man, in which case there is less competition for choice appointments). In some of the smaller spas, you can sign up twenty-four hours in advance. Try calling a day or two before your arrival to set up your first day's schedule. If you like an afternoon massage, try to get to the appointment desk early, and sign up for as many days in advance as they'll let you.

TREAT YOURSELF RIGHT

They say experience is the best teacher. All the same, here are some warnings I wish someone had given me beforehand.

Don't overdo exercising or dieting in your enthusiasm to get quick results. If your muscles begin to ache, don't try to be heroic. Pace yourself.

A good massage combats fatigue, relieves tension, promotes circulation, and removes toxins. The experts at Canyon Ranch suggest that you first spend ten minutes in the steamroom or whirlpool to loosen up; then follow the massage with a herbal wrap or bath.

A routine that alternates hot and cold treatments both stimulates and relaxes the muscles. First the whirlpool, then a cold shower or plunge in the pool. While all nerve endings are tingling, it's on to the steam treatment, sauna, or herbal wrap and, finally, the massage.

A massage can be a bit disconcerting the first time if you're inclined to be self-conscious. It will feel so good that you'll soon relax, but the therapist should always cover your private areas with a sheet.

A note to claustrophobics: if you have the slightest tendency toward claustrophobia, there are a number of confining situations that you might encounter at a spa. For instance, always try the handle inside your steam cabinet to be sure you can let yourself out if you're left unattended. Again, when I'm getting an herbal wrap treatment, I always have the attendant leave my arms outside so I can unwrap myself and flee if need be; or I tell her that ten minutes will be as long as I wish to be unattended, thank you.

RESORT, OR "DO-YOUR-OWN-THING" SPAS

With so many different types of people on the spa scene seeking so many different objectives, it's not surprising that there are spas to meet every need. For simplification, I have created three spa classifications, which I term resort, structured, and beauty spas. Let's talk about resort spas first.

At first glance, these "large recharge" establishments look like any other first-class resort. The spa is only one part of a huge complex, with sprawling acres of tennis courts, racquetball courts, golf courses, running tracks, diet lectures, and dancing after dark. You sign up for spa time just as you would for a tennis lesson or horseback riding.

The major distinction of a resort spa is a separate dining room or separate dining area for spa guests. This makes it much easier to stick to low-calorie meals and nonalcoholic beverages. However, dietary temptations are all around, especially if you choose to dine in the regular dining room with someone who is not on the low-calorie plan. After all, there is a limit to how often you can look at a marvelous dessert and say no.

Structured places offer all the spa amenities: sauna, whirlpool, steam room, and usually both indoor and outdoor pools. There are separate men's and women's pavilions for massage and other treatments. The regularly scheduled exercise classes usually are coed. They're big on beauty. The pampering and beauty treatments aren't far short of the kinds of indulgence that made life pleasant for Cleopatra, and the sports facilities probably would entice Marc Antony. Outstanding examples of resort facilities include The Spa at Palm-Aire, La Costa, Olympia Village, Doral Saturnia, Bonaventure, and Marriott's Desert Springs Resort and Spa.

Resort spas are usually more dressy than structured spas. Before going to Palm-Aire, I asked if I could wear jogging outfits to dinner and was told, "Yes, of course—nice jogging outfits." Luckily, I brought a pair of black linen pants. I wore them every evening; a "nice" jogging outfit just wouldn't have cut it.

STRUCTURED SPAS: DOING IT *THEIR* WAY

The structured spa has a more particular view of what leads to health, happiness, beauty, or a combination of the above. If you want to partake, you're expected to abide by the rules. These are total immersion spas: the entire facility is geared to weight loss and a complete health environment. Everyone is on a diet program, and almost everyone is there for the same reasons: to reduce, firm up, and have fun doing it, so you have a built-in support group. The food is low in fat and cholesterol, and low- or no-salt.

Some structured spas, such as the Golden Door, are exclusively or primarily for women; others, such as Canyon Ranch and The Palms at Palm Springs, California, are coed. Most are highly fitness-oriented: exercise classes hourly, from beginners to advanced. Massage and other pampering treatments run the gamut from wonderful to sublime. Spas that are heavily into fitness (Canyon Ranch, The Palms at Palm Springs, and The Oaks at Ojai) offer an unlimited choice of exercise classes as part of your basic fee, with pampering treatments extra.

Unlike the resort spas, the structured spa uses practically every moment to inculcate attitudes geared to better health. Thus, your evening programs are most likely to be lectures—but fascinating ones that will help inform you about a healthy life-style outside the spa.

House rules: most of these spas do not allow smoking in their main buildings. If you must light up, you'll have to do it outside (under a bush?) or in the solarium. No liquor is served on the premises; Perrier is *the* drink. However, there's no one to stop you from taking a ride or a jog to a four-star restaurant. You are your own keeper of the key.

If the discipline sounds chafing, remember that there are compensating fringe benefits. You'll get that sense of serene wellbeing that comes when you know someone is taking care of you. For a week or two, spa personnel schedule your activities and your goals and give you a definite means to accomplish them. They soothe your brow. They put food in front of you.

Sound familiar? It should. It's what people did for you when you were very young. Structured spas offer people leading highly stressful lives the chance to be a child again, if only for a few hundred hours. The pampering and privacy also give you the opportunity to discover yourself as you are—a beautiful human being.

BEAUTY SPAS: THE FAIRY GODMOTHER STRIKES AGAIN

The name means exactly what it says. Beauty is the be-all and end-all of the time you spend at one of these spas. Not that facials and massages are the only activities on the agenda. Far from it; there are exercise classes a-plenty. Usually, though, the programs are geared toward slower body toning. Workouts (a somewhat exaggerated term for the easygoing fitness sessions one finds at most beauty spas) are ordinarily in the morning. That leaves afternoons free for treatments and pampering. The entire atmosphere contributes to that special glow you take home with you.

Since this is the "Beauty Spa" section, it's as good a time as any to discuss the types of beauty treatments you can expect at spas, beauty and otherwise. Most spas offer a variety of treatments and techniques. Here are a few that may be unfamiliar to first-time spagoers.

Facial massages tone up the muscles of the face and stimulate the pores. Regular facials can't make wrinkles go away, but they can help stop them from getting worse. The procedure is the same almost everywhere. First, the aesthetician wraps your hair in a towel. Then she cleans your skin with a heavy-duty cream, which she removes gently with a sponge or a cotton pad. The therapist massages your face, moving from the base of your neck all the way up to your ears. She removes excess cream with a skin freshener. Most therapists give a neck and shoulder massage along with the facial.

At this point, you may opt for a facial mask. Most spas offer several types, such as a granular, honey-almond mixture or a mineral-clay type. The mask is left on for ten minutes while you listen to music in a darkened room. The therapist removes the mask, first with hot water, then with cold. After that, she tidies up your eyebrows with a tweezer and applies moisturizer for the finishing touch. It's heavenly!

For a complete body cleansing, you may want to try a *loofah scrub*, which removes dry and scaly skin. First a lotion made up of salts and oils is rubbed into your body. Then you are completely wrapped in hot sheets that have been doused with aromatic herbs and spices. Finally, you wash off these sweetsmelling scents in a Swiss shower (varying water temperatures and pressures), all of which leaves you relaxed, refreshed, and feeling more beautiful than ever.

A heated *herbal wrap* helps to remove the toxins from your body. After sipping mint tea, you are swathed in sheets saturated with a combination of herbs; then you're covered with blankets for additional insulation. Finally, you are left to sleep or relax in a darkened room for fifteen to thirty minutes, usually to the accompaniment of taped music or nature sounds. When the wraps come off, you feel physically and psychologically transformed.

Some spas offer a one-hour *cellulite wrap*, complete with contouring cream, cellophane suit, and massage. A facial with this is optional.

By now you should have a fairly good idea of what to expect when you go to a Spa Proper. Read on to find out exactly which one suits you best.

Criteria for designating a spa as "resort" are (1) the spa is just one element of a large resort-hotel complex or institutional setting, (2) dieters and nondieters can be accommodated at the same dining table, and (3) the environment is generally rule-free, with many options. There is usually a lounge serving alcohol on the premises.

Unless otherwise specified, cost is based on a one-week stay (high season), double occupancy, including tax, gratuities, and meals. An "affordable" spa costs up to $1,000 per week; a "moderate" one ranges from $1,000 to $1,700; "expensive" spas cost more than $1,700 per week.

Best Buys are indicated by an asterisk.

Resort spas are listed in the Directory.

3
SPAS PROPER: DIRECTORY

RESORT SPAS—WHY, WHERE, AND HOW MUCH

* AURORA HOUSE SPA
35 E. Garfield Road
Aurora, OH 44202
216-562-9171

A spa set within the framework of a renovated eighteenth-century house, furnished with lovely antiques. Open year-round.

RATES: Expensive. American Express, MasterCard, Visa.

LOCATION AND TRANSPORTATION: Aurora House is 20 miles southeast of Cleveland and 20 miles northeast of Akron. Complimentary transportation is provided from Cleveland airport.

EMPHASIS/PHILOSOPHY: The focus here is on beauty, pampering, and relaxing. Weight loss goal is 6–8 pounds weekly average.

DIET PROGRAM: 600–850 calories per day. Well-balanced, portion-controlled meals, featuring fish, chicken, and veal and lots of fresh fruits and vegetables. No salt or sugar used in preparation. Desserts consist of fruit sorbets, poached fresh fruit, or mousses. A vegetarian regimen is available, as are 750- and 1200-calorie-per-day programs. Calorie count is on the menu. Nondieters can get nouvelle cuisine and gourmet meals. Wine is available with dinner.

GUEST POPULATION: Coed. 30 guests. Not all guests are on a diet. "Lots of men come here for relaxation," says Michelle, one of the activity coordinators.

PACKAGES AND MINIMUM STAYS: There are 1-day/1-night and 3-day/2-night programs plus a Six-Day Package: in on Sunday after 2:00, out on Saturday after lunch.

MEAL SERVICE: No separate dining room for diet spa guests. There is table service for all meals in one of five charming dining rooms. A hostess is available to seat you.

DRESS CODE: A jogging outfit is perfect on weeknights. However, on weekends, men are required to wear jackets. The spa provides warmup suits and robes for guests during the day.

ACCOMMODATIONS: Lovely Victorian-style rooms and furnishings, with all the modern conveniences.

HOUSE RULES: Smoking only in the lounge area.

PHYSICAL FACILITIES: Whirlpool; sauna; Swedish steam cabinet; environmental habitat (cycle of sun, steam, warm breeze, rain); exercise rooms; massage rooms; indoor and outdoor swimming pools; golf course; beauty salon; and boutique. Spa area is open until 6:00 most evenings, until 9:00 on Tuesday and Thursday nights for any of your treatments.

ACTIVITIES: TREATMENTS, AND PROGRAMS: The 6-day package includes daily Dynastic exercise sessions; exercise workouts ⌐n Nautilus equipment; water exercise; yoga; steam bath; sauna; whirlpool; half-hour body massage; and environmental habitat. Beauty treatments include three facial treatments during the week, plus one each of the following during your stay: herbal wrap, cellulite wrap, thalassotherapy, salt glow loofah scrub, reflexology massage, pedicure, manicure, hairstyle, and makeup application.

A Day at Aurora House

8:00	Breakfast
8:30	Walk/jog
9:30	Dynastic exercise class
10:30	Yoga, steam bath, or whirlpool
12:00	Lunch
1:00–4:00	Beauty treatments
6:00	Dinner
7:00	Evening lecture

OPTIONAL COSTS: Hair-salon treatments, lash tinting, face and body waxing, special nail and facial treatments.

NICE TO KNOW: Joanne Liuzzo, director of Aurora House, has more than twenty years' experience in the health and beauty industry, including training in yoga, exercise techniques, and gymnastics. Joanne has gathered antiques, furniture, lights, and accessories from all over the East Coast to add unique charm to Aurora House.

*BEST BUY AND WHY: This spa is a "Best Buy" because:
- An unusual number of treatments are included in the one-week package.
- You will receive sufficient beauty care and pampering to send you home relaxed and rejuvenated.

BADEN-BADEN HEALTH RESORT
611 El Camino Real
Carlsbad, CA 92008
619-931-1411

The spa is part of the Olympic Resort Hotel just down the road from the famous La Costa Spa. It is located between Southern California's beautiful mountains and famous beaches. Open year-round.

RATES: Moderate. Seven-day Spa Special, Sunday to Sunday, saves you up to 31 percent. One-day program available, or come in any day and spend as little or as much time as you like. American Express, MasterCard, Visa.

LOCATION AND TRANSPORTATION: Carlsbad is 45 minutes north of San Diego and 2 hours south of Los Angeles. Transportation available to and from the San Diego airport (approximate charge $30 each way).

EMPHASIS/PHILOSOPHY: This spa provides a combination of European pampering with American awareness of nutrition and fitness. Part of the Baden-Baden health philosophy is attention to individual schedules that will provide good nutrition, hydrotherapy, massage, and exercise. They also offer a full range of beauty services.

DIET PROGRAM: The spa uses locally grown fruits, vegetables, herbs, and fresh seafood selections, for 3 meals totaling 1,000 calories per day. No red meat served on spa plan. According to the spa's manager, Wolfgang Seitzer, gourmet health food is served in a manner that is highly appealing to the eye. A rose on your plate might be made out of strawberries, for example. There are two options for calorie counting. For those who want to lose weight, the "light track" selection on the menu is based on a 1,000 calorie per day limit. Guests wanting to maintain their weight may choose "fitness track" selections based on a higher caloric intake. Weight loss varies, of course, with each individual. Wolfgang says that it is not unusual to achieve a 4½-pound weight loss during one week's stay.

GUEST POPULATION: Baden-Baden is able to accommodate 20 guests who are entitled to the same amenities as the guests of the resort hotel. The program is coed.

PACKAGES AND MINIMUM STAYS: The program is extremely flexible, subject to availability, and no minimum stay is required.

MEAL SERVICE: Spa program participants use the same dining room as the Olympic Resort Hotel guests. There is a separate area in the dining room for spa plan participants, who receive special vouchers that are given to the waitress to indicate that they are on the spa meal plan. The dining room is open to the public.

DRESS CODE: Jogging outfits are acceptable for breakfast and lunch; however, dinner is more formal and requires at least dress slacks and a nice blouse. Some of the male guests might be wearing a tie and jacket. The spa provides terry robes, which can be worn throughout the day. The spa boutique sells T-shirts, swimsuits, and exercise clothes. Sometimes the Southern California evenings are cool, and Baden-Baden recommends that guests come prepared with a sweater or jacket.

ACCOMMODATIONS: Guests are housed in five separate villa-type buildings surrounding a courtyard built around the pool and interspersed with trees and flowers. Rooms have both queen- and king-sized beds, and suites are also available. The rooms are luxurious and spacious with color cable TV, air conditioning, and heaters in each room. The decor can be described as French contemporary, with soft blue colors creating a soothing effect.

HOUSE RULES: Alcoholic lounge on premises. Smoking is allowed everywhere except in the spa treatment area.

PHYSICAL FACILITIES: Two outdoor pools, one a 25-meter lap pool, and one a recreational pool with outdoor Jacuzzi; a pitch 'n putt golf course with water and sandtraps (the 27-hole golf course at nearby Whispering Palms Country Club is twenty minutes away); and 5 tennis courts. Indoor facilities include a fitness center with Nautilus equipment; separate locker rooms for men and women, each containing a sauna and a steamroom; one exercise room. Eleven rooms in the lower salon comprise the spa facility area and are used for beauty treatments as well as for exercise. A full-sized gymnasium is open to all guests.

ACTIVITIES, TREATMENTS, AND PROGRAMS: Before beginning any program, you will meet with Wolfgang Seitzer for a personal consultation to discuss what you would like to accomplish during your week's stay at Baden-Baden. Your blood pressure is checked and you fill out a health questionnaire. Based on this interview, Wolfgang will design a program geared to your individual needs, such as recommending the appropriate level exercise classes. According to Seitzer, the spa intends to have a physician on staff in the near future. Included in the spa package are: 7 to 9 exercise classes per day, including such activities as olympic aerobics (vigorous), aqua aerobics, body shaping, moderate aerobics, tae kwon do (martial arts) for adults and for youth, stretch and relax classes, and yoga. Treatments included in the one week program are 6 fifty-minute massages, given either deep Swedish style or underwater style (done in a bathtub with jets of warm water applied by the massage therapist); 2 facials; a body facial; manicure and pedicure; seven body wraps; shampoo and styling; and a makeup application. Once a week guests attend a lecture on nutrition given by a dietician.

Here's what a typical day's schedule may include:

7:00	Walk or run on the sandy beaches of the Pacific (guests are taken by van daily to the ocean, which is four miles away)
8:00	Breakfast
9:00	Aerobic exercise
10:30	Tea break
11:00	Hydrotherapy, herbal wrap, body brushing, or body facial
12:00	Manicure or pedicure
1:00	Luscious, low-calorie lunch
2:00	Aquatics (summer only), swimming, or rest
3:00	Facial or other beauty treatments
4:00	Swedish or other massage
5:00	Turkish steamroom or Finnish sauna
6:00	Lectures, nutrition classes
7:00	Dinner

OPTIONAL COSTS: Tennis instruction is available at an additional charge. Personal consultations with a nutritionist and a wide range of beauty services are also available for added fees.

JUDY'S COMMENT: A nice touch here is that no matter what your individual goal—be it general rejuvenation, weight loss, or attention to skin care—you come away feeling very special, relaxed, pampered, and fit.

BONAVENTURE RESORT AND SPA
250 Racquet Club Road
Fort Lauderdale, FL 33326
Inside Florida: 800-432-3063
Outside Florida: 800-327-8090
Local: 305-389-3300

Located on a lake in the Bonaventure Country Club resort community, the spa is part of the 1,250-acre Fort Lauderdale Intercontinental Hotel complex. Open year-round.

RATES: Expensive. Credit cards: American Express, MasterCard, Visa.

LOCATION AND TRANSPORTATION: Bonaventure is 25 minutes from Fort Lauderdale airport and 45 minutes from the Miami airport. Pickup from both airports is available.

EMPHASIS/PHILOSOPHY: The Bonaventure Spa describes itself as providing more than a vacation: "Our spa is planned, designed, staffed [110 people], and committed to one goal; Bringing back the joy of living and the natural health and fitness you were born for."

DIET PROGRAM: 900 calories per day. Extensive menu of well-rounded, all natural foods. No sodium is added, and fructose is the only sweetener used in recipes. Calorie count appears next to each item on the menu. The spa claims that no red meat is served—but, indeed, it was offered twice the week that I was there (my husband loved it!). Some of my favorite entrees are: Baked Flounder Stuffed with Crabmeat (240); Veal Do Paij in Cumin Sauce (225); and Maylasian Chicken with Toasted Coconut and Sesame Seeds (220).

GUEST POPULATION: Coed. 110 guests. Guests come in all sizes and for all reasons. The week I was there a young matron (size 4) came for toning so her clothes wouldn't pinch in the waist. Famous folks who've checked into the Bonaventure Spa include *Dynasty*'s Linda Evans, who has made it glamorous to be over 40, and movie star Barbara Rush. Separate facilities for men and women.

PACKAGES AND MINIMUM STAYS: "The Perfect Day;" 3-day Sampler; 4-day and 7-day Fitness Plans; and several other packages. Check in any day you wish.

MEAL SERVICE: Spa guests eat in a special section of the Garden Room (right next to regular diners), which is located just off the hotel's lobby. Unfortunately, you must pass the dessert carts for the regular diners (and the heavily laden buffet tables at lunch) to reach

Courtesy of Bonaventure Hotel and Spa

your diet table. Hostess will seat you for dinner. Each table has its own bottle of Evian mineral water. Nondieters must sit in the spa dining area if accompanying a spa-goer (the reverse will not be accommodated). Nondieters may order from the regular menu; however, neither bread, rolls, or alcoholic beverages will be served in the diet section. All spa meals must be taken either in your room or in the spa dining room. No serving in the treatment area or at the pool.

DRESS CODE: The spa furnishes you with warm-up suits, maroon leotards, shorts and T-shirts, tank suits, terry robe, and bath slippers, all color-coordinated in burgundy shades. Guests seem to enjoy dressing up for dinner. "Jackets are requested, not required." Take your cue from that.

ACCOMMODATIONS: The guest rooms are located in 9 four-story buildings facing the lake or golf course. Most spa guests stay in spa buildings number one and two because of their proximity to the spa itself. The room decor is delightfully tropical with touches of rattan and lovely watercolor paintings. Rooms are spacious, with two queen-size beds. Each room has a large dressing room and giant cable TV. Ample closet space. Nice bath touches, which were generously replenished each day, included Lancôme soaps in pretty cases and small

Courtesy of Bonaventure Hotel and Spa

plastic bottles of shampoo, bubble bath, and fabric wash. Wonderful!

HOUSE RULES: No smoking in spa building. Smokers sometimes meet in the solarium area to light up. This being a resort spa, be aware of the alcoholic lounge next to the dining room.

PHYSICAL FACILITIES: There are two complete and separate spa facilities for men and women. Each has a large outdoor exercise pool (with ample deck space), roomy solarium adjacent to the pool, and outdoor whirlpools. Each area contains exercise room, massage rooms (15), sauna, Turkish steam room, and hot- and cold-water plunge pools. In addition, there are 9 herbal-wrap rooms and a gym. Beauty shop for the ladies; men's section has barbershop. Boutique located in the spa lobby. The complex boasts two 18-hole championship golf courses, 23 tennis courts, 5 racquetball courts, riding stables, and a large convention center.

ACTIVITIES, TREATMENTS, AND PROGRAMS; The 7-day program consists of a medical screening upon checking in; personal consultation with registered dietician; unlimited fitness classes—some of which may include morning stretch and energize, water classes, three levels of aerobic classes, and weight training. Treatments included in the 7-day program are: 6 body massages (one-half hour each), 4 herbal wraps, 1 loofah body treatment, 4 whirlpool baths, 3 Kerstin facials, 1 makeup application, 1 shampoo and set, 1 manicure, and 1 pedicure. Evening programs consist of lectures on nutrition, discussions

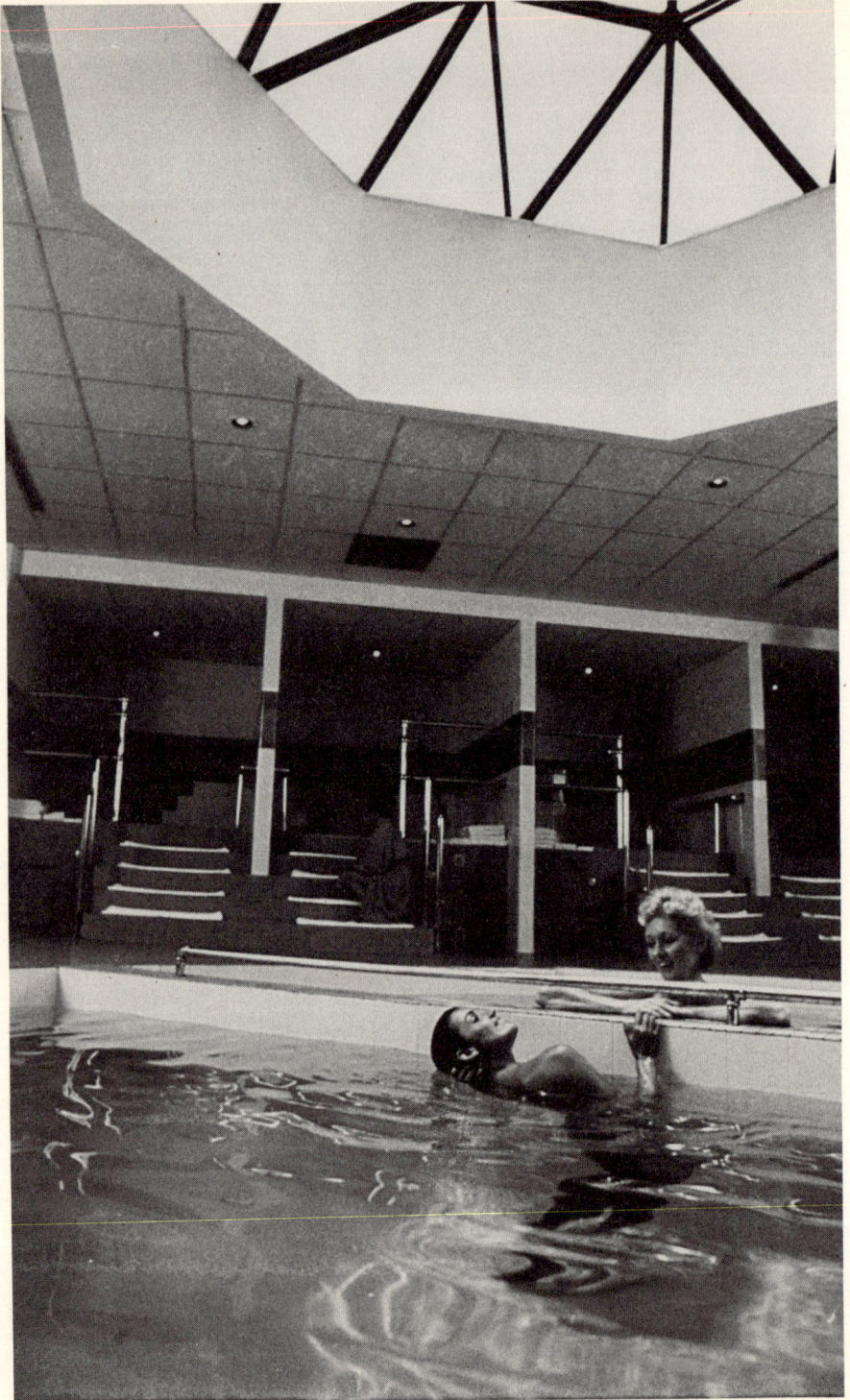

Courtesy of Bonaventure Hotel and Spa

on exercise, cooking demonstrations, fashion shows, bingo, card games—a potpourri of health, social, and cultural programs.

A Day at Bonaventure

7:00	Fitness walk
8:00	Fitness walk
8:00	Light workout (advanced)
9:00	Stretch and energize (beginner)
9:30	Total workout (intermediate-advanced)
	Water workout—(40 minutes) (beginners)
10:40	Low-impact aerobics I (beginner)
11:00	Waterobics (30 minutes) (beginner, intermediate)
11:15	Strictly aerobics (intermediate, advanced)
1:30	"Life-styles of the Fit and Beautiful" lecture
2:00	Advanced water (daily, 45 minutes)
2:20	Introduction to weights (beginner, intermediate)
	Low-impact aerobics II (beginner, intermediate)
3:00	Water workout (beginner, intermediate)
	Contour (beginner, intermediate)
	Motions (advanced)
3:40	Stretch and relax (beginner)
4:00	Ask the Trainer (coed)

OPTIONAL COSTS: Additional exercise classes or private class instruction, individualized fitness tape cassettes, fitness profile (medical evaluation with cardiovascular profile and weight/measurement chart, etc.), waxing treatments, and beauty salon services are available.

SPECIAL PACKAGES: All programs have reduced rates during the off season (May 12 to September 26). If you're in the neighborhood, "The Perfect Day" program offers a day of beauty treatments, unlimited fitness classes, and lunch for approximately $129 (high season) plus tax and gratuity. There's also an à la carte route. A $20 entrance fee ($10 with treatment) includes your locker, spa clothing, and use of all spa facilities. You can then purchase an array of beauty treatments on an item-by-item basis. Twenty-four hours' advance notice is requested for specific appointments.

NICE TO KNOW: Spa orientation tours are held twice daily, at 12:30 and 4:30. The 800 toll-free number will not connect you directly to the spa. Should you have any questions regarding spa programs, you may want to call 305-389-3300 and ask for the Spa Desk, but getting specific answers to questions has been like pulling teeth. Spa guests begin their fitness classes at 8:00, while hotel guests begin at 9:30. Anyone in the neighborhood can take the early morning walk/jog around the golf course; just meet in the hotel lobby at 7:00 A.M. One evening a week the spa bus takes guests to the Galleria shopping mall, which has stores such as Neiman Marcus and Saks.

JUDY'S COMMENT: This spa offers a wonderful opportunity for life-style reeducation. Complete medical attention is available at the distinguished Las Colinas Preventive Medicine Center. Guests can, with the help of the staff, design a highly individualized program. A full range of exercise classes is offered at all levels along with a large variety of sports activities. It is unusual that a facility of this magnitude also offers individual attention in every area.

THE CLIFF SPA AT SNOWBIRD
Snowbird, UT 84092
800-453-3000
801-742-2222, ext. 5900

The only spa in the continental United States in an alpine setting. The town of Snowbird is a skier's resort and summertime mountain-climbing community. Many come here for skiing and go to the spa on an à la carte basis. Ski and spa packages are your best bet. Open year-round.

RATES: Moderate. Credit card: American Express.

LOCATION AND TRANSPORTATION: The Cliff Spa is situated on 1,900 acres of snow country, at 8,000-feet altitude in the Wasatch National Forest. Persons with heart or respiratory conditions should take precautions to allow for altitude. Salt Lake City airport is 30 miles away, and bus, taxi, or shuttle service is available. Airport transfer is included in some spa packages.

EMPHASIS/PHILOSOPHY: This spa/resort combines skiing with the spa experience. The new 13-story Cliff Lodge houses patrons for the ultimate in a health-care vacation. The dream of Richard D. Bass, owner of Snowbird, is to integrate body, mind, and spirit through fun and relaxation. The summer activities emphasize mountain hiking, climbing, and general outdoor vigor, coupled with dance recitals, open air concerts, and lectures for a "total" person approach.

DIET PROGRAM: There is no professional dietician here, but the 1,200–1,500 calorie-per-day program is low-fat and low-cholesterol. Guests order from the spa menu and make their own choice whether or not to stick to the recommended calorie count. It is a fact that people will eat more at 8,000 feet and because of the sports activities will use more energy. The menu is portion-controlled. Chef Robert Sullivan has complete charge of all restaurants and menus. Average weight loss is 5–7 pounds, but that is mostly water. The idea is to reduce your intake permanently, but since no one is looking over your shoulder, it might be harder for some to adhere to this type of program.

GUEST POPULATION: Coed. 100 guests, about evenly divided between men and women. Separate locker facilities for men and women.

PACKAGES AND MINIMUM STAYS: There are 2-day/1-night, 3-day/2-night, 5-day/4-night, and 8-day/7-night packages. The spa is also open and available to resort guests on a per-day fee basis, currently $10 for use of facilities.

MEAL SERVICE: Five restaurants offer a choice of menus. Two, the Aerie and the Spa Cafe, offer spa menus, which are portion-controlled. A buffet is offered at breakfast, policy being that you're an adult and control your own appetite. A hostess will seat you at the more elegantly casual dinner restaurants, and tables are graced with fresh flowers and fine china. This is a very casual, relaxing place and the restaurants and meal service reflect that.

DRESS CODE: Jogging outfits are acceptable all day long, although some might wish to dress up for dinner at the more formal restaurants. Mountain casual is in vogue here. Pack at least two sets of leotards/tights or shorts/T-shirts, aerobic shoes and socks, swimsuit, walking or hiking shoes, bathrobe, cover-up, and thongs. If you are a skier, bring along appropriate ski wear.

ACCOMMODATIONS: The Cliff Lodge has 532 deluxe guest rooms situated around an 11-story glassed atrium that offers spectacular mountain views. The top two floors of the Lodge house the fitness center, a rooftop year-round swimming pool, and dancing under the stars! Spa patrons are housed on the ninth floor of the Lodge. All rooms have telephones, TVs, private baths, and daily maid service. Three condominium lodges, besides the full-service hotel, are also available on a daily basis if you prefer. Cliff Lodge has 38 smoke-free guest rooms for patrons who hate smoke!

HOUSE RULES: Alcohol is served in the restaurants but not allowed in the spa or on level 9. Smoking is allowed everywhere except in the spa and in the nonsmoking block of rooms.

PHYSICAL FACILITIES: The spa is located atop the Cliff Lodge and is the 27,000-square-foot centerpiece. Level 9 has the beauty salon, women's locker rooms, men's locker rooms, massage/facial stalls, herbal wrap stalls, steam and sauna rooms, and hydromassage. Level 10 houses the aerobics room, with suspended wood floor; exercise room with Keiser K-300 pneumatic resistance equipment; stretching room; heated outdoor swimming pool; whirlpool; and the Spa Cafe. A sundeck is located here, too. Herbal wraps are available. Skiing, bicycling, rock climbing school, backpack camping, summer tram rides, and a heliport for transportation to the golf course are other options. Four tennis courts complete the picture.

ACTIVITIES, TREATMENTS, AND PROGRAMS: The two-day/one-night program includes 1 massage, 1 herbal wrap, 1 facial, 1 spa pedicure, 1 shampoo blow dry/set, unlimited exercise classes, and daily morning hike. Meals are extra. For the three-day/two-night program add 1 more massage and unlimited tennis. Meals are extra. The five-day/four-night package includes 3 massages, 1 herbal wrap or parafango, hydromassage, 1 facial, 1 spa manicure, 1 spa pedicure, 1 hair and scalp treatment, 1 shampoo blow dry/set, 1 personal fitness consultation, unlimited exercise classes, unlimited tennis, and daily morning hike. Three spa meals are included as is airport transfer. Your best buy is the eight-day/seven-night package, which includes 3 meals per day at any Cliff Lodge restaurant and airport transfer, plus 5 massages, 2 herbal wraps or parafangos, 2 hydromassages, 2 facials, 1 spa manicure, 1 spa pedicure, 1 shampoo blow dry/set, 1 personal fitness consultation, unlimited exercise classes, daily morning hike, and unlimited tennis. Additional treatments, such as beauty or facials, cost extra. Therapeutic, Swedish-style massages incorporate elements of acupressure and shiatsu massage.

A Day at The Cliff Spa

Stretch class
Low impact aerobics
Breakfast
Mountain hike
Lunch
Break (sunbathing, etc.)
Water volleyball
Beauty treatments (facial, hydrotherapy, etc.)
Break
Dinner
Relax (no scheduled activities)

Times of classes are not given as they go on all day long, and you, furnished with your personal fitness evaluation, will decide how to spend your days. The key to this spa is flexibility.

OPTIONAL COSTS: Dermalogica and Thytomer beauty and facial products are used here and are available for sale. Ski/spa packages and stress management classes and lectures are available. A mountaineering center, summer arts festival, golfing, summer dance festival, concerts, and Octoberfest are some of the ways you can pass the time. Additional massages, hydromassage, herbal and parafango wraps can be had for extra fees. There is a fine-art gallery, book shop, and ski rental/repair shop.

NICE TO KNOW: This setting, high in the mountains, is a natural wonder and offers a chance for spiritual as well as bodily renewal. There aren't many nighttime activities scheduled, so guests can relax before a fire, see a movie, or just read quietly. Things are less structured here than at many spas because it is assumed you will want to take advantage of winter skiing or summer climbing activities. Lane Tietten, spa director, is formerly of the Four Seasons. Many couples and families take advantage of all that Snowbird and the Cliff Spa have to offer. A children's camp, for kids five and up, offers supervised play and learning in the mountain air. The Cliff Spa conference center can handle up to 900 people for meetings and programs.

* COOLFONT RE-CREATION PROGRAM
Berkeley Springs, WV 25411
304-258-4500

A wholistic health and education program set within a rustic resort of A-frame chalets in the mountains of West Virginia. The resort has two lakes and is surrounded by 1,200 acres of forest land. Open year-round.

RATES: Affordable. Credit cards: American Express, MasterCard and Visa. Winter rates from December through March.

LOCATION AND TRANSPORTATION: Two hours from Washington, DC, or Balitmore. Limousine service is available from airport to resort. Alternate transportation: Greyhound bus from Washington to Hancock (eight miles from resort). A Coolfont vehicle will pick you up in Hancock for a nominal charge.

EMPHASIS/PHILOSOPHY: Total mind and body awareness through yoga, nutrition, and exercise. Coolfont's philosophy is to imbue guests with a health program that they can fit into their own lifestyles. Owner Sam Ashelman, who opened the retreat in the early 1960s, believes Coolfont is for "renewing and restoring your mind and senses in a natural environment."

DIET PROGRAM: 750–1,200 calories per day. Well-balanced, portion-controlled meals feature fish, chicken, fresh fruit, and vegetables. Only natural food is used. No salt, no sugar. Average weight loss is 3 pounds in five days.

GUEST POPULATION: Coed. 20 guests. Most are from the Mid-Atlantic states.

PACKAGES AND MINIMUM STAYS: Five-Day Health Retreat program (in on Sunday, out on Friday after lunch) focuses on weight control, exercise, and stress management. There also are Fitness Weekends; Breathe Free 6-day plan to stop smoking; and Massage Workshops, a weekend program for partners.

MEAL SERVICE: Special diet for guests who are on the Health Retreat program. Meals, served in gourmet style, are for socializing.

DRESS CODE: Do your own thing. Jeans, a jogging outfit, or a long skirt for evenings are just fine.

ACCOMMODATIONS: A-frame chalets, cabins, and lodge rooms, some with fireplaces or cook stoves. Limited camping. No television. There are telephones only in lodge room accommodations.

HOUSE RULES: No smoking is allowed when the group is together. There is a lounge serving alcohol on the resort premises.

PHYSICAL FACILITIES: Massage rooms, hot tubs, sauna, an indoor pool, and a large exercise room. Outdoor facilities include a large lake for swimming, volleyball courts, basketball courts, tennis courts, miles of hiking trails, and horseback riding.

ACTIVITIES, TREATMENTS, AND PROGRAMS: Exercise classes consisting of stretch class, spot reducing, aerobics, Jazzercise, T'ai Chi (combination of ballet and self-defense), and body building. Nature hikes, classes in yoga, and cooking and tennis are also offered. A self-hypnosis program is part of the schedule. A wholistic evening program offers sessions on body chemistry balancing, a chiropractor's lecture, and seminars on reflexology and polarity massage therapies. Evening recreation includes square dancing and disco dancing.

A Day at Coolfont

7:00   Wake-up walk
8:00   Morning stretches
8:30   Breakfast
9:30   Post-breakfast jaunt
10:00 Healthy life-style discussions (weight loss, stress management, behavior modification)
11:00 Tone-up exercises
12:00 Aerobics
1:00   Lunch
1:45   Aerobic walk or leisure activity (honey facials, nature walk, gentle stretches, free time)
2:45   Body toning with "Stretchies"
3:45   Yoga
4:30   Free time to enjoy massage, sauna, and hot tub
6:30   Dinner
7:30   Moonlight walk
8:00   Evening programs (guest speakers, films, massage techniques, square dances)

OPTIONAL COSTS: Massages, facials, horseback riding. If you wish to remain longer in order to expand your wellness experience, you can combine the basic Five-Day Health Retreat with one of the other intriguing programs offered.

NICE TO KNOW: The Berkeley Springs area has an old mineral spring that dates back to the Indian times. The town can truly claim that "George Washington bathed here."

*BEST BUY AND WHY: This affordable spa is a "Best Buy" because:
- It has a top-notch wholistic education program, encompassing body fitness, nutritional instruction, and behavior modification principles.
- A wide variety of exercise classes are scheduled, and good recreational facilities are available.
- Time spent in this lovely forest setting has a restorative effect on the mind and body.

DORAL SATURNIA INTERNATIONAL SPA RESORT
8755 NW 36th Street
Miami, Fl 33178
800-331-7768
305-593-6030

A spanking new spa opened in September 1987. Built at a cost of more than $30 million, it reflects the mood and atmosphere of the Terme di Saturnia, Italy's renowned spa. Open year-round.

RATES: Expensive. Credit cards: American Express, Carte Blanche, Diners Club, MasterCard, Visa.

LOCATION AND TRANSPORTATION: Miami International Airport is close by, and pickup service is provided gratis.

EMPHASIS/PHILOSOPHY: Their philosophy is one of balance in life-style management. The four-part spa program incorporates fitness and exercise, diet and nutrition, stress management, and "the total you." The program is flexible, balanced, and allows for individual differences. Total European pampering with active exercise allows for a positive life-style change in a relaxed, luxurious setting.

DIET PROGRAM: 1,000 calories and 22 fat points per day. Calorie and fat count are given on all menus. A new fat-point system was developed for the Doral Saturnia. It is based on recent research, which showed that fats are easily converted into body fat; only 3 percent of the calories in fat are burned during metabolism. In contrast, 23 percent of the calories in complex carbohydrates are burned during metabolism. That means that an extra 20 percent of the calories are burned when you eat carbohydrates compared to when you eat fats. So you are better off eliminating as much fat as possible from your diet and sticking to complex carbohydrates.

The Doral Saturnia emphasizes this new basis for weight loss in all phases of its dietary program. The fat count is noted on the menu, discussed in lectures, and is the main point of a booklet given to you. It is also the basis for a new cookbook written by Cheryl Hartsough, R.D., the lead nutritionist, and Michael McVay, the chef, soon to be published.

A professional nutritionist will help you develop a realistic personal program. Menus are low in fat and calories and portion-controlled. Gourmet health food, low in salt and sugar, high in complex carbohydrates, is served. Based on Tuscan cuisine, emphasis is on fresh fruit and vegetables, whole grains, pasta, poultry, and seafood.

Courtesy of Doral Saturnia International Spa

Weight loss averages 4 pounds for women, 6–8 pounds for men.

GUEST POPULATION: Coed. 90 guests. Separate facilities for women and men. This spa has been very "in" since its opening.

PACKAGES AND MINIMUM STAYS: The following plans are offered: 7-Day Plan, 4-Day Plan, and the A la Carte Plan.

MEAL SERVICE: Two gourmet restaurants serve full spa menus, which feature sensational Tuscan low-calorie cuisine. The Ristorante di Saturnia is an open-space area with a four-story atrium effect. The Villa Montepaldi is a glass gazebo set in a formal garden. It is more private and elegant. Naturally, fresh flowers and fine china are on the tables.

DRESS CODE: Jogging outfits are acceptable at breakfast and lunch. Although jacket and tie are not required, most guests choose to "dress up" for dinner. An elegant "casual" look is definitely present here. The spa provides all exercise clothing for the duration of your stay. An extra bathing suit and pair of leotards might be handy, however.

ACCOMMODATIONS: Guests stay in lavish suites, overlooking the golf greens and lush gardens. All suites have private marble Jacuzzi baths. The 36 Luxe suites have living rooms, entertainment centers, and two marble Jacuzzi baths with dressing rooms. Five sprawling Supreme suites combine a Luxe suite with even grander amenities, and each of these is themed after an Italian city! Total of 48 suites. A special touch: each bathroom has heated towel racks! All rooms are decorated in modern Italian style, with a grand European touch.

HOUSE RULES: No smoking in the spa's public areas. A three-ounce glass of wine is served with dinner.

PHYSICAL FACILITIES: A 148,000-square-foot complex encompassing the Spa Centre and luxury hotel features such architectural elements as clay-tiled rooftops, formal Old-World gardens, trompe l'oeils, balustrades, and a 100-foot atrium. The fitness facilities include four exercise studios, two with spring-loaded floors for safe aerobic workouts. You'll find a large outdoor recreational pool with Jacuzzi and cascading falls for hydromassage, outdoor lap pool, and indoor exercise pool. There is an outdoor, climate-controlled, banked track with its own sound system for walking and jogging and an outdoor exercise trail, featuring exercise stations and lush tropical land-

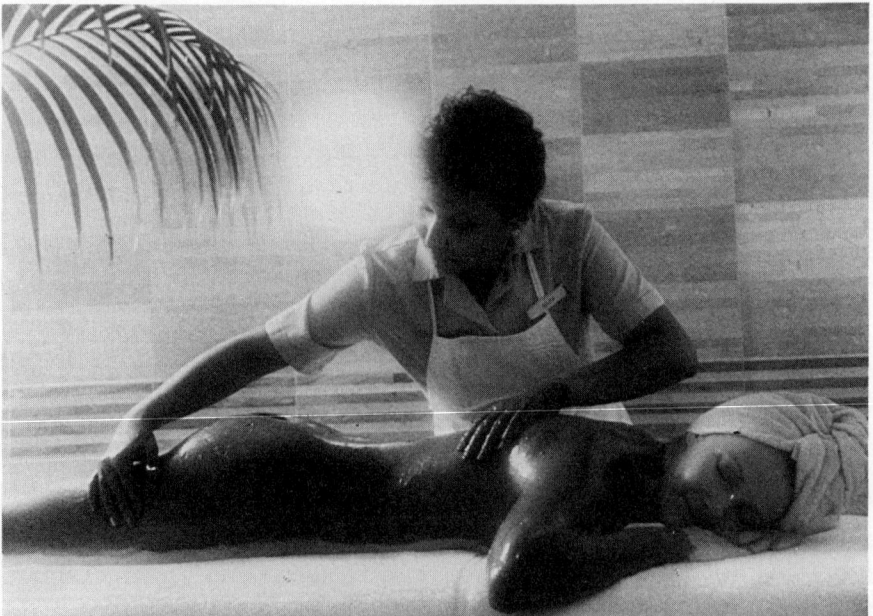

Courtesy of Doral Saturnia International Spa

scaping. Strength training uses David Fitness Equipment, European high-tech, resistance weight-training equipment that is light, quiet, and easy to use. Free weights, treadmills, exercise bicycles, Stairmasters, and rowing machines are available. Five championship golf courses, fifteen tennis courts, and a world-class equestrian center are nearby at the Doral Hotel. Beauty facilities include 26 massage rooms; European hydrotherapy pools; herbal wraps; Jacuzzis; and cool dips, separate for men and women; two Swiss showers; saunas; and a mineral-salt soak. Separate sundecks for men and women. The reading room is where you meet and mingle with other guests; it includes newspaper racks, books, backgammon, and billiards.

ACTIVITIES, TREATMENTS, AND PROGRAMS: Guests on the 7-Day Plan have a choice of emphasis: Health, Sports or Total Image. They all start out with a fitness test and exercise prescription. All include four one-hour massages. All have their choice of four personal, professional and sports services, which range from herbal wraps and beauty treatments to nutrition consultations and sports lessons. You may take as many exercise classes as can be fitted in with your other treatments and programs. Fifty different aerobic, stretching, and strengthening exercises are offered daily. All classes, guest lectures, and movies are included. According to the chosen emphasis, four or five additional services are offered. For instance, the Health Emphasis includes a total body fango mud treatment, hydrotherapy with hydromassage, computerized health-risk assessment, and nutrition consultation with dietary computer analysis.

OPTIONAL COSTS: The Terme di Saturnia skin-care line is available in the beauty shop, which has a U.S. exclusive on these highly regarded Italian products. An active-wear shop sells clothing, and a sundry shop is on the premises. Additional treatments include fango facials, body polish, cellulite treatments, wax treatments, hairstyling, face design, manicures, and pedicures. Golf, tennis, and horseback riding are available.

NICE TO KNOW: Adjacent to the Doral Saturnia is the famous Doral Hotel and Country Club, where you can golf, play tennis, walk, jog, or ride horses—all available to spa guests. After learning new eating guidelines at the Spa, guests are reinforced in their positive life-changes by receiving a personalized take-home nutritional plan, a spa newsletter, and a toll-free hot-line number if diet relapse seems imminent. Stress management is also a primary concern here, and the staff works with guests to help identify and relieve "hot" spots where stress is stored. Above all, a "total-image" philosophy prevails at Doral Saturnia, and life-style consultants frequently meet with guests to discuss how to maximize strengths and eliminate weak spots.

JUDY'S COMMENT: This special spa successfully combines the therapeutic and pampering treatments of European spas with the diet and fitness know-how of American spas.

EVOLUTION SPA AT
THE EQUINOX RESORT
Manchester Village, VT 05254
800-362-4747
802-362-4700

Spa program available 22 weeks a year; the resort is open year-round. The spa is part of a restored Revolutionary-era inn. This historic inn is now a twenty-million-dollar renovated resort with a full spa program, offering a medically supervised health and wellness option.

RATES: Expensive. American Express, MasterCard, Visa.

LOCATION AND TRANSPORTATION: The Evolution Spa is nestled at the foot of Mt. Equinox (part of Vermont's Green Mountains), which is lovingly called "The Grunt." The nearest airport is in Albany, New York, an hour and a quarter's drive from the spa. Limousine service can be arranged through the hotel. Bradley International Airport in Hartford, Connecticut, is a two-hour-and-ten-minute drive away.

EMPHASIS/PHILOSOPHY: Dr. Stuart I. Erner, M.D., medical director and creator of the Optimum Health and Beauty Program, states that his "medical philosophy emphasizes preventive health and total wellness as they relate to optimal nutrition, physical fitness, and psychological well-being." In addition, the Evolution Spa "doesn't stop at improving your body; we're also out to improve your mind with our unique Health Education Seminar series."

DIET PROGRAM: Consists of a well-balanced diet of 800–1,000 calories per day. According to Susan Thorne-Thonsen, the manager of the spa, the menu consists primarily of high-fiber, low-fat, moderate-protein, and complex carbohydrates (vegetables, fruits, and grains are stressed). Red meat is served, perhaps loin of lamb or grilled filet of beef with shallots. There are no calorie counts on the menu, but each serving is meticulously portion-controlled. The spa wishes to avoid excessive concern with calorie counting. Chef Ken Paquin does an outstanding job with the cooking and presentation of meals. Susan feels that is one of the high points of the program. Chef Paquin comes directly from the New York Culinary Institute and is a true artist.

A Typical Meal Plan:

BREAKFAST
Fresh-squeezed orange juice

Choice of:
Buckwheat pancakes with fresh fruit sauce
Hot oatmeal with skim milk
Bran and raisin cereal
One-egg omelet with spinach, mushroom, tomato, or cheese
Wheat toast
Decaffeinated coffee

LUNCH
(Always a first and second course for lunch)

First Course
Fresh fruit with Belgium endives and fitness vinaigrette *or* Chicken soup with pesto *or* Chilled terrine of sole with tomato sauce

Second Course
Fitness chef salad *or* Open-faced sandwich with tomato, mozzarella cheese, basil, and sprouts *or* Fresh tuna with lemon, tomatoes, and capers

DINNER
(Always four items)

Appetizer
Calamari in tomato cilantro with olive oil dressing *or* Avocado terrine with herb tomato *or* Grapefruit with crab salad and endive

Salad
Salad is the same for everyone. This particular evening a grated raw vegetable salad was served.

Entree
Papillote of sole with saffron or julienne vegetables *or* Veal medallion with orange and thyme *or* Breast of duck à l'orange

Dessert
Plain yogurt with fresh strawberries and blueberries with a sprig of mint
Decaffeinated coffee

All this and healthy too!

GUEST POPULATION: Coed. 12 guests. Since the spa had only been open for a month at the time of this writing, there had been only female guests, primarily from New York. There have been many inquiries from mothers and daughters planning to rendezvous at the spa in the future.

PACKAGES AND MINIMUM STAYS: There are 7-day/7-night and 3-day/3-night complete spa programs.

MEAL SERVICE: Spa diners eat in the same lovely dining room as all resort guests. You can choose to eat with other spa diners, alone, or with resort guests. There is a hostess to seat you. Meals are all sitdown service. Fresh flowers are on the table. Each evening Ron Levine, a pianist who has appeared at Carnegie Hall, plays classical music as well as contemporary favorites. The dining room is open to the public.

DRESS CODE: Jacket and tie are required for men at dinner. Ladies, take your cue from that. A pair of pants with a silk shirt is perfectly acceptable.

ACCOMMODATIONS: All accommodations are located in the 174-unit inn. The rooms range in price from $115 to $340 a night for the Cupola Suite or large Presidential suites. All the rooms are decorated in authentic colonial style, with stenciling on the walls, tie-back draperies, stuffed wing chairs, armoires with mirrors, and desks with Hitchcock chairs. The housekeeping staff goes to great pains to please you. You'll find a large bowl of fresh fruit upon arrival; turn-down bed service every night. Twenty-four-hour-a-day room service is available.

HOUSE RULES: Anything goes. One spa guest insisted upon wine spritzer with her meal each evening and no one batted an eyelash.

PHYSICAL FACILITIES: The Equinox Inn is a complete resort complex that includes a conference center with six meeting rooms, two outdoor heated pools, one indoor pool, 18 holes of golf, five tennis courts with clay and all-weather surfaces, two indoor platform tennis courts for winter play, five restaurants, and a lovely 14-acre pond. There is a charming shopping mall, filled with 18 shops and overflowing with antiques, along with a Vermont country store. The spa itself is filled with loads of tropical plants. There are separate spa locker rooms for men and women, with saunas. The indoor pool complex contains two Jacuzzis and one steam room, all coed. The massage rooms and the herbal wrap rooms are located in the spa facility, whereas the manicure, pedicure, facial, and hair treatments are all done across the street at the Equinox shops. There is a fresh fruit bar in the spa, serving natural fruit and vegetable juices. The exercise room is open all the time. It has Nautilus equipment, Lifecycle machines, semirecumbent bicycles, computer rowers, cross-country track machines, and free weights.

ACTIVITIES, TREATMENTS, AND PROGRAMS: Included in the 7-night Spa Plan is a complete medical analysis at the start of your visit. Seven exercise classes (at least one per day), featuring calisthenics, aqua slimnastics, low- and high-impact aerobics, aerobic dance, body sculpturing, and stretch and relax classes are also included. Classes are given in the exercise studio, which has a sprung dance floor. There are exercise activities for both summer and winter, such as cross-country skiing, tennis, fishing, swimming, and golf. The 7-night Spa Plan includes the following treatments: daily, half-hour Swedish massage; loofah scrub; two herbal wraps; two facials; one pedicure and manicure; and haircut with styling consultations. There are three daily health education seminars. And, of course, you get three calorie-controlled, gourmet spa meals each day.

A Day at Evolution Spa

9:00	Breakfast
9:45	Organized walk
10:15	Morning seminar (e.g., lecture on nutrition)
11:15	Exercise period
1:00	Lunch
1:45	Afternoon seminar (e.g., stress management and reduction)
2:45	Spa activities and/or recreational activities
6:00	Dinner
8:00	Evening lectures, films, or discussion groups led by the spa and culinary staff

STAFF POPULATION: Dr. Erner, medical director and founder of the Evolution Spa, is a board certified internist who specializes in the treatment of obesity and other eating disorders. There is quite an impressive health-related team at the spa. To implement the stress management and behavior modification for weight-control programs, there are two psychologists. Also on the team are two nutritionists and a physical therapist. As mentioned earlier, Susan Thorne-Thonsen comanages the spa with her husband, Roger, who is a tennis pro. Three full-time massage therapists are on staff.

NICE TO KNOW: It seems a shame that such a strong behavior and beauty program doesn't include more exercise classes in the spa package rates. The spa brochure is ambiguous regarding the number of exercise classes one can take daily. I was told, however, that seven classes are offered daily, and they are very loose about how many exercise classes you may attend. I would check this out before checking in.

JUDY'S COMMENT: A well-rounded program offering lots of healthy options plus gourmet health cuisine, cardiovascular exercises, educational seminars, and physical activities utilizing the area's many natural resources. A sound emphasis on developing individual awareness of an optimal life-style geared toward wellness.

FOUR SEASONS FITNESS RESORT AND SPA
4150 North MacArthur Boulevard
Irving, TX 75038
214-717-0700
800-268-6282 for general information
on all Four Seasons Hotels

Open year-round. This sprawling complex also includes the Las Colinas Preventive Medicine Center, a sports fitness facility, and a Four Seasons Hotel.

RATES: Moderate. American Express, MasterCard, Visa are accepted.

LOCATION AND TRANSPORTATION: Situated on 398 acres overlooking the rolling hills of the suburb Las Colinas, 20 miles from downtown Dallas. Courtesy transportation is provided to and from Dallas/Fort Worth airport.

EMPHASIS/PHILOSOPHY: The Four Seasons Fitness Resort and Spa is dedicated to the "rejuvenation of the mind and spirit as well as the body." By utilizing the vast array of treatments and facilities, guests can strive toward achieving the highest level of physical and emotional fitness.

DIET PROGRAM: The Four Seasons Hotels have been catering to health-conscious guests for several years. They have developed the Four Seasons Alternative Cuisine based on guidelines set by the American Heart Association. The use of complex carbohydrates is emphasized, consisting of low cholesterol (animal fat), low sodium, low fat, and high carbohydrates (which means lots of pasta, fruit, veggies, and grains). No red meat is served on the spa diet menu.

Jeanne Jones, author of *Diet for a Happy Heart,* is the nutritional consultant for all Four Seasons Hotels. She works in conjunction with Marilyn Goldman, who is the dietician at Las Colinas. Instead of emphasizing weight loss, the Las Colinas Center prefers to measure percentage of body fat changes.

Meals are based on a total of 1,000 calories per day. There are two menus to choose from: the regular menu given to all resort guests and the spa menu, which features the Four Seasons Alternative Cuisine selections. The spa food plan is based on an eight-day rotational program. There are several choices of entrees for each meal, and they are all nutritionally balanced. A sample of one of the eight daily spa menus follows:

BREAKFAST
Poached fruit crepe with cinnamon yogurt sauce (150)

LUNCH
Gazpacho (45) *or*
Duck consommé (10)
Chicken enchilada (225) *or*
Quesadilla (285)
Flan (110) *or*
Fresh fruit plate (70)

DINNER
Cold gingered carrot soup (100) *or*
Duck consommé (10)
Fish en papillote (215)
Poached pear marsala (125) *or*
Fresh fruit plate (60)

GUEST POPULATION: Coed: 25 guests. John Croll, executive director of the spa and resort, reports that the spa population is nearly 50 percent men and 50 percent women. The other week, he said, they even had some single men!

PACKAGES AND MINIMUM STAYS: There is no minimum stay. A variety of packages can be arranged. They include: a Golf 'n Spa Getaway and the Fresh Start Plan, each for 3 days and 2 nights; the Four Seasons health and Fitness Plan, consisting of 5 days and 4 nights; a 7-day/8-night package; the Discovery Weekend; the Honeymoon Package for 2 days and 1 night; and the Premier Day Plan for guests wishing to use the spa during the day only.

MEAL SERVICE: Resort and spa guests dine in the restaurant, called the Cafe on the Green, that overlooks the eighteenth hole of the golf course. Mr. Croll stresses the flexibility of the program in that spa-goers wishing to order from the regular menu or buffet, or to consume extra calories from the spa menu, are free to do so at their own discretion. There are four other restaurants in the resort hotel complex, all of them casual, and some overlook the golf and tennis courts. Most spa guests sit in the nonsmoking area of the dining room.

DRESS CODE: The atmosphere of the Four Seasons is friendly and casual. It is perfectly fine to wear a jogging outfit to any meal, including dinner.

ACCOMMODATIONS: Spa guests stay in deluxe rooms equipped with large bathrooms, hair dryers, full-sized bathrobes, and cable TV. All the amenities of a typical Four Seasons resort hotel are provided. The Four Seasons, known for its luxurious facilities and impeccable service, has created a plush, spacious environment in a contemporary style, filled with plants and light. Most guest rooms have balconies overlooking a wide expanse of hills in Las Colinas.

HOUSE RULES: No smoking is allowed in the spa or in any fitness or recreational area. There is a no-smoking area in the dining room, and an entire floor of the hotel is devoted to nonsmokers. Alcohol is served in all the restaurants.

PHYSICAL FACILITIES: The physical facilities are extensive. Outdoors there is the Las Colinas Tournament Players Golf Course (TPC), which has 18 holes; a park across the street for walking; a quarter-mile outdoor jogging track; eight outdoor tennis courts; a 25-meter outdoor pool; men's and women's outdoor sunbathing decks; an outdoor whirlpool. Some of the indoor facilities include a hair salon for men and women, and three boutiques—a pro racquet shop, a golf shop, and the spa fitness boutique. The latter sells fitness accessories, the R-K line of facial products, the Four Seasons line of toiletries, and Judith Jackson's aromatherapy products. There are three exercise rooms; separate men's and women's locker rooms with whirlpools, saunas, steam rooms, and cold plunge area; facial area; massage area; one-eighth mile indoor jogging track; 25-yard indoor pool, tanning parlor; seven racquetball courts; two squash courts; four indoor tennis courts. Special meeting rooms are available, equipped with computer links and closed-circuit television. Also on the premises is the Las Colinas Preventive Medicine Center (PMC). All this gives you an inkling of the myriad of outstanding facilities at the Four Seasons Fitness Resort and Spa.

ACTIVITIES, TREATMENTS, AND PROGRAMS: For spa guests staying eight days and seven nights, the week starts off with an evaluation of your health and a life-style profile at the PMC. This requires fasting for 12 hours on water and juice before a blood test is given. You are asked to fill out a detailed questionnaire on your life-style and habits. This information is sent to the lab and results are explained to you the next day. Some of the evaluative tests include: diagnostic exercise test; body mass assessment; pulmonary function test; and stress-level exam. The Preventive Medicine Center is open Monday through Friday only.

A wide range of exercise classes are held from 6:00 A.M. to 7:00 P.M. at three different fitness levels. Some of the exercise classes are aerobics, total fitness, conditioning, stretch and relax, waterworks, master swim classes, moms-to-be fitness class, and children's stretch class. Supervised weight-training facilities are offered all day long. Spa program participants are entitled to one complimentary private sports lesson of their choice. This might involve a golf, tennis or swimming lesson, weight training, or overall fitness consultation. Morning walks are seasonal and take place at 7:00 in the park.

Treatments included in the 8-day spa plan are two herbal wraps; one loofah salt body treatment; one facial; a shampoo, haircut, and blow-dry; a manicure and pedicure. In the evenings films are shown, and there are frequent lectures on topics such as healthy life-style management, skin care, and nutrition. Exploring the charming village of Las Colinas is another option for guests. The hotel will sometimes arrange shopping trips to the village.

STAFF POPULATION: Staff population is impressive, with John Croll heading up the team as executive director and a spa director who at the time of this writing was on maternity leave. Fitness Director Marilyn Goldman, the dietitian, has been with Four Seasons for four years. Among the many staff members are eight massage therapists and ten facialists. The Las Colinas Preventive Medicine Center has a full roster of physicians and health professionals.

OPTIONAL COSTS: There are 32 beauty treatments available. Private golf, racquetball, and squash lessons are offered at an hourly rate. Marilyn Goldman gives nutritional counseling upon request. Boutique shopping, of course, is always an enjoyable option.

NICE TO KNOW: The Four Seasons hotels have been catering to health-minded individuals since 1984 by accommodating guests with the Four Seasons Alternative Cuisine. The Byron Nelson Golf Classic is played at the Las Colinas Resort each year. According to Mr. Croll, the spa will provide workout clothes and athletic shoes if needed for the duration of your stay. Meal plans include gratuities. A confusing aspect is that Four Seasons Fitness Resort and Spa has a mailing address in Irving, Texas. However, when you call in they state that they are located in Las Colinas, Texas.

JUDY'S COMMENT: This spa offers a wonderful opportunity for life-style reeducation. Complete medical attention is available at the distinguished Las Colinas Preventive Medicine Center. A full range of exercise classes is offered at all levels along with a large variety of sports activities. It is unusual that a facility of this magnitude would also offer individual attention in every area. Guests can, with the help of the staff, design a highly individualized program, utilizing any number of the vast array of services and activities available.

GOLDEN DOOR "SPA AT SEA"
Cunard Hotels and Resorts
555 Fifth Avenue
New York, NY 10017
800-223-1946
212-759-5357

These permanent and comprehensive health and fitness programs are offered aboard the *Queen Elizabeth II, Vistafjord,* and *Sagafjord.* For the sake of brevity, this listing will detail the program aboard the *Queen Elizabeth II.* A staff from the Golden Door spa in Escondido, California, runs these programs (see listing of Golden Door Spa under "Structured Spas").

RATES: Expensive. The Spa at Sea program is offered at no additional cost to cruise passengers.

LOCATION AND TRANSPORTATION: The *QEII* makes 24 transatlantic crossings during the year as well as round-the-world cruises. Most departures are from New York City. Check Cunard for schedules and sailings of all three ships.

EMPHASIS/PHILOSOPHY: According to Deborah Szekely, founder of the Golden Door in California, "The program is more than a luxurious elective. It is an opportunity to combine the cruise adventure with an intensely personal journey designed to revitalize oneself in every aspect of life." The principles of the Golden Door are the basis of the program, combining fitness classes, health education, and low-calorie dining.

DIET PROGRAM: A well-balanced, low-calorie diet is available as fits your needs. A breakfast buffet and luncheon salad bar are set up for Golden Door participants. Breakfast consists of yogurt, muesli, and fruits; luncheons feature salad, a hot entree, fruit for dessert, herbal teas, and juices. Watch for the "Golden Door Menu Box" on

your regular luncheon and dinner menu, which gives the chef's nouvelle cuisine recommendations for low-cal, nutritious meal choices.

GUEST POPULATION: Coed. All 1,800 passengers are eligible to
participate in the program. There's a limit of 30 people per exercise
class.

MEAL SERVICE: Breakfast buffet and, periodically, a luncheon
salad bar are set up outside the Lido Lounge on the *QEII*. Dinner is
served in any of the three ship's restaurants: The Queen's Grill and
Lounge, the Princess Grill, and the Columbia Restaurant—all with
table service.

DRESS CODE: Tights, leotards, and shorts are ideal for exercise
classes. Folks dress up for dinner.

ACCOMMODATIONS: A variety of single and double accommodations, as well as suites, is available. All staterooms have shower and
toilet, wall-to-wall carpeting, individual climate control, six-channel
radio, telephone, and roomy closets.

HOUSE RULES: No smoking in the spa area.

PHYSICAL FACILITIES: Cunard has created a private and separate area on the sixth deck of the *QEII* that features a large, mirrored
exercise gym, massage center, Jacuzzi, sauna, a heated exercise pool
with teak platform for hydrocalisthenics, and three hydrotubs (coed).
Guests also have use of the ship's other exercise facilities, including
a gymnasium with Nautilus equipment, bicycles, treadmills, turkish
baths, massage/facial rooms, a full-service beauty salon, and a parcours track on the boat deck (4½ times around the deck equals one
mile).

ACTIVITIES, TREATMENTS, AND PROGRAMS: The Spa at
Sea offers six exercise classes daily (three different levels of fitness),
including DaVinci aerobics, water exercises, parcours, body toning,
yoga, and use of all spa facilities. Daytime lectures by the Golden
Door staff are offered on relaxation techniques, nutrition, biofeedback, and stress management.
      The Golden Door Service Desk is open daily (except Port Days)
from 11:00 A.M. to 1:00 P.M. You can stop by with your questions or
any request for individual advice from Golden Door specialists. Use
swimwear for water classes and in the pool and hot tubs. Dress for
all other classes is warm-up suits, leotards, or loose trousers, and
T-shirts.

STAFF POPULATION: All members of the Spa at Sea staff come
from the Golden Door in California.

OPTIONAL COSTS: Massages, facials, hair care, and beauty salon treatments can be found in the ship's salons.

JUDY'S COMMENT: What a way to cruise and grow slim!

THE GOLDEN EAGLE RESORT
Route 108, P.O. Box 1110-B
Stowe, VT 05672
800-626-1010
802-253-4811

The spa program is part of a rustic resort set among the birches and pines of the beautiful Green Mountains. The resort is open year-round, but the spa program is conducted summers only.

RATES: Affordable. Credit cards: American Express, MasterCard, Visa. High season extends from July 1 to September 20; early rates apply from May 17 to June 30.

LOCATION AND TRANSPORTATION: Located in scenic Stowe, Vermont. Courtesy van pickup from the bus and Amtrak station at Waterbury is available. Or use the shuttle service from Burlington airport, 45 minutes from the resort (approximately $25).

EMPHASIS/PHILOSOPHY: Rejuvenate, relax, and reawaken in the mountain air. According to the Golden Eagle, "Introduction to our program can result in establishing a lifetime of new eating habits."

DIET PROGRAM: 1,200- or 1,500-calorie diet plans. Portion-controlled, well-balanced meals utilizing fresh fruits, local produce, fiber foods, poultry, fish, and meat. Low fat, salt, and sugar with high fiber and carbohydrates. Weight loss expectancy? With hiking up the mountain trails and exercising, you can expect to lose several pounds during your stay.

GUEST POPULATION: Coed. 10 guests. Popular with young and young-at-heart couples. One partner can make use of the diet/exercise facilities while the other eats cheesecake and plays golf.

PACKAGES AND MINIMUM STAYS: The basic fitness package includes 5 nights; check in on Sunday or Monday.

MEAL SERVICE: Dinner is served in the Partridge Inn, a handsome, wood-paneled dining room with slat-backed chairs. The hostess

Courtesy of The Golden Eagle Resort

and friendly dining room staff help solo guests find comfortable seating. Room service is available.

DRESS CODE: Informal. A jogging outfit is appropriate.

ACCOMMODATIONS: Guest rooms feature oversized beds and contemporary furnishings. Some rooms have their own Jacuzzis or fireplaces. Balconies overlook a pond or the vistas of Mount Mansfield.

HOUSE RULES: Anything goes.

PHYSICAL FACILITIES: Universal gym, massage, sauna, whirlpool, indoor and heated outdoor pools. The grounds include a clay-topped tennis court, fishing pond (skating in winter), and hiking trails. The Stowe Country Club golf course, one-half mile away, offers reduced greens fees for spa guests.

ACTIVITIES, TREATMENTS, AND PROGRAMS: The spa fitness package includes nutritional consultation; therapeutic massages; unlimited use of the sauna, whirlpool, exercise equipment, indoor and outdoor pools, and tennis court; all fitness classes; and daily lectures. Exercise sessions include stretching and toning workouts, aquaerobics, danceaerobics, and yoga led by an instructor. The program is supplemented by hiking, bicycling, and tennis. Certified nutritionist Marie Russell offers meal planning to guests who request help.

A Day at the Golden Eagle

7:00	Wake-up
7:30	Morning stretch and walk/jog
8:00	Breakfast
9:00	Personal evaluation (cardiovascular, percent body fat, weight, measurements recorded)
9:45	Dance exercise and/or circuit weight training; ergometer bike exercises
10:45	Massage or foot reflexology
12:00	Lunch
1:00	Free time and reading
2:00	Afternoon stretch and nature walk
3:00	Free exercise (tennis, badminton, swimming, etc.)
4:30	Sauna, whirlpool, stretch
6:30	Dinner
Evening	Seminars on the role of exercise in a healthy life, or movie

OPTIONAL COSTS: Manicure/pedicure, facials, horseback riding, tennis lessons (elsewhere), and tours of Stowe and the surrounding countryside can be arranged.

NICE TO KNOW: Sandy Morningstar, spa program director, and the staff at the Golden Eagle are very accommodating. The 800 number is for reservations and basic information, but they'll have the staff people call you back to answer specific questions. A beauty salon is just across the road.

JUDY'S COMMENT: This resort offers a beautiful mountain escape where you can refresh your spirit as well as get your body in shape. Spa goers have the extra advantage of enjoying the country beauty and historic charm of old Stowe.

GURNEY'S INN,
THE INTERNATIONAL HEALTH
AND BEAUTY SPA
Montauk, Long Island, NY 11954
516-668-2345
516-668-2509

A European-style, full-service spa situated within the framework of a sprawling resort and conference center called Gurney's Inn. Smack-dab on the Atlantic Ocean at the tip of Long Island. Open year-round.

RATES: Moderate. Credit cards: American Express, MasterCard, Visa.

LOCATION AND TRANSPORTATION: Gurney's is 2½ hours east of New York City. The Long Island Railroad leaves from Manhattan's Pennsylvania Station, and Montauk is the train's last stop. Guests may fly from New York to nearby East Hampton. Gurney's provides courtesy transportation to local airports and railroad stations.

EMPHASIS/PHILOSOPHY: Gurney's Inn is dedicated to promoting fitness, conditioning, and stress reduction. According to Nick Monte, owner and founder of the spa, "Visitations to a true spa should be considered preventive health care and not mere fluff, which spas have been so long reputed to be. A real spa takes care of the whole person, body and mind ... it plants the seeds of individual health consciousness ... it gives the tools and the knowledge to enrich the quality of life and to combat degenerative disease."

DIET PROGRAM: 800–1,200 calories per day. The menu is a continental variety of low-calorie fare. All meals are low in fat, cholesterol, sugar, salt, and refined carbohydrates. The resident nutritionist will plan an individualized menu of only 800 calories per day or 1,000 if you're "working hard." According to Nick, "Our food is designed to appeal to all the senses while helping to achieve a weight-control program. We try to introduce a way of eating you can live with for the rest of your life." Many of the meals are based on the fresh fish that is abundant here at Montauk. Other dishes feature chicken, veal, and vegetables. No red meat is served. Homemade wholewheat hard rolls are prepared daily in the Gurney's Inn bakery. Calorie count is listed next to each item on the menu.

Here's what a daily menu at Gurney's Inn looks like.

LUNCHEON
Appetizers (Choice of One)
Fresh Raw Oysters with Lemon Wedges (35)
Fresh Little Neck Clams with Lemon Wedges (45)
Potato Leek Soup (65)

Salads (Choice of One)
Cucumber Yogurt Salad (35)
Hearts of Lettuce with Herb Dressing (35)
Caesar Salad (60)

Entrees (Choice of One)
Mushroom Stuffed Fish Rolls (150)
Salmon Mousse (120)
Vegetables au Gratin (150)
Broiled Peconic Bay Scallops (110)
Chef Salad (230)
Fresh vegetables available daily

Dessert (Choice of One)
Fruit Salad (60)
Apple Crisp (60)
Fresh Melon (35)
Fruit Flan (75)

DINNER
Appetizers (Choice of One)
Gazpacho Andalusian (75)
Antipasto with Mustard Sauce (60)
Zucchini Soup (40)

Salads (Choice of One)
Marinated Tomato Salad (25)
Spinach Mushroom Salad (10)
Haitian Vegetable Salad (35)

Entrees (Choice of One)
Chicken Pizzaiola (180)
Moussaka (220)
Seafood Paella Valencia (230)
Veal Marsala (190)
Fresh Fish of the Season (160)

Dessert (Choice of One)
Brandied seasonal fruit (85)
Custard (70)
Pineapple-Lemon Whip (75)
Ginger Apples (45)

Beverages A selection of coffees, teas, and mineral waters is offered, as well as light Chablis.

GUEST POPULATION: Coed. 60 guests. Lots of executives come here, using their vacation week to become fit and trim, along with veteran spa goers and professional dancers. Celebrity guests who pop in, and whose livelihood depends on looking good and staying trim, have included beauty expert Adrien Arpel, top models Cheryl Tiegs and Christie Brinkley, and actor/interviewer Dick Cavett. Barbra Streisand was spotted checking in as this book was being written.

PACKAGES AND MINIMUM STAYS: During peak season, early June to Labor Day, a minimum stay of four days is required. Available packages include a Seven-Day Rejuvenation plan, Executive Longevity five-day program, a couple of four-day plans, and a Day of Beauty.

MEAL SERVICE: Spa guests are served meals in a separate dining room. Large bay windows overlook the ocean. Guests can also take their meals in the main dining room of the Inn. This offers a good opportunity for the dieter and nondieter to "do their own thing" together. The main dining room is known for its Italian creations. Room service is available.

DRESS CODE: The stated policy is to "maintain an atmosphere of dignified leisure." We interpret this as "casual-dressy." No jeans or jogging outfits are found at dinnertime. Men are requested to wear jackets at dinner.

ACCOMMODATIONS: Spa guests use the same accommodations as resort guests. There are six guest buildings on the premises, four with ocean view and two buildings directly on the ocean (the Forward Deck and the Forward Watch). Accommodations run the gamut from rooms to suites to cottages. All guest rooms have a view of the ocean. Most rooms are large and wood-paneled with simple contemporary furnishings; most have double beds. A timeshare condominium program also is available.

HOUSE RULES: Smoking is allowed in sections of the dining room and outdoors. A lounge in which alcohol is served is on the premises.

PHYSICAL FACILITIES: The spa is surrounded by the Montauk Bluffs and boasts one of the cleanest and sandiest beaches on Long Island. Separate spa pavilions for men and women are located near the Inn. Each pavilion has indoor exercise rooms, massage rooms, steam rooms, saunas, hydrotherapy rooms, treatment wrap rooms, tanning lounges, and herbal wrap rooms. There's a large gymnasium with Nautilus and Universal equipment located downstairs in the women's pavilion. A full-service beauty salon for both men and women is located within the spa building. The king-size saltwater indoor pool is a coed facility. It is heated to 82 degrees and overlooks the ocean. Spa hours are 8:00 to 10:00, seven days a week.

Outdoor athletic facilities include a fifteen-station parcours to strengthen endurance; it winds along the beach and bluffs. Tennis and golf are nearby.

ACTIVITIES, TREATMENTS, AND PROGRAMS: Only general spa facilities are included in room rates. The wide range of therapeutic and beauty treatments may be had à la carte or as part of package programs. Upon arrival at the spa, you will meet with a physiotherapist who will evaluate your medical history and current level of physical activities. Based on these findings, an individualized exercise and treatment program that will be of maximum benefit will be prepared for you. Included in the Seven-Day Rejuvenation program are morning aerobic beach walks, choice of three exercise classes daily (all classes are coed), one health and fitness profile, and one private exercise class based on your Health Assessment Profile. Some of the exercise classes (which are held in the ladies' pavilion or on the roof) include Yoga Salute to the Sun, Awake and Stretch, Spot Gymnastics, Aerobic Conditioning, Aquatic Body Contour, Aerobic Water Class, Weight Training with Universal Equipment, and Hatha Yoga.

Some of the beauty and pampering treatments you'll be treated to during your week's stay include: a half-hour daily massage; two German thalassotherapies (immersion in tubs of body-temperature seawater filtered to remove impurities—this is what you're here to try!); two Italian fango mud packs; two body scrubs, two facials, one hair-conditioning oil treatment, one manicure, one shampoo and styling (cut, shampoo, and styling for men), one polish change, one pedicure, and one makeup application (treatment of choice for men). Milopa Products from Switzerland are used for all beauty treatments. The evening program consists of nightly musical entertainment as well as lectures on nutrition, reflexology, stress management, and dieting. Each evening there's a "P.M. Workout," which is available at no extra charge.

A Day at Gurney's Inn

7:30	Breakfast
8:15	Weigh and measure
9:00	Beach walk
9:20–9:50	Awake and Aware
10:00–10:40	Aquatic aerobics
10:40–11:20	Spot slimnastics
11:20–11:50	Thalassotherapy
12:00	Lunch
2:00–2:30	Private exercise session with fitness instructor
4:20–5:00	Yoga
5:00	Herbal wrap
6:20	Massage
7:00	Cocktails and dinner

STAFF POPULATION: The staff at Gurney's is impressive. It includes a registered nurse, a nutritionist, massage therapists and aestheticians licensed by the state of New York, aquatic instructors, and exercise physiologists.

OPTIONAL COSTS: There are extra fitness classes, additional facials, beauty services, and a host of other delicious treatments you may want to treat yourself to.

NICE TO KNOW: About a mile up the road from Gurney's Inn are the Walking Dunes. These dunes were the site of the 1920s film *The Shiek*, where Rudolph Valentino swept a maiden out of the sand and onto his horse.

JUDY'S COMMENT: It's a shame that Gurney's Inn does not have a toll-free number to answer questions about their extensive program. This could be a good start on the road to your own fountain of youth. Hats off to Joyce and Nick Monte, "Keepers of the Inn," for researching and gathering the secrets of European spas and implementing them here in the United States.

* HARBOR ISLAND SPA
West End, Long Branch, NJ 07740
Outside New York City or New Jersey: 800-526-2157
In New Jersey: 201-222-2600
In New York City: 212-406-1162

The spa is located within a large resort hotel set right on the Atlantic Ocean, with 300 feet of private beach. Open year-round.

RATES: Affordable. Credit cards: American Express, MasterCard, Visa. Low season is April 1 to the end of June; high season from the end of June through Labor Day.

LOCATION AND TRANSPORTATION: Harbor Island is one hour south of New York City and 90 minutes east of Philadelphia. From New York City, you can even take the Asbury Park Transit Bus.

EMPHASIS/PHILOSOPHY: Beauty and pampering, with weight-loss program if you desire. The spa describes itself as an adventure in good health, well-being, and self-help: "Through our facilities, we hope to improve peoples' lives—through exercise, diet, and nutritional awareness."

DIET PROGRAM: 600 calories and up per day. The certified nutritionist meets individually with guests when they arrive and sets up an appropriate diet plan. The spa caters to vegetarian, Pritikin, and specialty diets if arrangements are made in advance. Your hosts, Miriam Rosenthal and Ben Paisner, say, "All meals at Harbor Island are gourmet quality, whether diet or nondiet, and our guests often find they aren't able to tell the difference." Desserts include such delights as Diet Chocolate Mousse, which is only 47 calories!

GUEST POPULATION: Coed. 300 guests. You'll find a mixture of dieters and folks who merely want to unwind. Miriam Rosenthal pointed out: "Over the years [the spa] has attracted numerous stars of Broadway and the movies."

PACKAGES AND MINIMUM STAYS: Other than occasional singles weekends, stays are unstructured. Arrive any day and leave any day.

MEAL SERVICE: There is one dining room for all hotel guests, with a hostess to seat you. Dieters and gourmet diners eat together and sit at the same tables.

DRESS CODE: Since you're at a resort hotel, dressy-casual is the byword. Jackets are required for men at dinner.

ACCOMMODATIONS: Twin-bedded luxury rooms, many with an ocean view. Suites are also available. The modern seascape decor features whites, greens, and blues.

HOUSE RULES: Anything goes. There is a lounge serving alcohol on the resort premises.

PHYSICAL FACILITIES: Separate and complete spa facilities for both men and women, including massage rooms, saunas, steam rooms, whirlpools, heated indoor and outdoor pools, a private ocean beach, indoor racquetball and handball courts, a card room, a beauty salon, and a boutique. Tennis courts and an 18-hole golf course are nearby (free midweek).

ACTIVITIES, TREATMENTS, AND PROGRAMS: While a guest, you're entitled to daily half-hour massages and your choice of any or all exercise classes (warm-up, aerobics, slimnastics, yoga, water exercise, and more). Evening entertainment includes fortune and card reading, investment counseling seminars, makeup demonstrations, art instruction, dance lessons, bridge lessons, sing-alongs, and nightly dancing to a live orchestra. Guests have full use of all spa facilities.

A Day at Harbor Island

8:00	Breakfast
9:00	Daily walk (meet in lobby)
9:30	Bend and stretch class
10:00	Aerobicize class
11:00	Water class

12:00	Lunch and free time
2:00	Exercise class
2:30	Wand class
3:00	Swimming
4:00	Massage
4:30	Juice bar snack
7:00	Dinner
8:00	Evening entertainment

OPTIONAL COSTS: Facials, cellulite body wraps, reflexology massages, and "mitts and boots" treatments are available at extra costs.

SPECIAL PROGRAMS: Harbor Island offers Jewish holiday packages, for which kosher meals can be provided.

NICE TO KNOW: At Harbor Island Spa, the waiters and waitresses are trained in proper nutritional guidance and are available to assist you at each meal. The spa holds beach barbecues in July and August. Atlantic City and Monmouth Park racetrack are nearby for those who feel lucky.

*BEST BUY AND WHY: This affordable program is a "Best Buy" because:
- It offers a good, individually tailored food program for dieter and nondieter alike.
- A minimum of 10 fitness classes are offered per day.
- A free half-hour daily massage is included in the room rate.
- The lovely private beach provides a perfect spot for unwinding.

---

* THE HILLS HEALTH
AND GUEST RANCH
C-26, 108 Ranch
100 Mile House, B.C. VOK 2EO
604-791-5225

The Cariboo Gold Rush country is the setting of this guest ranch, which features a complete spa program, luxurious accommodations, and down-home Western atmosphere and activities. Open year-round.

RATES: Affordable. Credit cards: MasterCard, Visa.

LOCATION: The town of 100 Mile House is on the Cariboo Highway, 290 miles from Vancouver. Vancouver has the nearest international airport, with connecting flights to Williams Lake on Canadian Airlines International. Limousine service is available for a $10 fee. A highly recommended alternative is the incredible scenic train ride from Vancouver to 100 Mile House. Complimentary pickup is available at the train depot.

EMPHASIS: According to co-owner and codirector Pat Corbett: "We don't sell brass and marble ... no glitz and glamour here. We believe in results and our people have good results. We ask them what their goal is upon arrival. And then we help them toward that goal. We concentrate on inches more than pounds. The average loss during a ten-day stay is 6½ inches and 6½ pounds."

DIET PROGRAM: 1,000–1,200 calories per day for women, 1,000–1,600 for men. Caloric intake is determined after the intake interview. The Swiss chef prepares many dishes from his homeland. Two all-time daily favorites are the delicious, hand-kneaded bran bread and the homemade muesli. A favorite weekly entree is Hunter Style Veal. Lamb, poultry, and fish are also served.

GUEST POPULATION: This spa program caters to individuals and couples. Families with children are welcome at the ranch; however, only adults are allowed in the spa program.

PACKAGES AND MINIMUM STAYS: The 7-day Executive Renewal is the Best Buy upon which this write-up is based. Other packages range from weekenders to the 10-day weight loss program. You determine your own day of arrival. There is no required minimum stay.

MEAL SERVICE: When you step into the dining room, you feel like you are stepping back in time to the Cariboo Gold Rush at the turn of the century. That historical essence has been captured by using furnishings and accessories similar to those used by early settlers.

Spa guests are seated in one area of the dining room and have their own special menu.

DRESS CODE: Casual and Western clothes will make you feel right at home here.

ACCOMMODATIONS: Every individual or couple has a private Swiss-style chalet, with master bedroom, 2 loft bedrooms, full bath, complete kitchen, living room with color TV, and two private balconies.

HOUSE RULES: No alcohol is served. Smoking is permitted outdoors and in certain areas.

PHYSICAL FACILITIES: The resort is located on 380 acres of pla-
teauland between mountain ranges. All chalets are on a high ridge
overlooking the vast wilderness—the epitome of peace and quiet.

The common areas include the lounge, dining room, and special
rooms. There are seminar rooms, a massage room, a beauty treatment
room, an aerobic room, and the gym and fitness room. In the latter,
there are cardiovascular testing machines, a running machine, exercise bikes, hydraulic and free weights, and a rowing machine. The
wet area includes a 20 by 40 indoor heated swimming pool, two whirlpools, and two saunas (men's and women's).

Outdoors are horseback riding facilities and cross-country ski
trails. Golf, tennis, downhill skiing, and fishing are available nearby.

ACTIVITIES, TREATMENTS, AND PROGRAMS: The spa day
starts with a half-hour power walk before breakfast. Then exercise
classes begin. There's yoga stretch, high-energy aerobics, no-bounce
aerobics, aquaerobics, stretch 'n' flex and stretch 'n' strength. After
all that, spa guests are rewarded with a delicious lunch, followed by
a seminar on life-style. The afternoon is free for pampering and optional activities, such as riding. Evening activities begin with dinner.
Half the time there's a special class or seminar and the other half
there's a social event. One of the favorites is a hayride to the party-
size Teepee, where low-cal drinks and high-spirited musicians await
you.

Included in the 7-day Executive Renewal Program are a private
chalet, gourmet diet meals, daily exercises, unlimited use of spa facilities, daily tanning sessions, one manicure and pedicure, one facial
and skin treatment, and one daily 45-minute massage.

OPTIONAL COST: Sport activities, such as riding, tennis and golf.
Also, additional pampering treatments.

NICE TO KNOW: Pat's wife, Juanita, once won a free trip to anywhere in the world. She chose La Costa and they both went. This
trip made them realize that there was no spa in their region of Canada, so they founded their own, incorporating the theme of the local
Cariboo Gold Rush.

JUDY'S COMMENT: The unique, wilderness location of The Hills
sounds idyllic!

*BEST BUY AND WHY: This spa is a "Best Buy" because:
- It offers many exercise classes and programs daily.
- The accommodations are excellent.
- A daily massage is included.

INTERLAKEN RESORT AND COUNTRY SPA
Box 80, Highway 50 West
Lake Geneva, WI 53147
800-225-5558
414-248-9121

Nestled in the heart of Wisconsin's Lake District, Interlaken stretches across 90 acres of hills and woods on the shores of Lake Como. Open year-round.

RATES: Moderate. Credit cards: American Express, Carte Blanche, Diners Club, MasterCard, and Visa.

LOCATION AND TRANSPORTATION: Located on Highway 50, three miles west of downtown Lake Geneva. The spa is 65 miles from Chicago, 40 miles from Milwaukee, and 70 miles from Madison, Wisconsin. Private planes use Big Foot Airport at Walworth, WI, or the Delavan Airstrip in Delavan, WI.

EMPHASIS/PHILOSOPHY: Interlaken Country Spa presents you with an opportunity to experience total fitness. It features a fully equipped facility, perfect for physical conditioning, weight reduction, or pampering. You'll come away "looking terrific, feeling wonderfully refreshed, full of energy, a more beautiful you!" Interlaken's staff will work with you to identify your goals and design a program to meet your individual needs. According to Sheri Counselbaum, the director, the focus of the spa is not on elegance but on providing warm and caring attention to each guest.

DIET PROGRAM: Three delicious meals per day that add up to 1,200 calories. The chef cooks with no salt, low fat, and lots of Dash and natural herbs. Everything is weighed and portion-controlled. Red meat is a part of the menu. Meals are beautifully served and garnished with vegetables, parsley, and sometimes crab apples for show. A typical menu has selections of four to five items per category, with the caloric count next to each item. Chef Bob Wuerhle, originally from Germany, does an excellent job of preparing the meals for both the Abbey Resort (the sister resort of Interlaken) and for Interlaken. A typical menu might include:

Act III (Dinner)

OVERTURE
Chilled tomato juice (20)

Shrimp cocktail (80)
Chicken broth with tarragon leaves (18)

GREEN SCENE
Celery and shrimp salad (60)
Cucumber au vinaigrette (30)
Bibb lettuce garni (30)

MAIN STAGE
Broiled lemon sole (120)
Chicken breast almondine (170)
Broiled filet mignon (180)
Colorado brook trout (146)
Salmon steak Florentine (140)
Breast of duck with peppered oranges (146)

SIDE SHOW
Asparagus (15)
Carrots Vichy (16)
Broiled tomato (15)

ENCORE
Frozen blueberry yogurt (40)
Fresh pineapple (60)
Ambrosia (35)
Blueberry sherbet (25)
Chocolate mousse (40)
Apricot parfait (40)

What can you expect to lose on this program? Sheri reports that, of course, it varies among individuals, but there have been people who have lost up to 3 or 4 pounds during their four-day midweek stay.

GUEST POPULATION: Coed. 40 guests. Weekends are always packed with lots of couples, mother-daughter teams, and women friends. Guest ages range from 18 to 75.

PACKAGES AND MINIMUM STAYS: Midweek package, 5 days/ 4 nights, Sunday to Thursday; weekend package, 3 days/2 nights, Friday to Sunday. Spa plan participants are required to stay at least two nights. From October through June, Interlaken Country Spa offers the "Workout Weekend." The program runs from Friday to Sunday (3 days/2 nights) for two weekends a month. The Workout Weekend is offered at a lower cost than the regular packages and includes one facial or massage and a full schedule of exercise classes. Keep your eye open for this discount package; it is quite popular.

MEAL SERVICE: Spa guests eat in the Lake Bluff dining room, which accommodates all resort guests. Mealtimes are: breakfast, 7:00–10:30; lunch, 11:00–2:00; and dinner, 5:30–10:30. There is a hostess to seat you, which is particularly nice if you are alone and wish to sit with other spa guests. The dining room overlooks the villas and Lake Como and is light and airy with modern decor. Seasonal plants decorate each table.

DRESS CODE: Dinner in the Lake Bluff dining room is dressy-casual. The Lake Bluff room is the only dining area serving spa cuisine. For those of you desiring a regular dining menu, the more formal Newport dining room, open only on weekends, requires a jacket and tie. Check it out before checking in. Comfy terry robes and slippers are provided in your locker, to be returned at the end of your stay.

ACCOMMODATIONS: Spa guests stay in deluxe rooms usually located near the spa area. The newly decorated, modern rooms are gorgeous according to Sheri and come with all the amenities.

HOUSE RULES: Smoking is permitted everywhere. The spa would like to discourage smoking in the spa area, but at the time of this writing it is still permissible. Alcoholic beverages are served throughout the resort. The choice is yours.

PHYSICAL FACILITIES: Recreational facilities abound, with Lake Como providing summertime fishing, boating, water skiing, jet skiing, and rental of pontoons, motorboats, and sailboats. Wintertime offers snowmobiling, ice fishing, and skiing nearby. Other outdoor facilities include five tennis courts and two outdoor pools with coed sauna, steamroom, and whirlpool. There are four to five golf courses nearby, none of which are on Interlaken's grounds. Indoor facilities include a beauty shop right in the spa that provides hair care (no perms), facial, pedicure, and manicure services; the Geneva exercise room that accommodates 50 guests; a spa boutique that sells tights and leotards; the Carefree Merchant (gift shop); separate locker rooms with a coed indoor pool area; and massage and herbal-wrap rooms.

ACTIVITIES, TREATMENTS, AND PROGRAMS: Participants in the morning walk meet in the lobby at 8:00 where they do general stretches and warming-up exercises. Usually the group walks to Lake Geneva for a five-mile trek through the Williams Bay area, filled with beautiful homes and estates.

A typical exercise schedule would be:

9:30–10:30	Low-impact aerobics
11:00–12:00	Aquacise
2:00–3:00	and

4:00–5:00   Aquacise alternating with weight training or stretch-and-tone
5:30–6:30   High-intensity aerobics (Sheri stresses
that you should do the exercises at your
own pace in this class)

Beauty treatments included in the spa package: one 45-minute massage (Swedish, Esalen, shiatsu, and reflexology); one facial; a makeup
session; two herbal wraps; two mineral baths; and two tanning sessions. On occasion, an evening program, "Color Me Beautiful," is
presented by a local cosmetologist, or a plastic surgeon gives a two-
hour lecture on face-lifts.

STAFF POPULATION: Sheri Counselbaum, spa director, comes
from an exercise, music, and dance background. She exclaims, "I love
spoiling people every day." The spa is well staffed with eight massage
therapists, four cosmetologists, three exercise instructors, and a receptionist and spa attendants. At the time of this writing, there is no
dietician on staff.

OPTIONAL COSTS: A full range of beauty treatments is available
at the spa salon.

NICE TO KNOW: You may want to combine the midweek with
the weekend package. Sheri suggests that you talk to the reservation
people to plan this arrangement. She also says that the spa is quite
flexible about services and that some substitutions can be made.
Weekends are always packed (midweeks are lighter), so plan your
weekend vacation time well in advance. Gratuities are included in
your meal plan but not in your pampering treatments.

JUDY'S COMMENT: Good for a quick introduction to spa life.
The Workout Weekend is a terrific buy and most affordable! This
might be just the right place to try "going it alone" because of the
friendly attention provided by the staff.

Courtesy of La Costa Hotel and Spa

LA COSTA HOTEL AND SPA
Costa del Mar Road
Carlsbad, CA 92009
800-854-5000
or 619-438-9111
Life Fitness Program: 800-426-5483

The Spa itself is only part of a huge resort complex, which sprawls over 5,600 acres of condominiums and villas, shops, hotels, and parks. Open year-round.

RATES: Expensive. Credit Cards: American Express, Diners Club, MasterCard, Visa. A 15 percent service charge is added to all rates.

LOCATION AND TRANSPORTATION: Forty-five minutes north of San Diego and two hours south of Los Angeles. Transportation is available to and from airports.

EMPHASIS/PHILOSOPHY: La Costa describes itself as "the ideal place for toning up or winding down . . . for losing inches and pounds (or even gaining if you wish) . . . or for doing whatever exercise or relaxation activities you prefer. . . . There's a full range of things to do to keep your days and evenings as active or relaxed as you choose. From massages to herb wraps, to exercises or yoga, to diet lectures or dancing in the Continental after dark."

DIET PROGRAM: Individualized diets, 600–1200 calories, are suggested by the medical staff, usually with an 800-calorie minimum. The Spa Dining Room serves a well-balanced menu, low fat, no sugar, no salt. Dietetic products are used. For nondieters, no less than seven restaurants are available.

Executive chef Willy Hauser creates masterpieces of *cuisine minceur.* There is a calorie count on the menu, and you choose from three selections for each category. Some of my favorite entrees from the La Costa menu are: Medallion of Veal Princess, Halibut in Wine Sauce, Curry of Lamb, and Hungarian Beef Goulash (each of these entrees is 150 calories). There's an outstanding array of delicious desserts (most at 40 calories) such as: Hot Cherries Burgundy, Chocolate Mousse, Peach-Almond Parfait, Frozen Strawberry Banana Yogurt, Orange Sherbet, and Hot Spiced Pears. How many pounds can you expect to shed? If you manage to give up your cocktails, a pound-a-day loss is not uncommon. One Chicago North Shore man, an annual visitor, lost 7½ pounds in three days—not unusual for men. I was at La Costa for five days on the 600-calorie plan and (with bits of cheating) lost 2½ pounds—a fantastic weight loss for my small frame!

GUEST POPULATION: Coed. 1,800 guests. This is the spot where the beautiful people, including many men, come to stay beautiful. This flamboyant haven is a playland for the rich and the influential. La Costa advertises itself as a resort for people who hate to be bored, and is seeing a real growth in 35- to 49-year-old guests. Lots of young starlets and Las Vegas showgirls frequent La Costa, along with celebrities such as Johnny Carson, Ed McMahon (who has a home nearby), Carol Burnett, Dinah Shore, Jack Lemmon, Felicia Farr, James Garner, and Gore Vidal (who stays in seclusion until the pounds are dropped). Lots of high-powered clientele, sophisticated couples, financial wizards, and beautiful people; some come to see and be seen, others take all their meals in their rooms and remain in seclusion. The lively alcoholic lounge is a good spot to meet members of the opposite sex.

PACKAGES AND MINIMUM STAYS: The basic spa plans, 4-night and 7-night programs, include all meals, as well as use of all spa facilities and a host of services and treatments. La Costa may also be taken à la carte; that is, meals are European plan (not included in the room rate) and the myriad treatments, massages, and beauty services are purchased as wished. There is also a 24-hour beauty day, a 2-night sampler, and a 9-night life-style management program. Note: children under 18 are not permitted in the spa.

SPECIAL PROGRAMS: The Life Fitness program concentrates on diet, exercise, and stress reduction. It is a 7-day program, starting and ending on Sundays. First, the staff doctor performs certain tests and orders others, such as blood sugar and cholesterol level. After evaluating the status of your health, both a nutritionist and exercise physiologist meet with you to plan your diet and exercise program. You will meet with them again at the end of your stay, to assess your progress and plan your home program.

The Life Style Center is a separate building for the lectures and personalized services, such as Tai Chi or yoga. Life Fitness guests use spa or resort facilities for other treatments or activities, such as massages and golf.

An important part of the program is the follow-up. The Life Fitness counselor keeps in touch with letters and phone calls. You are encouraged to call if you feel yourself slipping from the program. You can return for remotivation or even for a reunion.

MEAL SERVICE: All meals for spa-goers are served either in the spa dining room or via room service (for which there is a charge). It seems incredible but room service is usually on time—like a Swiss watch. Poolside luncheon is also available for no extra charge. Watching the parade of formally clad waiters matching dinners to diners is a real treat—reminiscent of the scene at a European outdoor cafe. The spa dining room is located next to the Continental dining room and the bar. All tables have cloths, vases full of fresh flowers, and sugar and salt substitutes. The spa dining room can accommodate the nondieter, although no alcoholic beverages are served here. But should you need to entertain guests, or if your companion must have a cocktail, La Costa can arrange seating at what they call the "outside post" area. This buffer zone (consisting of a row of four tables) can accommodate spa diners, regular diners, and those who wish a cocktail. Strolling violinists add to the charm of your dinner. If you're a woman traveling alone and would like company, just talk to one of the hostesses and they'll be happy to seat you with a companion. The dieticians are on hand at all meals. They are all a true delight and really "know their stuff." Menus for the next day are distributed at dinnertime, and should you be dining in your room, the dietician contacts you by 9:00 P.M. to set up the next day's meal plan. I was given specific suggestions on how to balance my menu nutritionally. The care and kind attention of the staff dieticians is truly outstanding.

DRESS CODE: Daytime attire is provided by the spa. Women are given yellow togas and shoes, and La Costa provides white terry robes (as in European spas) to wear while moving about from your room to the spa. There are no dress restrictions in the spa dining room for lunch, but shorts, jeans, and sweatsuits are prohibited at dinnertime. The nonspa dining rooms have different dress codes, which you'll need to check out if you plan to use them. Most California folks dress low-key. If you're used to a country club way of life and accustomed to casual but expensive clothes, you'll fit right in here.

ACCOMMODATIONS: Spa accommodations consist of the Spa Building, Main Building, and Executive Homes. The buildings are two-storied, built around a U-shaped courtyard with a pool in the middle. Each first-floor room has its own lanai, with lounges, table, and chair. The 500 building is the newer structure, with more spacious bathrooms but no view of the pool, as compared to the 400 building. If you're an avid sun-worshiper and like to be closer to the dining room area, you may prefer the low 400 numbers. But if staying cool in the afternoon appeals to you, opt for the upper 400 numbers.

The pastel rooms are decorated in lovely shades of peach and greens. There are two deep and comfy lounge chairs with an ottoman—nice for lounging and daytime reading. There's a color television and built-in radio in every room plus your own digital alarm clock. Also a huge marble dining table is on hand for leisurely dining and pool viewing. A charming basket of La Costa products awaits you in your room, and the soaps are simply wonderful.

HOUSE RULES: Anything goes! I have never seen as many ashtrays in any other spa. There are smoking and nonsmoking areas within the spa. The poolside solariums are good for a smoke.

PHYSICAL FACILITIES: There are separate spa buildings for men and women (55,000 square feet), with some shared exercise classes. Each area has two sets of indoor, glass-enclosed but open to the sky, hot and cold plunge pools. There are two outdoor pools. One is 3½ feet deep, the other is 4 feet deep. Most swim classes are held in the 4-foot pool. Be sure to check with a fitness instructor as to class location. This is the only spa I've been to that allows nude swimming in the spa pool area (except during swim classes when you're expected to cover up). The men's and women's areas each have massage rooms, facial rooms, herbal wrap rooms, exercise rooms, tanning rooms, makeup rooms, whirlpool, sauna, and solaria. Hats off to the designer of La Costa's women's spa! The locker rooms are conveniently located and have all the right amenities. Each shower stall offers marvelous flavors of body gels—herbal, lemon, raspberry, strawberry, and coconut. La Costa shampoos and bath conditioners are always at your fingertips. Towels and suntan items are plentiful. Supplies appear like magic—the attendants are that good and that well trained!

Courtesy of La Costa Hotel and Spa

Spa hours are from 9:00 A.M. to 6:00 P.M., seven days a week. Spa accommodations and buildings are close to the jogging trail, and there's a central coed pool convenient for lunch. The La Costa schedule room is beautifully managed, but take note: they're open from nine to noon and from two to four in the afternoon.

Facilities at La Costa include swimming pools, a 27-hole golf course, 25 all-weather tennis courts, and horseback riding. There are seven gourmet restaurants and a movie theater. Dining, shopping (clothes, toiletries, miscellaneous), and evening social or educational programs take place in the main building. Movies and lectures are held in the auditorium. There is a nutrition center on the second floor of the main building, which is open from 1:00 to 10:00 P.M. At no added cost, a nutrition consultant will provide a computerized evaluation of your dietary pattern and make recommendations to improve your nutritional habits. You just call and make an appointment.

ACTIVITIES, TREATMENTS, AND PROGRAMS: Upon arrival

at La Costa you will see the resident physician, who will weigh and measure you, take a brief history, and discuss your dietary goals. I was surprised to learn that they still had my records with all vital statistics from my last visit—15 years before, no less! You have a choice of going to any or all of the exercise classes (no limiting here as at some permissive spas I know). Complimentary golf (no greens fees) and tennis privileges are included in the complete spa programs. Evening programs include diet lectures, dietetic cocktail parties, spa cooking demonstrations, backgammon and bridge lessons, and disco dance sessions.

For your enjoyment, I include a typical exercise schedule at La Costa.

Men's Daily Class Schedule

8:30	Walk
9:00	Men's fitness class
9:45	Water volleyball
10:20	Aqua-Thinics (pool exercise)
11:05	Aerobics (coed—ladies' gym)
11:45	Open gym
12:25	Yoga (coed—ladies' spa or open gym)
2:00	Men's fitness class
2:40	Water volleyball
3:20	Aqua-Thinics
4:05	Aerobics (coed—ladies' spa)
4:45	Specialized men's exercises
5:25	Open gym

Women's Daily Class Schedule

8:30	Walk
9:00	Stretch and flex (mat and bar work)
9:45	Costa Curves (rigorous calisthenics)
10:20	Spot reducing
10:20	Aqua-Thinics (pool exercise)
11:05	Aerobics (coed)
11:05	Aqua-Thinics
11:45	La Costa Special (advanced exercise)
11:45	Aqua-Thinics
12:25	Hatha-yoga (coed—beginning)
2:00	Spot reducing
2:00	Aqua-Thinics
2:40	Stretch and flex
2:40	Aqua-Thinics
3:20	Costa Curves (coed)
4:05	Aerobics (coed)

You will enjoy a wonderful array of beauty treatments during your stay at La Costa on the 4-day and 7-day women's programs:

4-DAY PROGRAM	7-DAY PROGRAM
Daily	*Daily*
Half-hour massage	Half-hour massage
Half-hour facial	Half-hour facial
Herbal wrap	Herbal wrap
Exercise classes	Tanning session
Makeup classes	Exercise classes
	Makeup classes
One Per Stay	*One Per Stay*
Loofah massage	Loofah massage
Collagen facial	Collagen facial
Manicure/pedicure	Manicure/pedicure
Oil treatment	Oil treatment
Polish change	Polish change
Private makeup	Private makeup
Eyebrow arch or wax	Eyebrow arch or wax
Skin analysis and review	Skin analysis and review
1 shampoo and set	2 shampoos and sets
1 spot toning treatment	2 spot toning treatments
	Special facial machine
	Orthion treatment

I found the facial products at La Costa to be heavily fragranced—too much so for my sensitive skin. You may want to bring along your own creams for the facials, or be sure to speak up if you have any skin sensitivity.

There's a staff of 47 to serve you. I was lucky enough to enjoy several hours at the skilled hands of Kristine, who has over 1,000 hours of massage therapy and is still going strong. Don't forget to let your able schedulers know exactly what your needs are for a perfect match-up.

STAFF POPULATION: An attentive and courteous staff, including a full-time M.D. and three dieticians, is at your service. La Costa's management is truly impressive for a U.S. resort.

OPTIONAL COSTS: Some of the beauty extras offered are leg, bikini, upper lip, and chin waxing; paran facials; facial peels; and high-frequency skin treatment.

NICE TO KNOW: La Costa was recently acquired by a Japanese consortium, after having undergone an 85-million-dollar restoration.

JUDY'S COMMENTS: La Costa rates an "A" for effective diet and weight control, glorious pampering, and an outstandingly courteous staff. The fitness and education programs lag far behind. A note on massage therapists: In my opinion, La Costa has some of the best Swedish-massage therapists found anywhere. How truly wonderful it would be if La Costa could create a central and self-contained spa and related educational area as well as a separate dining room that would keep temptation out of sight and out of mind! Still, it's the only place that offers you a closely supervised 600-calorie diet. The mention of the name La Costa conjures up thoughts of opulence, sports galore, nightlife, and celebrities—which is exactly what the spot has to offer. It's a truly permissive environment.

LE PLI HEALTH SPA AND SALON AT THE CHARLES HOTEL
Charles Square
Cambridge, MA 02138
617-868-8087

Open year-round. In the heart of the shops, cafes, jazz and folk clubs, theaters, and international restaurants of Harvard Square and by the shores of the Charles River, Le Pli is a three-level structure adjoining the Charles Hotel. This urban spa provides visitors with a place to relax and reenergize and the flexibility to take care of business or simply enjoy the many resources of the Cambridge and Boston areas.

RATES: Moderate. Rates can vary slightly depending on treatments and activities chosen. Gratuities are included in the price. Credit cards: American Express, MasterCard, Visa.

LOCATION AND TRANSPORTATION: Cambridge is right next to Boston. A short subway ride takes you to the center of the city. Complimentary limousine service to and from nearby Logan Airport in Boston is provided.

EMPHASIS/PHILOSOPHY: Le Pli makes an effort to show busy men and women that it is good for body and soul to relax and be pampered. Highly individualized attention provides each guest with an integrated program of European-style beauty treatments and fitness services. The spa tries to supply visitors with the "necessary tools to create a diet and exercise program tailored to specific goals and preferences," a program they can incorporate into their daily life once they return home. Owners Sydney and Silke Moss, originally from Europe themselves, were profoundly influenced by many spas in Germany and have imbued Le Pli with a European atmosphere.

DIET PROGRAM: The food served spa guests features low-fat cuisine totaling about 1,200 calories per day. Fish and vegetables are emphasized with an occasional chicken entry. Daily and seasonal menus use fresh New England ingredients. No beef is served, and special dietary requests are accommodated. Spa manager Marcy Baskin meets with each guest personally to design a meal plan for them. She follows the "Fit or Fat" system developed by Covert Bailey, where fat units rather than calories are counted. The spa believes in promoting reeducation of eating habits, resulting in gradual weight loss.

GUEST POPULATION: Coed. Maximum of 10 participants in the spa program. According to Baskin, the spa specializes in making people who come alone feel comfortable. Many of the guests on the spa plan come from New York City and have busy careers. At any one time, Le Pli is host to: hotel guests not on the spa plan but using spa services à la carte; people who have joined Le Pli as a health club; and spa program participants. Le Pli health club members consist of about 60 percent women and 40 percent men. Many are from the Harvard Business School or from the Boston area business community.

PACKAGES AND MINIMUM STAYS: There is a 6-night/7-day package, with arrival and departure days open. Weekend programs are available once a month. A 1-day spa package is the minimum program period. For those who live in the area, a 3-month weight and fitness management program is offered.

MEAL SERVICE: The meal plan at Le Pli works on a very individualized basis. Guests arrange with the spa to have their meals either in the spa cafe, one of the hotel restaurants, by the pool, or in their rooms. At the time of this writing, the spa food is prepared by special arrangement with Le Pli in the kitchens of the Charles Hotel.

DRESS CODE: The general ambience of the Charles Hotel, where spa guests stay, is relaxed and casual. The hotel provides a terry robe for use during your stay, and the spa provides a lovely white sweatsuit with the Le Pli logo on it for you to keep. Dressed in their terry robes, visitors can be seen in the hotel corridors heading for Le Pli. Most people wear their sweatsuits during meals. It is not necessary to bring much clothing unless you plan on participating in activities outside the hotel. A sweatsuit, exercise clothes, bathing suit, and pajamas are about all you need.

ACCOMMODATIONS: The guest rooms in the Charles Hotel are decorated in a style that is a blend of contemporary and antique themes. Rooms feature original artwork and luxury appointments including: an honor bar, three telephones, bathroom television and scale, writing desk, quilted down comforter, and telephone modems for computer hookups in some rooms. Twenty-four-hour-a-day room service is available.

HOUSE RULES: Smoking is not permitted in the spa area. Alcohol is available in the rooms and in hotel restaurants.

PHYSICAL FACILITIES: Le Pli occupies three different levels. On the first floor you will find an exercise studio with an aerobic sprung floor, the reception desk, weight room, luxuriously appointed showers and locker rooms, and private rooms where spa treatments are administered. Level two houses the spa cafe and the beauty salon, in which hair and skin care, makeup consultations, manicures, pedicures, and waxing services are provided. Level three, the top level of the building, is entirely devoted to the pool area. The pool is glass-enclosed and overlooks the Charles River. It has sliding glass doors which allows a maximum of fresh air and light to enter depending on the season. The pool has four lanes and is attended at all times. Next to it are a warm-up area, suntan booth, huge hand-tiled whirlpool, and a plant-screened sun terrace where spa-goers have their meals on occasion.

The spa has a full range of exercise equipment including KaiserCam II, Nautilus, free weights, rowing and bicycle ergometers, cross-country ski machines, treadmills, and Lifecycles. The equipment used for spa treatments is almost entirely imported from Europe. The spa boutique sells a full line of exercise clothing, Bioesthetique hair, skin and makeup products, and fitness equipment. The spa has a laundry room, but most guests use the valet service provided by the hotel for their laundry needs. In addition, the Charles Hotel has large conference and banquet rooms for business use. There is also a special enclosed area of 24 distinctive shops called Charles Square within the hotel.

ACTIVITIES, TREATMENTS, AND PROGRAMS: An Individual Fitness Analysis is included in the week package. This analysis is performed by an exercise physiologist and includes strength and flexibility measurements, body fat/muscle assessment, and a submaximal graded exercise test to determine fitness capacity. The physiologist will then design a total exercise program for you both while at the spa and to incorporate into your daily life after leaving Le Pli. Unlimited exercise classes come with the package. Among classes offered are body conditioning, stretch, jazz, ballet, yoga, aerobics at three different levels of difficulty, conditioning, stretch and run; hydro-exercise classes to music in the pool; and back care. At the time of this writing, 10 exercise classes a day are offered. One personal fitness training session also comes with the week program.

Beauty treatments included in the 7-day package are 6 one-hour massages (Swedish, athletic, shiatsu, or Polarity therapy); a one-hour facial; 2 body wraps of different types; 1 Italian fango mud treatment; 1 hydrotherapy treatment; 1 makeup consultation and application session; 1 shampoo and blow dry; a manicure and pedicure; and 1 hair and scalp consultation and conditioning.

STAFF POPULATION: Manager Marcy Baskin coordinates all programs at Le Pli and helps give the spa a caring and friendly feeling. All the massage therapists are certified. The beauty treatment therapists are specially trained by Baroness Hildegard von Mengeren, a leading spa expert in Europe.

OPTIONAL COSTS: Personal trainers will exercise with you. Private swimming and aerobics classes and jogging coaching are also available.

NICE TO KNOW: The spa gives guests copies of Covert Bailey's book, Fit or Fat. Le Pli means "fold" or "wrinkle" in French. Le Pli has been so successful that they intend soon to open another spa in Boston.

JUDY'S COMMENTS: A highly personalized, total program for independent spa-goers. Le Pli creates a restful retreat in the middle of a big city. The program offers beauty treatments with a European touch and an individual diet and fitness program designed to be followed in everyday life. The seven-day spa package includes a vast array of treatments and fitness instruction at quite a reasonable price.

MARRIOTT'S DESERT SPRINGS RESORT AND SPA
74855 Country Club Drive
Palm Desert, CA 92260
Spa/Hotel Reservations: 800-255-0848
Spa Appointment Desk: 619-341-1874

Surrounded by the Santa Rosa mountains, this is a year-round 400-acre resort and spa in the desert.

RATES: Expensive. Credit cards: American Express, Diners Club, MasterCard, Visa.

LOCATION AND TRANSPORTATION: Set in Southern California's luxurious desert community with easy access to fine shops, restaurants, and a wide variety of recreation, the spa is just 13 miles from the Palm Springs airport. Pickup is through American Limo (make prior arrangements before arrival) and will cost you approximately $10 each way.

EMPHASIS/PHILOSOPHY: Desert Springs is a European-style spa offering individually designed programs with emphasis on weight loss, stress reduction, and life-style reeducation. This is accomplished in a lushly beautiful setting under medical supervision in conjunction with the Eisenhower Medical Center. Because programs are individually designed, they are flexible and allow you to go at your own pace. Computerized body composition analysis and in-depth fitness assessments allow you to make the most of the exercise classes and services offered at the spa. The center is also a resort, which allows couples the option of both enrolling in the spa program or one enrolling and the spouse simply partaking of the many recreational offerings. Something for everyone!

DIET PROGRAM: Approximately 1,000–1,200 calories per day. Spa guests are seated in a separate section of the most elegant of several restaurants: Lakeview. The food is individually tailored to your nutrition program. Prepared by Chef Christian Chavanne, formerly of Las Colinas/Four Seasons, it is gourmet spa cuisine. Offerings are low in fat and calories and portion-controlled. A typical meal might include cream of carrot soup with ginger and dill, wilted spinach salad with smoked egg white, wild mushrooms, and herb vinaigrette, grilled boneless quail with juniper sauce, and a fresh fruit tart for dessert. Weight-loss totals are not yet available, but they are generally deemphasized because total life-style change is considered the target. Once this is achieved, pound loss will follow, according to spa director Jack Patterson, who commented: "It's hard not to lose weight if you follow the program and eat at the spa dining room and do not cheat." No red meat is served.

GUEST POPULATION: Coed. 150 guests, 75 percent women and 25 percent men at this time. Couples make up 30 to 40 percent of the population at any one time. Separate facilities for men and women.

PACKAGES AND MINIMUM STAYS: Packages include an 8-day/7-night Spa Program; 4-day Sampler and 4-day Deluxe programs; and a Perfect Day getaway. Guests staying at the resort can use the spa facilities on an à la carte basis.

MEAL SERVICE: Spa guests dine in a separate section of the

Lakeview, the Marriott's most elegant restaurant. The restaurant is California casual and features fresh flowers and fine china on the table. The resort itself has four other restaurants. The Lakeview is open to the public, but a hostess will seat you in the spa section.

DRESS CODE: The spa will furnish you with a warm-up suit, which is fine for breakfast and lunch. However, you might want to change into dress pants and a nice blouse for dinner. The spa provides all exercise clothing during your stay: warm-up suit, robe, slippers, shorts, T-shirt, or leotards and tights for the women. Bathing suits should be packed and an extra set of leotards and tights is not a bad idea.

ACCOMMODATIONS: Guest rooms are spacious and feature a refrigerator, minibar, telephone, TV, air conditioning, private bath with double sinks, daily maid service, and a balcony big enough for lounging. The resort has 920 rooms, including 65 VIP suites. Spa guests are housed in a separate section near the spa building. Each room is decorated in California casual with a European touch! The hotel resort has cantilevered wings with an eight-story atrium. All rooms feature beautiful views of the mountains, man-made lakes, and pools.

HOUSE RULES: Smoking is permitted in the hotel rooms but not at the spa facilities. You can smoke in the restaurants. Alcohol is permitted and served in the restaurants.

PHYSICAL FACILITIES: This spacious 27,000-square-foot spa has it all: lap and exercise pools, hot and cold plunge pools, individual whirlpool baths, Turkish steam room, Finnish sauna, an advanced 22-station fitness gym, aerobics room, exercise lawn, and walking and jogging paths. Power walks and hiking in the surrounding mountains and desert biking add special flavor. Spa guests are also guests of the resort and are welcome to enjoy the full range of activities, including a Ted Robinson-designed 18-hole golf course, a unique 12,000-square foot swimming beach with white desert sand sloping to a freshwater lake, 16 tennis courts, a stadium for tournament play, and a full-service tennis pro shop. Two outdoor heated swimming pools are used by spa and resort guests alike.

Facial rooms, massage rooms, and separate locker rooms for men and women are in the spa building. A beauty shop is on the premises. There are several boutiques scattered throughout the resort where one can purchase anything from exercise wear to formals. Shiatsu acupressure massage is available for men, and Swedish body massages are available for both men and women. An underwater massage is for women only, and women can have loofah body buffs and herbal wraps. Aromatherapy is offered, as are fitness and aerobics classes geared to your needs. Personal training sessions are available.

ACTIVITIES, TREATMENTS, AND PROGRAMS: At this writing, three separate spa packages are available, but note that extra days can be added to each of these and will include additional activities and treatments. Since this spa is new, I've been told that additional packages may be offered at a later date. For now, the packages are as follows. Four-Day Spa Sample includes accommodations at the resort, meals, medical screening on arrival, arrival and departure fitness consultation, individual program consultation, Swedish body massages, 1 private whirlpool bath, unlimited use of spa facilities, unlimited fitness classes, and use of the spa wardrobe. Four-Day Deluxe Spa Program offers all the above plus daily bottle of spa water, 2 facial treatments, 2 herbal wraps, loofah body buff, an additional private whirlpool bath, and unlimited tennis at the resort. Spa salon services are also included and include a shampoo/blow dry, makeup lesson, manicure, and pedicure for women; a shampoo/haircut, scalp treatment, manicure, and pedicure for men.

The Seven-Day Deluxe Program includes 7 nights' accommodations, all spa meals, medical screening, fitness and program consultations, unlimited access to spa facilities and classes, daily bottle of spa water, use of the spa wardrobe, and unlimited tennis. Treatments include: 4 facials, 6 half-hour Swedish body massages, 3 herbal wraps, 3 whirlpool baths, 1 loofah body buff, 1 underwater body massage for women or, for men, 1 shiatsu acupressure massage. Salon services included are the same as listed for the four-day Deluxe package. A special half-day "Conference" program is available for conventioneers on site.

OPTIONAL COSTS: Swedish skin care products by Kerstin Florian are used in the beauty salon and can be purchased. Famed hair stylist Jose Eber and his team operate this salon. Several boutiques and a sundry shop offer all kinds of possibilities for shopping, from bathing suits to lavish designer formal wear. Remember, this is in the heart of Southern California's luxurious and sophisticated desert resort area, and people dress very well although casually. For some spa-goers, tennis and golf time is extra, depending on the package you purchased. All beauty skin care and treatments can be purchased à la carte. Massage therapists are available to give you a massage in your room for an additional sum.

NICE TO KNOW: Because this is a hotel resort cum spa, many conventioneers come down, do a few days business, and elect to stay on for a while at the spa. Or, if time is short, they will use the spa's facilities and treatments on a per charge basis. Because this resort caters to vacationers and conventioneers as well as spa-goers, the onus is on you to follow through with your spa program. As one of the directors told me, no one follows you around to see that you're not eating spa meals, then cheating at other restaurants or consuming alcohol in the lounges. A concerted effort is made to change life-style habits, but this is a very relaxed and permissive resort, so willpower is necessary!

NEW LIFE SPA
Liftline Lodge
Stratton Mountain, VT 05155
802-297-2600
802-297-2534

A health retreat that encourages group spirit, set within the frame-work of a wintertime ski resort. The spa-ski program combines the elements of a fitness camp with the looks of a quaint Austrian inn. Open year-round.

RATES: Moderate. Credit cards: MasterCard, Visa.

LOCATION AND TRANSPORTATION: Located in the heart of southern Vermont's spectacular Green Mountain National Forest. Two hours northeast of Albany, where you may rent a car or take a bus to Manchester, Vermont, and be picked up by a spa driver. Or fly from Albany into Rutland, only 1 hour away. Driving times: 3½ hours from Boston, 4½ hours from New York City.

EMPHASIS/PHILOSOPHY: New options for health, good nutri-tion, and physical well-being, with emphasis on a positive self-image.

DIET PROGRAM: 800–1,000 calories a day. Jimmy LeSage, spa owner as well as premier chef, has worked out a tasty and workable diet. Low in fat, moderate in protein, and high in complex carbohy-drates. The folks at the spa call it a modified Pritikin program: how-ever, the menu does include chicken, fish, and veal, with lots of fruits and vegetables. New Life can easily accommodate guests who wish a strictly vegetarian diet. Each guest takes home a diet and recipe plan. LeSage calls the cuisine served to participants "gourmet style" and manages to include such dishes as Veal Piccata, Ratatouille, Onion Soup, and Salad Niçoise. What can you expect to lose? Many guests shed five pounds during their week's stay. But, according to Jimmy, "what gratifies you more than the loss of pounds at the end of your stay is the inch loss and the tune-up." Here's a sample menu from the New Life Spa:

BREAKFAST
Honeydew melon
Sprouted wheat French toast and Vermont maple syrup

LUNCH
Salad Niçoise

DINNER
Spinach salad with tahini dressing
Paprika chicken
Stuffed potato
Carrots with orange glaze
Chocolate mousse or strawberries Romanoff

All meals are served with decaffeinated coffee, herbal tea (hot or cold), and bottled mineral water from Saratoga Springs.

GUEST POPULATION: Coed. 30 guests. The guests range in age from 24 to 64, with some very fit and some not so fit. Most guests are there to get a "fresh start" on a fitness and right-eating program. It's reported that a frequent guest of the Golden Door in California prefers New Life: "It's less expensive and the setting is just as beautiful." Mel Zuckerman, owner of Canyon Ranch in Arizona, pops in to chat and compare programs.

PACKAGES AND MINIMUM STAYS: There is a 7-day/6-night program (in on Sunday, out on Saturday) from March to September. A 6-day/5-night program is conducted from January to March. Winter sessions, with plenty of skiing, go on from December to April.

MEAL SERVICE: There is a separate dining room for spa guests. The tables are decorated with pastel-colored tablecloths and small bunches of wild flowers in Perrier bottles. Through the dining room's picture window one can see the Green Mountains. No room service available.

DRESS CODE: Casual is the byword. Bring along a sweater or jacket as mornings and evenings are cool in the mountains. Hiking shoes are a must. Don't forget your ski togs for winter. Bring your ski equipment or rent it at the lodge. Tuck in a large towel or mat for yoga classes.

ACCOMMODATIONS: Spa guests stay in the two-story Glockenhof Austrian chalet at the base of Stratton Mountain. The rooms are decorated with touches of wood, reminiscent of the Tyrol. Each room has two double beds (covered with colorful comforters), a private bath with shower, and a telephone.

HOUSE RULES: No smoking allowed in dining room or spa facilities. Alcoholic lounge is located in the Liftline Lodge building.

PHYSICAL FACILITIES: There's a complete recreation building on the grounds called the Stratton Sports Center, which houses indoor racquetball courts, weight room, indoor lap swimming pool, indoor tennis, Nautilus room, steam room, Jacuzzi, and locker room facilities for men and women. In the basement of the Glockenhof building are massage rooms, facial rooms, saunas, hot tubs, and a small gymnasium. Outdoors you'll find another swimming pool, clay tennis court, and the mountains at your doorstep for hiking or downhill and cross-country skiing in winter. Golf is available nearby at Stratton Mountain Country Club. Both English and Western riding are offered at stables nearby. Liftline Lodge has an Austrian boutique.

ACTIVITIES, TREATMENTS, AND PROGRAMS: Package prices include all meals, unlimited exercise classes, use of all spa facilities, and two massages. Ski sessions include lessons, equipment, and lift. Jimmy LeSage, certified yoga instructor and consultant to the New England Cardiovascular Health Institute, promises each participant "a program that gives even the beginner a routine to take home." The regimen includes vigorous slimnastics, aerobics, spot toning, body dynamics, mountain walks, skiing in winter, yoga, and free time for hot tub, saunas, and massages. Is the routine too vigorous? We were told: "You can do any or all classes depending on how you feel each day. We stress listening to your body and not pushing it beyond its own boundaries. All of our classes are small and geared to individual instruction. We concentrate on proper body alignment to protect the lower back and proper exercise technique to reduce the chance of any injury." At evening seminars you discuss nutrition, exercise, cardiovascular care, and beauty tips, and share ways of building your own everyday New Life program.

A Summer Day at New Life

7:00	Wake-up
7:30	The Energizer (stretch and stroll)
8:00	Breakfast
9:00	Body Awareness
10:00	Body Conditioner
11:00	Brisk walk
12:15	Lunch
1:15	Health notes (mini lecture)
2:00	Body contour
3:00	Aerobics
4:15	Yoga
5:00	Free time (relax and reflect)

6:30   Dinner
8:00   Evening activity (may be a workshop, lecture,
      guest speaker, or movie)
10:00   Bedtime

The schedule for the winter spa-ski program is basically the same through lunchtime, with hours of 12:30–4:00 left free for skiing or workouts at the Stratton Sports Center.

OPTIONAL COSTS: Additional massages, facials, rental of ski equipment, and tennis lessons are available.

NICE TO KNOW: Jimmy LeSage graduated from Florida State University and moved to Vermont, where he worked as a chef in the kitchens of several restaurants. Because of his experience as a yoga instructor and his interest in natural foods, he decided he was perfectly suited to run a health spa. The young, energetic staff is friendly and caring and imbued with the New Life philosophy. New Life also offers an intensive program designed specifically for those who can maintain an accelerated pace. It consists of strenuous hikes and more strenuous aerobic workouts.

JUDY'S COMMENTS: An effective and enriching health experience from all viewpoints (even the yoga headstand). Sound nutrition and a good fitness program should add up to solid weight and inch loss.

THE NORWICH INN SPA
AND VILLAS
Route 32
Norwich, CT 06360
800-892-5692
203-886-2401

This classic country inn is set on beautifully landscaped grounds, overlooking an 18-hole golf course. The spa facility is located just a short distance from the Inn. Nearby are some of New England's most scenic and historic towns, such as Old Lyme, Essex, and Mystic Seaport. Open year-round.

RATES: Expensive. Credit cards: American Express, Carte Blanche, Diners Club, MasterCard, and Visa.

LOCATION AND TRANSPORTATION: Transportation can be arranged from the Groton airport as well as from the New London train station. Hartford is about 45 minutes away and New London is 20–30 minutes away. New York City is a 2½-hour drive.

EMPHASIS/PHILOSOPHY: The Norwich Inn offers a comprehensive program of diet, exercise, and beauty to reshape the body and spirit. Highly individualized attention is given to help guests reach their specific goals. The main concern is to reeducate participants on how to attain lifetime fitness through exercise and proper eating habits.

DIET PROGRAM: Guests learn how to eat correctly through portion control. Calorie counting is not emphasized at Norwich Inn. The dietician bases the menus on 1,200 to 1,500 calories per day for women and 1,800 to 2,000 for men. Complex carbohydrates, notably vegetables, fruits, and grains, with moderate amounts of protein, are prepared New England-style, with little fat, sugar, or salt. The protein consists of fresh seafood, chicken, and veal. Beef is not served. Seasonal specialties offered are locally grown fruits and vegetables, as well as soups flavored with fresh herbs.

GUEST POPULATION: Coed. 25 to 35 guests. Men and women work out together but use separate whirlpools, saunas, steam rooms, and changing facilities. Guests have included Mary McFadden, Michael Douglas, Placido Domingo, and Bill Blass.

PACKAGES AND MINIMUM STAYS: Three different spa programs are offered: a five-night/five-day program (arrive Sunday, leave Friday); the Norwich Revitalizer, a two-night program (starting either Monday or Wednesday, in at 4:00 P.M. and out by noon); and a one-day Revitalizer Plan, which is the minimum stay. Although there is no spa program per se on weekends, spa services are available on an à la carte basis.

MEAL SERVICE: Upon check-in, spa guests staying longer than one day are given their choice of two dining rooms, The Windsor Room or The Grill. The Windsor Room serves only spa cuisine. The Grill is the general dining room, which offers spa cuisine, an impressive list of regular entrees, and alcoholic beverages. Spa guests who are accompanied by non-spa-goers usually elect to dine in The Grill.

Both dining rooms have a classy, country atmosphere. The Windsor Room is done in relaxing sea-foam green. The Grill's decor is in tones of fresh green and watermelon pink. Most tables seat four to six people so that participants can get to know each other. Meal presentation is enhanced by fresh flowers and fine china. Chef Daniel Kucharski heads up the spa cooking-team and gives lecture/demonstrations once a week.

DRESS CODE: It is quite acceptable to wear jogging outfits for breakfast and lunch. Evenings are more formal: jackets are required for men in both dining rooms; ties are optional. Ladies, take your cue from that! The spa provides guests with their own lockers that contain a bathrobe, slippers, and a bag for bathing suits.

ACCOMMODATIONS: Norwich Inn has 80 villas and 65 rooms, both with a choice of rooms or suites. Guest room decor in the original inn was designed by Peri Wolfman, using Laura Ashley prints in warm shades of cinnamon, sand, and Nantucket blue. Guest rooms feature restored antique furniture, chintz print upholstered armchairs and sofas, country print wallpaper, ruffled drawback curtains, hand-woven rag rugs, and Chippendale mirrors. Step-stools accompany raised, four-poster beds in many rooms.

The villa suites have a sitting area with a fireplace, a kitchen area, and either one king-size bed or two double beds. The villa duplexes have a kitchen area, a dining area, and a living room with a queen-size Sico bed (a fold-down bed, similar to a Murphy bed). They also have a queen-size bed in the loft. These units were decorated using Ralph Lauren fabrics in tones of mauve and teal blue. All rooms are equipped with color cable television and ceiling fans.

HOUSE RULES: Children under the age of 18 are not allowed in the spa. Smoking is not permitted in the spa area. Alcohol is served in the Grill Room and the Prince of Wales Bar only.

PHYSICAL FACILITIES: Centered around a colorfully tiled workout pool are these facilities: exercise rooms, machine and weight rooms, and treatment rooms. Each locker room has its separate whirlpool, sauna, and changing area. There is an indoor, heated pool. Outdoor facilities include a PGA golf course, several jogging trails, and Har-Tru tennis courts. A spa boutique carries everything from leotards to bathing suits. Sundries are available at the inn boutique. A facility for hairstyling, manicures, or pedicures is forthcoming. For now, the concierge will be glad to take you to a local beauty salon for these services.

ACTIVITIES, TREATMENTS, AND PROGRAMS: The program for both men and women begins with a half-hour fitness evaluation. Clients are not weighed or measured. However, tests are administered to evaluate cardiovascular health, flexibility, muscular condition, and body composition. The results of this evaluation form the basis for an individualized exercise prescription, which is formulated by an exercise specialist.

You choose three fitness classes a day, which alternate with beauty treatments. Classes include low-impact aerobics, water workouts, body-sculpting exercises, free-weight instruction, stretching and flexibility exercises, body-awareness sessions, and yoga.

Your morning begins with a walk at 7:00 followed by breakfast, at which time you receive your individual, daily schedule of fitness and treatment activities. Each evening at 8:00 there are special lectures and programs. Topics such as stress management and cooking demonstrations by Chef Kucharski are presented.

In addition to fitness classes during your five-night stay, you will have the following pampering treatments: 2 full-body massages, 1 aromatherapy massage, 1 hydrotherapy treatment, 1 thalassotherapy treatment (seaweed wrap), 1 body scrub, 1 nourishing facial, 1 deep-cleansing facial, 1 paraffin hand treatment, 1 foot treatment, and 1 neck and shoulder massage.

NICE TO KNOW: The present structure of Norwich Inn was built in 1929 and soon thereafter became a haven for the rich and famous, drawing such personalities as George Bernard Shaw, Charles Laughton, and Frank Sinatra. Longtime residents of Norwich can recount stories of this landmark's celebrated guests, among them Edward, Prince of Wales.

Norwich Inn is now owned by Edward J. Safdie, creator of the well-known Sonoma Mission Inn and Spa in northern California and The California Terrace, in Monte Carlo, Monaco. He also owns The Greenhouse in Texas.

Safdie is the author of *Spa Food*, a collection of great spa menus and recipes, which is illustrated with beautiful color photographs.

JUDY'S COMMENT: The 6-day program is certainly well rounded, offering 18 fitness classes, 11 facial and body treatments, nightly seminars, and nutritious spa meals served in a separate spa dining room. To complete the package, I would like to see a beauty salon incorporated as quickly as possible.

OLYMPIA VILLAGE SPA
Oconomowoc, WI 53066
Outside Wisconsin: 800-558-9573
Inside Wisconsin: 414-567-0311

Olympia Village Spa is part of a 400-acre resort complex located in the heavily wooded lake country of southern Wisconsin. Open year-round.

RATE: Moderate. Credit cards: American Express, MasterCard, Visa.

LOCATION AND TRANSPORTATION: Only 2½ hours northwest of Chicago and 1 hour west of Milwaukee. Part of the Olympia Resort complex, the spa blends dramatically into its lovely setting of forest, hills, rivers, and lakes.

EMPHASIS/PHILOSOPHY: Total pampering while losing weight and inches.

DIET PROGRAM: 600–1,200 calories. The diet is well balanced and portion-controlled. Food is prepared with no salt, low-fat, and dietetic products. There are several choices for each course at lunch and dinner, with calorie count appearing next to each item on the menu. The food is delicious and beautifully presented. Some of my favorite edibles were Lobster and Shrimp in Creole Sauce; Beef Stroganoff (prepared with low-fat, plain yogurt); Pepper Steak and Pineapple Fluff. Olympia is one of the few spas where they have a 600-calorie count, which can be most effective for weight loss. One recent guest, new to the spa scene, was delighted to lose four pounds in four days on this regimen. This may not apply to all!

GUEST POPULATION: Coed. 50 guests. There are separate spas for men and women with a shared exercise area. Most of the spa guests are women, including high-powered executives, young mothers, and models such as Miss USA.

PACKAGES AND MINIMUM STAYS: There are 7-day and 4-day programs plus a little 2-day "sampler" as an introduction to the world of spaing.

MEAL SERVICE: Spa guests use a separate entrance to the diet dining room; in the early days you had to go through the main resort dining room. There is a hostess to seat you, and all meals are table service. A dieter and nondieter who wish to share a table will be served in the Garden Room, which is the resort dining room. You may have diet meals served in your room; the chef's extension is 185.

DRESS CODE: Since there is a separate entrance to the dining room, I would feel comfortable in a dressy jogging outfit, even for dinner, but the choice is up to you. The spa provides guests with warm-up suit, leotard, a robe, and shower scuffs for activities during the day.

ACCOMMODATIONS: Comfortable, contemporary rooms with two double beds, plush carpeting, and colorful decor. Suites have open fireplaces and private bars. In all, 500 rooms and villas.

HOUSE RULES: No smoking on the spa premises. Several alcoholic lounges on the premises, but it's a no-no! There is a large shopping mall attached to the resort, which offers many temptations. Bring your self-discipline along.

PHYSICAL FACILITIES: Well-equipped gymnasium with Nautilus equipment. Men and women's locker rooms each contain whirlpool baths, steam rooms, eucalyptus sauna room, and Grecian showers. There are two exercise rooms (for shared activities), massage rooms, facial rooms, and herbal wrap rooms. Indoor-outdoor pools (which are used for water exercises), indoor-outdoor tennis courts (which are lighted at night), an 18-hole golf course, and a wintertime ski school and slopes add to all-year enjoyment. There are also the usual amenities of a large resort hotel: movie theaters, night clubs, and boutiques. Spa hours are 9:00 A.M. to 6:00 P.M.

ACTIVITIES, TREATMENTS, AND PROGRAMS: The spa's full seven-day plan includes: 5 daily exercise classes; use of all spa facilities; 3 half-hour body massages; 1 full-hour massage for problem areas; 2 one-hour facials; 2 herbal wraps; 2 individual whirlpool sessions; 1 loofah cleansing; 1 pedicure and foot-care treatment; 1 manicure and hand care treatment; 1 shampoo with blow-dry and a scalp massage with oil treatment. And last but not least, a Lancôme makeup application and lesson on the day you check out. Lancôme beauty products are used for facials and makeup. The daily scheduled exercises might include an early morning walk (7:00, weather permitting), sunrise stretch, skinny dipper class, low-impact aerobics, rear echelon (spot-reducing exercises), and yoga. Exercise classes are 30 minutes long. A consultation with the dietician is also included. The evening programs are varied. There is an evening of bingo, the dietician might speak on nutrition and behavior modification, and there are movies and card games. Friday evening is a free night.

OPTIONAL COSTS: Makeup consultation, extra exercise classes, and extra-time massages are available.

NICE TO KNOW: One first-time spa-goer tells how the Olympia staff put her at ease. "They made me feel comfortable by explaining all the treatments and procedures." Here is a spot you may want to go the à la carte route. If you've been spaing before and know exactly what you like, you may be able to save yourself some money.

JUDY'S COMMENT: Olympia Village is a most complete resort. Besides the excellent spa and fitness program, there are a myriad of sports activities and "good life" options for vacationers. An extra dimension at Olympia Village is the winter program, replete with downhill and cross-country skiing, ice skating, and après-ski amenities.

THE PHOENIX FITNESS RESORT
111 N. Post Oak Lane
Houston, TX 77024
Outside Texas: 800-548-4700
Inside Texas: 800-548-4701
Local: 713-680-1601

The Phoenix is in a resort hotel setting. The entire Houstonian complex is located on 22 heavily wooded acres. Spa guests use the facilities of the Houstonian Health and Fitness Club and are housed in the club's intimate Ambassador House Hotel. Open year-round.

RATES: Expensive. Credit cards: American Express, Carte Blanche, Diners Club, MasterCard, Visa.

LOCATION AND TRANSPORTATION: Residential area of Houston. Courtesy service to and from airport.

EMPHASIS/PHILOSOPHY: The Phoenix is a progressive health, fitness, and beauty facility focusing on learning. The program will introduce you to weight-control principles that will remain with you long after your stay.

DIET PROGRAM: 1,000 calories per day. Emphasis is on complex carbohydrates and proteins—a well-balanced diet where no food is omitted. Everything served is absolutely fresh. Low salt, sugar, and fat. The spa will not serve less than 850 calories per day; however, they will adapt a menu for a vegetarian diet or if you have an allergy. Chef Vicki Dempsey prepares continental dishes that are lovely to look at as well as low in calories. Phoenix guests report that the meals are so satisfying it's hard to believe they're really on a diet. Chris Silkwood, the spa director, says, "Your weight loss for your week at the Phoenix should be about 2 to 4 pounds, and then you'll drop a pound or so upon returning home. We do not under any circumstances promote quick weight loss, starvation diets, or extreme heat treatments for the purpose of losing weight—it's just not safe or realistic."

GUEST POPULATION: Women only. 15–30 guests. There are two couples' weeks each year. Guests come here to shape up, start a diet, be pampered, recover from an operation or a divorce, or just escape from it all. One petite insurance executive from Boston (5'0" tall and 102 pounds) was sent here by her company as a reward for her outstanding performance in the line of duty. She toned up and felt "re-energized."

PACKAGES AND MINIMUM STAYS: The Phoenix offers an Ultimate Week, Fitness Week Plus, and Fitness Week. Check in on Sunday, out on Saturday.

MEAL SERVICE: Meals are served in the attractive mirrored dining room located on the first floor of the Houstonian. Fresh flowers adorn the tables. As one Chicago North Shore matron says, "It's like being in someone's private home." Lunch can be served poolside, weather permitting. No room service for your diet menu. A fitness staff member is on hand at all meals to answer any questions.

DRESS CODE: The spa provides T-shirts, shorts, pink and gray warm-up suits, terry robes, slippers, and caftans. For dinner most guests wear the caftan, or you can do your own thing. Jeans allowable.

ACCOMMODATIONS: Spa guests are housed in the Houstonian Club's Ambassador House. All rooms are single occupancy, with queen-size beds. Spacious rooms have subtle earth-tone colors, while rattan furnishings create a restful feeling. There is a lounge for spa guests where decaffeinated coffee and tea are always available. Your personal laundry is done daily.

HOUSE RULES: No smoking allowed anywhere on the premises. You must go outside to smoke.

PHYSICAL FACILITIES: In the midst of the metropolis of Houston, this is one of the most well-planned city resorts anywhere—a country club setting (everything but golf). The Phoenix's exercise rooms are located in the Houstonian Club, which is directly across from the Ambassador House. Facilities of the Houstonian used by Phoenix guests include an Olympic-size outdoor heated pool, indoor and one-mile outdoor jogging tracks, weight-training room, Nautilus equipment, whirlpool and Jacuzzi, racquetball courts, sauna, steam room, basketball, volleyball, and tennis courts. All massage treatments are given here. Adjoining is a boutique, specializing in fitness togs, and beauty salon.

ACTIVITIES, TREATMENTS, AND PROGRAMS: Some of the daily activities are a brisk walk/jog, stretch class, strength and tone class (spot exercises), cardiovascular and aerobic exercises, circuit training on weight equipment, in-water toning exercises, and fun dance classes. Each guest receives a body composition test upon arrival to determine ideal weight percentages. If you're not a strong exercise buff, or are presently out of shape, you needn't worry. Chris Silkwood says, "Ours is not a pie-in-the-face drastic approach to fitness. No one wants you to overexert." One apprehensive first-timer who considered herself a klutz didn't feel at all out of place because the staff and other guests were so supportive. Spa packages include daily massage, facials, manicure/pedicure, makeup sessions, paran treatments, hair treatments, and skin consultations. Evening discussions and lectures cover a variety of stimulating topics, such as lifestyle management, healthy cooking, fashion, and so on. Once a week there's a free evening for shopping at the Galleria or going to Gilley's (of *Urban Cowboy* fame).

A Day at Phoenix

6:30	Wake-up call; juice served to help pick up the blood sugar level before the walk
7:00	Brisk 2-mile walk to stimulate the heart early in the day and enhance overall circulation
7:30	Breakfast buffet
8:30	Extender—static, comfortable stretches to prepare the body for the day's activities
8:45	Toner—45-minute class, working with specific body parts for tone, strength, and overall definition
9:30	The Beat—30 minutes of low-impact aerobics
10:00	Juice break
10:30	Circuit training—45-minute class combining weight machines with walking for a toning and aerobic effect
11:30	Massage
12:30	Lunch
1:30	The Revive—relaxed toning exercises in warm water
2:30	Beauty treatments
3:15	Fruit smoothies to pick up blood sugar and energy level
4:30	Free time for tennis, racquetball, lap swimming, or relaxation
5:30	Additional walking or relaxation
6:30	Nonalcoholic cocktail hour
6:45	Dinner
7:30	Evening lecture or free time

OPTIONAL COSTS: Tennis lessons; complete cardiovascular exam available through the Houstonian Medical Center; individualized exercise cassette tape.

NICE TO KNOW: Chris Silkwood truly is the guru of fitness. Her down-to-earth philosophy holds that aerobic exercise is one of the most effective ways of burning off calories and reducing the layer of body fat surrounding the muscle layer. Brisk walking is a natural and

safe aerobic activity. Rapid walking burns the same number of calories as moderate jogging over the same distance. In line with this
belief, many spa guests find themselves walking as much as ten miles
a day by the end of the week. Spa guests also love the freedom of
being able to walk into the kitchen and chat with Chef Vicki about
diet and recipes.

JUDY'S COMMENT: The Phoenix gets the most low-cal brownie
points for doing the best job of helping guests incorporate Phoenix
weight control principles into the real world. Departing guests are
given notebooks to take home that contain menus, recipes, caloric
information, makeup tips, and a self-help reading list—plus a log book
for the number of miles walked. The spa's follow-up program features
a personalized letter or phone call from Chris, checking your progress
and offering reinforcement. It's not what you lose that counts—it's
what you carry home with you!

PONTE VEDRA INN AND CLUB
Ponte Verda Beach, Fl 32082
Outside Florida: 800-234-7842
Inside Florida: 800-432-3498
Local: 904-285-1111

This spa resort and hotel are beautifully situated on the white, sandy
shores of the Atlantic, amid tropical palm trees and flowers. Open
year-round.

RATES: Expensive. Credit cards: American Express, Carte Blanche,
Diners Club, MasterCard, Visa.

LOCATION: Midway between Jacksonville and St. Augustine, off
Highway I-95. Nearest major airport is Jacksonville, where complimentary pickup is available.

EMPHASIS/PHILOSOPHY: According to Theresa Clements, spa
director: "The Spa at Ponte Vedra is different from most spas due to
our oceanfront setting and our emphasis on *service.* We have one of
the best programs for health, fitness, nutrition, and beauty, and we
offer it to you in a very extraordinary way. The Spa is an important
part of our resort's tradition and reputation for genuine hospitality.
Combined with the highly trained and responsive staff of experts, we
will make you feel the specialness of the Ponte Vedra Spa experience."

DIET PROGRAM: 1,000 calories per day (1,200 calories for men). Hors d'oeuvres and side dishes feature fresh vegetables, such as vegetable paté and steamed artichoke with faux butter. Fresh local seafood and poultry are used in the main entrees. One delicious luncheon entree is sea salad with Florida lobster. Dinner favorites include flounder baked in parchment, and coq au vin. Red meat is occasionally offered, fresh fruits are often served as dessert. The spa bran muffins are so delicious that they are on all four restaurant menus.

GUEST POPULATION: Coed. The spa package is limited to 20 guests. Up to now, most participants were women who came specifically for the spa program. However, this has been changing since the recent opening of the new conference center. Many corporate wives, who accompany their husbands, choose to follow the spa program while their husbands are busy with meetings.

PACKAGES AND MINIMUM STAY: The Weekly Package is for 5 nights and 6 days, from Sunday at 3:00 P.M. until Friday at noon. There are also two 1-day programs: "A Taste of the Spa," from 6:45 A.M. to 6:00 P.M., and "A Day of Beauty," for 6 hours, mornings or afternoons. All spa services and programs are also available on an à la carte basis.

MEAL SERVICE: The spa dining room is often called the garden room, for it has plants indoors and out. There's an open feeling from all the glass used in its construction. Looking out, you see a trellised deck filled with flowering planters, and the gently breaking waves of the Atlantic.

The soft colors of the surf and sand are repeated in the interior decor. Fine linens and fresh flowers are always on the tables.

A spa participant may dine at one of the other Ponte Vedra restaurants. Selections from the spa menu are available at all of them.

DRESS CODE: Casual resort clothes are always appropriate in the spa dining room. Jackets are required in the other dining rooms— take your cue from that, ladies!

ACCOMMODATIONS: All guest rooms are spacious and luxurious. Each has glass sliding doors, with patio or balcony, overlooking the ocean. The soft decor features tones of peach, sand, and seafoam green. All have private baths.

HOUSE RULES: There are bars serving alcohol here as this is a resort hotel spa setting. Smoking is not permitted in the spa buildings and wherever else noted. You may request a nonsmoking guest room.

PHYSICAL FACILITIES: This 215-acre resort features two championship golf courses, and 15 all-weather lighted tennis courts with an elevated spectators' stadium. This is in addition to 4 swimming pools (2 heated), a large outdoor Jacuzzi, and a nursery for children between the ages of six months and six years.

The spa is located in two charming shingled cottages on the oceanfront. One cottage contains rooms used for massages, facials and beauty treatments, as well as the kitchen and dining room. The other cottage houses all the rooms and equipment used for exercising. The aerobics and Nautilus rooms are mirrored and overlook the lap pool, the Jacuzzi, and the ocean.

ACTIVITIES, TREATMENTS, AND PROGRAMS: There is no hectic schedule at Ponte Vedra, for they feel that this is your time to relax and pamper yourself. All activities are optional. Mornings are fitness time, with a walk, stretch and tone class, low-impact aerobics, and "Splash Dance," an aquaerobics class. Afternoons are beauty and leisure time, with pampering and personal services that you schedule yourself. Evenings are seminar time, with presentations on subjects such as stress management, nutritious cooking, and beauty.

Services included in the weekly program are fitness analysis and consultation; daily aerobic classes; unlimited use of Nautilus and weight rooms; all life-style seminars; 4 full body massages, 2 facials, 2 herbal wraps, 1 seaweed wrap, 1 body polish, 1 shampoo and styling, 1 paraffin manicure and pedicure, and 1 makeup demonstration and analysis.

OPTIONAL COSTS: Available for an extra fee are additional sessions of treatments included in the program, as well as waxings, eyelash tints, skin care, color and nutritional consultations, and fitness evaluations.

NICE TO KNOW: A beautiful fruit basket will be in your room upon arrival.

JUDY'S COMMENT: A wonderful place for couples to follow their own interests, whether it be golf, tennis or spaing!

SAFETY HARBOR SPA
AND FITNESS RESORT
105 N. Bayshore Drive
Safety Harbor, FL 33572
800-237-0155
In Florida: 813-726-1161

Right on scenic Tampa Bay near Clearwater, Florida. This resort is built over the Espiritu Santo Springs, which were discovered in 1539 by Hernando de Soto. There are four separate mineral springs, and each is reputed to be beneficial for a different ailment (arthritis, gout, and bladder). Of course, the spa makes no such claims and does not use the waters for treatments. The hot mineral springs flow directly into the bathhouse and are used for bathing. Open year-round.

RATES: Moderate. Considerable savings may be expected during off-season, May–October. American Express, MasterCard, Visa.

LOCATION AND TRANSPORTATION: Only minutes away from Tampa airport. Limousine service is available from airport, for a fee. Complimentary return service to airport.

EMPHASIS/PHILOSOPHY: Safety Harbor emphasizes total fitness for "body, mind, and spirit." It combines exercise, good nutrition, sports, and "taking the waters" into a sound, sensible health-improvement program.

DIET PROGRAM: No salt, fat-free, low-cholesterol diet for all. Calorie range from 900 up, as recommended by physician at check-in. Menu is portion-controlled. Fish and chicken are always available at dinner. Dietetic products are used. Bottles of white wine are allowed at the table if purchased at the bar and brought up by the maître d'.
　　Here's a typical Safety Harbor daily menu:

BREAKFAST	CALORIES
Fresh Florida Grapefruit Half with Strawberry Sauce	50
Eggwhite Omelet with Mushrooms and Green Pepper	85
Half Slice High-Fiber Bread	35
	170

LUNCH	
Asparagus Soup	50
Cold Poached Salmon with Dill Mustard Sauce	215
Spa Coleslaw	30
Potato Skins	60
Rainbow Parfait	10
	365

DINNER	
Endive and Carrot Salad with Dill Vinaigrette	40
Bouillabaisse	230
Steamed Broccoli Florets	25
Bananas Baked with Lime	90
	385

TOTAL DAILY CALORIES	920

GUEST POPULATION: Coed. 280 guests. All kinds of folks come here, from posh to plain, from young to old. Louis Nizer, well-known lawyer and author, is a regular visitor here. Safety Harbor also has served as training camp for professional boxers Mark Breland and Henry Tillman.

PACKAGES AND MINIMUM STAYS: There are two Total Fitness Plans: 8 days/7 nights and 5 days/4 nights. Other programs include: Medical Make-Over Weight Loss week; Risk Reduction week; Sports Plan (minimum 4 nights); Fitness Weekend (3 days/2 nights); a Perfect Day; and per day à la carte plan.

MEAL SERVICE: Dieters and nondieters sit at the same table. Table service with hostess to seat guests. Most guests are on a diet program. Room service is available.

DRESS CODE: Casual is the rule, but no shorts are allowed for dinner. Jackets are not required for men at dinner but many wear them on weeknights.

ACCOMMODATIONS: All very comfortable rooms, some newer and larger than others. A wide range of prices from which to choose.

HOUSE RULES: No smoking between treatments, but there is an alcoholic lounge on the premises, which opens at 5:00 P.M. and serves raw vegetables and low-cal popcorn.

PHYSICAL FACILITIES: Separate spa building houses massage rooms, sauna and steam rooms, exercise rooms, jogging track, Jacuzzi, and an impressive array of exercise equipment from Nautilus and Paramount machines to speed bags. There are three pools: an indoor mineral springs therapeutic pool and two outdoor pools. There is a 3-hole putting green on campus, with guests offered free golf daily at two nearby courses, Pelican and Tarpanwood. There are 7 outdoor tennis courts lighted for night play. A Lancôme Skin Care Institute, boutique, and beauty shop complete the array. Guests can walk for miles along the boardwalk on Old Tampa Bay.

ACTIVITIES, TREATMENTS, AND PROGRAMS: Medical examination upon arrival. Each day the guest is offered a half-hour massage and unlimited exercise classes (which are coed) and use of all spa facilities. Classes begin at 8:50 A.M. and might include body sculpting, circuit weight training, aerobic water class, radu (advanced aerobics), and a two-mile walk for the fit among us. Programs could include bingo, movies, bridge instruction, shopping excursions, and Sam the Man at the piano in the cocktail lounge.

STAFF POPULATION: Two physicians are on staff, as are a nurse, nutritionist, 11 exercise instructors, and no less than 50 massage therapists.

OPTIONAL COSTS: The cosmetology department with 19 full-time cosmeticians offers Lancôme products and all kinds of facials, lip and leg waxing, and peeling treatments. Boutique purchases and Maggie's Variety Store items are strictly à la carte, as are beauty shop services and sportswear from the tennis shop.

NICE TO KNOW: If you don't mind Florida summers, Safety Harbor is an incredible value from May to October, with a full week's stay running under $1,000.

JUDY'S COMMENT: Safety Harbor was purchased by Bright Star Holding Company during the summer of 1985. A complete renovation was undertaken to the tune of $11 million (at least). The entire interior was gutted, with completely new space made for a posh spa and beauty program. Some innovative changes place Safety Harbor among the Palm Aires, Bonaventures, and La Costas. The seedy but cozy place I intended to find exists no longer, but the friendliness is still there. Exercise classes have been increased: whereas they had three or four classes daily, they now have two classes per hour. Beginning with your 8 A.M. walk, classes are held every 40 minutes, ending the day with yoga and stretch class from 3:00 to 4:00. Evening entertainment now includes health lectures three times weekly, the bingo game, dancing twice weekly (to a 4-piece combo), and lots more social entertainment. But you can still taste the sulfur in the drinking water, which keeps you in touch with the fact that you're at a "watering spa."

THE SHOREHAM
Box 225, 115 Monmouth Avenue
Spring Lake, NJ 07762
201-449-7100

Flanked by the Atlantic Ocean and Spring Lake, this Victorian resort hotel has yesteryear's charm and today's spa. Open from May 1 to October 31.

RATES: Moderate. Credit cards: MasterCard, Visa.

LOCATION: The Shoreham is located at the very popular Jersey shore, less than a 2-hour drive from New York City and Philadelphia. The nearest airport is Atlantic City, where taxis and limousines are available.

EMPHASIS/PHILOSOPHY: The Shoreham focuses on individual

needs. Each spa guest has her/his own custom-designed program for both nutrition and exercise.

DIET PROGRAM: 1,000–1,200 calories per day. There is a special diet menu for spa guests based on a complex carbohydrate diet. Fresh fruits and vegetables are featured, as is fresh local seafood. Some favorite dishes include dilled shrimp, broiled swordfish, and sole en papillote.

GUEST POPULATION: The Shoreham attracts a dynamic forty-plus group, who love the variety of offerings. The spa program is limited to 15 guests. Coed.

PACKAGES AND MINIMUM STAYS: Most popular are the Week, Weekend, Weekday packages.

MEAL SERVICE: Spa guests are served in the fine Victorian dining room. They choose their meals from a special spa menu.

DRESS CODE: Casual during the day. Gentlemen must wear jackets after 6:00 in the lounge and dining room.

ACCOMMODATIONS: You'll always know you're in the right room at the Shoreham, for variety is the spice of life here! Each Victorian guest room has a distinct personality, with unique furnishings and decorating. The only constant is architectural: high ceilings and private baths.

HOUSE RULES: Alcohol is served on the premises. Smoking is allowed except where noted.

PHYSICAL FACILITIES: There is an outdoor pool. The Shoreham has a beach at the ocean, which is just a block away. Surfing, sailing and deep-sea fishing are available nearby, as are tennis and golf.

ACTIVITIES, TREATMENTS AND PROGRAMS: Included in the spa program are individually planned fitness programs; exercise classes, such as stretch and tone, low-impact aerobics, and aquatics; bicycling; brisk ocean and lake walks; three massages; one European facial; one herbal wrap; lectures on topics such as stress management, nutrition, fitness, and self-hypnosis.

In addition to the spa activities, the hotel staff offers an incredible potpourri of happenings. There are fashion show luncheons, music by all-time favorite bands, luaus, scavenger hunts, bingo, ballroom dancing, and movies. The staff conducts local excursions for shopping, antiquing, and browsing through arts and crafts shows. For those who want to try their luck, Atlantic City and the Monmouth Race Track are nearby. And for those who want to hear famous artists, such as Frank Sinatra and Liza Minnelli, there are trips to the Garden State Arts Center.

OPTIONAL COSTS: Extra massages and beauty treatments. Excursions, other than local, also may be extra.

NICE TO KNOW: You must make your reservations during the season. There is no way to reach the Shoreham when it is closed.

JUDY'S COMMENT: A good combination of diet, exercise, massage and showstopper evenings.

SONOMA MISSION INN AND SPA
P.O.Box 1447
Sonoma, CA 95476
Outside California: 800-358-9022
In California: 707-938-9000 or 800-862-4945

The spa is part of a charming resort hotel (a restored Spanish mission inn) located on 6½ landscaped acres of a residential area and surrounded by hills. Open year-round.

RATES: Expensive. Credit cards: American Express, Diners Club, MasterCard, Visa.

LOCATION AND TRANSPORTATION: Located in the heart of California's wine country, a few miles from Sonoma, and 45 miles north of San Francisco (allow an hour and a half from the airport). Spa will provide courtesy transportation from San Francisco International Airport.

EMPHASIS/PHILOSOPHY: The Spa at Sonoma Mission Inn describes itself as a tranquil world where cares and tensions vanish. In this relaxed environment, you can begin to rediscover a sense of well-being and new vitality. As a guest of the spa, you'll be totally pampered while developing a schedule for health, beauty, and fitness that suits your individual needs.

DIET PROGRAM: 800 calories ("losers"), 1,200 calories ("maintenance"), and 2,000 calories ("gainers"). All natural foods with lots of fruits, vegetables, and whole grains as well as fish and fowl. No red meat served. No dietetic products used. Chef Roland Muller prepares delicious low-calorie meals. Included in the fare are drinks such as blue nectarine smoothies and a red wine slush that's only 20 calories. Special herbal dressings and sauces add a nice touch to this nutritionally balanced menu. The spa also offers fasting days on Monday and Thursday, featuring six fresh fruit juices and sunflower seeds. According to the spa, "Fasting promotes maximum weight loss with minimum stress ... this highly effective program cleanses and rejuvenates the system." Some of my favorite delectable delights are: fresh bran muffins served each morning for breakfast, tofu and wild rice salad, grilled chicken breasts in mustard sauce, cantaloupe sundae (fresh fruit, no ice cream), and vanilla flan. It's hard to believe that anything that looks and tastes so delicious can be so low in calories. What can you expect to lose? Most guests on the 800-calorie plan lose four to five pounds. The inch loss is even better!

GUEST POPULATION: Coed. 15 guests. A diverse crowd comes here: tired executives, young mothers, magazine writers feverishly taking notes, and people from the entertainment industry. Olivia de Havilland once spent three weeks at the spa after gaining ten pounds while playing the Queen Mother in the TV movie *Charles and Diana—a Royal Romance.* Says Olivia, "In Beverly Hills, my hometown, the three-letter words are worse than the four-letter words. And the worst one of all is F-A-T!"

PACKAGES AND MINIMUM STAYS: The basic package at Sonoma is the 5-night Great Escape. Additionally, there are the 3-night Revitalizer, 2-night Beauty, 2-night Fitness, 1-night Mini Escape, and 1-day Getaway. Treatments and exercise classes are also available à la carte.

MEAL SERVICE: All meals are served in the Prive, a small dining room adjacent to the Inn's Provençal Dining Room. Participants in the juice fasting days can elect to take their juices in their rooms. The menu is set, with a calorie count beside each item listed. Rose-colored tablecloths (to match your complexion) and fine cream-colored china grace the tables. No spa meals served at poolside or in treatment areas. No spa room service available.

DRESS CODE: Dressy-casual is the style. Since you are in a charming deluxe resort hotel setting, slacks and sweaters are more suitable than a jogging outfit for dinner. The spa provides warm-up suits, terry robes, slippers, and kimonos, along with hats and mittens for your morning hikes. Bring along a sweater as you're in the foothills of the Valley of the Moon.

ACCOMMODATIONS: Charming bedrooms in subtle earth tones have queen-size canopy beds. Some of the room features are a commodious dressing room, comfortable upholstered furniture, spacious bathroom with generous counter space, a ceiling fan (thermostatically controlled), television, and an indispensable clock radio. Personal laundry and spa attire are picked up daily by maids in pink uniforms.

HOUSE RULES: Smoking is prohibited in the spa building and spa dining room.

PHYSICAL FACILITIES: Former owner Edward Safdie spared no expense in restoring this 1926 Spanish-style mission. The color pink is everywhere, from the walls of the Inn itself to the central fountain made of rare Norwegian pink marble and the award-winning Provençal Restaurant (which serves Inn and spa guests alike). The interior of this historic three-storied pink palazzo is reminiscent of early California missionary times. The separate spa building has been designed to harmonize with the California mission look of the Inn. Located on the first floor of the spa building is a large gymnasium for fitness classes and two smaller gyms that house Keiser Cam II and other weight equipment. The second floor of the spa includes the locker room and dressing area, guest lounge, and treatment area (massage rooms, herbal and cellulite wrap rooms, facial rooms, and whirlpool, sauna, steam room, and inhalator room). Water activities take place in the spa's four-foot heated exercise pool located outside in the courtyard. All this is augmented by the Inn's two tennis courts (lighted for night play) and Olympic-size pool. There is a boutique located in the hotel as well as in the spa.

ACTIVITIES, TREATMENTS, AND PROGRAMS: Most fitness classes are offered during the morning to allow you plenty of time for afternoon pampering. They include early morning hikes and yoga, aerobics classes, poolercize, and slimnastics (spot toning). Delicious treatments included in the package programs are full-body massages, facials, hydromassage, herbal wraps, manicure/pedicures, and hair and scalp treatments. The spa uses Kirstin of Laguna Beach products for all beauty treatments; these can be purchased in the spa boutique.

OPTIONAL COSTS: All beauty and body treatments are available à la carte. Golf, horseback riding, tennis lessons, tours of the local wineries, and even hot-air ballooning can be arranged by the Inn's concierge.

NICE TO KNOW: During your five-day Great Escape you have the spa all to yourselves during daytime hours. However, the spa is open on a coed basis to all hotel guests on weeknight evenings. The weekend program for couples is not a structured affair, and on weekends the spa is open to the public as well as to hotel guests. The 800 number will connect you directly to the spa itself—well-trained, cheerful receptionists answer your smallest question. There's never a sense of surliness or rushing—rather a true sense of pampering and courtesy. The original Sonoma Mission was built near natural thermal mineral springs and became a mecca for health seekers. Today, those natural mineral spring waters are used in the hydrotherapy and Jacuzzi treatments but not to effect health cures.

JUDY'S COMMENT: After your stay at the Sonoma Mission Inn spa, you can throw away your rose-colored glasses. You'll be in the pink of health and feeling rosy, a glow that comes from within, not from without.

THE SPA
AT FRENCH LICK SPRINGS
French Lick, IN 47432
800-457-4042
In Indiana: 800-742-4095
Local: 812-935-9381

The Spa is located within the framework of a gracious resort hotel set on 1,500 acres of lush woodland. Open year-round.

RATES: Moderate. Credit cards: American Express, MasterCard, Visa.

LOCATION AND TRANSPORTATION: Sixty-five miles from Louisville, Kentucky, airport. Hotel limousine service is available. Driving time from Indianapolis is about 2 hours.

EMPHASIS/PHILOSOPHY: The spa describes the central theme of its five-day program as follows: "To give you five uninterrupted days of diet, fitness, beauty, and pampering."

DIET PROGRAM: 1,200 calories per day. Well-balanced, portion-controlled meals feature fish and chicken. Dietetic products are used. Upon consultation with the chef, meals can be individualized. Spa director Gail Spencer says, "It's not unusual for guests to lose 3 to 5 pounds during their five-day stay."

GUEST POPULATION: Coed. When the spa first opened, they geared their advertising strictly toward women. Now, however, their literature is directed toward the men, too. According to Gail, "We are trying to change our image, as more men are beginning to appreciate the importance of proper fitness and body care. Of course, most of our guests still are women, which is true of most spas."

PACKAGES AND MINIMUM STAYS: For the 5-day/5-night basic program, check in on Sunday by 4:00 P.M., check out Friday after lunch. There is also a modified 5-day program and a 2-day program.

One may alternatively simply stay at the French Lick Springs Resort and use spa services à la carte. The Mini-Spa package is for any 2 weeknights.

MEAL SERVICE: Table service. Spa guests eat with regular guests in the resort's main dining room.

DRESS CODE: At this luxurious resort, dressy-casual is the byword. Nice trousers, caftans, or long skirts are fine. No jeans or jogging outfits. Spa provides robes for daytime use.

ACCOMMODATIONS: One area of the historic, turn-of-the-century grand hotel is reserved for spa guests.

HOUSE RULES: Smoking is discouraged during spa activities. There is a lounge serving alcohol on the premises.

PHYSICAL FACILITIES: Indoor and outdoor pools; separate saunas, whirlpools, and locker rooms for men and women; massage rooms; facial rooms; mineral water baths (not touted as having curative powers); exercise rooms (classes are coed); beauty salon; indoor and outdoor tennis courts; and two 18-hole golf courses.

ACTIVITIES, TREATMENTS, AND PROGRAMS: Included in your 5-day package are daily beauty treatments, massages, facials, and soaks in the Pluto Mineral Baths. Manicure/pedicures, cellulite body wraps, makeup and hair consultations are given intermittently during the week. Evening programs consist of lectures on self-motivation, wardrobe planning, and consultations with a dietician.

A Day at the Spa at French Lick Springs

7:00	Walk or jog
8:00	Breakfast
9:00	Aquatic exercise
10:00	Sauna, whirlpool, Pluto bath
11:00	Massage
12:00	Lunch
1:00	Skin care
2:00	Aerobic exercise
3:00	Scalp treatment
4:00	Yoga
5:00	Makeup consultation
6:30	Dinner

OPTIONAL COSTS: Wax treatments, boutique purchases, tennis and golf lessons.

NICE TO KNOW: French Lick has been a spa resort area for more than fifty years. It got its name because deer made use of the salt lick to refresh themselves. If you call the 800 number, they'll be happy to connect you directly with someone at the spa who can answer your questions.

JUDY'S COMMENT: This is a fairly new spa program that needs to be firmed up as to specific focus. I could not lose weight on 1,200 calories per day. The historic "Grand" hotel is under full-scale renovation at this writing and eventually should be a major attraction in itself.

THE SPA AT PALM-AIRE
2501 Palm-Aire Drive North
Pompano Beach, FL 33069
800-327-4960
In Florida: 305-975-6028

A 1,500-acre southern Florida condominium village and sporting paradise with separate spa hotel and spa building. Open year-round.

RATES: Expensive. Lower rates for off-season (summer). Credit cards: American Express, Diners Club, MasterCard, and Visa.

LOCATION AND TRANSPORTATION: Midway between Palm Beach and Miami. Thirty minutes from Fort Lauderdale airport; one hour from Miami airport. Taxis, airport limousines, and rental cars always available at either airport. No pickup service is provided.

EMPHASIS/PHILOSOPHY: Total mind and body approach designed to improve the quality of your life.

DIET PROGRAM: 800–1,000 calories per day: 800 suggested for women; 1,000 for men. The diet is well-balanced, low in sodium, cholesterol, and fat. There are several choices for each course at all meals, with the calorie count stated on the menu. The food is delicious and beautifully presented. A nice touch is the option of a glass of wine at dinner (50 calories). The sliced bagel thins and pita bread crisps are simply wonderful and have minimal calories. Dietetic products are used for scrumptious desserts. Bela, the dietician, is available to answer all your questions.

GUEST POPULATION: Coed. Two separate and completely furnished pavilions—one for men, one for women—accommodate 80 women and 30 men. There are separate his and her facilities for class

activities and treatments (mealtime is the only time they get together). The clientele consists of a maximum percentage of "doers"
and a minimum percentage of retired folks. And you may bump into
such exciting people as Paul Newman, Joanne Woodward, Billie Jean
King, Lee Trevino, or Elizabeth Taylor.

PACKAGES AND MINIMUM STAYS: The premier plans are the
7-day Complete Shape-Ups, one for men and one for women. Additional packages: Instant Tone-up (3 days/3 nights); golf and tennis
packages; and The Ultimate Day. Health and beauty services are also
available à la carte. It is not necessary to subscribe to one of the plans
to enjoy the spa, but the therapies, classes, and beauty treatments
may be difficult to schedule at a convenient time if the 7-day program
is filled with guests.

MEAL SERVICE: The dining room is divided into two areas: guests
on the diet program sit in the tiled area with a view of the golf course
and lots of greenery. The Peninsula Dining Room, which serves Continental cuisine, will also accommodate the dieter and the nondieter
at the same table. There is a hostess to seat you. It's a joy not to have
to pass a heavily laden dessert cart on your way to the table. Out of
sight, out of mind! There is room service for those on the diet plan.
Smoking is allowed in the dining room.

DRESS CODE: Men are required to wear jackets, but not ties, at
dinner. Ladies, take your cue from that. The spa provides red, green,
and black leotards (for swimming and exercising), warm-up suits, terry
robes, and pool shoes. You might want to bring along your own leg
warmers and a leotard or two.

ACCOMMODATIONS: Palm-Aire has created a separate and special spa environment. Accommodations, dining, and programs are all
under one roof. The Spa Hotel lobby acts as a central meeting place
for guests on the full spa program as well as those going à la carte.
There are hostesses stationed at the reception desk throughout the
day and early evening to answer your questions. All guests at the Spa
Hotel can meet in congeniality and have complimentary low-cal beverages and vegetable snacks in the lounge (a meeting room, not an
alcoholic bar), served daily between 5:15 and 8:00 P.M. It is easy to
make friends in this program because all Spa Hotel guests (whether
dieter or nondieter) can meet for lectures and programs three times
daily.
    Each spa bedroom is large and gracious, with a veranda, two
queen-size beds, and a lovely sitting area. The older rooms are tastefully decorated in greens and yellows, while apricot is the color for
the newer additions. Each double room has two complete bath-

rooms—his and hers. Wonderful! And there is ample closet space.

HOUSE RULES: No smoking in the spa building (solarium area only). No meal service poolside or in treatment areas.

PHYSICAL FACILITIES: The Spa Hotel architecture is a restful blend of off-white walls, stretches of glass, shingles, and concrete all contained in a modern, low-rise building. The hotel has a small, lovely pool. There is no linen or food service provided at this pool. The spa building is located just across a narrow but dangerously busy street (you need the agility of a mountain goat). There are complete and separate facilities for men and women. Each area has its own massage, facial, exercise, locker, and herbal wrap rooms; beauty salon and barber shop; outdoor exercise pool with a large solarium area; hot and cold plunge pools; and steam, sauna, and whirlpool areas. A half-mile parcours and an Olympic-size pool are shared spa facilities. There are two boutiques—one in the Spa Hotel and one in the spa building. For the sports enthusiast, there are five 18-hole championship golf courses, four racquetball courts, and thirty-seven tennis courts.

ACTIVITIES, TREATMENTS, AND PROGRAMS: Take your choice between a moderate or vigorous regimen. All workouts are geared to individual needs. There are 45-minute periods of aerobics I and II, water classes, vigorous conditioning with weights, spot specials I and II, stretch and relax classes, and yoga classes. The spa guest is allowed up to 10 exercise classes daily, depending on the chosen program. The spa provides daily exercise clothing, robe, and slippers.

The 7-day Complete Shape-Up includes medical evaluation, use of all spa facilities, 6 half-hour facials, 1 herbal wrap, 1 salt-glow loofah, 1 makeup consultation, 1 shampoo and set, 1 pedicure, and 1 manicure. Golf and unlimited tennis are included. Men as well as women take advantage of the skin-softening salt glows, loofah rubs, facials, manicures, and pedicures. Lancaster beauty products from Europe are used for the facials and cosmetics. No substitutions for facials are allowed, but alternate hypoallergenic cosmetics are available.

Included in the package are daily lectures, consisting of talks on toning and flexibility, nutrition, avenues to wellness, stress management, and life-styling. Evening entertainment is a potpourri of cultural lectures and slides, dancing lessons, bingo games, health lectures on how to avoid premature aging, relaxation therapy, and medical information on plastic surgery. Each guest is given a medical examination upon arrival as well as a take-home "Fitness Package," which includes five recipes from the diet program.

OPTIONAL COSTS: Body-fat test evaluation, private individual fitness instruction, and personal health and beauty services available.

NICE TO KNOW: Palm-Aire will connect a toll-free caller with the spa appointment desk or other spa personnel, unlike other large spas such as Bonaventure, La Costa, and Olympia, whose 800 numbers are strictly for taking reservations. For men there is a daily event scheduled at the Olympic pool called Volley War. From the sounds of joy coming from the pool, it sounds better than a floating crap game.

JUDY'S COMMENT: Ladies' spa director Carol Upper and Men's director Bill Freeman should be applauded for organizing such a beautiful and well-rounded (no pun intended) fitness, health, and beauty program.

THE SPA AT STOWE
P.O. Box 1198
Stowe, VT 05672
800-525-5606
802-253-9954

A relatively new fitness spa that offers activities, amenities, and accommodations in a picturesque Vermont ski resort setting. Open year-round.

RATES: Moderate. Credit Cards: MasterCard and Visa.

LOCATION AND TRANSPORTATION: Set in the historic village of Stowe, with Vermont's Green Mountains as a backdrop. Burlington International Airport is nearby, and airport transfer is included in all package rates.

EMPHASIS/PHILOSOPHY: Realistic life-style changes and lifetime fitness are the goals here. By learning your options (it doesn't have to be just taking aerobic classes) to keep fit, you'll be able to chart a new course for yourself. The program is flexible and assumes that everyone is an adult and will choose what is best for their life-style. Because of the spa's small size, they can individually tailor a program to fit you and make changes as required.

DIET PROGRAM: 800–1,100 calories per day. A daily menu lists food choices for the day, and you decide which you'll have. Meals are balanced, low in fat, high in fiber; calorie count is shown on the menus. Emphasis is on fresh fish, vegetables, and fruits. Average weight-loss monitoring is not done here, but it's hard not to lose if you stay within the allotted calorie count. However, some people find

Courtesy of The Spa at Stowe

it tough going to stay within the limits! Two chefs, Jim Ruggiero and
Keith Martin, share kitchen duties.
 A typical menu looks like this:

BREAKFAST
Fresh-squeezed orange juice (80)

or

Mixed fresh fruit (50)
Single poached or boiled egg (75)
served with whole wheat bread/toast (55)
or
Two pancakes (150)
Freshly brewed decaffeinated coffee or herb tea

LUNCH
Crepe florentine (135)
Greens with alternative herb dressing (34)
Sliced tomato (27)
Skim milk (88)
or
Cold poached salmon with cucumber dill sauce (161)
Tabouleh (83)
Skim milk (88)

DINNER
Garden salad (34)

Your choice of:
Roast Vermont turkey (388)
Broiled veal loin chop (276)
Grilled fresh Idaho trout (490)
Chef's special entree of the evening
Melon or mixed fresh fruit (60)

GUEST POPULATION: Coed. Only 25–30 guests are in the spa program per week, but "townies" also use the spa, which can accommodate 250–300 people. At this writing, 30 percent of the spa guests are men and about 40 percent are couples. Facilities are shared except for locker rooms.

PACKAGES AND MINIMUM STAYS: Choose among the following packages: 3-day/2-nights; 5-day/4 nights; 7-day/6 nights. All are considered fitness vacations.

MEAL SERVICE: Lunches are served in the Whip lounge and dinners in the main dining room of the Green Mountain Inn, featuring gourmet spa cuisine. The scene is eastern casual, country-antique, with fresh flowers and elegant china on the table. During warm weather, you can dine on the terrace.

DRESS CODE: Bring your own exercise clothes and jogging outfits. Everyone dresses New England casual at night, and dress pants or a nice skirt and blouse are fine. Bring your swimming suit for the summer months, but there is no indoor year-round pool at this writing. Ski togs are in order during winter months. You might need a sweater even in summer.

ACCOMMODATIONS: Guests stay at the Green Mountain Inn, which is listed in the National Register of Historical Places. Each room is furnished in Early American, with wood floors, country antiques, period prints on the walls, four-poster, canopied beds, and pretty floral wall coverings. All rooms have telephones, TVs, private baths, and daily maid service.

HOUSE RULES: There is no smoking or drinking in the spa itself, which is located a short distance from the Inn. The Inn, however, allows all worldly pleasures, so it's up to you.

PHYSICAL FACILITIES: The spa, a short walk from the Inn, has a full complement of fitness facilities: aerobics room; Nautilus room; equipment room with rowing machines, Lifecycles, stationary bikes, and motorized treadmill; coed steam room; sauna; whirlpool; tanning lounge; massage room; flotation tank; and racquetball/squash courts. The outdoor heated swimming pool (open only during summer months) is located at the Green Mountain Inn. Lakes and ponds are everywhere, and mountain hiking, bicycling, and winter skiing—downhill and cross-country—are offered. Tennis courts are close by

Courtesy of The Spa at Stowe

and available at extra cost to guests. Wind surfing and canoeing are also available to guests in summer. Ice skating and sleigh rides are winter favorites.

ACTIVITIES, TREATMENTS, AND PROGRAMS: The 3-day/2-night Weekender package includes the following: hotel accommodations and meals; 1 one-hour massage; 1 facial; an individualized exercise program, including unlimited exercise classes, Nautilus circuit training, guided hiking and bicycle tours, racquetball, squash, and aqua exercise; and unlimited use of spa facilities. The 5-day/4-night Spa Fitness plan includes all of the above plus nutritional counseling and evaluation, personal fitness evaluation, one more 1-hour massage, a manicure, two day trips, such as mountain biking, hiking, windsurfing, or canoeing, and evening and special activities. The 7-day/6-night Spa Fitness plan includes all of the above plus 1-hour massages; and three day trips. Extra nights can be added and include accommodations, three spa meals, unlimited fitness classes, one massage, Nautilus circuit training, a day trip, and use of all spa facilities.

A Day at the Spa at Stowe

7:30	Morning walk/jog
9:00	Breakfast
10:00	Weight training
11:00	Free time
12:00	Exercise class
1:00	Lunch
2:30	Biking or aquaerobics
4:30	Free time
5:30	Aerobic dance
7:00	Dinner

OPTIONAL COSTS: Beauty salon, extra massages, facials, personal fitness profile, and tennis are available. A sundry shop is on the premises. Boutiques and beauty supplies are available in the many village shops, which are very near the Inn. Merchandise ranges from exercise/ski equipment to New England style and casual/elegant country clothing. Antiques shopping, book stores, and knickknack shops are everywhere.

NICE TO KNOW: If you like a place with a sense of history, the Spa at Stowe in northern Vermont is a cosmopolitan, extremely comfortable place to stay. It combines a gracious country inn with a modern, flexible spa program. There are trips to the theater, concerts, antiques hunting, and skiing at famous Trapp Lodge and Mt. Mansfield. The full program includes a thorough evaluation administered by a medical team, followed by recommendations for exercise activities and guidelines to meet your nutritional needs for the week. One-on-one training supervision and guidance in some packages almost assure success. Corporate wellness programs, incentive meetings and seminars, and customized spa/ski trips can be organized for your group.

JUDY'S COMMENTS: The Spa at Stowe offers a unique ambience: small-town charm, world-class skiing, and all the pampering and fitness programs of a first-class spa. Go for it!

THE TUCSON NATIONAL RESORT AND SPA
2727 West Club Drive
Tucson, AZ 85741
800-528-4856
602-297-2271

Spa program open year-round. From 1965 to 1980, The Tucson National Golf Course was the site of the prestigious PGA annual event, The Tucson Open. Early in 1986 the property was converted to the Tucson National Resort and Spa, reflecting the facility's transformation into an exclusive resort/spa.

RATES: Moderate. Slightly lower June 1–September 30 and October 1–December 31. Extra day available on each plan for $169 to $235 depending on season. American Express, Carte Blanche, Diners Club, MasterCard, Visa.

LOCATION AND TRANSPORTATION: The resort's 650 acres are located in the foothills of the Santa Catalina Mountains. The resort is about eighteen miles (25 minutes) from Tucson International Airport and twelve miles from downtown Tucson. An inviting Southwestern atmosphere permeates the resort, highlighted by the 9,000-foot peaks of the surrounding mountain range, pure desert air, spectacular flaming sunsets, and cool, star-filled nights. For those who want to combine work and play, the resort features a 15,000-square-foot conference center, with meeting facilities for 3 to 300, and two ballrooms.

EMPHASIS/PHILOSOPHY: Steve Waguespack, assistant spa director, says, "We provide a lot of personal attention to all guests and try to show them, through education and individually tailored fitness programs, ways they can continue the benefits after they leave here.

Courtesy of The Tucson National Resort and Spa

We want our facility to be fun for guests, and our fitness and exercise classes are designed to be that way—not intense or rugged."

DIET PROGRAM: A low-sodium, low-cholesterol diet consisting of 800–1,200 calories per day. Menus include calorie count. A dietician is on staff to offer professional dietary consultation, nutritional help, and advice on combining exercise and weight-loss programs.

GUEST POPULATION: Coed. Accommodations for approximately 240. Spa guests are housed together with regular resort guests. Typically, about 35 to 40 women and 20 to 25 men participate in the spa's weekly program.

PACKAGES AND MINIMUM STAYS: There are 7-day/6-night and 5-day/4-night packages plus a special 1-day Day of Beauty for women and Day of Rejuvenation for men.

MEAL SERVICE: Dine with other resort guests in the resort's Catalina dining room. Spa-goers order from a separate menu.

ACCOMMODATIONS: Guests are located in 170 deluxe villas and suites with private balconies or patios, wet bars, and refrigerators. Many have fireplaces and complete kitchens. Suites are spacious, with distinctive Southwestern decor. Overall atmosphere is one of casual elegance. Room service available around the clock.

HOUSE RULES: None. As resort guests, anything goes.

PHYSICAL FACILITIES: The Tucson National Resort and Spa is a complete resort complex. The resort's claim-to-fame is its 27-hole USGA championship course, originally designed in 1960 by Robert Bruce Harris. All three courses (Green, Orange, and Gold) were remodeled in the early 1980s. Courses are located on 405 acres, with 188 traps, 10 lovely lakes, and tree-lined fairways.

The Tucson National is western headquarters for Golf Digest Instructional Schools, so pros abound and are available for lessons.

The resort/spa complex features a temperature-controlled swimming pool and three hydrotherapy pools. Six championship tennis courts, lighted for after-dark play, are a short walk from the main complex. The spa itself has separate women's and men's facilities, with a coed area for aerobics, nutrition, diet, and conditioning classes. A variety of services are available, such as Russian and Finnish baths, Orthion equipment, massages, herbal wraps, Scotch shower, loofah, tanning beds, and a full service beauty salon.

ACTIVITIES, TREATMENTS, AND PROGRAMS: Packages include deluxe room, daily meals, half-hour massage, half-hour facial, herbal wrap, nutritional counseling, 2 exercise classes, use of Roman pool, cold plunge, Russian bath (men), inhalation, sauna/steam cabinets (women), and Swiss shower. One of the following options is also offered daily: makeup, manicure, pedicure, shampoo, set or blow-dry, loofah, salt glow, soap scrub, Orthion, panthermal (ladies), Scotch shower (men), tanning session, unlimited tennis, 18 holes of golf including greens fees and cart rental. Seven exercise classes are offered daily, beginning with a morning walk at 7:00, for which a day's notice is required. Other classes include stretch and flex, aerobics (usually intermediate level but will modify to suit group), Aqua-fin-etics, body contour, stress management, and creative movement. Circuit weight training also is available.

Exercise-wise, a typical spa day might resemble the following:

7:00	Morning walk
9:00	Stretch and flex
9:40	Aerobics: low impact, usually intermediate level
11:00	Aqua-fin-etics: water aerobics Circuit training: instructors will assist you with a weight training program
12:20	Body contour: increases mobility and flexibility; isolates the abdomen, buttocks, hips, and thighs
2:20	Stress management and relaxation: deep breathing techniques and methods designed to relieve tension

3:40   Creative movement: a combination of stretch, aerobics, dance, and movement exploration

NICE TO KNOW: Doris M. Hogue, one of the most respected spa directors in the country, was for 15 years the ladies' spa director at La Costa. When the opportunity to take charge of a new spa presented itself, Doris moved to Tucson in 1985. She has also been with the Golden Door, the Spa at Palm-Aire, Olympia Village Spa, and Gurney's International. Doris believes that "eating right, exercising, and playing—all in moderation—will help us achieve our health and fitness goals."

JUDY'S COMMENTS: A good option for lots of fun with a moderate helping of fitness. Doris Hogue knows her stuff and is in charge of a world-class spa. Tucson National is a great spot for spaing and golfing, which could be a major consideration for couples.

* THE WOODS FITNESS INSTITUTE
P.O. Box 5
Hedgesville, WV 25427
304-754-7977

Open year-round. The Woods Fitness Institute is part of the Woods Resort complex in West Virginia's historic eastern panhandle. A 2,000-acre wilderness region called Sleepy Creek State Forest adjoins the resort.

RATES: Affordable. Choice, MasterCard, and Visa.

LOCATION AND TRANSPORTATION: The Institute is 90 miles from the Washington, D.C., and Baltimore urban centers. Transportation to and from the airport at Hagerstown, Maryland, is provided at a cost of $40 round trip.

EMPHASIS/PHILOSOPHY: Woods emphasizes life-style reeducation. Participants are shown how to develop personal habits that reduce the risk of life-style diseases such as obesity, hypertension, and cardiovascular illness. The weight-loss program is designed to improve greatly the physical condition of the guests as well as to effect substantial body toning and firming.

DIET PROGRAM: The diet program consists of approximately

1,000 calories per day. Complex carbohydrates comprise the dietary staples of the program. Little sodium, fat, or sugar are used. Whole grain breads, pastas, and potatoes are among the complex carbohydrates served. About 20 to 25 percent of the diet consists of protein. Sugar and salt substitutes are permitted.

GUEST POPULATION: The program can accommodate 30 to 35 men and women. The Woods Institute has been host to guests between the age of 17 and 78 who are of diverse orientations and backgrounds.

PACKAGES AND MINIMUM STAYS: The one-week program is the minimum length of stay. It includes seven nights and eight days, Sunday to Sunday. There is a special rate for those staying a full month. The average stay is three to four weeks.

MEAL SERVICE: Guests in the weight-loss program eat in the Woods Inn dining room along with the other guests of the resort. However, program participants eat at specially designated tables. The menus are preplanned, and everyone eats the same food. If a certain dish is really distasteful to one of the weight-loss guests, that person can move to a nondiet table and order something else.

DRESS CODE: Dress at the Institute is casual and comfortable, day and night.

ACCOMMODATIONS: The standard guest rooms come with TV, air conditioning, telephone, and a balcony overlooking the pool and pond. Deluxe accommodations have the above plus a cathedral ceiling, fireplace, whirlpool, and skylight. For stays of 28 days or longer, there are two special buildings called fitness cottages, where 16 long-term guests can be housed.

HOUSE RULES: Smoking is permitted everywhere except in the dining room. In the fitness cottages smoking is permitted contingent on the approval of all guests. There is a pub in the resort where alcohol is served.

PHYSICAL FACILITIES: The resort complex houses an extensive array of facilities among which are five outdoor lighted tennis courts, an Olympic-size outdoor pool, indoor tennis and racquetball courts, a gym, an exercise room, an indoor pool, a sunning room, whirlpools and saunas, a massage room, and a laundry room.

ACTIVITIES, TREATMENTS, AND PROGRAMS: Access to all facilities is included in the weight-reduction program package rate. Also included in the package are daily exercise classes: low-impact aerobics; stretching to classical music; weight training and swimnastics; escorted daily walks and hikes; lectures and discussions on nutrition, exercise, stress management, and life-style habits; film showings; and videotaped aerobic instruction.

An important component of the program, included at no additional charge, is a total fitness evaluation for each guest, conducted at the beginning of their stay. The tests measure coronary risk, blood composition, blood pressure, lung capacity, muscle strength, body fat, flexibility, and oxygen uptake. The results of the evaluation are used to determine a safe level of exercise for each guest.

OPTIONAL COSTS: Optional services and facilities offered include a private consultation with a registered dietician, Berkeley Springs massages and baths, use of tanning bed, golf course green fees, historical site tours, racetrack tickets, and tickets for theater and concert performances.

*BEST BUY AND WHY: The Woods Fitness Institute is a "Best Buy" because:
- It offers a complete fitness evaluation.
- There are a tremendous variety of facilities and activities.
- The low cost makes it possible to afford a long-term weight-reduction program.

NICE TO KNOW: There is no physician on staff. The Institute makes a point of requiring a physician's release form before enrolling in the program from anyone over the age of 35 or with health problems. For a supplemental charge of $175 per week, spouses or companions can accompany you and have full use of resort facilities, although food is at an extra cost. The Woods Fitness Institute program was designed in conjunction with the National Institute of Fitness in Ivins, Utah.

JUDY'S COMMENT: This program gives guests the opportunity to participate in a serious weight-loss program while vacationing at a fully equipped resort.

STRUCTURED SPAS—WHY, WHERE, AND HOW MUCH

Criteria for designating a spa as "structured" are:
1. The entire facility is dedicated to health, fitness, and well-being;
2. Diets are generally low in fat, salt, and cholesterol, and
3. There is no alcoholic lounge on the premises. At some, an occasional glass of wine may be offered.

Cost is based on a one-week stay, double occupancy, high-season rate, including tax and gratuities. Meals are included unless specifically stated otherwise. Best Buys are indicated by an asterisk.

Affordable: up to $1,000

Moderate: $1,000–$1,700
Expensive: $1,700 and up

AKIA
2316 Northwest 45th Place
Oklahoma City, OK 73112
405-842-6269

Located in the heart of the Arbuckle Mountains, this down-to-earth spa for women is geared to fitness and weight loss. Open spring and fall.

RATES: Affordable. No credit cards.

LOCATION: Akia is located in Sulphur, Oklahoma, approximately 90 miles south of Oklahoma City. Nearby airports are in Oklahoma City, and Dallas/Fort Worth. Pickup at the Oklahoma City airport can usually be arranged. Rental cars are also available. Route I35 brings you from either city to Sulphur.

EMPHASIS/PHILOSOPHY: Practicality and affordability are emphasized here. Akia was founded after Wilhelmina Maguire, a physiologist, visited a well-known coed spa. She was impressed with their program, but not their prices. So, together with her dietician friend, Jeanne Mayer, she decided to open an Oklahoma spa and offer some elements of the Canyon Ranch program at an affordable price.

Wilhelmina and Jeanne believe that the tools for good nutrition and moderate exercise should literally be taken home to encourage their continued use. To this end, they give guests copies of their spa recipes, and, for a minimal price, sell sets of rubber bands and surgical tubing, which are used in their exercises, as well as audiotapes of their toning exercises.

DIET PROGRAM: 950 calories per day. Average weight loss is 3 pounds in 5 days. Breakfast consists of cereal, fruit, and juice. Lunch is a high-protein shake. Guests have the option of substituting a fruit bowl for breakfast, and a sandwich, salad, or fruit bowl for lunch. Dinner features three or four courses, such as: vegetable hors d'oeuvres, gazpacho soup, Cantonese stirfry with rice, and fruit sherbet with fortune cookies. Low-calorie drinks and fruit are always available.

GUEST POPULATION: Women only. They range in age from 18 to 78, with the average age being 40 to 45. Some degree of fitness is required for the optional 10 miles of walking done daily. Eleven guests can be accommodated.

MINIMUM STAY: The shortest package is 4 days/4 nights, from Wednesday evening until Sunday afternoon. There is a 5-day/5-night package, from Sunday evening until Friday afternoon. The 7-day/7-night package begins and ends on Sunday evening.

MEAL SERVICE: Meals are served in the Southwestern-style dining room/sitting room, where there is a large, comfy table that seats all the guests at one time. Wilhelmina and Jeanne, the very congenial codirectors, do all the cooking and serving.

DRESS CODE: Casual and comfortable are the rule at Akia.

ACCOMMODATIONS: Guests stay in the native rock cabins. Each comfortably accommodates 3 women and has a bathroom. The decor is Southwestern. There are no TVs or telephones in the cabin. For your convenience, a telephone is located in the Main Lodge.

HOUSE RULES: No alcohol. Smoking is permitted outdoors only.

PHYSICAL FACILITIES: The main lodge is the center of activities. In it, meals are prepared and served, and the evening program is presented. There are 3 rock cabins and a duplex, half of which accommodates two guests. The other half serves as the massage parlor. In the courtyard is a large redwood deck, with chaise lounges for sunning. Bicycles are kept in the nearby bike barn.

The neighboring Chickasaw Indian Reservation plays an important role in the exercise program. It has many beautiful trails, perfect for the long walks that Akia advocates. It also has a lake and several freshwater streams, used for swimming during warmer weather.

Akia has no fancy exercise equipment. They utilize a few simple exercise aids that can be used almost anywhere, such as rubber bands for resistance exercises and surgical tubing for stretching exercises. These aids, as well as Akia's exercise tapes, are sold in the store, so that you can continue the exercises at home.

ACTIVITIES, TREATMENTS, AND PROGRAMS: The basic program consists of toning sessions, walks, and evening programs. Massages and beauty treatments are extra.

Walking is stressed as *the* natural exercise. Guests can walk up to 10 miles a day. However, each guest is free to choose how much she will participate in these or other exercises. Two toning sessions are offered every day: mornings in the pavilion by the lake, and evenings on the deck.

A Day at Akia

7:00   Stretching exercises

	Short walk
	Toning session
9:00	Breakfast
	Personal time
10:00	Park Adventure (a walk)
12:45	Lunch
	Personal time
2:25	Stretching exercises
2:30	Aerobic walk
	Juice Break
4:00	Muscle Tussle (toning exercises)
	Personal time
6:00	Cocktail hour
6:30	Dinner
7:30	Evening program
	Personal time

Personal time is often used for bicycling, swimming, or simply enjoying the company of the other guests on the sun deck.

The evening programs include a fashion show and a movie night, as well as lectures on skin care, weight control, nutrition, and self-massage.

OPTIONAL COSTS: Body polishes, a procedure using ground almonds and rose water, and massages are offered daily at an extra charge. Optional manicures and pedicures are offered on Thursdays only.

NICE TO KNOW: Since founding Akia, both Wilhelmina and Jeanne have become certified aerobics and fitness instructors. Each guest receives a complimentary Akia T-shirt.

JUDY'S COMMENT: This spa concentrates on fitness through diet, toning and walking—what a healthy way to spend a week and get started on a new life-style.

THE ARGYLE—A FOUNTAIN SPA
294 Country Club Road
Argyle, TX 76226
800-458-SPAS
817-464-7220

Located on a hilltop overlooking 14 acres of rolling countryside in Denton County, this Southwestern style spa combines the best of

European treatment methods with modern American fitness techniques. Open year-round.

RATES: Moderate. Credit cards: American Express, MasterCard, Visa. Each guest receives a $100 coupon, to be used for beauty, massage, or Kneipp water treatments or for use in the boutique.

LOCATION AND TRANSPORTATION: Thirty minutes north of Dallas/Fort Worth. Driving instructions: take Highway I35 to Highway 377, go south to Country Club Road, turn left. Limousine service is available from the Dallas/Fort Worth airport for approximately $50. Call spa for limousine reservations.

EMPHASIS/PHILOSOPHY: "The Argyle believes in your potential and realizes that the process of fulfilling your goals is a lifetime commitment.... Our ongoing programs of balanced nutrition and individualized fitness will help maintain your course to wellness and incorporate it into your personal routine. By limiting the number of guests, our highly trained and motivated staff are able to serve your needs on a personal level."

DIET PROGRAM: 800–1,000 calories per day for women. 1,250 calories per day for men. The average weight loss is three pounds per week. If you have special dietary requirements, an individualized diet can be arranged. The emphasis is upon complex carbohydrates, such as grains, fresh fruits, and vegetables. Fish and poultry are the primary protein sources. Red meat is rarely served. No sugar or salt is used; herb blends and artifical sweeteners are used.

From the looks and taste of the food, you would never think that so much can be done with so little. Food preparation and presentation is a fine art at the Argyle. The chef, Nancy Runyon, previously was at the Crescent Club, a daytime spa and health club in Dallas. She is assisted by Tom Edmonds. The chefs mingle with the guests to answer any questions regarding the recipes they prepare. In addition, they also teach cooking and nutrition classes. And, as if that weren't enough, at the end of your stay, they will give you all the recipes used during your time here.

Here are some of my favorite recipes from The Argyle.

CRUSTLESS SPINACH QUICHE

10 ounces fresh spinach,
   blanched
1 clove minced garlic
2 tablespoons unbleached flour
1 cup skim milk
Paprika to taste

2 teaspoons chopped onion
1 cup shredded low-fat cheese
½ teaspoon nutmeg
2 medium eggs (or 1 whole egg
   plus 1 egg white)

Heat oven to 350°. Sauté onion and garlic for 3–4 minutes. In a separate bowl, mix cheese, flour, and herbs. Combine eggs and add spinach and onion mixture. Combine with flour mixture. Mix well and pour into nonstick 9″ pan or quiche pan. Dust with paprika. Bake for 40 minutes or until center is firm to the touch. Yield: 6 servings. 120 calories per serving.

MEXICAN COLESLAW

4 cups shredded cabbage   2 cups shredded carrots
   (mixture of green & red)

Dressing:
³/₄ cup unsweetened apple juice   ²/₃ cup apple cider vinegar
¹/₂ teaspoon cumin   1 tablespoon low-cal mayonnaise
¹/₂ teaspoon celery seed   ¹/₂ teaspoon white pepper

Combine cabbage and carrots. Whisk dressing ingredients together. Toss together all ingredients and marinate at least 1 hour before serving. Yield: 8 servings. 41 calories per 1 cup serving.

BROILED FISH WITH MUSTARD

¹/₂ pounds fresh flounder or   Low-cal cooking spray
sole fillets   2 teaspoons low-cal yogurt
1 tablespoon whole grain   ¹/₂ tablespoon chopped fresh
   mustard   parsley
¹/₂ tablespoon chopped fresh dill   ¹/₈ teaspoon fresh ground pepper

Spray cooking sheet lightly with cooking spray. Arrange fillets on sheet. Combine remaining ingredients, spread evenly over fillets. Broil 3 to 4 inches from heat for 3–4 minutes. Serve with fresh lime wedge. Yield: 6 servings. 107 calories per serving.

PEACH CRUMB BAKE

2 cups sliced fresh peaches   ¹/₃ cup graham cracker crumbs
¹/₂ teaspoon ground cinnamon   Dash of nutmeg
2 tablespoons low-cal margarine

Heat oven to 350°. Layer peaches in bottom of an 8″ baking dish. Combine graham cracker crumbs, cinnamon, and nutmeg. Mix well. Blend in margarine and sprinkle mixture over peaches. Bake uncovered for 30 minutes. Yield: 4 servings. 76 calories per serving.

GUEST POPULATION: Coed. 40 guests. Most spa clientele are from the Texas/Southwest area as the spa is new and just getting started.

PACKAGES AND MINIMUM STAYS: The Seven-Day Vitalizer

starts on Sundays for 7 days and 7 nights. Check-in time is between 2:00 and 4:00 P.M. Check-out time is 3:00 P.M.

Some of the many special programs available are: the Daytimer, the Day of Beauty, the Taste of the Argyle (overnight), the Weekender, and the Seven-Day Smoking Cessation Program.

In keeping with Sue Goldstein's motto of "Never pay full price for anything," there's always a bargain available, be it a package or a treatment. For instance, during March, all treatments beginning with the letter "M" are half price: Massage, Makeup and Manicure. It's best to call for the current specials.

MEAL SERVICE: The meals are served in the dining room, an informal room with a panoramic view of the countryside. Usually the square tables are combined to form a larger table or a "U."

Breakfast is served as a buffet, to allow for both early- and late-comers. Lunch and dinner are sit-down meals. Both the menu and the calorie count are on a chalkboard.

DRESS CODE: Sweatclothes are fine for everything down here with shorts and tops for warmer weather. Bring your swimsuit and workout clothes. If you plan a day or evening in Dallas, bring the appropriate clothing.

ACCOMMODATIONS: The 20 double guest rooms are in two buildings on opposite sides of the courtyard. The rooms are spacious and decorated with deep teal carpeting and peach walls. The furnishings are rattan. The beds have duvet comforters, egg-crate mattress pads, and fluff-to-the-limit pillows. The bathrooms are large and exceptionally well planned: there are two vanities with sinks on opposing walls, so you and your roommate each have your own!

Each room is air conditioned with individual controls and has a TV and phone. VCRs are available for your use—just request one at the main desk. There's also a small refrigerator stocked with mineral water in each room. The spa will provide a roommate if both partners mutually agree.

HOUSE RULES: Smoking is permitted in designated outdoor areas. Alcohol is not used or permitted.

PHYSICAL FACILITIES: The Beauty Barn is the first building you see when you arrive. In it are the lobby/reception area, the aerobics studio, the equipment room, the beauty treatment rooms, the boutique, and the offices.

The main building is at the far end of the courtyard. It houses the main lounge, library, demonstration kitchen, spa kitchen, dining room, fitness testing area, Kneipp treatment area, and an indoor swimming pool. In front of this building is a gazebo-covered hot tub and an outdoor swimming pool.

Hiking and jogging trails twine through the 14 acres. Directly across the road is the Denton Country Club, which has an 18-hole golf course and 5 tennis courts. The spa will make arrangements for you to utilize these facilities. Racquetball courts are also located nearby.

ACTIVITIES, TREATMENTS, AND PROGRAMS: Included in all packages are the fitness classes and other scheduled programs. All beauty/pampering treatments are extra.

Fitness programs that are offered include high- and low-impact aerobics, hyrobics, stretch and tone, power walking, yoga, passive resistance, and specific body part conditioning. There is a fully equipped exercise machine room, complete with videos to guide you.

The menu of optional services is extensive: hair and nail treatments, facials, makeup, and waxings. There are four massage treatments available, including the therapeutic Swedish massage. The Kneipp water treatments run the gamut, from sitz baths to haysack wraps and wet sheet treatments.

Evenings are fun times at the Argyle. There are concerts, psychics, handwriting analyses, movies, games, and so on. The guest services director is forever finding new and different things to do.

If a group of spa guests wants to go to Dallas or Fort Worth for an evening, there are 3 spa cars available to take them.

A Day at the Argyle

6:30	Coffee's On
7:15	Countryside Walk & Stretch
8:00	Breakfast Buffet
9:00	Good Morning Stretch
9:45	Snack
10:00	Energizer—Low-Impact Aerobics
11:00	Body Shop—Shape & Tone Class
12:00	Lunch
1:15	Lecture or demonstration, such as "Fit or Fat," "Self-Massage," or "Low-Cal Cooking"
2:00	Hurray for Hips & Awesome Abs! or H2Ohhh!
2:45	Snack
3:00	Individual fitness consultations
4:00	Stretch & Relaxation or Yoga & Relaxation
5:30	Hors d'oeuvres and nonalcoholic cocktails Musical presentation
6:00	Dinner
7:00	Program: Starlight Concert, lecture on stress, makeovers, movies, and popcorn, etc.
8:00	Snack

STAFF POPULATION: The spa owner/director is Sue Goldstein, the diva of discounts. She is the author of *The Underground Shopper*'s series of books, one of which is the *Guide to Health and Fitness.* She followed her own advice—she combined the best features of the spas she researched with her no-nonsense approach to shopping. The result is The Argyle.

Her strong dollar sense is again apparent in the boutique, where everything is discounted 20 to 70 percent. They carry sportswear, aerobics outfits, toiletries, and jewelry. Guests may either purchase other items that catch their eye around the spa or Sue will tell them where to get them at bargain prices.

OPTIONAL COSTS: All beauty, massage, and Kneipp-therapy treatments are intentionally optional. Sue feels that you should pay only for what you want—and nothing more. In keeping with this philosophy, each guest receives a $100 coupon to be used for the treatments of their choice or in the boutique.

NICE TO KNOW: The Argyle has a pair of llamas and a pair of Akitas, the national dog of Japan, on the property. It also has the only animal spa that I know of. Your dog or cat can accompany you and enjoy a luxurious stay in an individual kennel or multilevel kitty condo! And don't feel you're neglecting your pet while you have your special treatments—it, too, can have a massage, facial, or manicure here at the Argyle!

JUDY'S COMMENT: Definitely the right spa for someone who wants to lose weight but doesn't want to leave home without their pet!

---

* BERMUDA INN FITNESS & REDUCING RESORT
43019 Sierra Highway
Lancaster, CA 93534
800-328-3276
805-942-1493

Located on 20 acres of parklike grounds in the foothills of the Tehachapi Mountains in the high desert country of Southern California. Open year-round.

RATES: Affordable. Credit cards: MasterCard, Visa.

LOCATION AND TRANSPORTATION: One-and-one-half hours' drive directly north of Los Angeles. Complimentary transportation to and from Lancaster's Fox Field, which may be reached from the Los Angeles airport via Desert Sun Airlines. Limousine service is available from LAX.

EMPHASIS/PHILOSOPHY: Bermuda Inn describes itself as America's best reducing-spa value, where you can lose weight and shape up while you vacation.

DIET PROGRAM: 700 or 900 calories per day, portion-controlled. The high-protein, low-carbohydrate menu features fresh fruits and vegetables, lean beef, fish, and poultry. Dietetic ingredients are used for delicious mousses and low-calorie desserts. No sugar, no salt. Breakfast meals are not included in the calorie count. Some of my favorite dishes include crepes, lasagna, and quiche. An open juice bar with coffee and herbal tea is available at all times. It is not uncommon for guests who stay an extended period to lose 25, 50, or even 100 pounds (for which awards are given). "Lose up to a pound a day the fun way" is Bermuda Inn's slogan.

GUEST POPULATION: Coed. 30 guests. Most guests come with weight loss as their main objective. Truly obese people feel comfortable here. Almost 90 percent of the guests are women. Well-known comedienne Nell Carter has dropped many pounds here. You can catch her praising the effectiveness of the program on evening talk shows. Sally Struthers and Ernest Borgnine also drop in at this California spa.

PACKAGES AND MINIMUM STAYS: Basic program is 8 days and 7 nights, although no minimum stay is required. Arrive or check out any day.

MEAL SERVICE: "Mocktail" hour's at 5:15 P.M. Guests may be served cottage cheese and cucumber dip on melba rounds. Most lunch and all dinner meals are table service. Room service is available on request.

DRESS CODE: Casual. Jogging outfits or caftans are just fine. Bermuda Inn suggests you bring along gym wear, swimsuit, beach towel, walking shoes, and a warm sweater or jacket as you're in "high desert" country.

ACCOMMODATIONS: Two-story motel building has more than adequate rooms. Each contemporary unit has a private bath, dressing room, television, and table and chair for your exercise gear. Full-service housekeeping is provided daily. For female guests arriving alone, shared accommodations can be arranged; they pair nonsmokers with like-minded.

HOUSE RULES: Smoking is permitted only in designated areas. The dining room has both smoking and nonsmoking sections.

PHYSICAL FACILITIES: All spa facilities are shared by both men and women. There are separate locker rooms provided for changing. Facilities include massage rooms, sauna, indoor Jacuzzi, outdoor swimming pool, indoor exercise pool, Nautilus, gym equipment, half-mile lakeside walking/jogging track (lighted at night), tennis courts, volleyball, croquet, and putting green. Beauty shop, boutique, and coin-operated laundry facilities are on the premises. Golf and bowling nearby.

ACTIVITIES, TREATMENTS, AND PROGRAMS: Initial interview on arrival to determine your diet, followed by daily weigh-in and blood-pressure check. Daily fitness activities include a half-hour morning walk, with your choice of fitness classes, including stretching, gentle exercises while seated, aqua aerobics, trim and firm, gentle water exercises, weights, cardio, and relax tape. Programs include bingo twice a week, arts and crafts, movies, shopping trips to Lancaster, fashion shows with guests as models, and evening dance classes and lectures on such topics as "Emotional Aspects of Overeating" and "Weight Reduction Techniques Through Nutrition and Exercise."

A Day at Bermuda Inn

7:00–10:30	Daily check-in with nurse for weight and blood pressure recording
7:00–9:30	Breakfast
Anytime	Desert walk or run on half-mile track
9:00–9:45	Stretch exercises
10:00–10:45	Cardiorespiratory exercises
11:00	"Sit and Fit" exercises
11:00–11:45	Aqua aerobics
12:00	Lunch
1:00–1:30	Body measurements
2:00–2:45	Aqua aerobics
	Toning exercise with weights
2:00–4:00	Shopping trip to Lancaster
3:00	Veggie break
3:00–3:45	"Trim and Tone" moderate exercises
4:00	Supervised walk
4:30	Relax tape
5:00	Casual gathering in lounge
6:00	Dinner
7:30	Bingo
8:30	Movie
9:00	Munch break

STAFF POPULATION: A medical doctor is on staff two days a week, and a nurse is present every day for weigh-in and blood pressure checks.

OPTIONAL COSTS: Bermuda Inn has a full-service beauty salon, and massages are an available extra at modest cost.

*BEST BUY AND WHY: This affordable program is a "Best Buy" because:

- It offers diet meals that are most effective for losing weight.
- Supervision by the medical staff is outstanding (a rarity even at some posh spas). Lots of tender loving care here.
- They offer room service—an uncommon bonus at moderately priced spas.
- It's refreshing to see people of all sizes here, not just starlet types with tiny derrieres.

JUDY'S COMMENT: A friendly and caring resort with an effective weight loss program not designed only for those who are already fit.

BIRDWING SPA
Route 2, Box 99, Litchfield, MN 55355
612-693-6064

This country-style spa is located on 300 wooded, rolling acres alongside beautiful Star Lake. Open year-round, including all holidays.

RATES: Affordable. Credit cards: MasterCard, Visa. The spa is available for group seminars.

LOCATION AND TRANSPORTATION: One-and-one-half hours west of Minneapolis–St. Paul on Highway 12. Nearest airport is Minneapolis–St. Paul. Shuttle bus from airport to Litchfield; courtesy pickup from Litchfield. Inquire at spa for more specific information.

EMPHASIS/PHILOSOPHY: According to spa owner/coordinator Elisabeth Carlson, "We try to maintain a luxury spa with professional staffing at affordable prices. I'm from Austria and we have brought European service to Birdwing."

"It's time for yourself" is Birdwing's theme. "Time for all those little things you've been meaning to do. And all those not so little things you've dreamed of doing. Like indulging in massages, facials, manicures and pedicures. Swimming, Jacuzzi, saunas and tanning indoors and out. Walking, running, biking, cross-country skiing and aerobics. Take it all in. Or take it easy. Our staff of nutritionists and fitness consultants will work with you to design a day-by-day schedule tailored to your needs, including health routines easy enough to work for you at home."

Birdwing uses the pampered approach to get people started on a healthy life-style.

DIET PROGRAM: 900–1,100 calories per day, according to your individual needs. Average weight loss is 5 pounds in seven days.

Melanie Lady, R.D., nutritional director, consults with you upon your arrival and is an excellent resource person for your questions about nutrition. The chef, RaeAnn Granlund, plans the menus, using only natural ingredients. Another dietician, Candace Huisman, turns these diet dishes into delights for the eyes by her attention to festive presentation. She also gives weekly cooking classes featuring seasonal food.

Some of my favorite recipes follow.

MANDARIN CORNISH HENS

2 3-lb. Cornish game hens
$1/2$ cup water
3 tablespoons fresh-squeezed
  orange juice
tarragon
$1/2$ teaspoon curry

$1/2$ teaspoon marjoram
$1/2$ teaspoon sage
$1/2$ teaspoon chicken bouillon
2 teaspoons reduced-sodium soy
  sauce

Remove giblets and wash hens. Split lengthwise. Place in glass 9 × 13 baking dish.

Combine remaining ingredients in small saucepan. Bring to a boil, reduce heat and simmmer 10 minutes. Pour over hens, cover and refrigerate 8 hours. Remove hens from marinade; reserve marinade. Grill over medium coals on each side, basting often. Done when leg moves easily. Serves 4. Calories: 133.

HEAVENLY CHOCOLATE BANANA DELIGHT

2 tablespoons part-skim ricotta
  cheese
$1/2$ teaspoon confectioner's sugar
$1/2$ medium banana, peeled and
  cut lengthwise into 4 slices

$1/8$ teaspoon almond extract
$1/2$ teaspoon flake coconut
$1/2$ teaspoon chocolate syrup
$1/2$ maraschino cherry

In small bowl combine cheese, sugar, and almond extract, mixing well. Arrange banana slices on plate, then drop mixture on bananas; then drizzle syrup, sprinkle coconut, and top with cherry half. Garnish with fresh mint. Yield: 1 serving. Calories: 113

GUEST POPULATION: Coed. Mostly women during the week. Some couples over the weekend. Eighteen guests are the limit in this intimate spa. They come from many walks of life, but what they have in common is an appreciation of the serene country setting and a desire to make a change in their life-styles. And they all appreciate the pampering while getting started in the right direction.

PACKAGES AND MINIMUM STAYS: A number of packages are offered: weekend, week, discounted extended stays, as well as special holiday packages. Call for the most current information.

MEAL SERVICE: A high-energy breakfast is served in bed. This option is very popular with weekend guests. Lunch and dinner are served in the handsome Tudor-style dining room, which overlooks picturesque Birdwing Bay. The European touch is apparent, with fine china and fresh flowers gracing the tables.

Only natural ingredients are used at Birdwing. Although all types of meat are used, the emphasis is upon fish and chicken. As it is such an intimate spa, there is no need for a printed menu. Dietician Candace Huisman goes over the menu with spa guests every day, making it a learning experience as well as an informative one.

DRESS CODE: Casual. Jogging outfits are perfectly acceptable. You may bring special sports equipment, such as skis and ice skates, or you may borrow it from Birdwing.

ACCOMMODATIONS: This lovely Tudor estate is trimmed in beautiful woods. The room decor features Early American furnishings. Each room has a color and personality all its own. Just like the White House, there's The Blue Room, The Yellow Room, The Green Room, and so forth through the rainbow!

All rooms are air conditioned and have daily maid service. There are no TVs or telephones, in keeping with the serene atmosphere. The phones and TV are in the social area. As this is formerly a private estate, bathrooms are shared by 2 bedrooms, except for the Master Suite. A delightful Continental touch is the bouquet of fresh flowers in each room.

HOUSE RULES: No alcohol is served at Birdwing. The nightly happy hour features exotic nonalcoholic fruit drinks in the gazebo during the summer and by the fireplace during cooler weather. Smoking is allowed only in your own room and outdoors.

PHYSICAL FACILITIES: The estate is perfect for long walks. There are meticulously maintained trails winding through the estate as well as alongside the 2 miles of shoreline. You may swim in the lake or in the heated outdoor swimming pool. In the wintertime, skiing is a favorite on the 25 kilometers of ski trails on the estate. Ice-skating on the rink is also a popular pastime

All facilities of the spa are in the main building, with the exception of the exercise rooms, which are a few minutes away. There is a full-service beauty shop, including a tanning booth, on the lower level of the main spa building. The massage room, Jacuzzi, sauna and laundry room are adjacent to the beauty shop.

ACTIVITIES, TREATMENTS And PROGRAMS: Included in the 7-day program are 2 one-hour massages, 1 European facial, 1 manicure and 1 pedicure, and 1 hairstyling. Aveda beauty products from nearby Minneapolis are used for skin care.

Two exercise classes are scheduled daily. Low impact aerobics are offered in the morning. A variety of exercises is offered in the afternoon, ranging from yoga to rubberband resistance classes.

There is a weekly program of speakers who address such topics as stress, healthy family life, personal development, etc. In addition, there are monthly guest speakers, who present programs and workshops. Some of the 1988 speakers were: Janet Hagberg, author of *Real Power*; Rubye Erickson, *Color Me Beautiful* consultant and speaker on inner and outer beauty; and Mary Ellen Pinkham, columnist and author of *Mary Ellen's Helpful Hints*.

A Day at Birdwing

8:00	Brisk walk for early risers
9:00	Breakfast
10:00	Individualized exercises, according to fitness level and areas of interest
11:00	Walk, swimming, canoeing, or skiing
12:00	Gourmet lunch
1:00	Talk by dietician or outdoor sport if it's too nice to stay inside
2:00	Leisure time
3:00	Low-impact aerobics, yoga, hydroaerobics, or long bike ride
4:00	Happy Hour Free time for sauna and Jacuzzi
5:30	Gourmet diner
6:30	Massages and beauty treatments
8:00	Special speakers or movies

OPTIONAL TREATMENTS: Extra massages and beauty salon services are available for an additional fee.

STAFF POPULATION: The spa coordinator, Elisabeth Carlson, owns the spa together with her husband, Richard. As a former model, she has a wealth of beauty experience from which to draw. Both Melanie Lady and Candace Huisman are registered dietitians. Melanie works with each guest to develop a personalized eating plan. She also speaks on nutrition and smart supermarket shopping. Candace teaches weekly cooking classes, using fresh seasonal foods. She emphasizes beautiful food presentation. RaeAnn Granlund is the chef who transforms all their marvelous recipes into reality.

NICE TO KNOW: Birdwing is open Thanksgiving and Christmas, for singles or couples who are alone for the holidays. This is indeed a rarity with spas. What a nice place to spend the holidays.

Elegant added touches are the imported herbal bath salts you find in the bathroom and the Birdwing T-shirts in your bedroom.

JUDY'S COMMENT: A lovely retreat open year-round. It has the kind of pampering and diet dining that makes it a great place to get a fresh start on a new life-style!

CAL-A-VIE
2249 Somerset Road
Vista, CA 92084
619-945-2055

Open year-round except the weeks of Christmas and New Years. This exclusive spa, where each guest is housed in a private cottage, combines European beauty treatments with an American awareness of fitness and nutrition.

RATES: Expensive. American Express, MasterCard, Visa. A $1,000 nonrefundable deposit is required to confirm your reservation.

LOCATION AND TRANSPORTATION: Cal-A-Vie is nestled in a secluded valley on 125 acres of rolling hills north of San Diego and one hour from the airport. Transportation to and from San Diego airport is provided at no extra cost. Flight information must be sent to the spa a minimum of one week before a guest's arrival.

EMPHASIS/PHILOSOPHY: The program at Cal-A-Vie is based upon European principles of body detoxification along with an American emphasis on life-style reeducation. William and Susan Power, the founders, tried "to create an environment where those interested in health and rejuvenation can change their attitudes and life-style. Our intensive program encourages proper rest, exercise, improved nutrition, reduced stress, and reenergized attitude." The spa aims to

Courtesy of Cal-A-Vie

meet "the changing needs of the individual seeking a viable means of equilibrium between mind, body, and spirit."

DIET PROGRAM: The menu is geared toward a diet of 800–1,000 calories a day for weight loss. Modification of calorie intake is also provided by adjusting the portions of the basic menu. Individual allergies and preferences are accommodated.

Chef Michel Stroot is a nationally recognized master of gourmet spa cuisine. He has developed his own special style of healthful food preparation called *cuisine fraîche.* Stroot's cuisine uses little fat and sodium and emphasizes whole grains, pasta, legumes, fresh fruits and vegetables, poultry, and fish. No beef is served. Most dishes contain seasonal produce and are seasoned with herbs grown in the gardens of Cal-A-Vie. Some of Chef Stroot's favorite spices are garlic, sage, rosemary, tarragon, and ginger. In the tradition of true master chefs, Stroot makes sure that meals are balanced aesthetically as well as nutritionally. Chef Stroot pays special attention to the colors and textures of the dishes served since he feels that food should heighten the senses. He is sincerely interested in trying to encourage guests to integrate healthy eating into their daily lives and willingly shares recipes. Examples of some of his wonderful creations are: Papaya Chicken Salad; Paillard of Turkey; Chicken Breast with Rosemary, Garlic, and Lemon; Lentil Vegetable Salad; and Bananas in Blueberry Sauce.

GUEST POPULATION: The spa can accommodate 24 participants. The calendar determines whether sessions are coed or not. For
approximately 16 weeks of the year, the program is for women only;
26 weeks are designated as coed sessions; about 8 weeks of the year
are devoted solely to men; and couples' weeks occur approximately 2
times a year. Cal-A-Vie has been host to such well-known women as
actresses Linda Gray and Catherine Oxenberg, model Christie Brinkley, and actor Larry Hagman.

MEAL SERVICE: Guests dine in the elegant French Provincial
dining room on fine china, with linen and fresh flowers at every meal.
The dining room has a beamed, cathedral ceiling, a giant stove fireplace, and French doors that open onto an outdoor dining area.

DRESS CODE: Guests are encouraged to leave their jewelry and
valuables at home. Cal-A-Vie provides almost all clothing needed during the program, such as jogging sweats, shorts, T-shirts, jacket, robe,
sandals, and rain gear. These items are returned to the spa at the end
of your stay. The ambience is relaxed and informal. Jogging outfits
can be worn at all meals.

ACCOMMODATIONS: The guest cottages—with terra-cotta roofs,
wide wooden plank doors, and window boxes brimming with flowers—
are reminiscent of villages in southern France. Each guest is housed

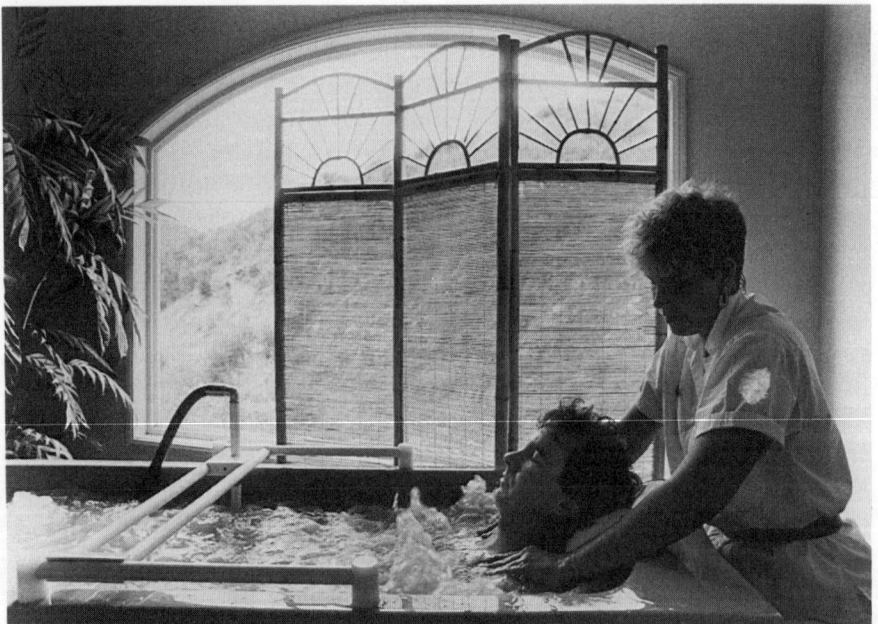

Courtesy of Cal-A-Vie

in a private, individually decorated cottage. Rooms are furnished with hand-carved pine furniture and have beamed ceilings and tiled bathrooms. The imported chintzes covering the duvets, pillow shams, and drapery are in soft tones of yellow, blue, rose, and green. Each cottage has a private deck that opens onto a vast expanse of wooded hills. The cottages have telephones and air conditioning but do not contain television sets. There are TVs with cable and satellite programs in a lounge in the Cal-A-Vie complex. Laundry service is provided. In the morning guests leave garments to be cleaned in their rooms; by afternoon the items are returned clean and ready to go.

HOUSE RULES: Smoking is not permitted in any public area of the spa. Four guest cottages are set aside to house spa participants who smoke. On arrival you will be served one glass of wine. Apart from that, no alcohol is served or available for purchase at Cal-A-Vie.

PHYSICAL FACILITIES: The architecture and interior design was created to achieve an environment of peace and tranquillity that reinforces the objectives of the spa program. All areas in the Cal-A-Vie complex possess a light, open quality that allows guests to experience the benefits of their treatments amid the spa's beautiful natural surroundings.

Beauty treatments are held either in the Beauty House or the Bath House. Massages, body wraps, water treatments, and other full-body treatments are performed in the Bath House. Guests also have the option of receiving massages outdoors on the sun decks. The Beauty House is reserved for services such as facials and hand, nail, and hair treatments.

There is a spa boutique that sells exercise and sportswear on the premises. The spa will provide you with most of the small toiletry items you may need during your stay.

There are a regular gym, two aerobics rooms with spring-loaded floor, and a weight-training gym room, which contains Nautilus and Keiser Cam II air-resistance equipment and computerized bicycles. Also among the indoor facilities at Cal-A-Vie are a Jacuzzi and dry and wet saunas.

The grounds are near hiking trails of various levels of difficulty (mountains or golf course). There is an outdoor Olympic-size swimming pool and one tennis court. Guests wishing to play golf may use the 18-hole course at nearby Vista Valley Country Club, where golf clubs can be rented.

ACTIVITIES, TREATMENTS, AND PROGRAMS: The week-long spa package includes 3 one-hour facials; 1 one-hour hair and scalp conditioning and massage; 2 one-hour hand and foot skin treatments; 5 one-hour massages employing shiatsu, Swedish, and other techniques; 1 thalassotherapy (seaweed wrap) application; 2 hydrotherapy sessions (underwater jet-stream massages); 1 one-hour Body Glo treatment (a full-body slough); 1 one-hour aromatherapy massage (essential oils); 1 reflexology session; 1 nail polishing; 1 makeup application; and 1 hairstyling.

At the beginning of every spa program, a treatment-orientation talk is given. The fitness program at Cal-A-Vie, included in the spa package, starts with a complete fitness assessment. This involves the administration of a battery of tests for flexibility, cardiovascular capability, upper and lower body strength, and the ratio of lean body mass to body fat. A Cal-A-Vie fitness expert enters the results of these tests, along with the guest's vital statistics, into a computer. The data is processed to yield an individualized daily diet and exercise program.

The Cal-A-Vie spa program includes an exercise regimen to match your level of physical proficiency. Guests have unlimited access to all exercise classes offered during their stay. The fitness classes given during a particular week may vary according to the needs of the spa population. At least four exercise classes a day are given. Classes emphasize nonimpact, rhythmic movements, body awareness and contouring; and posture and alignment. Exercise classes can include aerobic conditioning, water aerobics, stretching, calisthenics, yoga, and T'ai Chi. The more rigorous classes are held during morning hours. Also available are tennis, volleyball, swimming, hiking, and weight training.

Presentations are offered three or four evenings per week on topics such as stress reduction; low-calorie cooking with Chef Stroot; and nutrition and fitness.

Although every day's schedule is different at Cal-A-Vie, a typical day could go as follows.

6:30	Morning hike (mountains or golf course)
7:30	Warm-ups (half-hour)
8:30	Aerobics class
10:00	Shapes (intensified toning class with weights and rubber bands)
10:50	Break for juice with potassium
11:00	Stretch
12:00	Facial
1:00	Lunch
2:00	Abdominals class
3:00	Yoga or T'ai Chi
4:00	Pampering treatments
7:00	Dinner

STAFF POPULATION: The staff at Cal-A-Vie is highly experienced. Susan Power, the director, has a long history in fitness train-

Courtesy of Cal-A-Vie

ing. She began her career at Rancho La Puerta, after which she opened her own exercise center in California. She then returned to Rancho La Puerta as director and creator of a new fitness program. Chef Michel Stroot was trained in Belgium and was chef at the Golden Door for more than ten years. He is currently working on a book of recipes based on the cuisine at Cal-A-Vie. Linny Largent, formerly of the Golden Door as well, is the nutritionist and assistant chef. Patricia Miller, an international health and beauty expert, co-ordinates spa treatments.

OPTIONAL COSTS: The spa offers a full range of French à la carte beauty treatments. Golf at the nearby country club is available at an additional charge, as are private tennis lessons on Cal-A-Vie grounds.

NICE TO KNOW: Safe deposit boxes are available at the front desk. Many of the plants, flowers, and herbs used in the beauty treatments are grown in the spa gardens. "Ethereal" environmental music is piped into all beauty treatment areas. If you go with a spouse or partner, make certain your respective cottages are in proximity. There is usually much scurrying around at bedtime during couples' week as guests move about to join their partners for the night. Afternoons are devoted almost entirely to pampering treatments at this spa. The name Cal-A-Vie can be interpreted as follows: "Cal," as in California; "Vie," meaning "life" in French; thus, "California Life-style."

JUDY'S COMMENT: The luxurious accommodations, beautiful countryside, first-class spa cuisine, and extensive European-styled beauty treatments, along with a reasonable program of fitness activities, make this one of the nation's leading spas. Guests can expect to come away refreshed, relaxed, and reinvigorated.

CANYON RANCH HEALTH AND FITNESS RESORT
8600 E. Rockcliff Road
Tucson, AZ 85715
800-742-9000 (U.S.A.)
800-327-9090 (Canada)
602-749-9000

Nestled on 60 acres in the foothills of Arizona's magestic Santa Catalina Mountains. Open year-round.

RATES: Expensive. Credit cards: Discover, MasterCard, Visa.

LOCATION AND TRANSPORTATION: Only 30 minutes north of Tucson in a desert oasis. Courtesy service to and from airport.

EMPHASIS/PHILOSOPHY: According to Canyon Ranch, they "help people learn how to improve their health and well-being—by living the ideal healthful life-style while taking a vacation."

DIET PROGRAM: 1,000 calories per day for women; 1,200 for men, with emphasis on portion control. Well-balanced meals are low in fat, high in fiber, with no sodium or sugar (small amounts of fructose used). Gourmet menu may be diet or nondiet. One may eat as much or as little as desired. Two juice breaks daily. Several selections are available for each meal, and calorie count is on the menu. Jeanne Jones, well-known author and diet consultant, plans all the menus at Canyon Ranch. Jeanne is the one who says, "You should throw away all your scales and rely upon mirrors and tape measures as your guide to reality." Some of my favorite entrees are: Moroccan Chowder with Couscous, Cantonese Stir Fry, and Chicken Curry with Chutney. Some of these recipes can be found in the book *Fitness First: A 14-day Exercise Program for the New You*, written by Jeanne Jones and Canyon Ranch Fitness Director Karma Kientzler. I reproduce for your enjoyment typical menus for three days of Canyon Ranch's ten-day menu cycle.

Courtesy of Canyon Ranch Health and Fitness Resort

DAY 1

BREAKFAST
Blueberry Shake Breakfast (140)
French Toast (110)
    w/Pineapple-Peach Butter (95)

LUNCH
Consommé (15)
Curried Chicken Salad in Pineapple Boat (340)
Banana Cake (110)
or
Creole Vegetable Gumbo (200)
Fresh Fruit (40)

DINNER
Pasta Salad (65)
Eggplant Florentine (235)
Baked Apple w/Zabaglione Sauce (110)
or

Fresh Fish Veracruz (130)
Rice Pilaf (110)
Fresh Vegetables (30)
Fresh Fruit (40)

DAY 2

BREAKFAST
Carob Shake Breakfast (140)
Tropical Fruit w/Yogurt Sauce (85)
Bran Muffins (115)

LUNCH
Antipasto Salad (115)
Pizza (260)
Truly Fruity Cookie (60)
or
Salade Nouvelle (240)
Fresh Fruit (40)

DINNER
Carrot & Raisin Salad (60)
Swordfish Amandine (140)
Seven-Grain Pilaf (65)
Fresh Fruit (40)
or
Cheese Enchiladas (155)
Fantasy in Fruit (115)

DAY 3

BREAKFAST
Strawberry Shake Breakfast (140)
Bananas Canyon Ranch (135)
Canyon Ranch Bread (70)

LUNCH
Cold Blueberry Soup (50)
Mandarin Salad (355)
  w/Roll (70)
Custard (70)
or
Pita Pocket Sandwich (170)
Fresh Fruit (40)

DINNER
Salad of Young Greens w/Tarragon Vinaigrette (20)
Broiled Lobster Tail (70)
Scalloped Potatoes (100)
Fresh Fruit (40)
or
Tamale Pie (200)
Fresh Vegetable (55)
Heavenly Pudding (50)

GUEST POPULATION: Coed. 250 guests. Men account for 35–40 percent of guests. This spa is a favorite with many folks from all over the U.S.A.

PACKAGES AND MINIMUM STAYS: There are ten-night, seven-night, and four-night packages. No minimum stay is required from June 16 to September 15.

MEAL SERVICE: All meals are served in the light, Southwestern-style dining room. Beautiful plants, pottery, and other local artwork are featured. A hostess is available to seat you for both luncheon and dinner. A nice touch is the 24-hour beverage bar near the kitchen, which offers broth, herbal teas, and decaffeinated coffee. Perrier machines are scattered about the grounds for refreshing pickups.

DRESS CODE: Jogging outfits are perfect. You're in the mountains—bring along a sweater. Gentlemen, here's a chance to wear your ten-gallon hat!

ACCOMMODATIONS: Hotel-type accommodations are available, as well as casitas. The decor is Southwestern, with pastel tones. Telephone and television in each room. Single, double, and triple occupancy available.

HOUSE RULES: Smoking is allowed on the patios. No alcoholic beverages are allowed.

PHYSICAL FACILITIES: This spa has it all! The 62,000-square-foot, air-conditioned spa building has individual men's and women's areas. Each area has its own locker rooms, hot and cold plunge whirlpools, Jacuzzis, steam rooms, herbal-wrap rooms, and nude-sunbathing solarium.
    Indoor coed facilities include: 6 exercise rooms with aerobic flooring; an aerobic and strength-training room with Trotter treadmills, computerized bicycles and an extensive Keiser Cam II free-weight system; 3 indoor racquetball courts and 1 squash court; a rest/meditation room; the hiking and biking offices; an indoor pool; and skin-care facilities.

Courtesy of Canyon Ranch Health and Fitness Resort

Outdoor coed facilities include: 6 lighted tennis courts, one recreational pool, one 25-foot lap pool, one 75-foot lap pool, and a mile-long jogging track.

ACTIVITIES, TREATMENTS, AND PROGRAMS: Package programs include lodging and meals, use of all spa facilities, unlimited exercise classes, sports hiking and mountain biking, and presentations by medical, fitness, and nutrition experts. Included in the 7-night stay are your choice of 5 of these personal and sports services: full-body massage, European facial, 2 herbal wraps, manicure and pedicure, haircut, shampoo/set, makeup consultation and application, private tennis or racquetball lessons, or a round of golf. Also included are 2 professional health consultations ranging from nutritional assessment to hypnotherapy.

The day begins with a morning hike or jog through the foothills near the ranch. Mountain hikes are held daily. More than 30 coed fitness activities are offered daily, at all levels, including: stretch and relax yoga, body toning, strenuous and introductory aerobic classes, weight training, tennis clinics, and water exercise classes.

Evening programs consist of lectures by Canyon Ranch's full-time physician, resident dieticians, or exercise physiologists; nutrition talks; makeup and beauty consultations; and stress-management discussions.

SPECIAL PROGRAMS: The Life Enhancement Center is the new self-contained mini-spa for special programs. These programs focus on changing behavior, such as food-habit management, smoking cessation, or pain management. The Behavioral Health Department uses group discussions, private counseling, biofeedback, and hypnotherapy. The program is limited to 50, and runs for different periods of time.

OPTIONAL COSTS: Extra personal and sports services, which are listed above. Also additional professional health services. Horseback riding and golf are nearby.

NICE TO KNOW: It's interesting to note that entrepreneurs Mel and Enid Zuckerman, owners of Canyon Ranch, found themselves nearing fifty, overfed, overstressed, and asthmatic. A month's stay at the Oaks of Ojai, California, inspired them to purchase the old Double U Ranch and launch the Canyon Ranch Spa. Since then they have inspired a number of guests to open their own spas.

An East Coast Canyon Ranch is scheduled to open in mid-1989 in the Berkshires in Lenox, Massachusetts. It will be located on an estate named Bellefontaine, a replica of the Petit Trianon and grounds.

JUDY'S COMMENT: Canyon Ranch has the business savy to offer programs that appeal to a diverse clientele. The fitness program is outstanding. New wholistic health concepts are being introduced all the time. Whether you want to reduce or just plain relax, this is a wonderful place to do it.

*CARMEL COUNTRY SPA
Ten Country Club Way
Carmel Valley, CA 93924
408-659-3486

Six acres of lush mountain greenery surround this rustic resort. Open year-round.

RATES: Affordable. Credit cards: MasterCard, Visa. All treatments are extra.

LOCATION AND TRANSPORTATION   Eleven miles from Monterey and an easy drive from San Francisco. The Big Sur coastline alone is worth the visit.

EMPHASIS/PHILOSOPHY: Reduce, rejuvenate, relax. In Carmel country, there's space and time for getting back to nature.

DIET PROGRAM: 700–800 calories per day (not including breakfast). Well-rounded meals of fish, chicken, and veal; no red meat, salt, or sugar. Herbs and spices are used in the food preparation. Dietetic products are used. The main meal is served at midday to give you a chance to work off those calories. The guests themselves voted for this policy so their evenings would be free for the theater. Lots of fresh fruit salads and vegetables (many grown on the premises) are served, with a choice of fish entrees for the main luncheon meal. Dinners are light, usually soup and salad. Nutritional guidance is provided by lifetime guest and former owner, Ruth E. Ray, M.D., a specialist in bariatrics (the study of obesity). Expect to lose one pound a day; this spa has an excellent record for weight and inch loss.

GUEST POPULATION: Coed. 50 guests. Frequent visitors are Rubin Hills, president of Hills Brothers, and Mrs. Robert Mondavi of the Mondavi Vineyards (she goes there to gain weight). Lots of doctors, housewives, women in management, and executives fleeing stress come here.

PACKAGES AND MINIMUM STAYS: A 1-week stay is recommended; 3 nights is the minimum.

MEAL SERVICE: Breakfast is buffet with table service for lunch and dinner. There's a special treat every Sunday—an outdoor barbecue buffet consisting of barbecued chicken, fruit trays, huge cucumber and tomato salad, and a low-calorie punch. Delish! All the guests look forward to these Sunday picnics. No room service.

DRESS CODE: No formality here. Cover-up over bathing suit is just fine. A warm jacket or sweater and long trousers are a must, even in summer. Mornings and nights are chilly on the Monterey Peninsula.

ACCOMMODATIONS: Unpretentious but comfortable bungalows. Some rooms have king-sized beds, others twins. Telephone and TV in every room. No air conditioning needed as mountain air is quite cool.

HOUSE RULES: No smoking in the dining room. No alcoholic lounge on the premises.

PHYSICAL FACILITIES: These include a Jacuzzi, outdoor Olympic-size heated pool, exercise room, massage rooms, beauty salon, and fashion boutique. Golf, horseback riding, and tennis are nearby.

ACTIVITIES, TREATMENTS, AND PROGRAMS: All exercise classes and fitness activities are included in the week program. Most of the exercise classes are held indoors and are very low-key. Interspersed among the relaxed exercise schedule are such programs as informative health lectures, belly dancing, makeup application, stress reduction, and behavior modification.

A Day at Carmel Country Spa

7:00	Breakfast and vitamins
7:00–8:00	Weigh-in and consultation
8:00	Walk
9:30	Warm-up and Stretcherise
10:35	Aerobics
11:30	Aqua-Thin-Ics
12:30	Lunch (main meal)
2:00	Aqua-Thin-Ics
3:00	Toning, Dancercise, or resistance
4:00	Yoga or T'ai Chi
5:00	Happy Hour
6:00	Dinner
7:00	Evening activity

OPTIONAL COSTS: All treatments are extra. Beauty treatments include just about everything you've ever heard of such as salt-glow rubs, cellulite wraps, and lip, chin, and brow waxing. Don't miss Meredith's musical polarity massage and Katy's soothing facial treatment.

NICE TO KNOW: According to Director Frances Buller, folks come from all over the country to participate in this healthy and relaxing environment. Frances keeps track of her guests with a computerized zip-coder. She asked my zip-code number and then proceeded to tell me the names of other guests in and around my zip code who had visited the spa. Now that's downright friendly! Kim Novak and Merv Griffin live down the road; John Gardiner's Tennis Ranch is across the street. And, of course, Clint Eastwood was mayor of nearby Carmel.

*BEST BUY AND WHY: This affordable program is a "Best Buy" because:
- It offers the scenic beauty of the Monterey Peninsula.
- The food is excellent.
- It offers an effective and flexible exercise program.
- The staff is kind and accommodating.

JUDY'S COMMENT: This is just the spot to do your own thing—whether you want to lose weight, gain weight, or just plain relax. Carmel Valley is situated at the conjunction of zero degrees latitude and longitude. If you're searching for your center, this might be a good place to find it.

---

* DEERFIELD MANOR
R.D. 1 (Route 402)
East Stroudsburg, PA 18301
717-223-0160

Open May 30 to October 31. A lovely country house surrounded by 12 acres of beautiful woods.

RATES: Affordable. Credit cards: American Express, MasterCard, Visa.

LOCATION AND TRANSPORTATION: Located in the scenic Pocono Mountains of Pennsylvania, near the charming town of Stroudsburg, which offers flea markets, antiques shops, and summer theaters. The nearest airport is at Allentown, Pennsylvania. Limousine service is approximately $60 one way. The easiest way to get to the spa is to drive. Deerfield Spa is 90 minutes by car from New York City. The spa gives excellent directions in its brochure for traveling from Philadelphia; New England; Baltimore; Washington, D.C.; or Pittsburgh. By bus: Martz Trailways and Greyhound lines run from Newark, Philadelphia, and New York City to Stroudsburg.

EMPHASIS AND PHILOSOPHY: According to Frieda Eisenkraft, the spa's director, Deerfield Manor tries to create an environment where you can "lose weight, become healthier, and relax from the stresses of life in warm, supportive surroundings. Your weight loss and well-being are our main concern."

DIET PROGRAM: As of this writing, there are three types of dietary regimens; low-calorie gourmet, consisting of 600 calories per day; water fasts; and juice fasts. The spa discourages fasting and will only permit a fast to last a few days. Eisenkraft feels that low-calorie intake coupled with an exercise program is the best way to lose weight. It is possible that she will phase out the fasting program altogether. Average weight loss is 7–8 pounds for those who eat all three meals and 10 pounds for people who fast for a few days.

GUEST POPULATION: Coed. 33 guests, primarily women, varying in age from 18 to 80. Occasional couples slip in and thoroughly enjoy the program.

PACKAGES AND MINIMUM STAYS: The basic package is eight days/seven nights, from Sunday to Sunday.

MEAL SERVICE: The director closely monitors the daily meal selections of each guest. In the evening, spa visitors select their own meals, keeping the daily prescribed 600 calories in mind. There is a posted chart for all to see, making it easy to select your menu.

What I particularly appreciate is that there is a hostess to seat you at each meal, and guests are seated in the order of their arrival. There are vases of fresh flowers at breakfast and luncheon. Dinner is served on colored tablecloths with matching cloth napkins and lovely floral arrangements. All foods are attractively garnished and presented. Deerfield Manor strives for elegance at moderate prices.

DRESS CODE: For dinner anything goes "as long as you don't show up in a bathing suit," says Frieda. Sweaters are recommended for the cool fall evenings. Comfort is stressed at Deerfield Manor.

ACCOMMODATIONS: The rooms are cheerfully decorated with floral prints and coordinated bedspreads; most rooms have private baths with windows overlooking the tree-shaded grounds. According to Eisenkraft, the price of a room is based primarily on its size. There are no telephones or televisions in the rooms, but all are air conditioned.

HOUSE RULES: Smoking is allowed outdoors only. This includes an old-fashioned side porch that is readily accessible from either of the two lounges. There are no alcoholic beverages served on the premises. The cocktails that are served on Saturday night are made from fruit or vegetable juices only, naturellement!

PHYSICAL FACILITIES: There is an outdoor pool and an indoor gymnasium that accommodates 15 people comfortably. When they have a full house, classes are given in two shifts. There are two lounges with televisions. The larger lounge serves as a perfect place for lectures, movies, and other group activities. There is no laundry room on the premises; however, transportation is provided twice weekly to a nearby laundromat. There are many golf courses in the immediate area. Tennis courts are available at no extra charge at a camp next door to the spa. Lil, who is Frieda's all-around assistant, may be able to play tennis with you if you bring along your racquet.

ACTIVITIES, TREATMENTS, AND PROGRAMS: The program includes a choice of any or all exercise classes such as beginning stretch, calisthenics, low-impact aerobics, and regular aerobics. Afternoon activities could include pool exercises, volleyball, and yoga as the last class of the day. On the grounds are two walking trails, one 1½ and another 2½ miles long. Guests often take after-breakfast or after-lunch walks. The spa also offers afternoon shopping trips to the town of Stroudsburg, visits to the general store, or shopping at the flea market and antiques shops. Lil is in charge of the excursions, should you want to make special plans. Other afternoon excursions could include canoeing and tubing down the Delaware River. The spa will provide picnic lunches for these outings.

You are entitled to one massage with the week package; all other treatments are extra. The spa offers Swedish massages, deep-pressure massages, and shiatsu, as well as reflexology treatments in the special treatment room. Evening programs could include lectures on a variety of subjects such as antiques, flower arranging, and nutrition, and there are nightly showings of video films. Frequently, guests attend plays at one of the several local theaters.

OPTIONAL COSTS: Massages, excursions, use of golf courses, and theater excursions are additional.

NICE TO KNOW: Frieda likes to think of Deerfield as a bed and breakfast inn, offering good nutrition, beneficial exercise classes, and congeniality among guests. It's good to know that you can bring a radio or TV if they are played softly. Also, for immediate supply needs, such as toothpaste or tissues, there is a small general store within walking distance. Herbal tea is available all day. There is a separate phone for incoming calls for spa guests between the hours of 9:00 A.M. and 10:00 P.M. The phone number is 717-223-9070. Three pay phones are available for making outgoing calls. If, before leaving, you want your hair done, Malcolm's beauty shop is very convenient. Just call 717-839-8894.

*BEST BUY AND WHY: I consider this a "Best Buy" because:
- They offer an outstanding diet and fitness program.
- The price is more than affordable.

JUDY'S COMMENT: This informal and sociable spa has an excellent program, and there are a variety of off-spa activities to keep one happy. The Pocono Mountains setting is one of the loveliest to be found in the East.

EVERNEW
P.O. Box 183
Milton Village, MA 02187
617-265-7756
Mount Holyoke College
South Hadley, MA 01075
413-538-2000

Located on the 800-acre campus of Mount Holyoke College during summer break, this spa camp for women offers an extensive program in comfortable, unpretentious surroundings. Women only. Summer only.

RATES: Affordable. No credit cards.

LOCATION/TRANSPORTATION: Located in South Hadley, Massachusetts, 99 miles directly west of Boston. Nearby airports are Logan, in Boston, and Bradley International, in Hartford, Connecticut. Taxis and rental cars available there. Evernew will send detailed driving instructions.

EMPHASIS/PHILOSOPHY: The spa director, Barbara Slater, wrote: "I envisioned Evernew to be an affordable, health, versatile and fun vacation where women could come together to discover the importance of taking care of themselves while enjoying a little pampering.

"My plan was to offer a straightforward, common sense program for improving one's health and self-image from the inside out—where physical vitality and mental well-being would be the rewards for developing prudent eating habits and doing safe, invigorating exercise."

DIET PROGRAM: 1,200 calories per day. Average weight loss of 5 pounds in five days. The dietary goals are to help you learn how to reduce body fat and build lean muscle, as well as to lose weight. Meals are rich in fresh, natural ingredients and fiber, while low in fat, cholesterol, sugar, and salt.

According to Barbara, "We believe our menu will meet your nutritional as well as your emotional needs. And the meals, as delicious as they are healthful, will serve as examples for your own nutritional-management plan, and provide the momentum you need to develop prudent eating habits."

Here's a typical day's menu:

Breakfast
Fresh orange slices
Whole wheat french toast

Apple/cinnamon syrup

LUNCH
Vegetable cheese quiche
Mixed green salad
Honeydew melon with lime

DINNER
Chicken Tandoori
Herbed rice
Cucumber raita
Watermelon wedge

Here are some of my favorite recipes:

GAZPACHO

2½ cups low-sodium tomato
   juice
3 cups peeled tomatoes, coarsely
   chopped
1½ cups green pepper, diced
⅔ cup chopped onions
⅓ cup fresh parsley, minced

1–2 cloves garlic, minced
1 tablespoon Virgin olive oil
   (optional)
3 tablespoons wine vinegar
⅛ teaspoon cayenne pepper
½ cup cucumber, peeled and
   diced

Combine all ingredients except the cucumber in a large bowl. Puree one-third of the mixture. Add to remaining mixture and thoroughly chill. Mix well before serving. Top with diced cucumber.
Yield: 8 cups   Serving size: 1 cup   Calories per cup: 65

BRAN MUFFINS

Preheat oven to 400°. Grease twelve 2½″ muffin pans. Soften 1 cup bran cereal in 1 cup buttermilk. Add 1 large mashed banana and 1 egg. Beat well.

   Mix together 1¾ cups whole wheat flour and 1 tablespoon baking powder. Lightly fold into wet ingredients. Spoon into muffin pans. Bake at 400° for 35 minutes or until golden. 75 calories each.

GUEST POPULATION: Women only. Clients come from throughout the country as well as from Canada. It's a great place for networking with such a potpourri of professions represented—designers, engineers, accountants, realtors, homemakers, M.D.s, attorneys, marketing consultants, teachers, nurses, social workers and writers.

MINIMUM STAY AND PACKAGES: The typical stay is for 5 days, starting at 10:30 A.M. Sunday and ending at 10:30 A.M. Friday. The miniweek is from 10:30 A.M. Sunday until dinner Tuesday.

MEAL SERVICE: Meals are elegantly served in the dining room, which has a marvelous view of the lake. Guests are seated at round tables—very conducive to conversing.

DRESS CODE: Casual is the byword at this women-only spa. Bring your usual exercise clothes and shoes, sweatclothes, swimsuit, and light rain gear. Pack as though you were sending yourself to summer camp—just omit the labels! Optional equipment is: your bike, tennis racquet, golf clubs, for example.

ACCOMMODATIONS: Evernew utilizes the campus of Mount Holyoke College. So it's back to college and dorm life. Everyone has a private room for rest and solitude. Linens and bedding are provided. Laundry rooms are available.

HOUSE RULES: No alcohol is used or allowed. Smoking is not allowed in the buildings.

PHYSICAL FACILITIES: The Mount Holyoke College campus provides this beautiful setting: 800 lush acres of rolling lawns, secluded gardens, woodlands, and waterfalls. Numerous trails for walking and running intertwine the campus. The buildings are sprinkled along the lakeshore.

   The campus is not only beautiful but also very well equipped. The exercise room is huge and mirrored. There is a weight-equipment workout room and a sauna. The Olympic-size pool has 8 lanes for lap swimming. There are many types of courts, so bring your favorite racquet—tennis, racquetball or squash. There is an 18-hole golf course, as well as horseback-riding facilities.

ACTIVITIES, TREATMENTS, AND PROGRAMS: Evernew aims to combine expert individual attention with spirited group support in their fitness program. Proper body alignment and injury prevention techniques are emphasized along with how to improve your cardiovascular system and flexibility. Most important, they want you to learn how to enjoy exercising, for this new attitude will reap the most long-term benefits. One basic massage is included in the five-day program.

A Day at Evernew

6:30	Rise 'n' Shine
7:00	Sunrise Yoga or Power Walking
8:00	Breakfast
9:00	Positive Performance: all-round workout with aerobics
10:00	Aqua Conditioning: water exercises
11:00	Creative Movement
12:30	Lunch

1:30	Free time for massages, manicures, color consultations, reading, journal writing, relaxing, tennis, bike riding
3:00	Snack and workshops
4:30	Yoga
6:00	Dinner
7:00	Meditative twilight walk
8:00	Evening program
9:00	Snack

Mainstay of the afternoon and evening programs is the Synetics Creative Team, whose task it is to demonstrate how to manage creativity into practical solutions. They accomplish this by creating an atmosphere in which people feel safe enough to speculate, to be imprecise, and to wish. In this environment, ideas have a chance to grow and flourish.

Evernew also brings in a variety of speakers and performers. They include authors, storytellers, singers, songwriters, and consultants—on creative writing, image, wardrobe, and so on.

STAFF POPULATION: The founder/director is Barbara Slater, a private fitness consultant and lawyer. It was her dream to establish a program that would nurture women, guide them toward a healthier life-style, let them explore themselves, boost their self-confidence, and have fun at the same time.

The staff is carefully chosen for their ability to motivate, inspire, and teach, as well as for their warmth and generosity. Many of them come back every year. The staff includes certified aerobics and yoga instructors, certified massage therapists, estheticians (skin care practitioners), a registered dietician, and a manicurist. What they have in common is a highly contagious enthusiastic attitude.

OPTIONAL COSTS: Extra massages (Swedish, shiatsu and reflexology), facials, manicures/pedicures, waxings, lash tintings, makeovers, and individual sessions with consultants.

SPECIAL PACKAGES: The miniweek, from Sunday morning until dinner on Tuesday.

NICE TO KNOW: Evernew will again offer lessons in Ikebana, the Japanese art of flower arranging which is known for its wonderfully calming effect.

Barbara has just started the Evernew Network, a group that meets every 6 weeks for group discussion to help you maintain the Evernew spirit between sessions.

JUDY'S COMMENT: A rare program that combines affordability with practical weight loss hints and ideas.

FITNESS WORKS
180 South Lakeview Lane
Wayzata, MN 55391
612-474-1549

A "wellness retreat" at a woodsy, no-frills, 151-acre retreat center on Chubb Lake, Minnesota. Limited sessions; write for dates.

RATES: Affordable. Credit cards: Visa.

LOCATION AND TRANSPORTATION: Fitness Works uses the facilities of the Mount Olivet Retreat Center, nestled in woodlands adjacent to Chubb Lake, only 45 minutes from Minneapolis. Arrangements can be made for pickup at the St. Paul–Minneapolis airport.

EMPHASIS/PHILOSOPHY: Through workshops and exercise classes, you'll learn secrets of nutrition, stress management, and beauty to help you set a course for total fitness of mind and body. Mary Anderson, owner/director of Fitness Works (along with Sharie Frank and Bev Diekel) says: "Thin is a word we don't use. The idea isn't to scold you or shame you into losing weight, but to help you look and feel your best."

DIET PROGRAM: 900 calories per day. Portion-controlled, well-balanced meals. No salt, sugar, fat, additives, or red meat are served. Lunch features items such as a salad bar with peel-your-own shrimp, egg-lemon soup with tuna and snow-pea salad, or a Mexican feast of gazpacho and tostadas. Low-cal gourmet entrees include turkey cordon bleu, spinach lasagne, chicken casserole, and fillet of sole with almonds and oranges. Snack items include fruit kabobs and frosted bananas for midafternoon après exercise, while apples and popcorn may be served as a bedtime treat. Guests are encouraged to drink eight glasses of spring water a day and mark their progress on a wall chart above their name-tagged cups. Mary says you can expect a weight loss of "about 4 or 5 pounds at the end of the five-day session."

GUEST POPULATION: Women only. 30 guests. The diverse cross-section of guests has included senior citizens, housewives, bookkeepers, psychologists, a violin maker, a Playboy bunny, and women who are going through career or husband changes.

PACKAGES AND MINIMUM STAYS: There is only one program available: a 5-day session, in by 8:30 A.M. on the first day and out by 7:30 P.M. on the fifth day.

MEAL SERVICE: Guests eat together in an informal dining room at the Olivet Retreat Center. Meals are scientifically balanced and prepared by a registered dietician.

DRESS CODE: Shorts and T-shirts are fine—this is camp!

ACCOMMODATIONS: Spa-goers stay at the Mount Olivet lodge either in double rooms or in a six-woman dormitory with shared bath (for much less).

HOUSE RULES: Smoking is permitted only in the smoking room. No alcohol is available.

PHYSICAL FACILITIES: There are three buildings where activities take place. The main lodge houses the dining room (an airy, pine-paneled room with large windows overlooking the lake), and a gymnasium/auditorium where most exercise classes are held. The lodge contains a living room, lounges, and massage and beauty treatment rooms. Yoga classes are held in the conference building. Hot tub and minitrampolines are outside. Facilities include an indoor swimming pool, sauna, whirlpool, tennis courts, and several miles of scenic walking paths.

ACTIVITIES, TREATMENTS, AND PROGRAMS: All activities are included in the five-day session. Beauty services are additional. The five-day program begins with an initial recording of weight, measurements, and blood pressure. Daily exercise classes include yoga, morning walks, slimnastics, vigorous stretching class, toning and aerobics. The afternoon and evening lecture program includes such diverse topics as Stress Management, The Art of Self-Defense, Breast Self-Examination, Evaluation of Foods and Vitamins, Vegetarian Cooking Demonstrations, Beauty Make-Over Demonstrations, and Use of Personal Color in Wardrobe and Makeup Planning. Optional beauty services include massage, facial, manicure, pedicure, and make-up consultation.

A Day at Fitness Works

7:00	Wake-up call by trumpet!
7:30	Morning walk
8:00	Yoga
7:30–9:30	Breakfast and weigh-in
9:30	Midmorning walk
10:15	Power aerobics or stretch class
11:30	Lunch
12:30	Afternoon program
2:15	Low-impact aerobics
3:30	Pool exercises
5:30	Cocktails (nonalcoholic)

6:00   Dinner
7:00   Evening program
9:00–10:00   Movies in lounge

OPTIONAL COSTS: Massages, facials, makeup lessons, manicure/ pedicure, and hair-dressing are available.

NICE TO KNOW: Every session features a final evening's camplike awards ceremony, with comical prizes for The Most Water Drunk, Best Make-Over, Most Likely to Succeed, and Most Likely to Gain Weight—if there's an expectant mother in the group. Each guest takes home with her a cookbook containing all the recipes served so newly acquired, healthful eating habits won't be lost.

JUDY'S COMMENT: Fitness Works is a good place to have lots of fun and enjoy the camaraderie of fellow campers while getting your body in shape.

GOLDEN DOOR
P.O. Box 1567
Escondido, CA 92025
In California: 619-744-5777
800-231-5444

A tranquil Japanese retreat setting on 150 acres surrounded by the Miriam Mountains. Open year-round. A Golden Door program is also offered aboard the *Queen Elizabeth II*, the *Sagafjord*, and the *Vistafjord* (see Resort Spas).

RATES: Expensive. Personal checks only. MasterCard and Visa accepted in boutique.

LOCATION AND TRANSPORTATION: One hour northeast of San Diego. Courtesy limousine service to and from airport.

EMPHASIS/PHILOSOPHY: According to manager Rachael Caldwell, the spa was created to help guests develop a serene inner harmony, implementing the Oriental philosophy of physical fitness, proper nutrition, and beauty care. The Door provides a vigorous and challenging fitness routine for novices as well as for seasoned athletes.

DIET PROGRAM: The typical daily menu is 800–1,250 calories, including two juice breaks. The diet is well-balanced, low sodium, low cholesterol, portion-controlled, and only natural foods are used. Many

Courtesy of The Golden Door

of the vegetables are grown in their own organic gardens—and the happy chickens (which make better eating) are raised right up the road. Food is prepared with Spike, which contains salt. "Virtue-Making Days," consisting of fruit juices and sunflower seeds, are offered on Monday and Thursday, the traditional fasting days of Muslims and Orthodox Jews.

The chef, Christian Chanvane, will individualize any special dietary request. One young and trim Californian had the kitchen prepare for her a different soup for each meal of the day. This labor of love resulted in such delectables as Sweet and Sour Chicken Soup with Tofu, Cream of Pea Pod Soup, and Curried Carrot Soup. Wonderful! Some of my favorites are Golden Door Breasts of Chicken (served warm or cold for picnics), Fillet of Sole Florentine, and Seafood Curry. All of these recipes may be found in *The Golden Door Cookbook, The Greening of American Cuisine,* by Deborah Szekely with Michel Stroot, 1982, available by writing the Golden Door. Men, having greater calorie needs, are served meat during their stay. On this delicious, natural food diet, weight loss has never been dramatic for me, but the inch loss is spectacular!

Here's the recipe for a 2-calorie-per-tablespoon (!) Vegetarian Dressing Delight: 1 celery stalk, finely chopped; 1 tomato, medium size, peeled and quartered; 1/4 cup chives, chopped; 1/4 cup fresh parsley, chopped; 1/4 cup onion, chopped; 1 cup water; 4 tablespoons cider vinegar; 2 teaspoons vegetable seasoning. In a saucepan, bring all ingredients to a boil. Simmer 5 minutes. Puree in blender. Makes 2 cups. Chill before serving on green salads and all raw salads.

GUEST POPULATION: 39 women, with occasional men-only and couples-only weeks. The Golden Door has a rich and varied clientele, ranging from celebrities Lee Radziwill and Erma Bombeck (who is a reluctant participant in exercise classes but keeps everyone else in stitches) to a Manhattan secretary who saved up lunch money for years. The shape of the guests is as varied as their professions. The Golden Door acts as host to people from all over the world—you may find a princess from Portugal or an American executive based in Tokyo as your dinner mate.

PACKAGES AND MINIMUM STAYS: The Golden Door's basic package and minimum stay is one week, in on Sunday afternoon, out on the following Sunday after lunch.

MEAL SERVICE: Breakfast is served on a tray in your room after a vigorous 7:30 A.M. mountain walk. On Mondays, new guests meet in the dining room for breakfast. Lunch is served by the pool or in the dining room. Dinner is served in the dining room, preceded by delicious low-calorie concoctions. Of course, guests always have the option of meals in the serene setting of their own rooms. Potassium broth and juice delights are served twice daily, along with such raw vegetables as jicama (looks like a turnip, tastes like a fruit), cucumbers, sliced carrots, zucchini, and raw cauliflower fresh from the garden. Grapefruit segments, herbal tea, fresh lemonade, and decaffeinated coffee are available 24 hours a day in the Blue Guest Lounge.

DRESS CODE: The Golden Door provides the following items: beige warm-up suits with zippered pockets (wonderful!), shorts and T-shirts, nylon jacket, plush terrycloth robes, gloves and hat, yellow slicker, and Japanese wooden umbrella. For dinner most guests wear the starched blue and white Japanese yukata (summer kimono). I always bring along a heavy sweater or wrap because early mornings and evenings are cool. For Saturday night's gala dinner, do your own wardrobe thing—caftan, jeans, or ball gown. Jewels or no jewels—the choice is yours.

ACCOMMODATIONS: All rooms are single occupancy and decorated in lovely Oriental decor. Each room includes a niche containing a beautiful Japanese flower arrangement. The rooms are all the same size with luxurious appointments—only the scenery and location vary slightly. Rooms have sliding glass doors, some opening onto their own private waterfalls or sand gardens rippled to simulate water. Others have no private garden at all, but don't let that deter you. Reservations are booked so far in advance that it is not always possible to get the room you request. Rooms are assigned on a first-come, first-serve basis. There is no seniority here!

Courtesy of The Golden Door

There are no keys to the rooms nor any TVs, which is in keeping with the Oriental philosophy of inner peace and harmony. The staff will supply a daily newspaper if you request it, but they prefer that you leave the worries of the world outside the Golden Door. Upon arrival, valuables are placed in the vault, and you are completely freed of worldly possessions. Personal laundry is done daily by your assigned attendant. Should you forget some necessity, there is a shopping service into town three times a week. Your room has a wall hair-blower, so leave yours at home. It's interesting to note that couples' weeks are also on a single-occupancy basis. The staff enjoys watching the hurrying and scurrying between rooms after lights out.

HOUSE RULES: Smoking is permitted in your room, the Staff/ Guest Lounge, and outdoors. There is a no-tipping policy; however, most guests, if they have had an exceptional massage therapist or cosmetologist, will leave a gratuity. Some guests express their appreciation to the staff by sending boxes of candy or flower arrangements after their visit.

PHYSICAL FACILITIES: Deborah Szekely (pronounced "say-kay") has spared no expense in creating an authentic jewel of a Japanese setting. The rooms are situated around the Azalea, Bell, and Camellia courtyards—the simple ABCs of the Golden Door. Most first-timers are settled into A Court, which is very private but the most distance to travel—but walking can't hurt! There is a small kitchen in C Courtyard, which serves breakfast only.

The facilities include two outdoor pools (one four-foot exercise and one Olympic size); three exercise rooms, one with weight-resistance equipment; the bathhouse area, consisting of Japanese family tub (whirlpool); weigh-in room; two saunas; and an herbal-wrap room. (By the way, say hello to Gai, the sweet Japanese herbal-room attendant, when you check in for your wrap.) The beauty area consists of many facial, makeup, and manicure/pedicure rooms. There is no beauty salon per se—all the face and hair treatments are handled in these facial rooms.

The Blue Guest Lounge has 24-hour fridge service, TV, and videotapes (menus are posted in the gym, guest lounge, and dining room each morning), and the Staff/Guest Lounge offers TV and videotapes. There is a charming boutique, with lots of tastefully presented potpourri, managed by Hilda Rudolph assisted by Barbara. The Golden Door is one of the few spas of its size that has its own full-time tennis pro. All these facilities are made available without sacrificing the beauty of nature—the Japanese gardens, vegetable gardens with chickens roaming free, jogging trails, well-tended waterfalls, and, of course, the spectacular mountains at your doorstep.

SUNDAY CHECK-IN PROCEDURE: You are met by the limousine driver at the San Diego airport. It is a 45-minute ride to The Door. Once you cross over the wooden bridge, you will find a fantasy world. You surrender all your worldly possessions . . . your shoes are removed, white plastic scuffs are placed on your Cinderella feet, and you sip herbal tea and nibble dates. The hostess escorts you to your room and gives you a brief tour (which you should request if it is your first time here), and your luggage is brought to the room. Before unpacking, I usually change into the kimono provided, or my bathing suit. Then you proceed to the Blue Guest Lounge, where you chat with other guests and have fresh lemonade or herbal tea while waiting for your interview.

Mary Fagen, who has an in-depth yoga background, and is now the "Mother" of The Door, chats with you regarding your fitness level, takes a health history, notes any allergies to foods or cosmetics, and discusses your diet requirements. By the way, Mary, on our last Saturday night, shares with us some of the secrets of the Golden Door—an apropos farewell (if only we could take the chef home with us). After the interview, you proceed to the bathhouse to be weighed and measured. One first-time guest was horrified at the prospect of being measured au naturelle. The Door's response is simply to suggest you wear the same attire when you are measured at the end of the week. Following weigh-in and measure, there is free time to unpack, sunbathe, walk the grounds, meditate, and chat with other guests.

While waiting in the Blue Guest Lounge, most of us put on our name tags, which we are encouraged to wear for the first few days. The ringing of the Japanese gong at 6:30 signals the cocktail hour. There are all kinds of low-calorie appetizers in myriad colors, all works of art, filled with spinach Florentine or herbed yogurt. There is open seating for dinner. After dinner, Mary Fagen welcomes everyone and gives them an opportunity to introduce themselves to the group. After dinner there is the nightly walk to the gates and back, so bring along your sweater or shawl.

ACTIVITIES, TREATMENTS, AND PROGRAMS: Everything is included in your rate except tennis lessons—and the choices seem infinite! Within the framework of the marvelous fitness program, you are scheduled for a daily one-hour massage in the privacy of your room and a daily one-hour beauty treatment, which includes facials, boots and mitties, hair-care requests, and waxing. All Golden Door products are used for facials as well as makeup. A half-hour herbal wrap using Kneipp products can be scheduled daily. At least once during the week the following pamperings are offered: manicure, pedicure, a 1-hour makeup lesson, a 1-hour facial demonstration showing the guest how to use The Door's products, and a quickie hair analysis. Each evening from 8:00 to 10:00 guests may enjoy the Japanese hot tub and receive a brief neck and back rub before bed.

Daytime programs could consist of a lunchtime fashion show by the pool with staff members as models, a cooking demonstration, or the CPR class. Evening programs take place after the nightly walk and could include a crafts evening, a body language or creativity lecture, a program on stress management, a nutrition lecture, or a dance recital.

A Day at The Door

6:00   Wake-up call. Coffee/tea available in Blue Guest Lounge
6:30   Stretch and warm-up class out by the pool
6:45   Mountain walk. The guests begin together, then divide into novice, experienced, and expert groups
7:30   Breakfast

Most exercise classes are divided into three levels, especially the Da Vinci, which is aerobic movement, and the Spot Toning class. All classes are 45 minutes. Three to four exercise classes per hour are offered in the mornings.

8:30   General warm-up, stretch, or T'ai Chi
9:00   Ongoing exercises

10:00	Beauty hour
11:00	Weight-training class
12:00	Kneipp herbal wrap
12:30	Makeup, manicure, or pedicure
1:00	Lunch by the pool, in the dining room, or in your own room
2:00	Aqua aerobics
3:00	Golden Door Special. Every day is different—Shape-Up Class, Bar Fun, Stretches with Finney, Tap Dancing Delight (with trunks of red and black, silver shoes, and feather boas—you feel like Ginger Rogers!), or creating your own take-home exercise cassette
4:00	Yoga
5:00	Massage in your room
7:00	Cocktails and dinner
8:00	Evening program
9:00	Japanese hot tub and minimassage

STAFF POPULATION: The staff to guest ratio is three to one—there are twelve fitness instructors, a superb chef with four assistants, ten beauticians, and seven massage therapists. Special hurrahs should be given to the team of gardners who tend the grounds so beautifully, setting the scene for the entire experience.

OPTIONAL COSTS: Tennis lessons from Vera, the pro, boutique purchases, and Tecate bread for the trip home are your only extras.

NICE TO KNOW: The atmosphere at the Golden Door is casual, and the staff calls guests by first names. There will be lovely surprises waiting in your room each day, including a sample of Golden Door cosmetics, a $25 gift certificate for boutique shopping, Deborah's book, *Secrets of The Golden Door,* Erich Fromm's *The Art of Loving,* and your own personalized stationery. If you have dinner in your room, Mary Fagen may pop in just to say goodnight and make sure you're comfortable. The gold "massage" plaque functions as a "do not disturb" sign, I discovered after my fifth visit!

If you are looking primarily for expert beauty treatments and hair care, look elsewhere—The Door's real strength lies in its atmosphere and fitness program. However, the cosmetology department is skillful enough to do a heart-shaped bikini wax! Tennis racquets are provided, and you can play in your bathing suit if you wish—real freedom here. On departure, hair care is available from 7:00 A.M. so you can leave looking your best. A charming wicker basket of Golden Door chicken and fruit and cheese is provided for the plane ride home.

JUDY'S COMMENT: Thank you, Deborah and staff, for creating such a special retreat of peace and beauty. Some of the "plain" folks that frequent here are: John Denver, Craig Claiborne, and Bill Blass for men's week; Dyan Cannon, Kim Novak, and Olivia Newton-John.

*GRAND LAKE SPA HOTEL
Route 207
Lebanon, CT 06249
203-642-6696

Situated across from Grand Lake on 75 secluded acres of meadows, lawns, and trees, this affordable spa specializes in quick weight loss in a simple, country environment.

RATES: Affordable. Credit cards: American Express, MasterCard, Visa.

LOCATION: Lebanon is 25 minutes southwest of Hartford. The spa hotel provides complimentary pickup service from the airport, train or bus station in Hartford.

EMPHASIS/PHILOSOPHY: According to owner/director Natalie Skolnik, "We can provide a lovely vacation spot where diet-conscious people can enjoy great facilities in a relaxing country setting, dine on fabulous food and be pampered by a caring, trained staff. Everyone should be able to have the luxury of losing pounds and inches without paying luxury prices."

DIET PROGRAM: 650 calories per day for most guests. Average weight loss is 7–10 pounds per week. Higher daily calorie amounts as well as juice fasting are available, although neither option is very popular. The gourmet food is cooked without sugar, salt, or fat with the emphasis on vegetables, chicken and fish.

GUEST POPULATION: Coed. Most guests are women and there are many mother-daughter teams. The spa can accommodate 110 guests.

MEAL SERVICE: All meals are served in the elegant dining room by your waiter, who is specifically trained in the Grand Lake art of caloric limitation. At every meal, you have only to show him your card, which has your name and "calorie count" written on it. After that, limiting your calories becomes *his* responsibility! You can't even bribe him for extras—he would be fired on the spot.

DRESS CODE: Casual clothes are the norm here.

ACCOMMODATION: There are 85 motel-like guest rooms, each with a private, tiled bath. All have at least 2 beds, and several have 3 beds. Guests have their choice of single or multiple occupancy. Roommates can be arranged. There are phones, TVs, radios, and individually controlled air-conditioning units in each room.

HOUSE RULES: No alcohol. Smoking not allowed in dining room, lobby, and program rooms.

PHYSICAL FACILITIES: There are four 2-story buildings, set in a U-shape, as well as an enormous outdoor pool and two outdoor tennis courts, with a full-time pro. Indoors there is a complete fitness center, including a swimming pool, hot tub, sauna, massage and exercise rooms. Grand Lake's beautiful, natural facilities are, of course, the lake and surrounding countryside.

ACTIVITIES, TREATMENTS, AND PROGRAMS: The 7-day spa plan entitles guests to: a half-hour massage on every full day of your stay; an evaluation of your dietary needs, performed by a nurse; a physiology lecture before taking exercise classes; a makeup application and consultation; free group tennis lessons; unlimited exercise classes (three classes a day plus a morning and afternoon walk); access to all spa facilities; and participation in lectures, films and all other spa programs.

The spa makes good use of local recreational activities. The numerous activities offered at no extra charge are: boating and fishing on the lake; cross-country skiing lessons in the winter; ice skating; winter sleigh rides and moonlit ski tours.

STAFF POPULATION: Natalie Skolnick was a diet counselor for the Diet Clinic in Manhattan, Westchester and Riverdale. When she saw a need for a highly structured diet spa in the area, she founded Grand Lake Spa Hotel. Her motto is, "Hate me today, but you'll love me tomorrow." Newspaper and magazine reviews have lauded her for achieving such a high-average weight loss.

The Grand Lake miracle workers—a team of licensed massage therapists—will do wonders for your aches and disposition. There is a registered nurse on the premises at all times.

OPTIONAL COSTS: Guests may have their hair styled, manicures, pedicures, facials and waxings performed in the beauty salon; a complete fitness evaluation and consultation; golf and downhill skiing nearby; individual tennis lessons; and courses on stress management and nutrition.

NICE TO KNOW: Frozen spa dinners are available for purchase.

JUDY'S COMMENT: Grand Lake offers a solid weight-loss program and a great variety of activities at a reasonable price.

*BEST BUY AND WHY: This affordable spa is a "Best Buy" because:
- A good individually tailored food program is offered to the dieter.
- A minimum of five fitness classes is offered per day in addition to two walks.
- Six free daily massages are included in the 7-day program.

---

* HARBOR ISLAND SPA
7900 Larry Paskow Way
North Bay Village, FL 33141
In United States: 800-SPA-SLIM
In Canada: 800-548-9100
Local: 305-751-7651

One of the grandmamas of spa hotels, located on Harbor Island at 79th Street Causeway on beautiful Biscayne Bay. Open mid-October to Labor Day.

RATES: Affordable. Credit cards: American Express, MasterCard, Visa.

LOCATION AND TRANSPORTATION: Between Miami and Miami Beach on Biscayne Bay. Only 20 minutes from Miami International Airport. Taxi or limousine service available to and from airport.

EMPHASIS/PHILOSOPHY: Owner/director Larry Paskow describes his aim at Harbor Island: "to combine everything great about European health spas with all the accoutrements of a jazzy, good resort hotel—then add a personalized diet regimen, and let 'em live it up in the lap of luxury!"

DIET PROGRAM: Emma, the dietician (who's been here for years), helps plan your individualized diet upon arrival. Well-balanced meals from 600 calories up. Emma suggests 800-calorie-minimum diet fare. Dietetic products are used. There are no calorie counts on the menus—just trust Emma. Menu selections are made the night before. You choose from four entrees each day. Some of my favorite main courses included Cheese Blintzes in Fruit Sauce, Baked Chicken Cacciatore, Baked Vegetable Loaf, and Southern Style Baked Chicken.

Meat entrees are offered twice weekly. Desserts include low-cal pound cake, ice cream, mousses, and fresh fruits. Kosher cuisine is available. For those of you used to your Sunday lox and bagels and the *New York Times,* both are available here. How much can you lose? Even a sedentary person cutting back to 800 calories a day (remember it's all salt-free cooking) should be able to lose a couple of pounds.

GUEST POPULATION: Coed. Approximately 300 guests. Most guests are on the diet program; some are here just for rest and relaxation. This is the place where a friend of mine met her heart's delight in the telephone booth. She needed change and he obliged—they've been a twosome ever since.

PACKAGES AND MINIMUM STAYS: Harbor Island has it all: 8-, 7-, 5-, and 4-day stays. Three nights are the minimum, but during the off season shorter stays are possible if space is available. From May through August a special "pay for 7 days, stay for 11 days" plan is usually in effect—that's 4 days free!

MEAL SERVICE: Formal service in the dining room. Dieters and those folks just here to relax all eat at the same tables. You'll sit at the same table for each meal and have the same waiter throughout your stay. Emma comes around at each meal to see that you're happy. Room service is available at extra charge.

DRESS CODE: Weeknights are casual. On weekends, jackets are required for men.

ACCOMMODATIONS: Your choice of three types of accommodations. There are rooms in the main building (convenient for older folks) and the high-rise Tower Building (larger, with balcony and a small pool). The most expensive rooms are the poolside lanais, in typical Florida art deco style. All rooms have color TV and maid service. Harbor Island will accommodate three or four persons in some rooms.

HOUSE RULES: A glass of wine may be available at dinner, but no alcoholic bar is on the premises.

PHYSICAL FACILITIES: Spa facilities, separate for men and women, are located on the lower level of the main building. You'll find a fully equipped gymnasium, two outdoor swimming pools, sauna, steamroom, indoor and outdoor Jacuzzis, whirlpools, facial rooms, herbal-wrap room, and massage rooms. Other amenities include a beauty shop, makeup classes, a jewelry shop, a boutique, card rooms, an auditorium where movies are shown, dance studios, and a lounge for nightly entertainment and dancing. Outdoor facilities include three tennis courts (lighted at night), a putting green, and driving net with greens fees adjustment at any golf course three times a week.

ACTIVITIES, TREATMENTS, AND PROGRAMS: Included in a one-week stay are: an examination by a physician on arrival; a consultation with Emma, the dietician; a daily half-hour massage; and all exercise classes, including Slimnastics, yoga, posture classes, Dancercise, aerobics, and water exercises. One facial and one herbal wrap are included during your week stay. The spa is closed on Sundays. Evening entertainment includes dancing and shows nightly, and guests usually have a chance to participate in their own talent show— a fun mixer!

A Day at Harbor Island

8:00	Morning walk-jog, usually across the Causeway Bridge
8:45	Breakfast
9:30	Dancercise
10:00–11:00	Aerobics
12:00	Lunch
2:00	Yoga
3:00	Water exercise
4:00	Free time
6:30	Dinner
8:00	Dancing and entertainment

OPTIONAL COSTS: Private tennis lessons or longer massages (most reasonable).

NICE TO KNOW: Harbor Island is not conveniently located for walking into town. You need a car to get around. However, there are nice walkways and paths all along the grounds for jogging or walking. Houseboats are docked adjacent to the spa grounds. Some may be for rent—check at the hotel.

*BEST BUY AND WHY: This affordable spa is a "Best Buy" because:
- Rates are incredibly low for the accommodations, services, and activities offered.
- There's a good, structured exercise program and lots to do.

JUDY'S COMMENT: Wow! Eleven days for seven—one of the best spa buys around.

*LAKE AUSTIN RESORT
1705 Quinlan Park Road
Austin, TX 78732
Outside Texas: 800-847-5637
In Texas: 800-252-9324
Local: 512-266-2444

This 15-acre complex in Texas hill country is located on the shores of scenic Lake Austin. Open year-round except Christmas through New Year's.

RATES: Affordable. Credit cards: American Express, MasterCard, Visa.

LOCATION AND TRANSPORTATION: Located 25 miles northwest of Austin, seat of the University of Texas. Courtesy Austin airport pickup and return. Driving time from Dallas is 4 hours; from Houston, 3 hours.

EMPHASIS/PHILOSOPHY: Lake Austin Resort, formerly called The Bermuda Inn, has changed its name as well as its image. The emphasis used to be strictly on weight loss (typical of a "fat farm"). Now this affordable spa has incorporated structured fitness programs along with complex carbohydrate dietary cuisine. Deborah Evans is director of both Lake Austin and its sister resort, the Bermuda Inn of California.

DIET PROGRAM: 900–1,200 calories per day (not including breakfast). This portion-controlled, nutritionally balanced, Southwestern-style cuisine features fresh vegetables, fruits, fish, lean beef, turkey, and chicken. Foods are low in fat, salt and sugar, high in fiber and complex carbohydrates. Dietetic products are used (although they're being phased out and replaced with natural products). Breakfast is buffet style, consisting of many choices, including such items as whole wheat tortillas (with a wonderful hot sauce), poached or scrambled eggs, cereal, delicious bran muffins (60 calories each), wheat thins (30 calories each), and orange juice. Breakfast is fit for a queen at an English countryside manor. Dieter beware! Since at this writing the breakfast calorie count is not included in the total count for the day, it would be nice if simple charts were provided to show guests how many calories are in the breakfast items they're consuming.

Lake Austin is glad to accommodate vegetarians. Any changes in diet have to be okayed in advance by the staff nurse, as no substitutions are allowed at mealtime. Guests plan their next day's lunch and dinner menu (with choices from two entrees per meal) by writing their names and selections on a sign-up sheet in the dining room. No sign-up, no food! A fruit salad alternative is always available for lunch. Nurse Lee says: "I tell all my new people not to eat too many fruit salad plates since we serve fruit for dessert with fructose, and fruit is harder to burn off than greens or proteins." There's a nonalcoholic cocktail hour with low-cal hors d'oeuvres every day. A coffee and herbal-tea bar is open at all times.

How many pounds can you lose? Annie from Boston tells me she lost 5 pounds in seven days, "but I was really working—walking miles every morning and not missing a single exercise class." The week I was there I lost only 1½ pounds—exercising hard and fasting during my first day. My inch loss wasn't too impressive either. Perhaps I was in good shape to begin with and unaccustomed to eating so much food! The resort advises that average weight loss is 1½ to 2½ pounds per week. Perhaps it was that unlimited salt-free popcorn offered at the movies that did me in!

For your enjoyment, here's Lake Austin Resort's weekly menu:

LUNCH—12:00 Noon   DINNER—6:00 P.M.

MONDAY

Chicken Taco and Fruit *or* Fruit Plate with choice of cheese, soup du jour	Lettuce Wedge with Tomato Salad Lemon Braised Chicken *or* Fresh Fish with Scampi Sauce Steamed Asparagus Fresh Fruit

TUESDAY

Salad Bar with cheese and fresh fruit *or* Fruit Plate with choice of cheese, soup du jour	Mixed Green Salad Sliced Turkey Breast with Cranberries *or* Fresh Fish Steamed Green Beans Fresh Fruit

WEDNESDAY

Tuna Salad and Fresh Fruit *or* Fruit Plate with choice of cheese, soup du jour	Caesar Salad Baked Fresh Fish Italiano *or* Bermuda Inn Lasagna Sauteed Squash Fresh Fruit

THURSDAY

Salad Bar with Turkey and Fresh
  Fish *or* Fruit Plate with choice
  of cheese, soup du jour

Spinach Salad
Chicken Breast Teriyaki *or*
Ground Sirloin
Oriental Vegetables
Brown Rice
Fresh Fruit

FRIDAY

Chinese Chicken Salad with fresh
  fruit *or*
Fruit Plate with choice of cheese,
  soup du jour

Hearts of Palm Salad
Baked Breaded Fish *or*
Tenderloin Fillet with
  Mushrooms
Steamed Broccoli
Fresh Fruit

SATURDAY

Spinach/Mushroom Quiche with
  fresh fruit *or*
Fruit Plate with choice of cheese,
  soup du jour

Cole Slaw with Italian
  Horseradish Dressing
Barbecued Chicken *or*
Fresh Fish Rose
Corn on the Cob
Chocolate Mousse

SUNDAY

Seafood Salad with Fresh Fruit *or*
Fruit Plate with choice of cheese,
  soup du jour

Hearts of Artichoke Salad
Roast Cornish Game Hen *or*
Shrimp Kabob
Baked Potato
Fresh Fruit

GUEST POPULATION: Coed. 70 guests. Almost everyone here is from Texas with some Oklahomans and a few Easterners sprinkled in. There's a good variety of ages, from University of Texas students to lots of mother-daughter teams, a number of career women in their early twenties and thirties, and a few couples. The week I was there two young men from Saudi Arabia (thirteen and sixteen years of age) had returned to Lake Austin for a month's stay. People's sizes vary as do their ages—from trim and slim to obese. It doesn't seem to matter at Lake Austin—there is a friendly ambience for all. Many guests stay on for long periods. "Well, why not?" says one slim San Antonian, "we call this pleasant spot the poor man's Greenhouse."

PACKAGES AND MINIMUM STAYS: The basic package is a 7-day stay, from Sunday to Sunday.

MEAL SERVICE: All meals are served in the casual atmosphere of the dining room, which overlooks Lake Austin. There's no hostess to seat you—but such a friendly place—not to worry! There are tables of four, with natural sugar packets and Lake Austin's own seasoning shaker (tastes bitter to me) at your fingertips. As mentioned earlier, breakfast is all buffet while most lunch and dinner meals are served by friendly waitresses. At lunchtime, Peggy comes around to each table and gives out the daily ration of vitamins. For evening meals, fresh flowers are added to each table. No room service available.

DRESS CODE: The resort provides you with a small plastic-handled, drawstring sack (sorry, no lunch inside). However, do bring along a large tote bag for your personal stuff and clothes you may want to change into, such as a simple cover-up. This was helpful to me since there's no separate spa building or locker rooms where you can change out of a wet bathing suit. All the exercise rooms and halls are very air conditioned, so bring along your leg warmers. I found my shower cap came in handy at massage time, especially if you don't want your hair covered with oil. At dinnertime you see all sorts of casual wear from caftans to leotards to Bermuda shorts.

ACCOMMODATIONS: All accommodations are situated up on the hill facing the lake, so just going back and forth to your room is exercise in itself. The comfortable and cheerful rooms all have knotty pine walls, a ceiling fan, two queen-size beds, a desk, and a commodious double dresser. Closet and drawer space is more than adequate. Each vanity has two sinks, leaving little counter space for your hair dryer or toothbrush. There's no clock radio, so for those of you who need it, tuck in a travel alarm clock. The resort provides morning wake-up calls, of course. Rooms 127–140 have unobstructed views of the hills and the lake.

HOUSE RULES: Smoking is permitted in designated areas. No smoking is allowed in dining room, spa, or exercise areas.

PHYSICAL FACILITIES: Neither a separate spa building nor separate locker room facilities exist here. The main building houses the dining room, living room–lounge with card tables and TV, boutique, beauty salon, two exercise rooms (the Yellow Rose, which faces the lake, is the largest, while the Blue Bonnet accommodates smaller groups), the Nautilus equipment room, nurse's office, and two massage therapy rooms. The building also contains two hot-plunge whirlpool areas with a small three-foot-depth pool of indoor water classes. There are two small shower/changing rooms near the exercise area and two bathrooms off the dining rooms. All four of these bathrooms

are for men or women—whoever gets there first. There's a large outdoor pool with Astroturf deck overlooking the lake and pier. In the
adjacent public park, there is a concrete parcours where ten laps equal
one mile. There are three coin-operated laundromats as well as a coin-
operated diet pop machine.

ACTIVITIES, TREATMENTS, AND PROGRAMS: Medical exam
by a nurse on arrival consists of weigh-in, measurements taken, medical history, and blood pressure check. This is the only spot I've been
to where nurses are on duty seven days a week and where you can
weigh in and be measured early in the morning. There are two levels
of exercise classes offered at each session. You may choose from 16
different fitness classes per day, ranging from light stretching to challenging workouts. Guests may participate in these classes fully, par-
tially, or not at all. No part of the program is mandatory, but full
participation is suggested to receive maximum benefit. Some of the
other activities and programs available at Lake Austin are: occasional
fashion shows from the boutique (where guests can serve as models
and receive a 30 percent discount toward purchase); and Lake Austin's own excursion boat, which provides daily trips on the lake. Some
evening programs include viewing video movies (Tuesday, Thursday,
and Saturday), which are shown accompanied by huge bowls of all-
you-can-eat, air-popped popcorn. If you're susceptible to the aroma
of fresh popcorn (and who isn't?), it's hard to resist! Other programs
include Jazzercise three evenings a week (Monday, Wednesday, and
Friday) led by Verna, who is an inspiration to us all. She is sixty-three
years old with the energy, vitality, and figure of a youngster. Allow
plenty of free time for browsing in the boutique. Wendy and Cindy
will help you choose flattering styles from their large array of exercise
togs, caftans, and bathing suits.

A Day at Lake Austin Resort

7:00	Supervised hill-country walk
7:30–9:30	Weigh-in & measurements
8:00–9:00	Breakfast
9:00–9:45	Strictly Stretch (moderate)
10:00–10:45	Weight training (all levels)
10:00–10:45	Total Tune-up
11:00–11:45	Waterworks
11:00–11:45	Aerobics (all levels)
11:00–11:30	Hill-country walk
12:30–1:30	Lunch
2:00–2:45	Rear-End Round-Up (advanced)
2:00–2:45	Station aerobics
3:00–3:45	Total Tune-up (advanced)
3:00–3:45	Waterworks

4:00–4:30	Stretch and relax
5:30–6:00	Casual cocktails
6:00–7:00	Dinner
7:45	Evening program

OPTIONAL COSTS: All treatment, including massages, facials, hair and nail care, reflexology treatment, and complete beauty salon care, are extra. Massages are scheduled every hour from 3 P.M. into the evening hours. Here's a rare spot where you can sign up for your massage appointment in advance by phoning before your arrival. Another unique feature is the staff's willingness to accept cancellations at the last minute (most spas require 24-hour notice on cancellations).

NICE TO KNOW: Should you be touring or off on business, the resort will pack you a light brown-bag lunch: Monterey Jack cheese cubes, hard-boiled egg, melba toast crisps, and an apple. There's a splendid orientation program held each afternoon in the main lounge. The fitness instructors are all young and enthusiastic. For the most part, I think the exercises are paced too quickly to be effective for good toning control. According to Vic, a dynamic fitness instructor, "The best way to burn off fat is to get the heart rate going; that means aerobic activity. Reshaping the body through toning exercise does not burn off fat." I thoroughly agree!

*BEST BUY AND WHY: This affordable program is a "Best Buy" because:
- It offers a new fitness image and schedule where guests may participate in as many classes as desired—all geared to your individual fitness level.
- The lovely accommodations and Lake Austin setting offer fishing and boat-watching—which are exceptional extras.
- If you have lots of pounds to lose and want to do so in an attractive and affordable environment—this is the place. Most medical weight-control centers, which cater to the obese, are much costlier and often have less attractive surroundings.
- The real beauty of this spot is the fact that all kinds of folks come here—whether fat or fit, it's easy to feel right at home.

JUDY'S COMMENT: This could be an outstanding program. The one drawback for me was the overabundance of food. The spa should include breakfast, as well as the popcorn, veggies, and cocktails, in the total calorie count!

LAKESIDE HEALTH RESORT
32281 Riverside Drive
Lake Elsinore, CA 92330
714-674-1501

Located on a five-acre, parklike setting among English walnut trees just across the street from Lake Elsinore in the foothills of the Ortega Mountains. Open year-round.

RATES: Affordable. Credit cards: American Express, MasterCard, Visa.

LOCATION AND TRANSPORTATION: In beautiful Southern California, 75 miles southeast of Los Angeles. Complimentary service to and from Ontario airport.

EMPHASIS/PHILOSOPHY: This spa conducts a trifold health program, involving nutrition, fitness, and behavior modification.

DIET PROGRAM: Your choice of a 500-, 750-, or 900-calorie-per-day diet. The high-protein, low-carbohydrate diet meals feature fish, fowl, red meats, fresh fruit and vegetables, soups, and dietetic desserts. At cocktail hour guests socialize over diet sodas and raw vegetables. What's your weight loss expectancy? Up to a pound a day on the 500-calorie program, according to the spa.

GUEST POPULATION: Coed. 76 guests, mostly women. Lakeside seems to draw a large group from the Los Angeles area. All guests are on diets.

PACKAGES AND MINIMUM STAYS: One-week, 2-week, and even 4-week packages are available although the spa will accept weekenders and 2-night guests too.

MEAL SERVICE: Very informal dining atmosphere, with open seating and table service for meals. No hostess in the dining room.

DRESS CODE: Casual. Jogging suit is perfect.

ACCOMMODATIONS: There are 40 rooms, with single, double, triple, or quadruple occupancy. Every room has a sitting area and color TV. The casual, comfortable rooms are all on ground level and face the courtyard. Daily maid service is provided. Roommates can be arranged.

HOUSE RULES: None. No alcoholic bar on premises.

PHYSICAL FACILITIES: You'll find a whirlpool, a sauna, heated indoor and outdoor pools, herbal wrap rooms, an exercise room, a gymnasium, tennis courts, a sun deck area, a beauty shop, and a boutique. There is a laundromat on the premises.

ACTIVITIES, TREATMENTS, AND PROGRAMS: Upon arrival, you meet with the resident nurse who helps you plan your diet and exercise regimen. Daily activities include weigh-in and blood pressure check with the nurse each morning and your choice of the following exercise activities (some offered more than once a day): yoga stretching, warm-up exercises, slow-paced exercises, intermediate and advanced aerobics, Jazzercise, aquatics, body conditioning, Tahitian and Hawaiian dancing, and volleyball. Daily walks and bike riding are recommended. Available services include massage, tanning, and a full-service beauty salon. Evening programs include cooking and food demonstrations, classical concerts, astrological forecasts and readings, makeup demonstrations, bingo, bridge, and movies on the large screen television.

A Day at Lakeside

7:15	Morning stretch and walk
7:30–9:00	Breakfast
9:00	Gentle stretch and tone
10:00	Low-impact aerobics
10:00	Pool exercises
11:00	Better backs and bellies
12:00	Lunch
1:00	Bike ride or walk to Lake Elsinore
2:00	Pool exercises
3:00	Sit 'n' Fit body conditioning or Dance exercise
4:00	Relaxation
5:15	New guest orientation
5:30	Happy hour (appetizers and low-cal beverages)
6:00	Dinner
7:00	Evening program

OPTIONAL COSTS: Massage, facials, herbal wraps, hairstyling, and makeup classes.

NICE TO KNOW: The young staff is particularly enthusiastic and most helpful. Lakeside offers pre- and post-surgical care for patients undergoing cosmetic surgery by providing single rooms, room service for all meals, and supervision for a weight-control program. They carry no sundries in the boutique, so come well prepared.

JUDY'S COMMENT: Effective diet and exercise program. Prices are among the lowest for a complete month's stay.

---

*LIDO SPA
40 Island Avenue
Venetian Causeway
Miami Beach, FL 33139
800-327-8363
305-538-4621

The Lido Spa is located on Belle Island, the first island of Venetian Causeway, which connects Miami Beach to Miami and overlooks Biscayne Bay. Open November 1–May 1.

RATES: Affordable. Credit cards: American Express, Carte Blanche, Diners Club, Discover, MasterCard, Visa.

LOCATION AND TRANSPORTATION: Only 20 minutes by car from Miami airport. No pickup service available, but the Lido Spa will return you to the airport free of charge.

EMPHASIS/PHILOSOPHY: Rest, relaxation, and weight loss. Chuck Edelstein, owner of the Lido, promises, "You will find . . . at the Lido Spa all of the ways and means to better health and a glowing, more youthful appearance, as well as all of the facilities for a really fine vacation."

DIET PROGRAM: The Lido guarantees weight loss! But they don't say what you can expect if that doesn't occur. A nondieter's menu is also available. All meals are salt- and sugar-free. Fat-free and special diets are also available; individualized diets are worked out with the dietician. Fruit and vegetable juices are served as a midafternoon snack. Dietetic products are used.

GUEST POPULATION: Coed. 150–200 guests. Although there are guests of all ages, many are senior citizens on a winter holiday. According to a recent survey, one-third of the guests are at the Lido for weight loss, one-third are there to "get in shape," and one-third are there just for good old R & R.

PACKAGES AND MINIMUM STAYS: Come anytime and leave anytime. Rates are by the day and vary by 20 percent depending on the season.

MEAL SERVICE: There is a separate area in the main dining room for dieters. A salt substitute is on hand at all the guest tables.

DRESS CODE: Do your own thing. Jackets are optional, and a nice shirt is "just fine," says spa director Pat Little.

ACCOMMODATIONS: The lovely, contemporary rooms overlook the gardens and Biscayne Bay. There are three rate levels: Garden View, Poolside, and Deluxe Lanai, with a very modest dollar difference among them.

HOUSE RULES: There's no bar on the premises, but a glass of wine may be offered with dinner meals.

PHYSICAL FACILITIES: A complete spa building has separate facilities for men and women, including massage rooms, Jacuzzi, saunas, steam rooms, mineral baths, fully equipped gymnasiums, bicycles, walking machines, rowing machines, and much more. There are two outdoor heated Olympic-size pools (fresh water and saltwater) and a relaxing hot tub. Other features include a beauty salon, barbershop, dance studio, card room, and boutique. Outdoor diversions include a fishing and boating dock, driving range and putting green, and shuffleboard courts. Tennis and 18-hole golf are nearby.

ACTIVITIES, TREATMENTS, AND PROGRAMS: A free medical checkup is given upon arrival. Daily activities include a free half-hour massage and use of all spa facilities. Water exercise classes are held four times weekly. Afternoon and evening programs include health lectures on yoga, diet, and nutrition, and arts and crafts; there is dancing and entertainment nightly. Free golf and tennis are offered nearby.

STAFF POPULATION: The staff physician, together with the dietician, will individualize your program and supervise your weight loss. There are 14 massage therapists, 2 exercise instructors, 2 cosmeticians, and a social director.

NICE TO KNOW: The Lido Spa is well located for enjoying the entertainment and shopping that nearby Miami has to offer. Set on a private residential island, the Lido is surrounded by many walkways to the other small islands that make strolling and jogging a delight.

* BEST BUY AND WHY: This affordable spa is a "Best Buy" because:
- Everyone here is on a healthy salt-free diet.
- It offers a free daily massage.
- Free medical examination is available to every guest.
- The refreshing breezes and lovely view of Biscayne Bay restore both mind and body.

JUDY'S COMMENT: A well-rounded, bargain vacation! While trimming and toning, you'll also enjoy nightly club acts, live music, bingo, discussion groups, cards, lectures—you name it.

MONACO VILLA
371 Camino Monte Vista
Palm Springs, CA 92262
Telephone: (619) 327-1261

Located in a lovely European-style villa just north of town with a magnificent view of the mountains. Closed July through mid-September.

RATES: Affordable. Credit cards: MasterCard, Visa.

LOCATION AND TRANSPORTATION: Ten miles from Palm Springs airport. Courtesy transportation provided.

EMPHASIS/PHILOSOPHY: Reduce and recharge or just plain relax in this health-encouraging, motel-like oasis.

DIET PROGRAM: Women 500–750 calories per day, men 750–900 for weight reduction. There is also a plan for guests who do not wish to lose but are interested in healthful food. All meals are prepared salt-free and low in cholesterol. High-protein or gourmet cuisine, with lots of fresh fruits and vegetables. Anne Cobin, owner, director, and chef, is the guiding light in this low-calorie culinary adventure. Anne says, "I have long believed that a nutritional, well-balanced, portion-controlled diet, along with satisfying results in inches and weight loss, does not have to be dull." Some of your meals may include such universal favorites as broiled chicken, fresh fish, and gourmet dishes such as tournedos of beef, veal piccata, shrimp scampi, and crepes Florentine. Outstanding luncheon menus include seafoods and delectable salads. (The day I was there, I ate a delicious stuffed acorn squash salad filled with chopped chicken and veal and fresh vegetables.) Anne serves lovely desserts, such as orange lemon chiffon whip, baked Alaska, and chocolate mousse. Brewed decaffeinated coffee and iced tea are served after your meal. At 4:30 P.M. a pick-me-up of bouillon or potassium broth is served. For cocktail hour, Anne may serve low-fat yogurt dip with jicama and other crudités, or perhaps a seafood dip with crab claws. Fruit juice or no-sodium tomato juice are the usual beverages. Can you really lose weight on all this gourmet dining? Sure. The motto (and goal) of Monaco Villa is "lose a pound a day, the gourmet way."

GUEST POPULATION: Coed. 16 guests. Marty and Anne Cobin have welcomed all sorts of folks. Their diet program is designed not only for those who wish to reduce but also for diabetics, people with cardiac conditions or high blood pressure, and those who only desire to live a longer, healthier life. There have been mother-daughter teams, and one young man, Anne tells me, who was truly obese stayed at Monaco Village for two months. By the time he left, he had lost 40 pounds. Lots of elderly couples stay at the Cobins' for their annual vacation. The Cobins cater to the young and the young at heart. "We get a lot of repeat clientele," says Anne, "perhaps because we are more of a loving and caring family setting and not just another impersonal resort."

PACKAGES AND MINIMUM STAYS: The minimum stay is two nights.

MEAL SERVICE: You may breakfast in your room if you like. Lunch may be served by the pool or in the dining room. There is no set schedule for mealtimes. Since Anne does most of the cooking, it's difficult for her to "run like a Swiss clock." Sevenish is the cocktail hour, and guests meet in the homey environment of the Cobins' dining room, which is light and gay with pink table linens, fine china, fresh flowers on the table, and candlelight for dinner. It's like being entertained in someone's home.

DRESS CODE: Casual. Caftan or pants suit is just fine.

ACCOMMODATIONS: Spacious and attractive rooms with cheerful floral bedspreads. Adequate bathroom and dressing areas. All rooms have a nice desk area (to jot a note to friends back home) and all come equipped with color TV and direct-dial phones. The rooms are immaculate!

HOUSE RULES: No smoking in the dining room.

PHYSICAL FACILITIES: The architecture is simple and contemporary. All the rooms face a U-shaped courtyard filled with lush greenery and flowers. Located in this garden oasis are the Olympic-size pool and hot-jet therapy pool, as well as a large deck area with chaise lounges. There is a small gym located just off the courtyard. Golf and tennis are available nearby.

ACTIVITIES, TREATMENTS, AND PROGRAMS: There is a full program in the morning, including yoga, pool exercises, calisthenics, and aerobics. Classes are held on the grassy expanse near the pool. A lot of the guests like to walk or work out in the gym on their own. Massages by the professional staff are available. Evening programs include discussions on health and nutrition, cards, and specially arranged tours.

NICE TO KNOW: Monaco Villa is within walking distance of the fine galleries and shops in Palm Springs.

JUDY'S COMMENT: Anne Cobin and Monaco Villa prove to me that diet food can be sublime as well as effective in aiding weight and inch loss. Surely, Anne is the Michel Guerard of Palm Springs.

NATIONAL INSTITUTE OF FITNESS
202 North Snow Canyon Road
P.O. Box H
Ivins, UT 84738
801-628-3317
801-628-4338

A spa program located within a futuristic dome complex set in the mouth of Snow Canyon's towering red sandstone cliffs (6,000–9,000 feet elevation). Open year-round, except Christmas to New Year's week.

RATES: Affordable. Credit cards: MasterCard, Visa.

LOCATION AND TRANSPORTATION: The Institute is located two hours drive northeast of Las Vegas and six hours southwest of Salt Lake City. You may fly into St. George, Utah, from either city, and airport pickup is included in your cost.

EMPHASIS/PHILOSOPHY: According to Marc Sorenson, Ph.D., and his wife, Vicki, their aim is to help you lose weight, gain stamina, and feel like a new person. They also teach you how to maintain that slimmer body you'll return home with.

DIET PROGRAM: Meals contain 900–1,000 calories per day, on a modified Pritikin nutritional program. Menus are low in fat, low in salt, and low in sugar. Lots of fresh fruits and vegetables, white meat (veal and chicken), and fish are used in preparation. A typical daily menu might consist of fruit crepe for breakfast; salad, soup, and low-fat cottage cheese with fruit for lunch; and your choice of lasagne or chicken Polynesian stir-fry for dinner. How much can you lose? The average is 3–6 pounds a week for women, 4–8 pounds for men.

GUEST POPULATION: Coed. 60 guests. According to the Sorensons, guests range in age from 14 to 84. Some come to lose weight, others come just to get in shape or stay in shape.

PACKAGES AND MINIMUM STAYS: The minimum one-week

program runs from Monday to Sunday. Two-, three-, and four-week packages also are available.

MEAL SERVICE: All guests dine together in the main dining room, cafeteria-style, after waiting in the buffet line.

DRESS CODE: Very casual. Shorts or slacks are fine for dinner. Bring along a warm sweater or jacket for the cool mornings and evenings.

ACCOMMODATIONS: Guests stay in new but spartan-furnished single, double, triple and even quadruple rooms. All rooms feature a large, comfy chair, coffee table, private bath, color TV, and phone, with daily maid service.

HOUSE RULES: Smoking permitted outdoors only.

PHYSICAL FACILITIES: Indoor heated pool, hydroswirl bath, aerobic dance area, Olympic weight-training room, three exercise rooms, cardiovascular training center with motorized treadmills, computerized exercise bikes, minitrampolines, indoor racquetball court, tennis court, and lots of jogging paths and mountain trails. A beauty salon is available.

ACTIVITIES, TREATMENTS, AND PROGRAMS: Upon arrival, each guest receives an orientation and fitness evaluation, which includes blood-pressure test, body-fat-composition test, flexibility test, strength test, weigh-in, and a cardiovascular endurance test on a treadmill. You are then assigned to a fitness group at your own level and geared to your exercise capability. Daily activities include two walks plus classes in slow stretching, aerobics, low-impact aerobics, dancing, slimnastics, weight training, and minitrampoline. Programs include discussions on weight control, nutrition, and fitness.

A Day at NIF

6:15	Warm-up
6:30	Daily walk
8:30	Swim exercise
	Tennis instruction
	Orientation
9:15	Breakfast
10:00	Slow stretch yoga
10:45	Aerobics class
11:30	Slimnastics
12:15	Free time/rap session
1:00	Lunch
1:20	Weekly shopping trip
2:30	Weight training

          Low-impact aerobics
          Minitrampoline
  3:30   Racquetball instruction
          Personal weight training
  4:30   Free time for nap, massage, makeover, etc.
  5:30   Dinner
  6:15   Free time
  7:30   Evening walk
          Social activity
  8:30   Tennis instruction

STAFF POPULATION: Marc Sorenson holds a Ph.D. in exercise physiology from Brigham Young University and writes a weekly newspaper column called "Dear Dr. Fit." His wife, Vicki, instructor and makeup consultant, was a first runner-up in the Miss Utah contest.

OPTIONAL COSTS: Massages, makeovers, and trips to nearby Grand Canyon, Zion, and Bryce Canyon national parks are available.

NICE TO KNOW: Hiking here is a particularly wonderful experience. Snow Canyon is considered a "geological paradise." You may find bits and pieces of ancient pottery among the caves, pictographs from nomadic tribes, and carved dates left by early pioneers. *Butch Cassidy and the Sundance Kid* was filmed here.

JUDY'S COMMENT: This no-nonsense facility boasts a well-thought-out fitness and nutrition program set in mountain surroundings. Don't expect to be cuddled or pampered at NIF.

---

* THE OAKS AT OJAI
122 East Ojai Avenue
Ojai, CA 93023
805-646-5573

This diet and fitness resort is located in the center of the artist colony of Ojai, once the setting for Shangri-la in the movie *Lost Horizon*. It is a sister spa to The Palms at Palm Springs. Open year-round.

RATES: Affordable. Credit cards: MasterCard, Visa. All treatments are extra.

LOCATION AND TRANSPORTATION: Ninety minutes north of Los Angeles by car and forty minutes south of Santa Barbara airport. The Oaks provides van service twice a week to LAX for $25 each way.

Courtesy of The Oaks at Ojai

EMPHASIS/PHILOSOPHY: Physical fitness is their forte, with a strong diet program. Both The Oaks and its sister spa, The Palms at Palm Springs, are owned by Sheila Cluff, doyenne of physical fitness. Both spas have similar programs and philosophies—it's the locations that differ.

DIET PROGRAM: How many pounds can you expect to lose? According to The Oaks brochure, you can expect to lose up to two pounds every day for three days. 750–1,000 calories a day is the standard, but 600 calories as well as 1,500 calories (athlete's portion) can be arranged. The morning potassium broth, afternoon raw vegetable break, and late-day juice break are all included in the total daily caloric count. Meals are prepared with all natural products—no salt, no sugar, no dietetic products. The calorie count is printed on the menu, which is posted in the dining room. The guest has the option of substituting the Calorie Cutter Salad or the Cleansing Salad for each meal. If you order either of these salads, you will not be served the first course or dessert. Two Calorie Cutters or Cleansing Salads per day will bring total calories for the day down to approximately 600. A Calorie Cutter is a cold plate with lettuce, cottage cheese, and either tuna, chicken, or turkey, plus vegetable garnishes (250 calories). A Cleansing Salad is a high-fiber salad of shredded cabbage, carrots, alfalfa sprouts, orange, apple, and sunflower seeds (240 calories).
    Some of my favorite entrees from The Oaks menu include

Shrimp Oriental, prepared with pineapple juice and sherry and, of course, no rice (210 calories); Chicken à l'Orange, seasoned with caraway seeds, crushed rosemary, and orange rind (155–175 calories); and Vealburgers Stroganoff, prepared with mushrooms, dill weed, and low-cal sour cream (224 calories). Some of the tempting desserts (but, oh, so low in calories) are pineapple-coconut sherbet, prepared in the blender and poured into freezer trays (40 calories) and Colonial apple custard, made with fresh apples, cinnamon, and eggs (40 calories). This unusual apple recipe came from Donna Bennett, an assistant manager of The Oaks. Eleanor Brown is the consulting nutritionist and is responsible for other delightful recipes. Her book, *Recipes for Fitness,* as well as recipes printed on index cards, may be purchased by writing either The Palms at Palm Springs or The Oaks at Ojai.

Here is a typical weekly menu at The Oaks.

SUNDAY		MONDAY	
LUNCH		*LUNCH*	
Green salad	(35)	Green gazpacho	(35)
Shrimp Oriental	(210)	Chicken à l'Orange	(155)
Pineapple-coconut sherbet	(40)	Pineapple-banana cup	(40)
DINNER		DINNER	
Mushroom soup	(20)	Seafood cocktail	(55)
Vealburgers Stroganoff	(224)	Sesame tofu with	
Fresh fruit ice	(25)	brown rice	(215)
		Strawberry crepe	(50)
Total 554		Total 550	

TUESDAY		WEDNESDAY	
LUNCH		LUNCH	
Split pea soup	(50)	Marinated tofu salad	(40)
Chicken sandwich	(200)	Veggie-stuffed peppers	(240)
Fresh apple jell	(40)	Strawberry-pear torte	(25)
DINNER		DINNER	
Clam chowder	(75)	Mushroom soup	(20)
Steamed veggies		Turkey salad divan	(245)
with mozzarella	(200)	Fresh fruit slices	(40)
Colonial apple custard	(40)		
Total 610		Total 605	

THURSDAY		FRIDAY	
LUNCH		LUNCH	
Onion soup	(30)	Minestrone	(40)
Oaks Cold Plate	(250)	Spinach pie	(175)
Fresh Fruit	(25)	Green salad	(35)
DINNER		DINNER	
Antipasto salad	(35)	Country slaw	(40)
Fettucine	(225)	Fried chicken	(190)
Tortellini	(40)	Green beans	(15)
		Pear Brown Betty	(35)
Total 605		Total 570	

GUEST POPULATION: Coed. 80 guests. The clientele at The Oaks varies from week to week. One young guest tells us there are usually a lot of career girls there. More and more men are participating in this program, from young execs to doctors and lawyers. This spot draws an avid bridge crowd, and you can usually pick up a good game. Guests who hang out here, from TV star Charlene Tilton of *Dallas* fame to just plain career-minded folks, enjoy the superior fitness and diet program.

PACKAGES AND MINIMUM STAYS: The minimum stay is two nights. However, there is a reasonably priced Spa Day program (without room accommodation) and a Mini-Spa Day for groups of 10 or more.

MEAL SERVICE: A breakfast buffet, consisting of orange and grapefruit segments, half a date muffin, and your vitamin packet is served in the lounge, located off the dining room. The dining room is airy with lots of windows. Seating is casual and you may sit wherever you like. There is table service for lunch and dinner. Lunch is either served at the pool or in the dining room from 12:00 noon to 1:00 P.M. Dinner is from 6:00 to 7:00 P.M., and a member of the fitness staff is on hand to make announcements about the evening program and the following day's schedule. A recently adopted policy at The Oaks allows one to have lunch or dinner served in one's room. Each table in the dining room has an interesting assortment of condiments, including Dr. Jensen's natural seasoning (for sale at the front desk or at your favorite health food store), cayenne pepper, parmesan cheese, and cinnamon. A full-service, nonalcoholic bar is available 24 hours a day.

DRESS CODE: Pack casual clothes and workout attire. For dinner, jogging outfits are just fine.

ACCOMMODATIONS: Guests are housed in a wood and stone

renovated mansion, which is the main lodge, or in cottages scattered about the grounds under the live oak trees. The cottages are newer facilities and therefore have larger bathrooms. The rooms are "California Contemporary," unpretentious and pleasant. Triple occupancy rooms are available, and The Oaks will provide a roommate should you want to share expenses. Since there is no separate spa building with locker rooms, all changing must be done in your room.

HOUSE RULES: Smoking is permitted only in your room or outdoors.

PHYSICAL FACILITIES: The Coral Spa, which consists of a large, carpeted exercise room with whirlpool and sauna, is located on the first floor of the main lodge. All spa facilities are shared by both men and women. The beauty salon, four massage rooms, and two facial compartments are in a wing off the lobby, which also houses the boutique. The large outdoor pool is surrounded by colorful plantings, with the warm whirlpool nearby. Tennis courts are available across the street in the village park, but you need to bring your own game. Laundry facilities are available on the grounds for guest use.

ACTIVITIES, TREATMENTS, AND PROGRAMS: You may choose from 16 different fitness classes per day, seven days a week, including pool class and ranging from light stretching to aerobics, weight training, yoga, walking, and challenging workouts. You may participate in as few or as many of these classes as you wish. The fitness staff is superb—each member of the team is a real pro. Although the clientele are mainly female, male guests are welcome. Evening programs consist of lectures on nutrition, stress management, cosmetic surgery, money management, and arts and crafts demonstrations.

A DAY AT THE OAKS

6:00	Body dynamics or mountain hike
7:00	Brisk walk
7:30	Nature walk
8:00	Body awareness
9:00	Cardio combo
	Fitness potpourri
10:00	Body dynamics
	Pool
10:45	Broth break
11:15	Creative Aerobics
	Pool
12:00	Lunch
1:15	New guest orientation

2:00	Body conditioning
	Pool
3:00	Aerobic body contouring
	Weight training
3:45	Vegetable break
4:00	Yoga
5:15	Body dynamics
5:30	Happy hour (juice cocktails)
	New guest orientation
6:00	Dinner
7:00	Evening programs (wide variety)

OPTIONAL COSTS: All treatments, which include massage, facial, makeup design, and cellulite wrap, are extra, as are exercise cassette tapes, boutique purchases, and beauty salon services. All the facial and skin care products used at The Oaks and The Palms are by Vera Brown. The products are all natural, with no preservatives. Vera gives a great deal of her love, time, and money to the Junior Blind Association. All these wonderful products are even labeled in Braille. Tennis lessons are available at the Ojai Racquet Club, which is just down the road, at a nominal rate.

NICE TO KNOW: The Oaks features an unusual boutique, stocked with antique jewelry and gifts from around the world as well as the usual sportswear. Sheila Cluff, the owner, tries to pop in once a week, either Monday or Saturday. When she is there, she takes time to visit with guests and teach an exercise class. Bart's Corners Bookstore is a fascinating place to visit—an indoor/outdoor treasure house of used books and magazines. Books are available on a 24-hour, honor system basis. There are bookshelves on an outer wall where one can choose a book and toss the coins through the wire fence. Honorable, indeed!

*BEST BUY AND WHY: This affordable program is a "Best Buy" because:
- It offers an effective and realistic diet program.
- The guests may participate in as many fitness classes as they desire.
- The personnel and staff are accommodating.
- The location and setting are beautiful, with nature trails that lift your spirits.

JUDY'S COMMENT: The charming art colony of Ojai offers a delightful respite from everyday pressures. This is, indeed, an affordable Shangri-la.

Courtesy of The Palms at Palm Springs

THE PALMS AT PALM SPRINGS
572 N. Indian Avenue
Palm Springs, CA 92262
619-325-1111

This homey spa, sister to The Oaks at Ojai, is conveniently located near tempting shops and boutiques in the heart of Palm Springs. The central courtyard, which is surrounded by purple bougainvillaea, is reminiscent of Moorish Spain. Open year-round.

RATES: Affordable. All treatments are extra. Credit cards: MasterCard, Visa.

LOCATION AND TRANSPORTATION: Just a short taxi ride from the Palm Springs airport and less than a two-hour drive from Los Angeles.

EMPHASIS/PHILOSOPHY: Physical fitness is their forte, with a strong diet program. Both The Palms and its sister spa, The Oaks at Ojai, California, are owned by Sheila Cluff, doyenne of physical fitness, who offers similar programs and philosophies at both locations.

DIET PROGRAM: How many pounds can you expect to shed? According to The Palms brochure, "Even if you don't exercise at all, you still should achieve significant weight loss here. Our nutritionally balanced diet menu is designed to help you lose on average 2½ pounds a week." About 900 calories a day is the standard fare, but additional high carbohydrate foods are available. The morning potassium broth, the afternoon raw vegetable break, and the late day juice break are all included in the total daily caloric count. Meals are prepared only with natural products—no salt, no sugar, no dietetic products. The calorie count is printed on the menu, which is posted in the dining room.The guest can substitute the Calorie Cutter Salad or the Cleansing Salad for lunch and/or dinner. If you order either of these salads, you will not be served the first course or dessert. Two Calorie Cutters or Cleansing Salads per day will bring total calories for the day down to approximately 600. A Calorie Cutter is a cold plate with lettuce, cottage cheese, and either tuna, chicken, or turkey, plus vegetable garnishes (250 calories). A Cleansing Salad is a high-fiber salad of shredded cabbage, carrots, alfalfa sprouts, orange, apple, and sunflower seeds (240 calories).

Some of my favorite entrees from The Palms menu are: California Chicken Curry (185 calories); No-Pasta Lasagna prepared with sliced eggplant, low fat cottage cheese, and red wine (155 calories); and Crab Quiche (175 calories). Some of the delectable desserts are Fitness Flan, prepared with eggs, skim milk, and honey (80 calories); Orange Zabaglione (38 calories); and Sheila's "Cheesecake" Supreme (40 calories). Recipes printed on index cards may be purchased by writing The Palms or The Oaks at Ojai. There follows for your enjoyment a typical weekly luncheon and dinner menu.

LUNCH		DINNER	
		SUNDAY	
Costa Rican soup	(30)	Onion soup	(30)
Salad Niçoise	(230)	Palms vegetarian burrito	(200)
Fruited yogurt	(40)	Garden salad with	
		guacamole	(35)
		Pineapple-strawberry	
		sherbet	(40)
			Total 605
		MONDAY	
Turkey soup	(35)	Country slaw	(35)
Macaroni and cheese	(180)	Chicken teriyaki	(175)
Lettuce and tomato	(15)	Corn cobbette	(40)
Carrot bread	(40)	Potato crisps	(20)
Fresh fruit ice	(25)	Watermelon slices	(30)
			Total 595

TUESDAY

Split pea soup	(35)	Tabouli	(50)
Veal Crepes Florentine	(200)	Orange roughy à la	
Marinated veggies	(20)	Borenstien	(140)
Pita bread	(20)	Baked potato with sour	
Orange oat cookie	(30)	cream	(50)
		Fresh broccoli	(15)
		Fruited flan	(45)
			Total 605

WEDNESDAY

Egg Drop soup	(25)	Cucumber Borani	(25)
Sweet and sour chicken		Spaghetti with veal sauce	(210)
salad	(140)	Bread stick	(20)
Whole wheat popover	(35)	Asparagus spears	(10)
Ambrosia	(50)	Frozen blueberry yogurt	(40)
			Total 605

THURSDAY

Vegetable soup	(35)	Green Salad with dressing	(35)
Palms pizza	(200)	California chicken curry	(185)
Veggie garnish	(20)	Brussels sprouts	(15)
Frosted grapes	(45)	Onion roll	(30)
		Cheesecake	(40)
			Total 605

FRIDAY

Creamy carrot soup	(35)	Green salad with	
Frosted turkey sandwich	(215)	house dressing	(35)
Fresh fruit plate	(50)	Shrimp Oriental	(220)
		Fruited tofu	(50)
			Total 605

SATURDAY

Albondigas	(50)	Green salad with dressing	(35)
Vita tostada	(200)	Turkey kabob	(175)
Fresh pineapple slices	(50)	Veggie rice pilaf	(40)
		Squash medley	(20)
		Apple banana crepe	(35)
			Total 605

GUEST POPULATION: Coed. 90 guests. The week I was there, there were a lot of young, dynamic, career-minded women taking advantage of this fine program. There were also some young and young-at-heart couples—a good cross section of age and sex. The clientele's shapes and sizes varied as did the ages.

Courtesy of The Palms at Palm Springs

PACKAGES AND MINIMUM STAYS: The minimum stay is two nights. Check in or out any day of the week.

MEAL SERVICE: The dining room is light and airy, with lots of windows and crisscrossed bamboo wallpaper. There is no gong to call you to meals, but everyone magically appears. You may sit wherever you like. Breakfast is served buffet style, with grapefruit or orange segments, one-half date muffin (25 calories), and your vitamin packet. Should you require an egg for breakfast, it is necessary to get an egg "ticket" from the nurse. There is table service for lunch and dinner. Lunch is either served at the pool or in the dining room from 12:00 to 1:00, dinner is from 6:00 to 7:00, and a member of the fitness staff is on hand to make announcements about the evening program and the following day's schedule. Dr. Jensen's natural seasoning (for sale at the front desk or at your favorite health food store), cayenne pepper, Parmesan cheese, and cinnamon are among the interesting assorted condiments on each table. No room service.

DRESS CODE: Casual is the key.

ACCOMMODATIONS: Check out your room before checking in; there are three types. The least expensive are adjoining doubles, where four persons share one bath. The Palms will provide roommates. The lodge rooms or poolside cabanas are priced in the middle range. The "luxury" accommodations are the private cottages with private patios, a few of which have a high wall around the patio for sunbathing au naturelle. All luxury rooms have two double beds, TV, telephone, and air conditioning. The cottages and lodge rooms have better bathroom space with a counter for toiletries while the poolside rooms have a freestanding sink and no countertop.

HOUSE RULES: Smoking is permitted only in your room or outdoors.

PHYSICAL FACILITIES: Exercise classes, the pool, and the whirlpool are all coed activities. The Azul Spa is located in the same building as the dining room. It contains one large exercise room and separate men's and women's showers and saunas. The two-storied main building houses the front desk, the nurse's office, beauty salon, and boutique. The second floor houses the massage rooms, facial rooms, and the Winner's Circle, which is the lounge area for TV and lectures. There is a 24-hour open kitchen with herbal tea, decaffeinated coffee, lemon slices, and lots of ice cubes. The second floor outside porch is where we meet for the morning walks and do warm-up stretches. It is also a nice resting spot for weary bones at sunset, viewing the pool and bougainvillaeas. There is an outdoor Olympic-size pool (water classes are held in the shallow end) and an outdoor whirlpool. A do-it-yourself juice bar by the pool is open all day. Laundry facilities are on the premises.

ACTIVITIES, TREATMENTS, AND PROGRAMS: You may choose from 16 different fitness classes per day, seven days a week, including pool class and ranging from light stretching to challenging workouts. You may participate in as few or as many of these classes as you wish. Massages, facials, skin, nail, and hair care are à la carte. Tennis and golf are available nearby. Evening programs consist of lectures on nutrition, stress management, cosmetic surgery, money management, and arts and crafts demonstrations. The week I was there, they had a three-night seminar on "Planning Your Wardrobe." Many guest lecturers are brought it from the outside.

A Typical Day at the Palms

7:00	Brisk walk of three miles
7:30	Nature walk—slower, paced with time to admire nature
8:00	Breakfast
9:00	Body awareness—a moderate stretch
10:00	Body dynamics—the most challenging of the fitness classes
10:00	Creative aerobics
11:00	Aquatoning—pool exercise

12:00	Lunch
1:15	Body conditioning
2:00	Body shaping
	Aquaerobics
3:00	Aerobic body conditioning
4:00	Yoga
5:30	Happy hour—juice cocktails
	New guest orientation
6:00	Dinner
7:00	Evening programs

OPTIONAL COSTS: All treatments—including massage, facial, makeup design, cellulite wrap—as well as exercise cassette tapes, boutique purchases, and beauty salon services are extra. All the facial and skin care products used at The Palms and The Oaks at Ojai are by Vera Brown. The products are all natural with no preservatives (which means they won't last forever on your shelf). As noted before, Vera gives a great deal of her love, time, and money to the Junior Blind Association, and her products are even labeled in Braille.

NICE TO KNOW: All treatments and exercise classes are offered seven days a week. Should you plan to arrive after lunch is served, you can phone ahead to one of the three full-time nurses and arrange for your lunch to be waiting for you. If you must depart early in the morning, request the kitchen staff to prepare a box breakfast.

JUDY'S COMMENT: This is a perfect place for a first-time spa experience. The professionalism of the fitness staff is truly a joy! Sheila Cluff is a noted authority on physical culture. She has been teaching fitness for over 18 years in schools and on television, and to look at her is to know that she is the "Guru of Fitness."

REGENCY HOTEL-SPA
10101 Collins Avenue
Bal Harbour, FL 33154
800-327-0556
305-865-2311

The Regency Spa is located directly on the ocean within walking distance of deluxe shops and condominiums. Closed June to October.

RATES: Affordable. No credit cards.

LOCATION AND TRANSPORTATION: The spa is six miles from Miami airport.

EMPHASIS/PHILOSOPHY: The Regency describes itself as "a spa to reduce weight . . . and have a good time." That says it, I guess.

DIET PROGRAM: The staff dietician individualizes a diet program for each guest upon arrival. Well-rounded, portion-controlled meals feature fish, meat, and poultry, with plenty of fresh fruits and vegetables. The spa cooks with pure Florida spring water, which it buys in large bottles directly from the spring. Food is prepared 80 percent salt-free and without sugar. Dietetic products are used. The menu offers a number of choices at each meal, but calorie counts are not given. Mineral water is always available. The spa has its own bakery and rotisserie to make things fresh and tasty. Kosher meals are available.

GUEST POPULATION: Coed. 325 guests. Most folks are Jewish seniors who are young at heart. According to Jimmy Feyko, executive general manager, people come for a variety of reasons: "About 30 percent of the guests come to lose weight, 30 percent come to get into shape, and the remainder are there for just plain rest and relaxation." On the other hand, the brochure claims that 75 percent are on a reducing diet, so either way, you can't go wrong. The Regency is not built to accommodate persons in wheelchairs or those using crutches or two walking sticks.

PACKAGES AND MINIMUM STAYS: Rates are by the week, rising in midwinter and declining in spring. A $10 surcharge per day is made if guest checks out in less than one week. Bonus free days and other promotional incentives are offered in fall and spring.

MEAL SERVICE: Table service for all meals, with a hostess to seat you. Dieters and nondieters sit at the same table. Room service is available for a charge.

DRESS CODE: Jackets and ties are required for men at dinner.

ACCOMMODATIONS: Most rooms are twin-bedded, with television and air conditioning. There are a limited number of oceanfront rooms with terrace at a higher rate.

HOUSE RULES: Anything goes except alcohol. There is no alcoholic bar on the premises, and no wine is served with meals.

PHYSICAL FACILITIES: Whirlpool baths, steam rooms, saunas, mineral baths, massage rooms, a gymnasium with full equipment, and the spa's own sandy beach add up to full spa pleasure. Golf is nearby, and guests are allowed three free rounds during their week stay.

ACTIVITIES, TREATMENTS, AND PROGRAMS: The steamroom, sauna, mineral baths, and well-equipped gymnasium are yours to use. There are two daily exercise classes, both coed. A mild stretching class is held in the morning, and an aquatics session is held four days per week. As an incentive, the Regency Spa offers its 14-day guests one free half-hour massage daily on weekdays, twelve whirlpool baths, and a complimentary medical examination. All guests can enjoy dancing to the Regency Orchestra at dinner and live entertainment most evenings.

NICE TO KNOW: Nearby Bal Harbor has a wealth of posh shops, including Cache, Neiman Marcus, Gucci, Bonwit Teller, and Saks Fifth Avenue. Guests are expected to tip employees in accordance with a suggested tip list.

JUDY'S COMMENT: Regency Hotel-Spa has a wonderful location convenient to beach and shops. The program could use a bit more structure, but it seems to work for the faithful who return year after year.

SLIM INN AT CARIBOU LODGE
Caribou Lodge-on-the-Lake
Lac Supérieur, Québec, JOT-1PO Canada
819-688-5201

The Slim Inn program is offered from June through September. In the winter it is a ski lodge. Caribou Lodge-on-the-Lake is a cozy, pine-paneled lodge in the heart of Canada's Laurentian Mountains and on the shores of tranquil Lac Supérieur. A small, congenial program offers weight loss and relaxation in a beautiful setting.

RATES: Affordable. Credit cards are not accepted; pay by personal check. A $100 deposit before arrival is required.

LOCATION AND TRANSPORTATION: The lodge is 75 miles north of Montreal. For approximately $13 Canadian a bus will take you on a two-hour ride from Montreal to the town of St. Faustin. The spa provides transportation from St. Faustin to the lodge. The easiest way to reach the lodge from Montreal is by car.

EMPHASIS/PHILOSOPHY: Slim Inn offers guests a sensible, calorie-controlled diet program in a relaxed and casual atmosphere. Brigitta Stromberg-Parizot, the director, has designed an easygoing program that provides gourmet spa cuisine and lots of rest, relaxation, and camaraderie among participants. Brigitta wants to avoid putting any pressure on her guests. She has designed the program so that its only truly structured aspects are calorie intake and the hours at which meals are served.

DIET PROGRAM: Meals are based on a 1,000-calorie-a-day limit. They are prepared with great finesse by Richard Parizot, husband of Ms. Stromberg-Parizot. Chef Parizot creates artistically presented, well-balanced meals that are tasty and satisfying. Food consists of vegetables and grains, fish, veal, and chicken. Little salt, fat, or sugar are used. Beef is served once a week. Salt and pepper shakers are on the tables, but guests are urged to use salt in moderation. Soda water, plain water, coffee, and tea are available at all times. No snacks are served. An example of a day's meal plan would be:

BREAKFAST
Grapefruit
Poached egg
Toast
Skim milk

LUNCH
Tomato Juice
Lobster
Tomato and mushroom salad

DINNER
Consommé
Entrecote
Broccoli
Cauliflower
Salad
Fresh pineapple
Coffee or tea

GUEST POPULATION: Women only. 12 guests. The Slim Inn program caters primarily to busy career women seeking rest and relaxation. There are no other guests at the lodge during the spa program.

PACKAGES AND MINIMUM STAYS: A 1-week stay, seven days and six nights, is the required minimum.

MEAL SERVICE: Brigitta reports that mealtimes provide a nice opportunity for guests to socialize and give each other moral support. Everyone eats at one big table. The country ambience is enhanced by the addition of a large bouquet of fresh flowers on the table.

DRESS CODE: As part of providing a restful environment, guests are encouraged to dress very casually at all times. The women can throw robes over their bathing suits and run up to the lodge for lunch. A sweater or light jacket is recommended for cool summer evenings.

ACCOMMODATIONS: Each woman has her own room, which is simple but comfortable. The rooms are furnished with double beds of pinewood, a bureau, wardrobe, and sink with mirror. Air conditioning is not needed, and there are no telephones or TVs. To bathe, it's necessary to use one of the three baths or the one shower located in the hallway. Stromberg-Parizot says that this arrangement works out well. In fact, in wintertime, when the inn becomes a ski lodge, these same facilities accommodate 44 skiers. There is a maid who makes the beds on a daily basis.

HOUSE RULES: The rooms of the lodge are large and airy so that smoking is permitted everywhere except in the dining room during mealtimes. Alcohol is not served.

PHYSICAL FACILITIES: The Slim Inn program is conducted entirely inside the Caribou Lodge, which contains the guest rooms, dining and exercise rooms, and TV lounge. A large, screened-in porch overlooking the lake is a favorable relaxing area among the guests. The lake itself is one of the amenities, with its weathered dock and waterfront lawn cots. Laundry is done either in the sinks of the rooms or during one of the excursions to nearby St. Laurent. Small supplies can be gotten at a general store that is within walking distance, or in one of the local towns during a shopping trip. Money is spent on obtaining high-quality foodstuffs, not fancy equipment, says Brigitta.

ACTIVITIES, TREATMENTS, AND PROGRAMS: One nonaerobic toning and firming class a day is given by Brigitta. She also takes guests on brisk walks around the lake. Most of the women take daily swims in the warm, clear water of Lac Supérieur. Frequent excursions to the towns of St. Faustin and St. Jovite are made for shopping and browsing at local handicraft boutiques. Antiques and items made by silversmiths, potters, and weavers are sold. A terrycloth robe is provided by the lodge for use during the program. Once a week a beautician gives a class on how to make and apply your own facials. She also will give you tips on hair care and styling. There is no predetermined wake-up hour. The program is flexible enough to allow guests time to choose their own activities, such as reading, playing games, and knitting. Fifteen minutes before each meal, Brigitta rings a bell. Breakfast is served at 9:00 A.M., lunch at 1:00 P.M., and dinner at 6:30 P.M.

STAFF POPULATION: Brigitta Stromberg-Parizot and Richard Parizot both come from Sweden, where they were raised in the Swedish tradition of hiking, skiing, and other outdoor activities. Richard has developed a highly refined continental-style health cuisine. It is based on nutritional principles and culinary techniques he learned during his training in Switzerland.

OPTIONAL COSTS: Use of a laundromat in a nearby town and the services of the beautician at her local salon will most likely be the extent of your nonprogram expenses.

SPECIAL PACKAGES: Lodging and all three meals are complimentary on Saturday for guests staying more than one week.

NICE TO KNOW: According to Stromberg-Parizot, her program appeals primarily to women in their forties. Younger women frequently seek a more structured or "exciting" program. A note from a physician attesting to your good health on a 1,000-calorie-a-day diet is required before arrival. Kitchen doors are kept locked "unobtrusively" between meals. When it becomes cool enough in the evenings, the fireplace in the lounge is lighted to add to the comfortable, cozy feeling of the lodge. Guests can make and receive phone calls from the main phone at the front desk. A pay phone is available.

JUDY'S COMMENT: Situated in a remote mountain area, the Slim Inn at Caribou Lodge is a low-keyed, weight-reduction program. It provides overstressed women with a place to truly unwind in a warm, supportive atmosphere.

SOUTHWIND HEALTH RESORT
Route 2, Sandtown Road
Cartersville, GA 30120
404-975-0342

Open year-round. A restored 20-room Victorian mansion situated on 16 beautiful, wooded acres bordering Lake Allatoona.

RATES: Moderate. Credit cards: American Express, MasterCard, Visa.

LOCATION AND TRANSPORTATION: Southwind is 45 minutes from downtown Atlanta and Hartsfield International Airport. The spa provides transportation to and from the airport for a fee of $20 each way.

EMPHASIS/PHILOSOPHY: Doreen MacAdams, the owner and director of Southwind, describes the goals of the program as follows: "The spa experience is more than a pampered vacation in the coun-

Courtesy of Southwind Health Resort

try. It's a program to change your life's direction. Here, you can acquire the habits of healthy living and the motivation to make the most of what life offers. It's a whole new outlook on the possibilities of happiness." Southwind offers an individually tailored program that stresses total life-style reeducation. The spa focuses on weight loss, self-image improvement, energy enhancement, and stress reduction.

DIET PROGRAM: The calorie limit ranges from 800 to 1,000 calories per day. Newly arrived Chef Mary Roegge uses no red meat, sugar, or salt in preparing three low-fat, high-fiber meals a day. She uses fresh fruits and vegetables, fish, chicken, and veal. There is also a 9 P.M. snack, consisting of hot-air-popped popcorn or half an apple or orange.

Here's an example of a typical Friday night dinner:

APPETIZERS
Bellini Spritzer
Consommé Bellevue
Marinated mushrooms

SALADS
Romaine with radishes,
  zucchini, and tomato
Curried avocado

ENTREES
Lobster Newburgh
Chicken Paprikash
Scallops en Brochette

VEGETABLES
Polonaise of
   cauliflower
Minted baby carrots

DESSERTS
Fresh pineapple wedge
Strawberry sorbet
Fudge ripple

At Southwind calorie reduction and increased exercise maximize weight loss. According to Doreen MacAdams, female guests lose an average of five to eight pounds during a week's program.

GUEST POPULATION: 16 guests. Women only for the weeklong program. Weekend programs are coed.

PACKAGES AND MINIMUM STAYS: The 3-day, 3-night weekend program is the minimum stay required. There are special couples weekends and stop-smoking weekends. Full week programs involve check-in on Sunday, check-out on Saturday. The new 10-day package starts Thursday of one week and ends Sunday of the next.

MEAL SERVICE: Menus do not contain calorie counts, but any item you choose to eat is within the prescribed caloric limits. Southwind has established a tradition of using name cards to seat the guests. Placement of the cards is rotated at each meal to enable all the guests to meet each other. Dining ambience is rather formal in the spacious dining room, with twelve-foot ceilings. Tables are set with beautiful linen, fine china, and fresh flowers. Soft music enhances the atmosphere.

DRESS CODE: Attire at the spa is casual. Even shorts are acceptable. After the beauty makeover on Friday afternoon, guests may want to dress up a little for Friday evening dinner.

ACCOMMODATIONS: All rooms are double occupancy. There are no telephones or TVs in the rooms. A pay phone is located on the second floor. Central air conditioning and maid service are provided. Room decor is country Victorian, with lots of pinewood furniture. The mansion is carpeted throughout. Rooms are decorated in light mauve, peach, and pink tones.

Courtesy of Southwind Health Resort

HOUSE RULES: Smoking is not permitted in the buildings, pool, or deck areas. Guests can smoke outside only. Kir Spritzer and Bellini Spritzer are offered as two appetizer options during the week-long program.

PHYSICAL FACILITIES: All beauty services (massages, pedicures, and facials) are located in the manor house. As of this writing, there is no beauty shop to accommodate hair needs. These services can be arranged in a nearby town. As of this writing, there is a small boutique which carries specialty T-shirts and Southwind logo sweatshirts and other miscellaneous items. The exercise and fitness programs take place in a turn-of-the-century general store! There is an outdoor heated pool especially designed for water aerobics. In back of the house is a covered hot tub used year-round. Two nature trails are located on the 16-acre estate. A 4-mile trail parallels the lake and a 2¹/₂-mile trail goes through wooded terrain. There is a laundry room on the premises.

ACTIVITIES, TREATMENTS, AND PROGRAMS: Daily exercise classes are included in the room rate. These include morning fitness walks at three different levels of difficulty; beginning and advanced aerobic classes; water aerobic exercises, emphasizing lower back care and flexibility; and body sculpting exercises, where abdominal and upper-leg areas are emphasized. Treatments include 3 half-hour Swedish massages, 1 facial, and 1 beauty make-over. Two to three lectures and seminars are interspersed in the daily beauty and exercise regimen. The lectures cover such informative topics as nutritional awareness, relaxation techniques, strategies for success, stress analysis, cooking classes, the benefits of exercise, consumer education, and designing a personal fitness program. One private consultation with a dietician to establish an individual dietary plan is also included.

A Day at Southwind

8:00–9:00	Supervised fitness walk on nature trails
9:15–10:00	Breakfast
10:00–11:00	Morning seminar
11:45–12:15	Aerobics
12:30–1:30	Lunch
1:45–2:30	Water aerobics classes
2:30–3:30	Individual beauty consultations, massages, facials
3:30–4:30	Body-sculpting exercises
4:30–6:00	Relaxation and free time
6:00–7:00	Dinner
7:00–8:00	Seminars
8:00–whenever	Leisure time

STAFF POPULATION: The Southwind staff is quite impressive. Owner/director Doreen MacAdams is an R.N. and M.S.N., joined by Chef Mary Roegge. Two physicians are on call 24 hours a day. They give lectures once or twice a week on prevention of heart disease and coronary risk factors. A staff psychologist lectures on self-image, and the full-time hypnotherapist speaks on stress reduction. There are several massage therapists and exercise instructors. Also on staff are a dietician, physical therapist, facialist, guest relations manager, and assistant manager.

OPTIONAL COSTS: Additional massages and facials are available. Private consultation with one of the physicians is also possible for an additional fee. For hairstyling, manicures, and pedicures participants can choose to go to a local beauty salon.

NICE TO KNOW: Scheduling at Southwind works on a 10 day on/ 2 days off basis: the 7-day program is given one week and the following week only the 3-day weekend is offered. These 2 programs are combined to make the 10-day package. Single rooms are not available, which is surprising given the cost of the program and the emphasis on maximal relaxation. The spa will pair you with a roommate if necessary. Medical release forms from your doctor are required—a good idea that benefits both spa and guest.

JUDY'S COMMENT: Southwind offers a unique, well thought out program that combines extensive exercise with lowered caloric intake, varied seminars, and basic pampering treatments. This well-rounded approach helps guests acquire that inner and outer glow most of us seek. Southwind also offers the tools to achieve total life-style reeducation.

*SUN SPA
3101 S. Ocean Drive
Hollywood, FL 33019
800-327-4122
305-921-5800

A modern three-story hotel directly on the ocean at Hollywood Beach, Florida, is the home of Sun Spa. Open mid-October to mid-April.

RATES: Affordable. No credit cards; cash and checks only.

LOCATION AND TRANSPORTATION: The spa is 8 miles from Fort Lauderdale/Hollywood International Airport. Taxi to spa.

EMPHASIS/PHILOSOPHY: Sun Spa tries to provide a glorious vacation with a residual feeling of good health every day of the year. Their slogan: "Sun Spa is the place the seekers of health call home."

DIET PROGRAM: 800 calories and up per day. All meals are prepared salt-free, but salt is available on the table. Dietetic products are used. The diet is well-balanced, and several choices are available for each meal. Snacks are served at 3:00 P.M. and at 10:00 P.M. The dietician will individualize your program.

GUEST POPULATION: Coed. 200 guests. A wonderful seaside resort for spry, young-at-heart folks. Most guests are on a diet program.

PACKAGES AND MINIMUM STAYS: The basic program is 1 week. Rates peak in winter and decline in spring. It is often difficult to book in the winter as some folks return season after season. Usually, the spa offers a bonus free week with each paid week from mid-October to mid-December.

MEAL SERVICE: There is a hostess to seat you, and you sit at the same table for all your meals, getting to know your waiter and your neighbors. The dietician is present at every meal to help you with selections. Food is of high quality and simply presented.

DRESS CODE: Jackets and ties are required for men at dinner. Take your cue from that, ladies.

ACCOMMODATIONS: Comfortable, twin-bedded rooms, each with its own balcony.

HOUSE RULES: No alcoholic bar on premises. A glass of wine is served with dinner on Wednesday evenings, but is available at no other time.

PHYSICAL FACILITIES: Separate and complete penthouse spa facilities for men and women, with shared exercise classes. Facilities include whirlpool, steamrooms, sauna, solarium, Nautilus, passive and active reducing equipment, indoor and outdoor swimming pools, daily golf, shuffleboard, and Roman pools. The hotel also has a beauty salon and boutique.

ACTIVITIES, TREATMENTS, AND PROGRAMS: Rates include all exercise classes, consisting of stretch and relax, moderate calisthenics, and water exercise classes; a half-hour massage daily; and use of all spa facilities. Ladies receive a complimentary facial and makeup treatment during their stay. The medical examination is free after a 7-day stay. The spa pays your greens fee for golf at the Hollywood Beach Hotel and Country Club. There is entertainment and dancing nightly with a live band. Shows, movies, and card parties are always available. Sabbath services are held every Friday evening.

NICE TO KNOW: Sun Spa provides a "Helpful Tips" booklet. There is always a hot shuffleboard game available. Coke and Tab, as well as wine, are allowed at the dinner table.

*BEST BUY AND WHY: This affordable spa is a "Best Buy" because:
- At this wonderful location you can walk the Atlantic Ocean beach for miles or stroll conveniently to nearby shopping centers.
- The food is of very high quality.
- Management keeps the grounds impeccably clean.

JUDY'S COMMENT: This is a no-frills spa (certainly not a La

Costa), but the staff is capable and caring. The medical and health staff is unusually large, with a full-time doctor and nurse, two dieticians, and no less than sixteen massage therapists to take good care of you.

WOODEN DOOR SPA
Lake Geneva, WI
Mailing address:
P.O. Box 830,
Barrington, IL 60010
312-382-2888
camp numbers 414-248-9556 and 248-3600

The Wooden Door is a "return-to-nature" fitness retreat. It has a summer-camp-like setting on 54 heavily wooded acres right on Lake Geneva. An intermittent schedule of 12 weeks is conducted from January to October.

RATES: Affordable. Credit cards: MasterCard, Visa. This is one of the lowest priced spas you'll find anywhere. If you like "rustic," you'll not only enjoy the Wooden Door, but you'll spend very little.

LOCATION AND TRANSPORTATION: The spa is situated two hours north of Chicago. Limousine service is available from O'Hare airport.

EMPHASIS/PHILOSOPHY: Jill Adzia, Naomi Stark, and Shirley McAlear, founders and managers of the Wooden Door, describe their goal as "to help each participant find her full potential both physically and mentally in a stress-free rustic setting."

DIET PROGRAM: The spa's nutritionist has designed a 900-calorie-per-day program that is portion-controlled; the meals are well-balanced, low in fat and sodium, and high in fiber and carbohydrates. Meals feature chicken and fish, fresh fruits, and vegetables. No red meat, sugar, or caffeine are served. A supplemental food table is available for those requiring more calories. A five-pound weight loss during the 6-day stay is not unusual.

GUEST POPULATION: Women only. 70 guests—all ages and stages.

PACKAGES AND MINIMUM STAYS: The minimum "short week" stay includes 6 days and 5 nights. Arrive before noon Sunday, depart on Friday before lunch. An orientation program is held after your early dinner on Sunday.

MEAL SERVICE: All meals are buffet style with servers. Lunch is the most substantial meal.

DRESS CODE: Campy casual. Bring along your own insect repellent, flashlight, and exercise mat.

ACCOMMODATIONS: Guests are housed in large airy cabins, complete with bathroom, that accommodate two to four women. Bring your own bed linens or your own comfy sleeping bag for the bunk bed that you'll sleep in.

HOUSE RULES: No smoking in any building. Smoking is discouraged but allowed outdoors.

PHYSICAL FACILITIES: The air-conditioned gym and the gazebo by the lake are used for exercise classes. There are hiking/jogging trails, cross-country skiing in the winter, a pier for sunning/swimming/boating, tennis courts, shuffleboard and volleyball courts, a sauna, and the Little Store for sundries. Massages, manicures, and beauty services are available à la carte.

ACTIVITIES, TREATMENTS, AND PROGRAMS: There are classes for just about every level of fitness—sunrise yoga class, aerobics to music, stretching and toning, weight training, beginning ballet, self-defense techniques, assertiveness training—as well as makeup lessons and wardrobe planning classes. Evening programs consist of movies, lectures, fashion workshops, stress management, and campfires.

A Typical Day at the Wooden Door

6:00	Sunrise yoga class
7:00	Walk or jog groups
8:00	Breakfast
9:00–10:00	Exercise classes (slow- and fast-paced)
11:00	Advanced aerobics or yoga
12:00	Dinner
1:00	New Directions
2:00	Exercise
3:00	Weight training
4:00	Personality profile or nutrition chat
5:00	Supper
7:00	Evening program
8:00	Movie and snack

OPTIONAL COSTS: Massages, manicures, and pedicures are extra.

NICE TO KNOW: The city of Lake Geneva, only an easy mile's walk away, and surrounding areas are of historic interest and contain many antiques and fun shops and boutiques. In summer, there are lots of waterfront activities including sailing, waterskiing, and fishing. Winters are great for cross-country skiing, and the great hiking trails are always there for using.

JUDY'S COMMENT: The Wooden Door is like camping out—lots of fun, most affordable, and most effective.

BEAUTY SPAS—WHY, WHERE, AND HOW MUCH

A "beauty" spa is so designated because its primary emphasis is on beauty treatments combined with proper nutrition and exercise. Often the exercise program is geared toward the gentler types of body toning.

Cost is based on a one-week stay, double occupancy, high-season rates, including taxes and gratuities. Meals are included unless specifically stated otherwise. Best Buys are indicated by an asterisk.

Affordable: up to $1,000
Moderate: $1,000–$1,700
Expensive: $1,700 and up

THE GREENHOUSE
P.O. Box 1144
Arlington, TX 76010
800-637-5883
817-640-4000

This luxurious retreat was created by Neiman Marcus and Charles of the Ritz. A great, glass-enclosed private world in a Shangri-la of exotic gardens, patios, pools, and gymnasiums. Open year-round, except for four weeks in fall and two weeks in summer.

RATES: Expensive. Credit cards: American Express, MasterCard, Neiman Marcus, Visa.

LOCATION AND TRANSPORTATION: The Greenhouse lies midway between Dallas and Fort Worth. Make arrangements in advance for courtesy pickup at the airport.

Courtesy of The Greenhouse

EMPHASIS/PHILOSOPHY: The Greenhouse emphasizes restoring a woman's beauty. They say, "You'll experience a health and beauty program carefully planned for your total well-being."

DIET PROGRAM: Choose 850, 1,200, or 1,500 calories per day. The 850-calorie program should result in a loss of three to five pounds. The 1,500-calorie program is intended for those who wish to gain! Meals are salt-free, well-rounded, and nutritious, presented haute cuisine style. Included in the calorie counts are delicious crudité snacks. Dietetic products are used for some desserts. No carbonated water is used because of its high sodium content. The famous Greenhouse menus created by the late Helen Corbitt have been implemented by her talented protégés, combining the best of classic French cuisine with their own innovative ideas. Helen Corbitt's *Greenhouse Cookbook* (Houghton Mifflin) can be purchased at The Greenhouse boutique and at all Neiman Marcus stores. Dieting guests report they eat so much that it's hard to believe they're dieting.

GUEST POPULATION: 40 guests. This spa caters strictly to ladies. The Greenhouse has its fair share of professional women, socialites, new mothers, and famous faces who have felt right at home here. Some of the celebrities, past and present, include Brooke Shields (sans her Calvins), Lady Byrd Johnson, the late Duchess of Windsor, and the late Princess Grace. Most of the guests in this posh environment are repeaters, but first-timers are made to feel most welcome.

PACKAGES AND MINIMUM STAYS: The minimum reservation is for one week, Sunday to Sunday. Check in between 1:00 and 6:00 P.M.; check out by noon.

MEAL SERVICE: Your day beings with breakfast in bed at 7:00 A.M. Lunch is informal by the indoor pool, with formal dinner service in the dining room. Lunch and dinner may be taken in your room if you choose. All meals are experiences in gracious dining, with bone china and Waterford crystal. After-dinner coffee is served in the drawing room prior to the evening program.

DRESS CODE: Although the policy is casual evening dress, everyone dresses for dinner—from simple linens to extravagant silks! According to one recent visitor, "some of the dowager queens remain in their room most of the day preparing for the evening gala. Many wear their jewels weeknight evenings—it's almost a better display than the Neiman Marcus jewelry fashion show."

ACCOMMODATIONS: Guest rooms are located down walkways leading from the two-story, glass-enclosed atrium. Rooms are totally luxurious and tastefully done in pastel colors. Each room has a canopied bed fit for a queen, separate dressing area with wall-to-wall mirrors, your own air controls, makeup mirrors, and radio and TV. Each private bath has a sunken tub and a maid to draw the water when you ring a bell! (Very continental, indeed.)

HOUSE RULES: No smoking in the dining room. "Alcoholic beverages are prohibited," as stated in The Greenhouse brochure. Because of this strict no-drinking policy, guests have been asked to leave—their money was fully refunded. They really mean it.

Courtesy of The Greenhouse

PHYSICAL FACILITIES: You'll find state-of-the-art exercise rooms, facial rooms, makeup rooms, separate beauty salon, saunas, steam room, whirlpools, and boutique (chock-full of elegant dinner clothes and the latest chic fashion items).

ACTIVITIES, TREATMENTS, AND PROGRAMS: Toni Beck, well-known fitness authority and author, directs the exercise program. Toni heads a superb staff and has recently incorporated more aerobic exercise into the traditional program. Guests are taught how to monitor their resting heartbeat. A typical day includes 7:40 A.M. morning walk or jog around the one-sixth-mile track or the neighboring golf course; morning wake-up exercises around the pool; stretch and flex class, which is vigorous stretching and toning consisting of 45 minutes of leg lifts and tummy tighteners; choice of two pool classes a day, one in the morning and the other in the afternoon; and a dance or aerobics class at the end of the day.

Beauty treatments are scheduled through the day; massage, manicures and pedicures, beauty class, facials, and much more are all included. Hair care includes relaxing scalp massages, stunning French braiding, conditioning treatments, and expert styling. Makeup and skin care products are by Charles of the Ritz. The after-dinner hour is devoted to special entertainment and programs. Join an author, artist, or expert on fashion, jewels, or travel in the drawing room. A Neiman Marcus fashion coordinator/advisor is on hand for fashion shows to expedite your purchases. Limousines are available to take you to the famous Neiman Marcus store in downtown Dallas or anywhere else for only $45 for three hours.

OPTIONAL COSTS: Charles of the Ritz makeup purchases, smashing boutique items, and services of the tennis pro are available every afternoon.

NICE TO KNOW: Everyone speaks in whispers at The Greenhouse and you never seem to see anyone. Upon first checking in, one guest reports, "My friend and I thought we were the only guests in the place—it's oh, so quiet. We went to the exercise class and were shocked—the Greenhouse was full of people!" A full-time doctor and nurse are on the premises. They will come to your room for individual checkups. According to one pleased guest, the doctor will give you vitamin B-12 shots if you feel tired or weak. All at no extra cost.

JUDY'S COMMENT: After a week at The Greenhouse, you look as if you have had a complete face-lift—sans surgery. How special!

HRH MIND AND BODY
BEAUTY CENTER
RR3, Box 19-C
Scotts Corners, Pound Ridge, NY 10576
914-764-8161

The spa is located in a beautifully renovated eighteenth-century house in a serene natural setting. Weekend programs only.

RATES: Moderate. No credit cards.

LOCATION AND TRANSPORTATION: The spa is only one hour from New York City. Take the train to New Canaan, CT, and use the courtesy limousine from there.

EMPHASIS/PHILOSOPHY: HRH specializes in developing your beauty potential through fasting techniques. Initials stand for Health, Relaxation, and Hair.

DIET PROGRAM: Meals are light, vegetarian and Oriental, and many guests fast on distilled water for the weekend, broken with vegetable broth on departure day. In preparation for the weekend, a guest's diet should consist of many fresh fruits and vegetables, with minimal use of red meats, flour, sugar and alcohol.

GUEST POPULATION: Women only. 6–8 guests.

PACKAGES AND MINIMUM STAYS: There is only the 3 days/2 nights weekend program: in on Friday evening, out Sunday afternoon.

DRESS CODE: Very casual. HRH suggests you bring along an exercise outfit, comfortable walking shoes, warm socks, a sweater, writing paper, and toiletries.

ACCOMMODATIONS: Guests are housed in the charming, renovated mansion in rooms with an Oriental decor. There's only one private room; otherwise, roommates may be assigned if desired. Most guests sleep in large rooms separated by Japanese screens. Each Japanese-style "room" contains a futon mat for sleeping, a table, a chair, a lamp, and an Oriental flower arrangement. All bathrooms are shared.

HOUSE RULES: No smoking allowed. No tipping for professional services.

PHYSICAL FACILITIES: Facilities include a Jacuzzi, herbal steam sauna, rural hiking trails, and a library.

ACTIVITIES, TREATMENTS, AND PROGRAMS: Included in the weekend program are: two massages (choice of Swedish or shiatsu), yoga classes, gentle aerobicise class, steam/sauna, Jacuzzi, meditation class, stress workshop, nutritional advice, and evening lectures on fasting and wholistic-health-related subjects.

An HRH Beauty Weekend

Friday Evening
  7:30 Remove the body and mind stress of the week
     with a Stretch/Yoga class

8:30	Private steam/sauna, Jacuzzi, and body massage
10:00	Protein broth, herbal tea, and bedtime

Saturday

7:00	Organic juices and a brisk hike in the beautiful Pound Ridge Reservation
8:00	Grain and fruit breakfast
8:30	Stretch/Yoga class
9:30	Private steam/sauna, Jacuzzi
10:30	Aerobicise class
12:00	Vegetarian luncheon
1:30– 5:30	Body massage, Chanel facial, pedicure, and manicure
6:00	Light nutritive Oriental dinner
7:00	Meditative twilight walk (season permitting)
8:00	Body awareness lecture/workshop
9:00	Private steam/sauna, Jacuzzi, and motor table
10:00	Herbal tea and bedtime

Sunday

7:00	Organic juices and a brisk hike in the beautiful Pound Ridge Reservation
8:00	Grain and fruit breakfast
8:30	Stretch/yoga class
9:30	Aerobicise with light weights
10:30	Private steam/sauna and Jacuzzi
12:00	Gourmet Oriental luncheon
1:30	Herbal body wrap
3:30	Nutritional lecture/workshop
4:30	Chanel makeup lesson and hair design consultation

OPTIONAL COSTS: A full range of beauty salon services are available and include facial, manicure, pedicure, hand and foot massage, haircut, expert hair color, makeup lessons, complete beauty makeover, and much more.

NICE TO KNOW: The library at HRH contains extensive information on health, nutrition, and beauty. Chanel products are used for all beauty treatments. HRH is a beauty facility during the week, with live-in programs reserved for weekends.

JUDY'S COMMENT: A beautiful weekend in its utter simplicity!

*IXTAPAN RESORT HOTEL AND SPA
Paseo de la Reforma 132
06600 Mexico City, D.F.
800-223-9832
Reservations 905-566-28-55

The spa is part of a 42-acre resort complex located in the historic village of Ixtapan de la Sal. Emperor Montezuma is known to have "taken the waters" here back in the sixteenth century. High altitude setting. Open year-round.

RATES: Affordable. No credit cards. The favorable rate of exchange makes Ixtapan an exceptional value.

LOCATION AND TRANSPORATION: Situated 85 miles south of Mexico City on a first-class road. Hotel limousine service is available from Mexico City for a reasonable charge.

EMPHASIS/PHILOSOPHY: The weeklong Beauty Clinic is geared to rejuvenation in mind and body. "You can become a new woman by losing pounds, reducing inches, and toning the entire body."

DIET PROGRAM: 800–1,200 calories per day. The well-balanced diet includes lots of chicken and fish. Salt shakers are on the table. One delighted guest lost seven pounds in one week.

GUEST POPULATION: Coed. There usually are 50 to 60 women guests in the weeklong program. According to the spa director, however, men can also be accommodated in the diet and pampering program. There are two separate and complete spa facilities, one for men and one for women.

PACKAGES AND MINIMUM STAYS: The Week of Beauty program begins with Sunday check-in and ends Sunday after lunch. No spa meals or program on Sunday.

MEAL SERVICE: The Hotel Ixtapan provides a separate diet dining room for spa-goers, with table service at each meal. Dinner is by candlelight. The food is simply presented sans garnishes.

DRESS CODE: Early mornings and evenings are cold because of the high altitude, so bring a heavy sweater or coat. The spa provides cotton housecoats; the rest is up to you. For dinner, dressy casual clothes or caftans are fine.

ACCOMMODATIONS: Rooms are either in the hotel's main

building or in chalets. All rooms, from Junior to Presidential suites, have touches of pre-Hispanic decor.

HOUSE RULES: Anything goes.

PHYSICAL FACILITIES: Separate men's and women's spa buildings contain exercise rooms, Nautilus, massage rooms, facial rooms, steam baths, sauna, 20 private Roman baths, solariums, and beauty/barber salons. Outdoor facilities include a freshwater pool, tennis courts, thermal mineral water pools, and a whirlpool for do-it-yourself mud treatments. (The mud is located at the side of the pool; you place the mud where you want it on your body and it dries, tightening the pores.) There are all the amenities of a deluxe resort hotel: beauty salon, 9-hole golf course, tennis courts lighted for night play, putting greens, old-fashioned carriage rides, gift shops, and boutiques.

ACTIVITIES, TREATMENTS, AND PROGRAMS: Three diet meals and use of all spa facilities are included. Daily group exercise classes consist of stretching calisthenics, water classes, and spot exercise class. Daily treatments include a 50-minute massage, one paran bath, a 50-minute facial (consisting of all kinds of flavors—cucumber, apple, avocado), and daily treatments for hair, hands, and feet. The final day includes manicure, pedicure, and shampoo and set before departure. Evenings are spent enjoying live entertainment, mariachis and folklore ballet, concerts, and disco music found in the hotel's Aztec-inspired nightclub.

A Day at Ixtapan

8:15	Breakfast
	Rhythmic gymnastics
	Aquatic exercises
	Consommé
	Steam bath and body massage
	Electrotherapy or vibrator
1:00	Lunch in the Diet Dining Room
	Rest period for a walk, sunbath, or nap
	Facial
	Scalp treatment
	Nail treatment
	Juice
	Roman bath (private)
7:00	Supper in Diet Dining room

BEST BUY AND WHY: With or without peso devaluation, this program is a not-to-be-passed-up buy! This is the only beauty spa I've encountered that is inexpensively priced, yet includes so much.

NICE TO KNOW: You keep the same schedule for six days with the same treatment therapists who are thoroughly trained and "refreshingly unspoiled." Sundays are free to sightsee—a time to enjoy the local color. You can visit the baths where Montezuma bathed and the hot water "Green Lagoon," which was sacred to the Aztecs. The toll-free number is always busy, but at these prices and with this program, keep trying!

JUDY'S COMMENT: One delighted client lost 7 pounds in twelve days and felt deliciously beautiful and invigorated. "Montezuma's revenge" does not exist here. One can't afford to stay home!

THE KERR HOUSE
17605 Beaver Street
Grand Rapids, OH 43522
419-255-8634
419-832-1733

The Kerr House is a restored Victorian mansion nestled on the scenic Maumee River. Open year-round.

RATES: Expensive. Credit cards: American Express, MasterCard, Visa.

LOCATION AND TRANSPORTATION: Thirty miles south of Toledo and twenty minutes from Toledo Express Airport. Complimentary transportation is provided from the airport.

EMPHASIS/PHILOSOPHY: The main goal of Kerr House is rejuvenation with peaceful living and a renewed spirit of well-being. Laurie Hostetler, founder and director, says, "You don't need to punish yourself or suffer in order to get in shape or lose weight. Learning to eat properly, to enjoy natural foods, and to regain flexibility should be a pleasant experience."

DIET PROGRAM: 750–1,000 calories per day. Portion-controlled, well-balanced gourmet meals featuring fish, fowl, and fresh fruits and vegetables. All natural foods—no salt, no sugar, no white flour, no additives. They claim that it is quite easy to lose three to eight pounds during your 5-day stay. Some favorite dishes among guests are delicious homemade granola, cheddar cheese soup, and eggplant parmigiana.

GUEST POPULATION: Primarily for women, 8 guests. Occasional weeks and weekends that include men.

PACKAGES AND MINIMUM STAYS: The basic program is a "short week," running from Sunday through Friday afternoon. Weekends are available on request.

MEAL SERVICE: Breakfast in bed is a nice way to start the day! Table service prevails for luncheon and dinner. Dinner is served in an elegant dining room with linen cloths and fine porcelain china and crystal. A harpist plays on occasional evenings during your candlelight dining hour.

DRESS CODE: Caftans and dressy pants are perfect for dinner. The spa provides leotards, bathing suits, terry robes, and slippers for day use.

ACCOMMODATIONS: Comfortable single and double rooms with private baths, all beautifully furnished in Victorian style. All bedrooms have stained glass windows, armoires, antique bureaus, and old paintings.

HOUSE RULES: No smoking is allowed in bedrooms, as Kerr House is listed on the National Register of Historic Places, and they wish to take no chances. Smoking is allowed only in the Cafe (the informal dining room).

PHYSICAL FACILITIES: Massage rooms, facial rooms, exercise room, mineral baths, whirlpool, hot tub, sauna, an elegant parlor for group programs, a beauty salon, and a jewel-like boutique are on the premises. An outdoor pool, tennis courts, and golf are available nearby. There are paths along the old Miami and Erie Canal towpath for brisk walks or jogs.

ACTIVITIES, TREATMENTS AND PROGRAMS: Activities include use of all spa facilities, hatha-yoga, deep breathing exercises, stretch class, minitrampoline, low-impact aerobics, and walks along the river. Treatments include a daily one-hour massage, European facials two or three times a week, body wrap/herbal wrap once during the week, one manicure/pedicure during the week, and one hair care and makeup application before departure. Lectures are offered on stress management, nutrition, reflexology, graphology (handwriting analysis), and wholistic health.

A Day at Kerr House

7:00	Wake-up with breakfast served in bed
8:00	Exercise class
	Body appreciation, posture, relaxation techniques, breathing exercises
10:00	Morning treatments
	Massage, facials, reflexology, whirlpool, sauna, herbal wrap, body wrap, mineral bath

12:30	Lunch served in the Cafe
1:30	Quiet time
2:30	Group discussion, often with a guest speaker
4:00	Walk or outdoor activity
4:30	Afternoon exercise
5:30	Relax and dress for dinner
6:30	Dinner in the formal dining room
7:30	Varied evening activities
11:00	Lights out

NICE TO KNOW: The decor of The Kerr House is absolutely charming. Stained glass windows, wood-burning fireplaces, and hand-carved woodwork are reminiscent of a gentler era. The walkways along the river, where canal boats once traveled, make an inviting route for walkers and joggers. Paddleboat rides on the river are a frequent diversion for guests.

JUDY'S COMMENT: Designed for The Edwardian spirit (and nonsmoker) who loves and needs a genteel environment. It's hard to find this kind of soothing ambience, even within the world of spas.

MAINE CHANCE
5830 E. Jean Avenue
Phoenix, AZ 85018
602-947-6365

Elizabeth Arden's 110-acre beauty oasis with rolling green lawns is nestled at the foot of Camelback Mountain overlooking the city of Phoenix. Open from the last week in September to the end of May.

RATES: Expensive. No credit cards.

LOCATION AND TRANSPORTATION: Situated near Phoenix. Complimentary chauffered limousine service from the airport.

EMPHASIS/PHILOSOPHY: Beauty is a combination of health, individual charm, and grooming. Here, you'll receive an education in basic beauty habits that should become a way of life. The health and beauty regimen at Maine Chance is designed to make the most of each guest's natural assets and to concentrate on areas where she needs improvement. Elizabeth Arden believed that woman could remain beautiful forever through proper diet, exercise, and careful attention to her beauty regimen.

DIET PROGRAM: The Loser's Diet is 950 calories per day. It consists of a well-balanced selection of garden-fresh vegetables and fruits, lean meats, and fish. In the morning there's a snack break of potassium broth; in the afternoon fresh fruit juice is served. "Gainers," of course, are served appropriate mouth-watering additions to every meal and nutritious snacks in between. The Maine Chance desserts, known throughout the world, feature cheesecake, apricot mousse, Baked Alaska, and a variety of soufflés. (All this and lose weight too!) As one young matron says, "Meals are a special event." The same guest lost 6 1/2 pounds and 7 1/4 inches on her first visit.

GUEST POPULATION: Women only. 50 guests. Maine Chance attracts women from all over the world, and many of them return on a regular basis. Their interests are wide and varied: women with husbands at home and women with careers. There are busy hostesses, brides-to-be, students, women in the arts, business, politics, and education. Women from all over find that Maine Chance has something to give them. You may share some beauty tips with such notables as Joan Kennedy, Christina Ford, and Ava Gardner.

PACKAGES AND MINIMUM STAYS: The minimum stay and basic package is 1 week. Check in on Sunday, late afternoon; check out on Sunday after breakfast,

MEAL SERVICE: You begin your day with breakfast in bed served on a well-appointed tray (allowing you time to look at your schedule for the day). Tables and breakfast trays are set with Royal Adderley china and crystal. Luncheon is served on the flower-filled outdoor terrace under the shade of huge yellow umbrellas. Should you want to sunbathe, you can have cottage cheese and iced tea out by the pool. In the evening there's time for nonalcoholic happy hour and a chance to enjoy the companionship of fellow guests. Dinner is a formal and leisurely affair, served in the dining room, where windows on three sides let you enjoy the twinkle of city lights from Phoenix far below. The Georgia O'Keeffe mural, monogrammed silver, and linens create the feeling that you are a most welcome guest in a gracious and beautifully staffed private home. There are designated tables in the dining room for smokers. Luncheon and dinner may be served in your room.

DRESS CODE: You'll find your class uniform in your room when you arrive—a tank suit for exercise and pool and a pink terry cloth robe. Do pack soft slippers or sneakers to wear going between classes. The reservations manager suggests you bring along a shawl or wrap as the evening mountain air is cool. She goes on to say, "For dinner at Maine Chance we wear at-home caftans and pajamas, easy hostess gowns, or simple cocktail dresses." You'll be comfortable with diamonds or without any night of the week.

ACCOMMODATIONS: Guest accommodations are located in the main house as well as in cottages placed strategically about the grounds. Your room is a pleasant retreat, with its own distinctive decorative scheme, ample closets, books, and flowers. There are flowers everywhere, every day, breathlessly fresh and fragrant! Treasured French and Italian antique furniture and objets d'art are tastefully used for guest accommodations as well as in the main house. Each guest has her own personal maid who will help you unpack and who magically appears when you need her. There are different priced accommodations available, both single and double. The staff at Maine Chance will try to give you the same room on return visits if you so request.

HOUSE RULES: Elizabeth Arden believed that a quiet place is necessary for your well-being. This concept of peace, serenity, and privacy pervades the atmosphere.

PHYSICAL FACILITIES: Maine Chance is tucked away at the end of an unpaved road. There are no signs to indicate that a unique beauty resort is located here. This is your first clue that everything has been thought out, with your personal pleasure and comfort in mind. The main house, guest houses, and treatment areas all nestle into famous Camelback Mountain. By Elizabeth Arden's own design in 1945, each building is strategically located to afford the best possible view of the magnificent mountain. One young mother explains, "There are beautiful views everywhere—from the massage table or the Ardena wax table, from the tennis court, or from your own room." The Main Chance gardens offer both beauty and whimsy—places for you to muse and be amused. Viewed from the air, Main Chance appears a study in shadings and textures of green, dotted here and there with chalk white houses and turquoise pools. A lot of thought went into the planning, and the special setting makes you feel special.

The treatment complex includes the chart room (where all scheduling is done), exercise rooms, exercise pool, whirlpools, saunas, steam cabinets, and extensive beauty areas for facials, massage, Ardena wax treatments, and hair and nail care. There are outdoor and indoor swimming pools and an outdoor tennis court. A smashing boutique with a large selection of evening wear—in case you didn't bring your own—completes the fantasy.

ACTIVITIES, TREATMENTS AND PROGRAMS: The "Class" day begins early each morning and lasts until midafternoon. The program lasts a full six days and includes a balance of pampering and improvement that has been meticulously thought out with your special needs in mind. The exercises were developed by Marjorie Craig, who believes in gentle exercise geared to toning and flexibility rather than pounding aerobics. The staff takes into consideration your age and condition before placing you in any exercise class. Four classes are offered daily, one of which is a water exercise session. Some of the daily treatments (devised by Pablo Mazzoni for Elizabeth Arden) are facial, massage, scalp massage and hair treatment, whirlpool, steam cabinet, and sauna. Other beauty treatments you'll enjoy during the week include hand and foot massages, makeup classes, manicure/pedicure, shampoo and set, and the unique Ardena paraffin wax wrap (two per week).

The purpose of the Ardena wrap is to rid the body of excess water and impurities. First, you climb naked into a trough lined with wax paper. If you tend toward claustrophobia, leave your arms hanging outside. The attendant pours warm melted paraffin over your body, putting a bit more where the skin is thickest. Then you are wrapped in wax paper and covered with a blanket to keep the warmth in. You are given ice chips for your brow and lips. The treatment lasts about thirty minutes, and when you are "properly baked," the wax paper is removed and the wax is easily peeled off. You skin feels refreshed, you feel renewed (you may even lose a pound or more), and you trot off to your massage.

Evening programs arranged by your hostess might include an evening meeting with the chef or a lecturer on Southwestern Indian culture. Bingo is a weekly event, with beautifully wrapped prizes from the boutique. Then again, you may prefer good conversation in the drawing room or hopping off to Scottsdale for shopping.

A Day at Maine Chance

7:30	Breakfast in bed
9:30	Mat exercise (simple limbering and toning; you'll learn to move every muscle as nature intended)
	Steam cabinet (on alternate days sauna, Ardena wax, bath, or whirlpool)
10:00	Massage
11:00	Water exercise
11:30	Face treatment (cleansing, toning, and moisturizing)
12:30	Hair and nails (daily scalp treatment)
1:00	Luncheon
2:30	Makeup class
3:30	Mat exercise
4:00	Scotch shower (alternate sprays of hot and cold water)
6:45	Happy Hour
7:00	Dinner
10:00	Bedtime

STAFF POPULATION: Each guest has her personal attendant, and the staff-to-client ratio is 2 to 1. One first-time visitor from Houston drawled, "The personnel really seem to like what they do—they're gentle and seem happy. They're discreet and don't intrude. If you don't want to talk, they don't chatter."

OPTIONAL COSTS: Private tennis lessons can be arranged with a pro from John Gardiner's Tennis Ranch (located just the other side of the mountain). You can go there for morning instruction or an instructor may come to Maine Chance for a late afternoon lesson.

NICE TO KNOW: The founder, Elizabeth Arden, was born a Canadian truck driver's daughter who built a mutli-million-dollar beauty business. Every detail at Maine Chance was beautifully planned and well thought out by her. For example, leg-waxing and defuzzing treatments are included in your week's stay, [and aren't at other comparable posh spas]. Don't be put off by the stringent telephone interview—it's for your own benefit. Maine Chance maintains an Old World charm and graciousness that precludes guests being addressed on a first-name basis.

JUDY'S COMMENTS: From the moment the chauffeur meets you at the airport in Phoenix, personal responsibilities, chores, and obligations are left behind. All routine decisions are made for you, freeing you to begin your beauty renaissance.

TWO

NATURAL HEALTH RETREATS

4
Caring for
the Whole Person

In case you haven't noticed, there's a revolution going on. It's a non-violent one and its leaders have strange-sounding titles such as naturopath and homeopath. Its rallying cries are simple: natural is better; you are what you eat; back to the basics; treat the whole person. Its opponents are powerful and entrenched: chiefly, the organized medicine establishment and the fast-food industry—those forces that, intentionally or not, keep us fat, supposedly happy, and depending on others to cure what might not have ailed us in the first place if we had understood what was good for us.

Many of the health and fitness revolution's followers have a crusading enthusiasm, and even you may be among the revolutionary ranks if:

- You're worried about nitrates or other cancer-causing agents in your food.
- You've started reading the fine print on packaged foods.
- You're eating less red meat than you used to.
- You take massive doses of vitamin C when you have a cold.

Admit it. Today you probably accept, or at least wonder about, ideas that you would have laughed at—or ignored—a few years ago. Take a closer look at what's going on today in nutrition and fitness and ten or twenty years from now you may be thankful you did.

THE WHOLISTIC TRUTH

Wholistic (or holistic) is the term used to describe healing methods from acupuncture to Zen macrobiotics that deal with the whole person: body, mind, emotions, and spirit.

Wholistic healing is based on the belief that, given the right enviroment—air, food, water, space—the healthy person can maintain what's often called "high-level wellness" and the sick can heal themselves.

The wholistic approach rests on the idea that the patient is responsible for his own health. This idea is as old as Hippocrates. But in recent years a combination of blind faith in modern medicine and neglect of good health practices has resulted in an abdication of patient responsibility. Nutritionist Lillian Grant observes that many sick people approach a doctor much as they approach a car mechanic. "Here's the machine; fix it fast," they say. The wholistic physician, rejecting that attitude, insists that each individual take charge of his or her own well-being.

The wholistic practitioners pay attention to how you eat, breathe, stand, sit, laugh, and cry rather than relying on lab tests, drugs, and surgery. To treat every aspect of well-being, many practitioners go far beyond what traditional medicine considers its province. "We get people to read books," says Dr. Donald Tubesing, director of the Duluth, Minnesota, Institute for Whole Person Association (IWPA). "Or we find places for them to do volunteer work, or we'll send them to health farms, marriage encounter weekends, and workshops. We often put people in touch with support groups." When a problem does require medication or surgery, patients are given appropriate direction at IWPA: "Whatever they need—laboratory tests, or a swift kick—we try hard to listen and respond."

The practice of dealing with the whole person is refreshing in our age of "specialists." Too often, traditionally trained physicians are ignorant of basic nutritional facts and other vital aspects of preventive medicine. Their training is geared to the treatment of disease, not to the maintenance of good health. We're hard put to find a doctor today who isn't narrowed into a speciality—the knee, wrist, nose, throat, etc. Such doctors are often, unfortunately, oblivious to the rest of you.

Wholistic practitioners, on the other hand, believe that illness is your body's way of telling you something. What it is saying is that something is wrong with your way of life—possibly a too-rich diet or too much stress, our number-one enemy. They see disease not as something you "catch," but as something you have had a hand in creating—and as something you can take a hand in curing.

NUTRITION

Belief in the value of vegetarianism and organic foods is the core of the wholistic philosophy, which harks back to a simpler way of life. First, it was artisan-craftsmen who cultivated their own fresh herbs in little clay pots and ground their grain the hard way, with stone mortars and pestles as their great-grandmothers did. Then, vegetarianism caught on with teenagers squeamish about chewing on what could have been someone's pet. Finally, with the rising price of meat—and current findings of medical research about the effect of diet on the most common "killer" diseases—hale and hearty bread-

winners and little old ladies began hopping onto the fruit and vegetable bandwagon. Purists won't eat chicken, fish, whole milk, or
eggs—anything of animal origin.

Natural food proponents point out that food can cause or cure
disease, depending on where it comes from, what it's made of, and
how it's prepared and consumed. Fresh greens from the good earth
have unequaled therapeutic power. They're high in vitamins A and
C, iron, and potassium. They're easily digested and neutralize acids
in your system.

Organically grown vegetables are the staple of all these places.
Some serve cheese, eggs, milk, and even chicken or fish twice a week,
depending on their particular philosophy. (Meadowlark in Hemet,
California, is one of these, as is Rancho La Puerta in Tecate, Mexico.)
The dairy products are usually low-fat, such as skim milk, cottage
cheese, and yogurt. (Rancho La Puerta serves acidophilus milk, a cross
between Bulgarian buttermilk and yogurt.)

Most vegetarians avoid not only red meat but all processed foods.
They use brown whole-grain products that haven't had the nutrients
bleached out.

Rancho La Puerta serves a marvelous Tecate Brown Bread. The
Golden Door has this version, which can be found in Deborah Szekely's book, *Secrets of the Golden Door.*

WHOLE WHEAT TECATE BREAD

2 packages yeast
4 cups warm water (105–115°)
2 tablespoons honey
½ cup polyunsaturated oil
7½–8 cups stone-ground whole
wheat flour

Place yeast in a very large bowl. Add warm water and stir. Blend in
honey and oil. While beating with an electric mixer, add flour gradually until dough pulls off the beaters cleanly. Turn dough out onto
a floured board and knead until dough is no longer sticky. To knead,
fold the dough toward you, pushing the outer edge of the dough
down, toward you, and then away from you with the heel of your
hands. The dough is ready when it is silky and feels slightly bouncy.
The kneading will take about 8–10 minutes.

Place the dough in an oiled bowl, turning the dough once to oil
the top. Cover with a clean cloth and allow to rise in a warm, draft-
free spot until doubled in bulk: about 1 hour. You can check to see
if dough is ready by pressing the top with your finger. If a dent re-
mains, the dough has risen enough.

Punch the dough down; divide it in half and roll each half into
a 12″ × 15″ oblong. Starting at the narrow end, roll dough up, jel-
lyroll fashion. Seal seam and fold over each end 1″. Place, seam side
down, in a greased 9″ × 5″ × 3″ bread pan. Cover and allow to rise
again until doubled in bulk: about 1 hour.

Bake in a preheated 375° oven for 50–60 minutes, or until the loaf is well browned and has a hollow sound when rapped on top.

Cool bread on racks. To freeze, wrap in moisture- and vapor-proof wrapping paper, pressing out as much air as possible.

While I'm at it, here's my own favorite healthy dessert bread recipe:

JUDY'S WHOLE WHEAT ZUCCHINI BREAD

3 cups whole wheat flour
4 teaspoons baking powder
1/2 cup polyunsaturated oil
1/2 cup honey
4 eggs
1 cup milk
2 teaspoons vanilla

1 cup red apple, chopped
1 cup chopped nuts
2 cups grated zucchini
1 cup crushed pineapple, drained
1 cup chopped dates

Line two 9" × 5" loaf pans with waxed paper. Mix flour and baking powder together and set aside. Cream oil with honey and add eggs, one at a time, beating after each addition. Add milk alternately with flour mixture. Stir in zucchini, nuts, pineapple, dates, and vanilla. Pour into baking pans and bake at 350° for 40–45 minutes, until brown on top and a toothpick inserted in the middle comes out clean. Allow to cool 10–15 minutes in the pans. Finish cooling on a rack.

This bread freezes well and is good at breakfast or later in the day with tea. Approximate calories per loaf, 2,224; per slice (14 slices to the loaf), 158.

I freeze these breads and give them as hostess gifts, along with natural clover honey. Your guests will beg you for more!

FASTING

Fasting, in a way, is easier than dieting. When you're dieting, you have to think constantly about food: what to eat, what not to eat. While preparing or ordering low-cal food, you're likely to feel like Ulysses with the siren Circe beckoning him to disaster. There you are, surrounded by food, and you have to measure it in stingy amounts or blow your diet. When fasting, you can remove yourself from temptation altogether.

When you fast, you lose weight by abstaining from calories and you purify your body by getting rid of accumulated wastes and poisons. Fasting gives your gastrointestinal system a rest so your body can concentrate its energy on clearing out unwanted waste residues built up from years of stress, junk foods, and inadequate exercise. At the same time, you'll probably lose several pounds by getting rid of excess liquids lodged in your body cells and held there by salt you've been eating. Wholistic practitioners say it takes three days to detoxify a body that has been filling up with junk food for years.

Some natural health retreats offer colonic cleansing or a daily enema flushing to help get rid of impacted wastes. The prospect may not sound appealing, but colonic cleansing is actually not at all unpleasant; it is easier and more soothing than a Fleet enema. Colonics leave you feeling like a new person. Most retreats offer both methods. Check to see whether or not it's compulsory.

But be careful. I would not advise anyone—particularly an older person who lacks the resilience of youth or a teenager still in his or her "growing" years—to go into a fast without close expert supervision. In addition, if you have heart disease, bleeding ulcers, diabetes, gout, hypoglycemia, or any condition requiring medical care, you are not a good candidate for fasting. If you don't know what you're doing, fasting can be injurious to your health.

At natural health retreats you'll be under the watchful eyes of experts. Your teachers will break you into the fast gradually, easing you away from standard food and onto raw vegetables and juices, then air and water if you're up to it. Afterward, they'll bring you back to reality gradually to give your body a chance to readapt to food. Most retreats send you off with instructions for returning to a normal diet at home.

Another word of warning: in the early stages of fasting, you may experience mild fever, nausea, headaches, diarrhea, depression, fatigue, darkened urine, bad breath, and/or profuse perspiration. Don't be alarmed. These symptoms go along with the sudden release of accumulated toxins and will subside as the crisis passes, leaving you purified and full of new vitality.

WHAT TO EXPECT AT NATURAL HEALTH RETREATS

First, let's talk about what not to expect. You generally won't find the fancy resort facilities, pampering treatments, and expensive exercise equipment available at deluxe mainstream spas. Exercise at most natural health retreats is more low-key: brisk walking, yoga, and minirebounders (small trampolines). Meditation is often emphasized. Massage may or may not be available.

Two high-powered fitness retreats should be mentioned here as exceptions to the rule because of their heavy emphasis on vigorous exercise along with their vegetarian, wholistic-based philosophy. They are Ashram in California and Rancho La Puerta in Mexico. Both are also more expensive than other vegetarian retreats.

Most natural health retreats are quite small and take only a limited number of guests. Many have a communal flavor. You may share chores and learn how to prepare the foods. The atmosphere is usually casual and family style. Because of the simple menu and accommodations, the cost is usually relatively low.

The two constants at natural health retreats are a vegetarian diet and an educational emphasis. The weight control benefits of such a diet are obvious; it takes a heap of string beans to equal the caloric count of one chocolate eclair. But vegetarians attribute more positive values to their diet than the mere absence of fattening foods. They believe that eating the natural way can help rejuvenate your mind, body, and soul and build up resistance to disease.

5
NATURAL HEALTH RETREATS: DIRECTORY

WHY, WHERE, AND HOW MUCH

The chief criterion for inclusion in this category is that major emphasis is placed on diet and nutrition. A vegetarian program is basic to virtually all of these facilities. Fasting may or may not be part of the program.

Cost is based on a one-week stay in high season, double occupancy, including tax and gratuities. Meals are included unless specifically stated otherwise: Best Buys are indicated by an asterisk.

Affordable: up to $1,000
Moderate: $1,000–$1,700
Expensive: $1,700 and up

THE ASHRAM
P.O. Box 8009
Calabasas, CA 91302
818-888-0232

A Spartan retreat located in a secluded valley surrounded by mountains and running streams. Open year-round.

RATES: Expensive. No credit cards.

LOCATION AND TRANSPORTATION: The Ashram is 30 minutes west of Los Angeles and 10 minutes from the Pacific. Pickup service is scheduled at 12:00 noon Sundays at the Marriott Hotel, 5 minutes from Los Angeles Airport, or at 12:45 P.M. at the Valley Hotel Hilton (corner of San Diego and Ventura freeways). Return transportation is provided the following Saturday at noon, so flights home should be booked no earlier than 2:00 P.M.

EMPHASIS/PHILOSOPHY: Here you'll encounter an intensive program of exercise and diet in the pursuit of health both within and without. 'Ashram" means spiritual retreat. Dr. Anne Marie Bennstrom, founder and renowned preventive health authority, says, "We come to this type of place not so much to lose weight, but to restore our broken connection between ourselves, our inner selves, and nature. If your mind is awakened, your body will follow."

DIET PROGRAM: There's no calorie counting on the Ashram's vegetarian fare. The diet consists of fresh raw fruits and vegetables, nuts, juices, and herbal teas. No coffee or saccharin is served. Breakfast consists of freshly squeezed orange juice; lunch is generally yogurt and cottage cheese with fruit or vegetables; and dinner is a make-it-yourself salad with Hidden Valley dressing. Two juice breaks consisting of zucchini, parsley, and celery are offered each day. A weight loss of 10 pounds for the week is not uncommon.

GUEST POPULATION: Coed. 10 guests. Celebrity guests have included Barbra Streisand, Zsa Zsa Gabor, and Raquel Welch.

PACKAGES AND MINIMUM STAYS: The basic and only program is for one week: 6 nights and 7 days. Arrive Sunday afternoon; depart Saturday after lunch.

MEAL SERVICE: Informal meal service is provided in the dining room.

DRESS CODE: Very informal. The Ashram furnishes sweatsuits, T-shirts, robes and caftans. They suggest you bring walking shoes, a bathing suit, and a jacket or sweater for cool mornings and evenings. Except for personal items, they discourage bringing clothing or belongings.

ACCOMMODATIONS: Guests stay in pleasant double rooms with a Mexican flavor. If you come alone, you will be expected to share a room with a stranger. There are three bathrooms, which are shared by all. There are no room telephones or TVs at this retreat.

HOUSE RULES: No smoking is allowed. Personal cars on the premises are not permitted. Phone calls are discouraged.

PHYSICAL FACILITIES: A two-story stucco building serves as headquarters at The Ashram. Besides guest accommodations, the first floor has a comfortable living room with library shelves and a fireplace, kitchen, and dining room. Upstairs are the weight room and gymnasium, which has a wall of windows overlooking the hillside.

Behind the building is a small, heated pool and a geodesic dome where yoga and meditation sessions are held; there is an attached solarium. A volleyball court is on the grounds. The retreat is surrounded by miles of hiking trails.

ACTIVITIES, TREATMENTS, AND PROGRAMS: You will be thoroughly checked by the resident chiropractor upon arrival. Daily activities include two meditation sessions; two hikes (2½ hours and 1½ hours long); a one-hour weight training class and gym workout; one hour of pool exercises; a half-hour jog; and one hour of exercise to music (stretching and aerobics). Each guest receives a one-hour massage daily—you need it! Occasional volleyball games, evening movies, discussions about health and nutrition, and home follow-up suggestions round out the day's events.

A Day at The Ashram

6:30	Morning meditation
7:00	Wake-up
7:30	Breakfast
8:00	Morning hike
11:00	Gym and workout with weights
12:00	Water exercise
1:00	Lunch
1:30	Free time for resting and sunning
3:00	Massage
4:00	Walk/jog
4:30	Exercise to music
5:30	Evening walk
7:00	Yoga and meditation
8:30	Dinner
9:00	Evening program
10:00	Bedtime

OPTIONAL COSTS: Colonics and enemas (highly recommended by the Ashram) are extra.

NICE TO KNOW: Dr. Anne Marie Bennstrom, who founded the Ashram in the mid-seventies, holds a medical degree from Sweden but does not practice in the United States. She was formerly associated with the Golden Door. Staff members stay with the guests round the clock and are readily available for consultation. Tears from pain and exhaustion are common responses to the strenuous activities at The Ashram, but sharing these feelings and experiences produces a strong camaraderie among the participants in the program.

JUDY'S COMMENT: If you're ready to be toughened in mind and body and you love vegetarian food, sharing bathrooms, and being at one with nature, try The Ashram.

BLUEGRASS SPA
901 Galloway Road
Stamping Ground, KY 40379
502-535-6261

Open from April to early November only. Located in the lush blue-grass horse country of Stamping Ground, Kentucky, is a tranquil wholistic fitness retreat just a few miles north of Lexington. The "Manor House," an antebellum mansion in Greek Revival style, is surrounded by 30 acres of rolling hills and farmland. Clustered nearby are some of the guest houses.

RATES: Moderate. MasterCard, Visa.

LOCATION AND TRANSPORTATION: The Bluegrass is just north of Lexington, Kentucky, with free transportation available to and from Lexington airport. The spa is 65 miles from both Louisville and Cincinnati. Ground transportation from these cities is available for $30 each way.

EMPHASIS/PHILOSOPHY: Bluegrass Spa exists as a wholistic and tranquil center for renewal. Its programs are based on life enhancement; its environment supports a dedication to the individual's well-being. Since Bluegrass is small and intimate, the emphasis is on catering to each individual's needs and goals.

DIET PROGRAM: Modified Pritikin program 900–1,200 calories per day. Fish, chicken, and vegetables are served but no red meat. Meals are low in fat, high in fiber, low in sugar, and without salt. Most vegetables and herbs come from the spa's own organic garden. According to the chef/director Nancy Rutherford, "Counting calories is unimportant . . . if you eat fat, you get fat . . . Here you'll enjoy eating spa cuisine with a touch of Southern elegance." Both weight loss and maintenance and nondiet plans are available (with larger portions of food given to nondieters).
   A typical Bluegrass spa menu would consist of:

BREAKFAST
Baked Cinnamon Grapefruit with Blueberry Bran Muffins (150)

10:30
Tangerine Snack (39)

LUNCH
Shrimp-Asparagus and Grapefruit Salad with Horseradish Dressing
   (200)

NATURAL HEALTH RETREATS   239

3:30
Banana Popsicle (58)

DINNER
Spicy Confetti Slaw (58)
or
Cheese Potato Soup (54)
Chicken à l'Orange with Wild Rice (245)
or
Sweet and Sour Stir Fry Veggies with Brown Rice (274)
Cheesecake with Fruit Sauce (138)
or
Chocolate Mousse (50)

GUEST POPULATION: Coed. 8 to 12 guests. Couples do come, but there are usually more women than men. Often there are mother-daughter teams.

PACKAGES AND MINIMUM STAYS: The basic one-week program includes 6 days and 6 nights. A two-week program (at a discount) is also available as well as a "spa day" offering. There is no minimum stay requirement.

MEAL SERVICE: Your meal schedule begins with breakfast at 8:15, followed by vegetable or fruit snack at 10:30, lunch at 12:15, vegetable or fruit snack at 3:30, and dinner at 6:30. Dinner is served by candlelight in the spa's elegant dining room (part of the original mansion built in 1813) and is utterly romantic. The service is elegant, with fine crystal and china, lace tablecloths, and fresh flowers.

DRESS CODE: For dinner, jogging outfits are acceptable despite the formal ambience of the setting. According to Rutherford, "The mood at Bluegrass Spa is informal, and comfort is the watchword—so bring clothing you can relax in." The spa suggests you bring an outfit to wear "on our afternoon or evening out on the town." Casual pants or even a jogging outfit would be fine for an evening at nearby Red Mile Racetrack.

ACCOMMODATIONS: No telephones or televisions are in the rooms in order to maintain the feeling of relaxation and inner serenity. It is possible to use the receptionist Anna's telephone. Yes, the rooms are air conditioned. Diverse types of accommodations are available. For example, there are three or four rooms with private baths, as well as charming double rooms that share showers, sinks, and commodes. Some rooms offer fireplaces, others are furnished in brilliant colors with white wicker furniture and antiques, and still others offer intimacy and Kentucky memorabilia. The rooms are designed to add

to the guests' feelings of tranquillity and total comfort. Those planning to stay an extra week are guests of the spa from Friday night
until Saturday evening dinner. Maid service is available every day
except Saturday.

HOUSE RULES: The spa doesn't permit the use of alcohol or tobacco on its grounds.

PHYSICAL FACILITIES: Outdoor facilities include pool area, outdoor exercise pavilion, tennis court, nearby golf course, nearby riding
stable, and an ample supply of bicycles (a lot of biking and walking
are done on the small country roads). Indoor facilities include laundry
room, beauty salon, sauna, and Jacuzzi.

ACTIVITIES, TREATMENTS AND PROGRAMS: Rates include
all exercise and fitness classes, all lectures, workshops, and other classes—10 or more each week. Lecture topics can range from hearing a
trans-medium speak to a look at the birds and flowers of Kentucky.
Walking tours are scheduled three times a day. Guests have unlimited
use of the library and audio- and videotapes, unlimited use of bikes,
free transportation to all spa outings, and admission to all sports and
games (golf and horseback riding at small extra charge). Treatments
included in your weekly program are: three 1-hour Swedish massage,
one spa special facial, and choice of one bodywork or beauty treatment from the list of available services.

A Day at Bluegrass Spa

7:00	Morning bell
7:15	Guests gather for stretching, followed by a walk/run
8:15	Breakfast
9:00–9:45	Wake-up head-to-toe stretching
10:00–10:30	Love Me, Love My Cardio-Aerobics
10:30–11:15	Put That Back Where it Belongs toning
11:30–12:00	Letting go of stress relaxation
12:15	Lunch
12:45	Brisk walk
1:15–1:45	Short lecture e.g., "Caffeine—the Ac-ceptable Addiction"
2:00–6:00	Choose from: What Goes Up! (mini trampoline) Aquacizes (pool exercise) Massage & physical therapies Beauty works Sauna-Jacuzzi Outings

Workshops
Yoga
6:30 Dinner
7:30 Evening stroll
8:00 Program and dancing, "Introduction to Meditation," etc.

STAFF POPULATION: Cathleen Lindhardy has been a registered nurse for twelve years and is currently working on a medical anthropology degree. Cathleen is well versed in New Age techniques. She gives all kinds of massages including: Swedish, shiatsu, Traeger, reflexology, and polarity and teaches T'ai Chi and stress management.

OPTIONAL COSTS: There are 25 optional treatments, including bodyworks, hand and foot treatments, and waxing and tinting lashes and brows.

NICE TO KNOW: Bluegrass is just beginning its spa boutique, which as of this writing sells sweatsuits and postcards, with more items scheduled in the near future. In the meantime, if any of the guests need anything, Nancy goes to town daily. A golf country club is right around the corner, with 18 holes for a small greens fee. It is my understanding that Charles Rutherford is available to give golf lessons as well as to play tennis with guests desiring a partner. Should any of the guests desire to go riding, a nearby farm offers both Western and English styles. The three daily walks are taken along the quiet, country roads surrounding the spa since the grounds themselves are too hilly for fast-paced walking. It's nice to know that this spa allows you to use your own discretion regarding gratuities. Personally, I always leave a tip when receiving any service, but it might be a good idea to ask Nancy or Anna about protocol. Another nicety is that the spa gives out recipes for their guests to take home. The Bluegrass Diet can be comfortably followed in daily life, according to Nancy Rutherford.

JUDY'S COMMENT: This is a wholistic and individualized experience in weight loss and developing a lifelong program of health and fitness. The program enables guests to find tranquillity in a lovely environment.

CREATIVE HEALTH INSTITUTE
918 Union City Road
Union City, MI 49094
517-278-6260

The Institute lies on the banks of the Coldwater River near Union City, a small village abundant with wildlife and natural beauty. Open year-round.

RATES: Affordable. No credit cards.

LOCATION AND TRANSPORTATION: Situated on 300 acres, 30 miles south of Battle Creek, Michigan, and about three hours by car from Chicago. Transportation is provided from Battle Creek by the Institute if advance notice is given.

EMPHASIS/PHILOSOPHY: Optimum health through raw foods and natural methods is the aim of this nutritional learning center. The Institute was formerly called Hippocrates Midwest and was associated with the Hippocrates World Health Organization of Boston, which was founded by Ann Wigmore, N.D., D.D. Beliefs are based on the concept that the body is self-healing and self-regulating when provided with the proper conditions. They subscribe to the teaching of Hippocrates: "Let food be thy medicine."

DIET PROGRAM: The vegetarian diet consists solely of raw seeds, nuts, fruits, vegetables, and sprouts. Everyone fasts the first three days of the program. ("Learn to put a garden in your glass," says the Institute.) Seeds are ground up to make seed cheeses. Fermented wheatgrass (Rejuvelac) functions as a cleanser of the system. According to Mavis Haughey, founder/director, the average weight loss during the two-week program can be 19–24 pounds if you participate in walking and exercise. There is no calorie counting on the Living Food Diet.

GUEST POPULATION: Coed. 18 rooms house 36 guests. Most guests come to cure illness. However, those folks who want to lose weight or detoxify feel comfortable in this center of learning. All guests must be self-sufficient and ambulatory.

PACKAGES AND MINIMUM STAYS: One week is the minimum— in on Sunday before 1 P.M., out on Sunday, although an intensive weekend is sometimes available. The recommended stay is 2 weeks for the complete "learn by doing" program. Every Sunday there is an Open House, when guests and the public may enjoy the lovely raw buffet as well as a tour of the grounds. A 4-week stay is suggested for people with serious health problems.

MEAL SERVICE: Casual, buffet-style service at all meals.

DRESS CODE: Informal; jogging outfits or sweatsuits are fine.

ACCOMMODATIONS: Private and semiprivate rooms, with four to a bath. No telephones or television. Radios are allowed at very low volume.

HOUSE RULES: No smoking on the premises.

PHYSICAL FACILITIES: There is an exercise room and acres of gardens, where most of the food you'll eat is grown organically. A health food store is on premises.

ACTIVITIES, TREATMENTS, AND PROGRAMS: There are five exercise hours per day, which offer aerobics, yoga, breathing, and so on. Classes and evening programs include lectures and films on topics such as juice fasting, indoor organic gardening, positive thinking, the roll of enzymes, colon health, faith in nature, and occasional live entertainment. This is a "learn by doing" program, and after the first three days of fasting you will sprout your own sprouts and plant your own wheatgrass and greens.

A Day at the Creative Health Institute

7:30	Group exercise class
8:30	Breakfast
10:00	Green drinks
11:00	Class
12:00	Lunch
1:30	Class
3:00	Green drinks
5:30	Dinner
7:30	Class

OPTIONAL COSTS: Colonics, reflexology, massage.

NICE TO KNOW: The Institute is set in a beautiful natural setting replete with birds and small wildlife, very conducive to nature walks and reflection. Guests are invited to participate in the organic gardening that supplies much of the produce eaten and sold.

JUDY'S COMMENT: This is a good introduction to vegetarianism and detoxification, which can be quite difficult for a healthy person to pursue at home. For those so motivated, the testimonials of health reversals with this natural approach are impressive indeed!

Courtesy of The Heartland Health and Fitness Retreat

THE HEARTLAND HEALTH AND FITNESS RETREAT
Gilman, IL 60938
Chicago reservations office: 312-266-2050
815-683-2182

A rustic retreat set on the 31-acre Kam Lake Estate, which boasts a 3-acre lake and beautiful woods and meadows. Open year-round.

RATES: Moderate. Credit cards: American Express, MasterCard, Visa.

LOCATION AND TRANSPORTATION: Located 80 miles south of Chicago in the heart of the Midwest. Courtesy transportation is provided from O'Hare Airport and downtown Chicago to the spa.

EMPHASIS/PHILOSOPHY: Through a carefully designed program of sensible eating, vigorous exercise, and stress management techniques, you'll achieve a new level of fitness and the ability to make desirable life-style changes.

DIET PROGRAM: 1,200 calories daily for women, 1,500 for men. According to Susan Witz, Director of Nutrition, "Calories don't really matter if you modify your style of eating and increase your physical activity on a regular basis." Menus are mainly vegetarian, including fresh fruits, vegetables, and whole grains; fish is served twice a week. No sugar, no salt, no white flour is used. I was also told that toasted sesame seeds and a lot of kelp are used in the preparation of meals in lieu of salt. For those desiring to lose more weight, a blitz plate (consisting of greens, raw vegetables, and low-fat cottage cheese) is available for dinner. Ethnic foods such as Turkish dishes with bulgur wheat, Greek and Israeli salads, and Japanese vegetable sushi (vegetables wrapped in seaweed) are served. Delectable natural desserts such as sorbet (a frozen concoction of fresh fruits and dairy products), baked flan, fresh strawberries, and tofu cheesecake are also featured. Heartland can accommodate special diet needs—for marathon runners or those with allergies, for example—if advance notice is given. How much can you lose? Michael Livesay, Director, who got the program off to a good start, says, "With this vigorous regimen, a pound a day is not unheard of."

Here is an example of one day's fare at The Heartland:

BREAKFAST
Melon slice with lime
2 Heartland muffins
Mock cream cheese

SNACK
Vegetables with yogurt dip

LUNCH
Endive salad with buttermilk dressing
Grilled trout
Brown rice
Green beans

SNACK
Fruit cup

SUPPER
Dilled carrot soup
Corn crepes with spinach soufflé
Grilled tomato with feta cheese

DESSERT
Baked apple with cranberries and walnuts

GUEST POPULATION: Coed. 28 guests. A mix of professionals, executives, and homemakers, mostly from the Midwest.

PACKAGES AND MINIMUM STAYS: There are 5-day and 7-day packages plus a 2-day weekend plan—in on Friday afternoon, out Sunday afternoon. For the 5-day program, check in Sunday between 3:00 and 4:00, check out Friday by noon.

MEAL SERVICE: All meals are served in the charming wood-paneled dining room with floor-to-ceiling windows that overlook the lake.

DRESS CODE: The Heartland provides robes, sweatsuits, shorts, T-shirts, slippers, jackets, rainwear, hat and gloves, and even leisure wear! For dinner one may wear the spa's togs or one's own casual outfits.

ACCOMMODATIONS: The main house has a country inn ambience, with hand-pegged wood floors, wood-paneled walls, chintz-patterned furniture, and cozy fireplaces in both the living room and library. Guest rooms are small but comfortable with two double beds, bath, bedside tables—a Laura Ashley look, perhaps. Each room comes equipped with a clock radio and cassette player. No TV or telephones in the rooms. They'll provide a roommate if you wish.

HOUSE RULES: No smoking anywhere indoors.

PHYSICAL FACILITIES: An underground tunnel leads from the main house to the three-story converted barn that serves as a fitness and treatment center. The first floor houses separate spas for both men and women, which include whirlpools, saunas, steam rooms, cold plunge pools, showers, locker rooms, massage rooms, and facial rooms. The second floor is the gymnasium, which houses the Super Circuit Training Course (Cam II equipment, Exercycles, StairMaster, and rowing machines). All the non-high–tech exercise activity takes place on the third floor—a huge, mirrored room with ballet bars. The barn overlooks an Olympic-size covered pool of four-foot depth, good for both water classes and lap swimming. Two outdoor tracks (one with a twenty-station parcours, the other encircling the lake) offer the walker/jogger beautiful vistas. Summer activities include outdoor tennis, and in winter there is cross-country skiing and ice-skating on the lake. A boutique is on the premises.

ACTIVITIES, TREATMENTS, AND PROGRAMS: Upon arrival each guest receives a health evaluation assessment, consisting of a body fat test and dietary analysis. Daily exercises include calisthenics with floor mats, pool exercise, Super Circuit Training Class (using Cam II machines), alternating aerobic activity with stationary bicycles and trampoline, free weights class, spot or body toning, folk dancing, jazz exercise, and a special fun dance class. Included in your rate are a daily half-hour massage and one facial. Additional massages and personal care services are available at modest cost. An impressive lecture schedule covers such topics as techniques for dealing with stress, cardiovascular health, preventing disease through sound nutrition, how to eat out and still stay fit, how to look and feel young, personal financial planning, and assertiveness training. There also are cooking demonstrations by the chef. Widescreen video movies are shown nightly.

A Day at The Heartland

7:00	Wake-up
7:15	Morning stretch and walk
8:00	Breakfast
9:00	Race walking or Heartbeat (light to intermediate exercise)
10:15	Snack
10:30	Waterworks (pool class, all levels)
12:30	Lunch
1:15	Heartland Institute (lecture)
2:00	Major Motion (intermediate to advanced exercise) or Free Weights
3:15	Snack
3:30	Apparatus muscle training (all levels)
4:30	Yoga (all levels)
6:00	Supper
7:00	All the Fun Moves or evening walk
8:00	Heartland Institute (lecture)
8:30	Dessert/Games/Movies

OPTIONAL COSTS: Facials and beauty care are extra. Makeup products are by Rene Guiont, distributed by Aida Thibiant, the well-known Beverly Hills cosmetician whose clients include Jane Fonda, Eva Gabor, and Rod Stewart. No preservatives are in these products.

NICE TO KNOW: Susan Witz, nutritionist and educational director, tells me that there are 30,000 marathon runners in the United States today, and the staff at Heartland feels that that merits a special target program. This is one of the few spas I've come across that offers a supervised program with gravity inversion boots (not good for those with high blood pressure). Heartland has its own greenhouse for growing herbs, and the fresh artesian well that feeds the lake is used for all drinking and bathing. There's a lovely contemplation spot near the well.

JUDY'S COMMENT: I'm most impressed with the fact that Heartland spa has incorporated concepts that guests can adapt to their own at-home regimen. Many spas fall short in this regard.

KRIPALU CENTER FOR YOGA AND HEALTH
P.O. Box 793
Lenox, MA 01240
413-637-3280

A yoga retreat on the 350-acre former Shadowbrook Estate. The Center has a private beach right on Lake Mahkeenac and views of the Berkshire Mountains. Open year-round.

RATES: Affordable. Credit cards: MasterCard, Visa.

LOCATION AND TRANSPORTATION: The Center is one hour east of Albany, New York. Fly into Albany or Hartford, Connecticut, airport. Limousine service or buses are available to Lenox.

EMPHASIS/PHILOSOPHY: Here you'll find a blend of Western and Eastern approaches for integrating mind and spirit; ways as ancient as yoga and as modern as biofeedback. Kripalu says, "The guidance and teachings of Yogi Amrit Desai provide the zest for life that is the spirit behind the Health Center. Yogi Desai has dedicated more than thirty years of his life to living and teaching the art of leading a vital, healthy, and integrated life-style through yoga. His presence conveys an inspiring message of what it means to live life fully."

DIET PROGRAM: The Center serves three vegetarian buffets daily, consisting of fresh, natural foods. There are soups, salads, homemade breads, and varied entrees rich in fiber and protein and free of preservatives. The Raw Juice Fasting Program, according to Kripalu, "gives your digestive system a period of rest and gives your body the opportunity to gather and focus its healing energy according to your individual requirements for rejuvenation." The diet program includes a raw juice diet, nutrition and cleansing workshops, and instruction in yogic purification techniques. The Conscious Eating for Permanent Weight Loss diet concentrates on "learning to give up dieting" and learning how to satisfy your mental and emotional needs are well as physical needs and learning to maintain weight loss through conscious eating."

GUEST POPULATION: Coed. There are over 40 guest accommodations.

PACKAGES AND MINIMUM STAYS: There is a wealth of programs at Kripalu Center: 2-night, 3-night, 6-night, 9-night, 13-night, 20-night, and 27-night. Each has particular objectives and specific courses. During July and August there is a 6-night minimum stay.

MEAL SERVICE: Meals are served buffet style, with servers for all three meals. Silence during meals is advocated to "create a contemplative atmosphere."

DRESS CODE: Casual and modest. Bring walking shoes and books.

ACCOMMODATIONS: Deluxe accommodations—semiprivate and private rooms—are limited. The "standard" accommodations are dormitory-style, with bunk beds or foam mats on the floor. Bring your own bed linens, towels, and pillow for dorm living.

HOUSE RULES: No smoking, alcohol, or nonprescription drugs allowed.

PHYSICAL FACILITIES: Guests enjoy a host of health and recreational facilities: sauna, hot tub, whirlpool, solarium, racquetball courts, large dining room, lounges, library, and jogging trails through the mountains. There is lake swimming in summer, and winter sports include ice skating, cross-country skiing, snowshoeing, and downhill skiing (bring your own equipment). There is a wholistic health center on the premises and a store that sells health foods, books, and tapes on vegetarian diet and wholistic health attitudes.

ACTIVITIES, TREATMENT, AND PROGRAMS: All programs include three meals daily, a morning walk, two yoga classes, one Danskinetics class (aerobics), use of the sauna and whirlpool (with separate facilities for men and women), and use of all Center facilities such as the reading room, solarium, meditation room, racquetball courts, jogging trails, and lake swimming. Evening programs include lectures on planning a balanced vegetarian diet, the body digestion process, and maintaining weight loss.

A Day at Kripalu Center

5:45	Wake-up walk or guided meditation or group walk
6:40	Yoga class
7:30	Breakfast
8:30	Lecture (sharing session)
10:00	Workshop or nature walk
11:45	Danskinetics (aerobics) or yoga relaxation
12:45	Lunch
1:30	Free Time
2:30	Workshop
4:30	Yoga/Meditation
5:30	Dinner
7:15	Satsanga (gathering for inspiration, dancing, chanting, and lecture) or evening workshop

OPTIONAL COSTS: Massages, foot reflexology, consultation, and treatments with wholistic health practitioners are extra.

NICE TO KNOW: No colonics here. Fasters are encouraged to hike and take yoga classes. Kripalu Center makes available a wide variety of programs including wholistic health education, prevention and rejuvenation through physical fitness, yogic diet, yoga therapy, counseling, communication skills, stress reduction, and other personal growth programs. The Center also trains yoga teachers, health professionals, therapists, counselors, and social workers as well as laymen interested in learning about yoga and wholistic health practices.

JUDY'S COMMENT: Kripalu Center is a renowned, respected retreat and health center with a long record of success in combating the onslaught—physical and emotional—of modern society. If you're interested in new ways to cope, try this.

MEADOWLARK HEALTH & GROWTH CENTER
26126 Fairview Avenue
Hemet, CA 92344
714-927-1343

Meadowlark is a twenty-acre estate, with rolling lawns and shady trees nestled at the foot of the San Jacinto Mountains. Open year-round, except the first two weeks of September and Thanksgiving week.

RATES: Affordable. No credit cards. Guests are required to prepay at the beginning of their stay. All treatments are extra.

LOCATION AND TRANSPORTATION: The Center is 100 miles southeast of Los Angeles. Fly into Ontario or Palm Springs airport; Pickup may be arranged from either at nominal charge.

EMPHASIS/PHILOSOPHY: Meadowlark describes the objective of its services as: "The rediscovery of the Whole Person. In this sense, an individual's health is regarded as a balance of well-being in body, mind, and spirit. An integrated combination of medicine, psychology, spirituality, and the arts provides the means of attaining this higher level of wellness." Each guest is encouraged to assume responsibility for his or her own health and well-being.

DIET PROGRAM: Well-balanced meals consist of complex carbohydrates (fresh fruits and vegetables, grains, seeds, and nuts). Fish and chicken are served twice a week, along with certified raw milk, yogurt, cottage and natural cheeses. No processed foods, caffeine, white sugar, or flour are used. Supervised fasting is available, but first-time fasters are required to enter a two-week program. An examination by a doctor is necessary to begin fasting, and a $25 charge is made for a "Faster's Kit." Although weight loss can be achieved by fasting, Meadowlark sees the process as "a truly rewarding experience, emotionally, spiritually, and psychologically."

GUEST POPULATION: Coed. 18–24 guests. Guests come to learn about wholistic practices, for spiritual renewals, and to learn effective coping mechanisms for today's stressful life demands.

PACKAGES AND MINIMUM STAYS: A 1-week stay is required. A 2-week stay is required for first-time fasters. Arrive on Sunday between 2:00 and 4:00 and depart on Sunday after breakfast.

MEAL SERVICE: Informal, family-style meals.

DRESS CODE: Very casual. You're in the high desert, so it's cool in the evenings. Bring along a sweater or jacket.

ACCOMMODATIONS: Private single and double rooms and rooms with shared baths are available. The rooms and cottages are comfortable; they do not contain TV and telephones.

HOUSE RULES: No smoking or alcohol allowed on the premises.

PHYSICAL FACILITIES: There is heated outdoor pool, Jacuzzi, parcourse fitness system, bicycles, exercise room, and a main building where lectures and programs are held. There's an interdenominational chapel on the grounds and a wholistic medical center adjacent, which offers acupuncture, polarity massage, and homeopathic medicine. Meadowlark also has a beauty salon.

ACTIVITIES, TREATMENTS, AND PROGRAMS: Activities include toning exercise and swimming exercise classes, yoga, movement to music, meditation techniques, art classes (such as "play with clay"), psychosynthesis (guided imagery, working with chalk to music), and hiking. Programs include body awareness, nutrition, cooking class, journal writing, dream analysis, biofeedback, and a workshop for fasters.

A Day at Meadowlark

7:00	Morning walk/jog
8:00	Breakfast
9:30	Yoga
10:30	Life-patterns discussion
12:30	Lunch

1:30   Play with Clay
3:00   Nutrition and health
4:00   Tea
4:45   Meditation
6:00   Dinner
7:15   Evening program

STAFF POPULATION: There are two physicians and a nurse on the staff, including Evarts G. Loomis, M.D., who is the founder and executive director of Meadowlark. Dr. Loomis, who established Meadowlark in 1958, believes: "Mental and emotional tensions coupled with toxins in the body lie at the root of illness . . . The human body has an innate, root wisdom with which it maintains or recovers its own perfection when it is allowed to function unhindered."

OPTIONAL COSTS: For fasters, additional costs include an initial consultation with a physician to set up the program and the $25 Faster's Kit, plus an extra $5 a day for meeting with the doctor twice a day. Medical consultations are available at the wholistic medical center. Massages and biofeedback sessions are also available.

NICE TO KNOW: Meadowlark will make no exceptions in their basic diet but can accommodate those who cannot eat wheat, corn, or dairy products. Since there are several hills and stairs that have to be maneuvered at Meadowlark, full participation in the program is not possible for those with severe walking problems. No radios are permitted, but bring your tape recorder for storing class information and lectures.

JUDY'S COMMENT: A healthy combination of nutritious foods, medically supervised fasting, and wholistic programming make Meadowlark a unique find.

- **BEST BUY AND WHY:** This affordable program is a "Best Buy" because:
  - It offers a fitness and diet retraining program that can be "taken home" and put into practice.
  - The attentive staff offers individual attention in helping you assume a responsible plan for your own health and well-being.
  - There is a wholistic medical center in proximity if you choose to delve deeper into learning about wholistic principles.
  - The invigorating desert air and climate offer a respite from everyday stress.

Courtesy of New Age Health Spa

NEW AGE HEALTH SPA
Neversink, NY 12765
914-985-7601
New York only (800) 682-4348

A colonial-style resort located on the edge of a forest in a mountain setting on 155 acres in the Catskill Mountains. Open year-round.

RATES: Affordable. Credit cards: American Express, MasterCard, Visa.

LOCATION AND TRANSPORTATION: By car, two and one-half hours from Manhattan. From La Guardia, Kennedy, or Newark airports, you can take the Short Line bus to Liberty, New York, then taxi to the resort in Neversink.

EMPHASIS/PHILOSOPHY: The program, based on the nutritional philosophy of naturopathic physician Paavo Airola, brings physical, mental, and spiritual awareness to guests by means of lectures, classes, and—most importantly—nutritional guidance. New Age believes strongly in the use of fasting along with enemas.

DIET PROGRAM: Six different fasts and diets are offered:

1. The Water Fast is either 100 percent water or a combination of water and lemon with honey.

2. Fresh Juice Fasting. 350 calories per day. Fresh fruit and vegetable juices are served alternately.
3. Spartan Diet. 450–500 calories per day. Consists of fruits, green salad, steamed vegetables, and grains (brown rice or millet).
4. Lite Diet. 600–650 calories per day. Consists of fruits, vegetables, fertile egg dishes, dairy products, grains, and tofu.
5. Pro-Lite Diet. 850 calories per day. Same as the Lite Diet, with fish and chicken added to the evening meal.
6. Pro-Lite Plus Diet. Calorie count is unlimited and dependent on your choices. All natural foods, including lacto/vegetarian with chicken, fish, and luscious desserts. No chemicals or additives are used in food preparation.

Guests utilizing the Water or Juice Fast plans commonly lose a pound per day.

GUEST POPULATION: Coed. 72 guests. You'll find a variety of ages and shapes. Most come to lose a few pounds, some just come to detoxify their bodies. Recent visitors have included teachers, office workers, businessmen, models, nurses, and wealthy seniors.

PACKAGES AND MINIMUM STAYS: New Age offers a Short Week (5 days for the price of 4) in the winter "off" season. There are 2- or 3-day minimums over holidays, but other than that check in and out whenever you wish.

MEAL SERVICE: Separate areas of the dining room are designated for the different groups of dieters: the Fasters, the Spartans, the Lites, the Pro-Lites, and so on.

DRESS CODE: Be as casual as you wish. A jogging suit is fine.

ACCOMMODATIONS: Guests stay in rustic cottages surrounding the main building, which was the old Neversink Inn. Some rooms are motel-style with full baths while others are bungalow-type with shower only. There are no radios or TVs in guests rooms.

HOUSE RULES: No smoking is allowed. Guests are not permitted to swtich from a fast to a solid diet during their stay. A daily enema is mandatory for fasters.

PHYSICAL FACILITIES: There are indoor and outdoor pools, sauna, steamroom, two exercise rooms, Nautilus, and a spa building called The Barn (which has massage rooms and a beauty salon) where all exercise classes and treatments take place. Hiking trails abound, and golf and tennis are nearby. Cross-country skiing is available in season. A fully array of massages, loofah rubs, beauty services, and even astrological consultations are available, as is a boutique.

ACTIVITIES, TREATMENTS, AND PROGRAMS: Activities include a weigh-in, calisthenics/aerobics classes, sauna time, yoga, aquatics, weight-training, and an afternoon walk. Evening programs consist of lectures on wholistic medicine, herbal medicine, stress management, the psychology of fasting, overcoming self-destructive behavior, guided meditation, biofeedback, astrology, makeup demonstrations, basic food management, and recipes and food preparation. Theater games and sing-alongs provide diversion. Directors Stephanie Paradise and Werner Mendel are available for private consultations.

A Day at New Age

7:30	Nature walk
8:00	Weigh-in
8:30	Yoga meditation
9:00	Breakfast
9:45	Orientation twice weekly for new guests
10:30–11:30	Exercise classes
12:30	Weight training
1:00	Lunch
2:15	Guided nature walk or sports
3:15	Exercise workout and aquatic exercises
4:15	Yoga meditation
6:00	Dinner by candlelight
8:00	Workshops, lectures, or entertainment
9:30	Tea
11:00	Lights out

OPTIONAL COSTS: All treatments are extra and include massage, facial, manicure, pedicure, hair treatments, skin peeling, eyelash tinting, paraffin waxing, skin diagnosis, makeup consultation, and body wrapping. A resident astrologer will tape your chart.

NICE TO KNOW: Much of the success of the program is due to the lasting influence of Graeme and Elsa Graydon, the husband-wife team who founded New Age. The new hosts, Stephanie and Werner, carry on the nutritional emphasis but have advanced aerobic exercise as a twin cornerstone to the program.

JUDY'S COMMENT: New Age Health Farm will offer you a learning experience in wholistic health practice that could change your life-style forever.

*NORTHERN PINES HEALTH RESORT

P.O. Box 279
Raymond, ME 04071
207-655-7624

An eighty-acre retreat located on the shores of Crescent Lake in the middle of a pine forest. Open January to mid-March and mid-May to the end of October.

RATES: Affordable. Credit cards: American Express, MasterCard, Visa. Guests are expected to pay on arrival. Rates are somewhat higher in July and August.

LOCATION AND TRANSPORTATION: Northern Pines is in the Sebago Lake region of southern Maine, 45 minutes by car from Portland International Airport and a three-hour drive from Boston. Pickup service is available from Portland airport and major bus depots for a nominal charge.

EMPHASIS/PHILOSOPHY: The aim here is to guide each guest toward optimum health and well-being through a wholistic approach to conscious living.

DIET PROGRAM: The vegetarian diet (based on the nutritional principals of the late Paavo Airola, Ph.D., N.D.) is a mixture of fresh fruits and vegetables, nuts, seeds and grains, milk, vegetables, oils, kelp, wheat germ, and brewer's yeast. Fish and eggs are served twice a week. Supervised fasting is encouraged but not mandatory. A 48-hour diet of raw fruits and vegetables is required before beginning the fasting regimen, which consists of spring water, organic fruit, and vegetable juices. Fasters usually lose about one pound for each day of fasting. Liquids are not permitted to be taken until one hour after meals.

GUEST POPULATION: Coed. 30 guests in summer; 15 guests in winter.

PACKAGES AND MINIMUM STAYS: The basic program is 1 week; arrive Sunday evening, depart Sunday afternoon. Northern Pines also has a midweek Monday through Friday package, a weekend program, and daily rates.

MEAL SERVICE: Buffet style for all meals. Guests interested in food preparation are encouraged to participate.

DRESS CODE: Very casual. Bring cold-weather gear in winter and campy costumes in summer.

ACCOMMODATIONS: There are some heated rooms in the main lodge. Most guests live in rustic log cabins, some with and some without baths. All cabins have maid service and electricity, and overlook the lake. You can bring a roommate, be paired up, or opt for a single. Meals and programs occur in the main lodge.

HOUSE RULES: No smoking in any buildings.

PHYSICAL FACILITIES: The main lodge has a great room (with a piano) that is used as library/meditation room/lecture room. Other facilities include a private beach and dock, boating, hot tub, Samadhi Isolation Tank, sauna, organic garden, and nature trails. Cross-country ski trails abound—bring your own skis. Golf and tennis are nearby.

ACTIVITIES, TREATMENTS, AND PROGRAMS: Daily exercise activities include warm-ups, aerobic dancing, walking/jogging, and yoga. Classes in natural health are held daily, including sessions on wholistic diet and practices, rebirthing, meditation techniques, applied kinesiology, stress management, relaxation techniques, yoga, spiritual growth, enlightenment, ecology, herbology, body care, and art classes that focus on using the intuitive right side of the brain. Personal services such as reflexology, eye iridology, and hair care are available at an hourly rate. Canoeing, swimming, and sailing lessons are available. Films and fireside powwows take place in the evenings.

A Day at Northern Pines

6:45	Rise and shine
7:00	Warm-up exercises
7:30	Jog or walk
8:45	Breakfast
10:00	Classes on various aspects of natural health
11:30	Swim and relaxation
1:00	Lunch
1:30	Rest
2:00	Activity—water sports, herbal walks, private therapy, etc.
4:30	Yoga, exercise, meditation
6:00	Supper
7:30	Evening program—evaluation, sharing, films, entertainment
9:00	Informal fireside period

OPTIONAL COSTS: For modest sums, you may have a facial, massage, hair treatment, Isolation Tank or Rebirthing session (a one-to-one experience with a facilitator using deep-breathing techniques to reduce stress), and colonic irrigation. Side trips to Portland for summer stock theater and to other Maine attractions are planned from time to time.

NICE TO KNOW: If there is interest among guests, Northern Pines plans such summer excursions as canoe trips down the Saco River, picnic trips to the ocean, berry picking, and drives along the coast. Kingsley Pines children's summer camp, under the same ownership, is only two miles away, and many parents send their 7-to 15-year olds there while they enjoy Northern Pines. Northern Pines was built in the 1920s as a single women's vacation camp.

*BEST BUY AND WHY: This affordable program is a "Best Buy" because:
- It has a well-thought-out wholistic health program.
- The fasting program is carefully supervised—most important in my book!
- This rustic setting encourages physical exertion as well as spiritual renewal.

JUDY'S COMMENT: An idyllic rustic retreat and a wonderful program!

OPTIMUM HEALTH INSTITUTE
OF SAN DIEGO
6970 Central Avenue
Lemon Grove, CA 92045
619-464-3346

A school of nutrition located on four acres of parklike grounds, nestled on a hilltop with its own organic gardens. Formerly associated with the Hippocrates World Health Organization, the Institute terminated that relationship and adopted its new name in January, 1983. Open year-round.

RATES: Affordable. MasterCard, Visa; no personal checks.

LOCATION AND TRANSPORTATION: Ten miles from the San Diego Airport.

EMPHASIS/PHILOSOPHY: Hippocrates taught that wholesome, natural foods could restore and maintain vibrant health. Experience with a "live food" program, eliminating meat, dairy products, and all processed and cooked foods, "has confirmed for us at the Institute, and thousands of others, that perfect health is a natural state. The human body is self-regenerating and self-cleansing, and if given the proper tools with which to work, it can maintain itself indefinitely without illness, pain, or degeneration."

DIET PROGRAM: The diet consists solely of raw fruits, vegetables, and sprouts. Everyone fasts the first three days of the program. "Learn to put a garden in your glass," says the Institute. Seeds are ground up to make seed cheeses. Fermented wheatgrass (Rejuvelac) functions as a cleanser of the system, and you're allowed to drink as much of this as you want—it's loaded with enzymes. One young California cosmetologist trying to kick the junk food habit lost about ten pounds in two weeks. She said she never felt better; her whole aura was different—calm and relaxed.

GUEST POPULATION: Coed. 90 guests. Most who come here are already aware of wholistic health principles; others come as a last resort to attain "wellness." Testimonials of illness reversals are impressive. All guests must be self-sufficient and ambulatory.

PACKAGES AND MINIMUM STAYS: One week is the minimum, but the recommended stay is three weeks, which will include the entire curriculum of the "learn by doing" program. Fractions of a week are not permitted. Check in on Sunday between 2:00 and 4:00 P.M., out on Saturday by 11:00 A.M.

MEAL SERVICE: The first three days comprise the detoxification program. The Institute shows you how to use their electric wheatgrass juicers. The rest of the week meals are casual and buffet style. Watermelon is served at every breakfast, once you're off the fast.

DRESS CODE: Very casual. Jogging outfits are perfect. Bring clothing for both warm weather and occasional cold nights. Old bath towels and hangers are useful, as is your favorite unscented soap.

ACCOMMODATIONS: There are motel-type rooms, private and semiprivate, and a dormitory with bunk beds. Each room has a bath, but no telephone or air conditioning although hilltop breezes keep things comfortable. The Institute will provide a roommate of the same sex.

HOUSE RULES: Smoking and incense are not allowed at the Institute. All residents are expected to care for their own rooms and help for one hour daily with chores.

PHYSICAL FACILITIES: The beautiful grounds are surrounded by lemon grove trees, which provide shaded areas for relaxation. Fourteen one- and two-level structures house guests, kitchens, exercise rooms with minitrampolines, living room and lounge. There is an outdoor Jacuzzi. Organic gardens provide a lot of the fruits and vegetables used in food preparation.

ACTIVITIES, TREATMENTS, AND PROGRAM: A daily morning exercise session out on the lawn (stretching and Bates Eye Exercises) is led by Institute Director Raychel Solomon. She says, "At the Institute we share with you nature's secrets of health and youth and teach you how to understand and care for your body." The first week's classes may include reflexology, mental purification, digestion, wheatgrass planting, emotional detoxification, food combining, sauces/recipes, and sleep technique. Second and third week classes may include natural beauty care, organic gardening, advanced detoxification, sprouting for traveling, natural beauty care, and menu planning. Evening programs might include visualization and relaxation techniques led by Raychel, or sitting around the piano and signing favorite songs.

OPTIONAL COSTS: Massage, high colonics, class tapes, books, Rejuvelac juicer, and chiropractic consultation are extra.

NICE TO KNOW: According to one Institute convert, "Everything smells of wheatgrass (including your breath and urine)—it's a nice, clean smell." If you don't wish to put in your daily hour of duty, you can substitute a $20 contribution. Guests willing to work three hours a day get a $30 reduction on their room rate. The chef at the Institute liberally uses Dr. Bernard Jensen's "Quick Sip" natural seasoning (available at most health and food stores). An open house every Sunday (open to anyone) features a tour of the grounds, a lovely raw food buffet including mock chicken or tuna ($2.50 donation), and a lecture by Raychel or a guest speaker, as well as testimonials; Raychel urges guests to be positive and not talk about their own problems; but the impact of raw food can't help but prompt lively discussions of topics such as flatulence among the guests.

JUDY'S COMMENT: For the serious health-seeker who desires preventive measures this retreat might be a godsend. You'll get a good introduction to natural, raw vegetarianism, which, by the way, is hard to maintain at home unless you are highly motivated.

* PAWLING HEALTH MANOR
P.O. Box 401
Hyde Park, NY 12538
914-889-4141

A fasting/vegetarian retreat located in a colonial mansion in a peaceful setting on the shore of the Hudson River near Hyde Park. Open year-round.

RATES: Affordable. Credit card: MasterCard. All fees are payable in advance.

LOCATION AND TRANSPORTATION: 100 miles north of New York City. Limousine service is available from Kennedy or La Guardia for a charge. Or take Amtrak from Grand Central to Rhinecliff station.

EMPHASIS/PHILOSOPHY: The focus here is on losing weight through supervised fasting. The program features detoxification, juice regimens, educational programs, and natural food. The retreat's exercise philosophy is "the less you do while fasting the better." There is no medical advice given at Pawling. They suggest that you consult with you physician prior to coming.

DIET PROGRAM: There is a choice of low-cal vegetarian meals or fasting for those who qualify. If fasting, Pawling suggests that you do so for four days, from Tuesday to Friday. For those four days the menu reads: cold water, ice water, warm water, hot water, and ice cubes for dessert. The total caloric input is *zero* (no problem counting calories). On the fifth day you break the fast with oranges and a fruit platter. For the evening meal you may have a salad, steamed vegetables, and a baked potato. No dairy products, eggs, or grains are served. On Saturday, the final day, there is a lovely food demonstration buffet, which gives you an idea of how to continue your health regimen at home. The folks at Pawling practically guarantee that fasters will lose ten to twenty pounds in the first week!

GUEST POPULATION: Coed. 30–50 guests. The well-known operatic soprano Grace Bumbry is a frequent visitor here. "It may be okay for Luciano Pavarotti to have the traditional girth associated with opera singers," says Grace, "but it doesn't appeal to me." Shirley Verrett, also of the Met, often accompanies her friend Grace.

PACKAGES AND MINIMUM STAYS: One week is the minimum—check in Sunday afternoon, check out the following Sunday morning. At the Sunday evening orientation, they let you know exactly what to expect.

MEAL SERVICE: Room service only.

DRESS CODE: Extremely informal. Don't bring too many clothes. Do bring along a radio, personal stationery, and plenty of reading material.

ACCOMMODATIONS: Attractive single and double rooms in the main house or in the motel annex. Private baths are available in most

262 THE SPA BOOK

rooms. If you come alone, Pawling will do their best to arrange for a roommate if you wish. Television sets may be rented, and telephones are located in the hallways of the living areas.

HOUSE RULES: No smoking on the premises. According to the Pawling Health Manor, the program is effective in helping to overcome the smoking habit quickly and easily.

PHYSICAL FACILITIES: There is an outdoor heated pool, solariums with showers for nude bathing, a small gymnasium, and nature trails for walking. In addition, you'll find Nautilus equipment, a Jacuzzi, steamroom, sauna, tennis and racquetball courts, massage and suntanning facilities, beauty services, and a boutique.

ACTIVITIES, TREATMENTS, AND PROGRAMS: The daily routine beings with a visit from Dr. Robert Gross, Ph.D., a biochemist and nutritionist, who checks the pulse and blood pressure of each guest, answers questions, and remedies any problems that might arise due to the novelty of fasting. Daily lecture workshops are held on body biochemistry, nutrition, fasting, yoga, detoxification, vegetarianism, and food selection hints for an at-home regimen. The Saturday "going home" program consists of a food demonstration and buffet, where guests are taught how to adapt it to the world back home. During the afternoon, guests are free to relax, reflect, or take short trips into the nearby towns to shop or sightsee in this rustic area. Evening programs consist of video movies, makeup clinics, or seminars.

OPTIONAL COSTS: The services of a fine beauty salon, featuring Chanel products, include: facials, pedicures, manicures, hand or foot massage, haircut, expert hair color, makeup lessons, and complete beauty make-overs. Massages are also available!

NICE TO KNOW: Joy Gross, Pawling's director, is author of the books *Improved Fitness in 30 Days* and *The Vegetarian Child.* Theresa, the administrator and reservations manager, is lovely and very available to speak with if you have any questions concerning the program or procedures.

*BEST BUY AND WHY: This affordable program is a "Best Buy" because:
- As compared with other fasting spas, Pawling provides outstanding supervision in both fasting and "breaking-the-fast" techniques.
- Bob and Joy Gross assume real responsibility in helping their guests return home with an insight into proper eating habits.
- The lovely setting on the Hudson River establishes a sense of peace and tranquillity.

JUDY'S COMMENT: Wonderful supervision! Pawling wants you to lose weight, then break the fast with proper instruction.

POLAND SPRING HEALTH INSTITUTE
RFD 1, Box 4300
Poland Springs, ME 04274
207-998-2894

This health institute is beautifully situated on a gentle hill, overlooking lakes, streams, woods and meadows. It is affiliated with the Seventh Day Adventists. Open year-round.

RATES: Affordable. No credit cards.

LOCATION: Poland Springs is 35 miles from Portland, via Route 26. The nearest major airport is Portland. Complimentary transportation is available.

EMPHASIS/PHILOSOPHY: This program stresses the importance of eight factors for a healthful and positive life—good nutrition, exercise, water, sunlight, clean air, rest, temperance, and trust in God. Poland Spring aims to reeducate the mind and recondition the body. Principles of preventive health care are also emphasized.

DIET PROGRAM: This is a vegetarian program with no calorie count. No meat is served and dairy products are optional. Breakfast and lunch are large, nutritionally complete meals. Guests are encouraged to eat nothing or at most a very light dinner in order to obtain maximum weight loss. A former guest's description of this meal plan is: "Breakfast like a king, dinner like a queen, and nothing in between." The average weight loss is a pound a day.

GUEST POPULATION: This program is limited to a maximum of eight men and women in order to assure individual attention.

SPECIAL PACKAGES AND MINIMUM STAYS: A one-week stay is the minimum. If a guest is more than 20 percent overweight, a three-week stay is recommended. For people with coronary heart disease, there is a one-month program. There is also a two-week smoking cessation clinic.

MEAL SERVICE: The small size of the groups allows meals to be served at one big table in the dining room. When the weather is nice, meals are often served on the sunny porch.

DRESS CODE: Casual clothes are fine in this homelike atmosphere.

ACCOMMODATIONS: All guest rooms are in the Manor, the main building. There are private as well as semiprivate rooms. They are immaculately clean and simple in decor.

HOUSE RULES: No smoking. No alcohol used or permitted.

PHYSICAL FACILITIES: The institute is located on 90 acres of rolling hills. The main building is the Manor, which contains the guest rooms, kitchen, dining room, seminar rooms, and physical therapy rooms. The staff house and medical clinic are located nearby.

ACTIVITIES, TREATMENTS, AND PROGRAMS: A complete physical with laboratory and cardiac tests administered by the full-time staff physician is highly recommended. The charge for his workup averages $250 and is usually covered by a guest's individual medical insurance. After this physical, the physician implements regimens to counteract excess weight, diabetes, hypertension, depression, arthritis, or stress.

The weight-reduction program includes one daily massage or water treatment (steam bath, whirlpool, contrast spray or hot pack); stretching exercises; and health-education classes, lectures, and demonstrations.

The primary mode of exercise here is walking. Walks are geared to the physical condition of each guest. Gradually both the distance and the speed of the walks are increased to better condition the participants. Other local recreational activities are swimming in the lake and canoeing during the summer; and ice skating and cross-country skiing during the winter.

STAFF POPULATION: The spa directors are Richard Hansen, M.D. and his wife, Ulla Hansen, R.N.

OPTIONAL COSTS: None.

NICE TO KNOW: This retreatlike program has a strong spiritual emphasis, for which guests should be prepared.

JUDY'S COMMENT: Poland Spring Health Institute offers a personal and supportive life-style improvement program in a beautiful pastoral setting.

Courtesy of Rancho La Puerta

RANCHO LA PUERTA
P.O. Box 69
Tecate, Baja California, 92080, Mexico
800-443-7365
Spa number: 706-654-1155

"The Ranch" is the oldest residential fitness retreat in North America and nestles in the foothills of the Sierra Madre Mountains just half a mile across the U.S. border. Open year-round.

RATES: Moderate. No credit cards. Full payment is due 30 days prior to arrival. All treatments are extra, but exchange rates makes them a bargain.

LOCATION AND TRANSPORTATION: The Ranch is one hour south of San Diego, on 150 acres and at an altitude of 2,000 feet. The sun shines 341 days a year on the meadows, mountains, and gardens of the spa. Courtesy transportation is provided to and from the airport, although the Ranch is easily reached by highway (border open from 6:00 A.M. to midnight).

EMPHASIS/PHILOSOPHY: Long before it was popular, the Ranch touted the concept of wholistic health and personal fitness. Deborah Szekely, founder and owner of the Ranch (as well as the Golden Door in California) says, "The aim of Rancho La Puerta is to instill a permanent fitness attitude that you can take with you when you leave."

DIET PROGRAM: The vegetarian menu provides 1,200 calories per day for men and 1,000 calories per day for women. Eggs, fish, and cheese are included, supplemented by nuts, grains, beans, and natural foods grown in the spa's organic gardens. The calorie count can be increased for those who wish to maintain or gain weight. The low-cholesterol, low-calorie, low-sodium, high-energy natural diet contains no white flour or refined sugar. Recent statistics show that 40 percent of Rancho la Puerta guests who sign up for the weight-reduction/fitness program lose a minimum of three pounds a week; many lose far more. If you work very hard and eat very little, you may end up winning the weekly maximum-weight-loss contest.

GUEST POPULATION: Coed. 135 guests. The Ranch describes itself as an "Equal Opportunity Spa," and more and more men are responding to the fitness explosion and participating in the program. For the most part, guests are in good shape to begin with. The Ranch has served as a vegetarian refuge for intellectuals from Stanford and Berkeley as well as for such folks as Herschel Bernardi, Dyan Cannon, Cliff Robertson, Dina Merrill, William Buckley, and Giorgio di Sant'Angelo.

PACKAGES AND MINIMUM STAYS: One week, Saturday to Saturday, is the minimum package, but a shorter stay may be possible depending on availability. You may come as early as you like, but rooms aren't ready until 2 P.M. You must vacate your room by 11 A.M. on the following Saturday, but feel free to stay for a full day's activities. Couples weeks are scheduled three times a year.

MEAL SERVICE: Continental breakfast is served poolside in summer, in your room in winter. Lunch is buffet style, and there's a listing of each dish with its calorie count. You are free to eat as much or as little as you want. Dinner is family style, with guests joining in to serve each other. Juices and veggies are served twice daily. Open seating at most meals and a hostess at dinner.

DRESS CODE: Casual—a jogging outfit is perfect. Bring along a sweater in fall, winter, or spring. It's a good idea to bring along rain gear too (rubber tote boots and hooded parka).

ACCOMMODATIONS: The Mexican influence is evident in all three types of accommodations: rancheras (most with fireplace and sitting areas); haciendas (small homes with fireplace, living room, bedroom, and kitchenette); and villas (condominiums with two bedrooms, living room, and bath—a good buy if three want to share). All are decorated with Mexican one-of-a-kinds. Some of the lodgings have fireplaces, but none have room phones or air conditioning. Three telephones are located in the main lodge. If you're coming alone and wish to share accommodations, the Ranch will try to provide a roommate. Children are welcome. Most rooms are not carpeted, so do bring your slippers.

HOUSE RULES: No smoking in spa buildings or dining room.

PHYSICAL FACILITIES: No less than 80 buildings are scattered among the winding paths, roads, and jacaranda trees. There is a separate, air-conditioned spa building with massage rooms, herbal wrap rooms, and facial and beauty treatment areas. Also included in this fitness haven are: six indoor and outdoor exercise gyms; five outdoor pools; four men's and women's saunas; four Jacuzzis; Swiss sunbathing bins (for bathing au naturel); six outdoor tennis courts (lighted for night play); two-mile-long fitness parcours (with 20 exercise stations); hiking trails; a state-of-the-art weight room; an outstanding and well-stocked health library; beauty salon and boutique. A neighbor maintains a small Mexican curio shop on the ranch grounds.

ACTIVITIES, TREATMENTS, AND PROGRAMS: You have your choice from among 30 different moderate or vigorous exercise classes daily. Most classes are held in the outdoor, shaded pavilions, where even in summer cool breezes provide a respite from the heat. Every hour there's a choice of at least three classes. At the Ranch there's sex equality in reverse, with four classes per day for men only led by male instructors. Massages and beauty treatments are extra but incredibly low priced. Evening programs run the gamut from consciousness-raising weekend symposiums to weeknight movies, folk dancing, craft classes, off-the-loom basketry weaving, camera clinic, Indian pot painting, kinesiology lectures, and seminars on money management, how to remember names, and will and estate planning. Seminars know no bounds and include transactional analysis, self-love training, developing personal creativity, behavior modification in food intake, creative midlife retirement, assertiveness training, and an experiential-awareness workshop.

A Day at Rancho La Puerta

6:00	Yoga
6:30	Mountain hike
7:00	Meadow hike
7:30	Weigh-in

7:30–9:00	Breakfast
8:00	Stretch-awake exercises
9:00	Aerobics
	Body awareness
	Stretch
	Kinetic toning
10:00	Aerobic circuit training
	Body contouring
	Modified kinetic toning
11:00	Absolutely Abdominals
	Waterworks
	Aerobic circuit training
	Yoga workshop
12:30–2:00	Luncheon
2:00	Advanced fitness training
	Back care
	Waterworks
3:00	Bottom line
	Weight training
	All That Jazz
	Stretch and relax
	Painting on Silk
4:00	Aerobics
	Absolutely Abdominals
	Running clinic
	Aerobic walking clinic
	Yoga
	Vegetable garden hike
5:30–6:00	Cocktails Rancho la Puerta style
6:00–8:00	Dinner
8:00	Guest speaker, always challenging
	Craft classes
	Films
	Billiards and games in recreation center

NICE TO KNOW: Visitors from the United States need a Mexican Tourist Form. The Ranch will send this, or check with your travel agent. Also bring a passport, birth certificate, or voter's card to prove U.S. residency. The Ranch does not accept guests who weigh 35 percent more than accepted norms. Try to arrive as early as possible to weigh in and arrange for your beauty treatments as appointments fill up quickly. Orientation tours are offered at 5 P.M. (the hostesses for the week are former guests themselves). Should you tire of the vegetarian fare and have a yen for the best grilled shrimp and chicken around, try the El Pasato restaurant in town. Jose Parrata and his

Courtesy of Rancho La Puerta

entire family (great-grandma, too) will do their best to see that you're happy. Of course, you may not win the weight-loss contest at the end of the week but it may be worth it.

JUDY'S COMMENT: One of the world's great spa experiences, I call the Ranch the "world of reality." The instruction and variety of classes are superb. Since food is served buffet style, you must be your own policeman, which is a good introduction to self-discipline and fitness. The landscape of Baja California also contributes to the special quality of a week at Rancho la Puerta.

REGENCY HEALTH RESORT
2000 South Ocean Drive
Hallandale, FL 33009
305-454-2220

This oceanfront health resort provides what they call "the natural essentials for health and vibrant living: good air, pure water, sunshine, natural foods, exercise, sound sleep, rest and relaxation, recreation, entertainment, and, if you desire, supervised fasting." Open year-round.

RATES: Affordable. Credit cards: American Express, MasterCard, Visa.

LOCATION: Hallandale is north of Miami and directly south of Hollywood. The Fort Lauderdale airport is a 15-minute taxi ride away.

EMPHASIS/PHILOSOPHY: This medically supervised program emphasizes weight loss and life-style reeducation. The latter is done through seminars on behavior modification geared to eliminating smoking, alcohol, and food addictions.

DIET PROGRAM: The food plan is designed to retrain eating habits and detoxify the body. There is no calorie counting. The diet is strictly vegetarian. No dairy products are served. Fresh fruits, vegetables, nuts, seeds, and grains comprise the dietary staples of this program. Food is purchased fresh daily, whenever possible from organic producers. The food is served in proper vegetarian combinations. The spa also offers supervised juice and water fasting. They claim guests can lost 10–20 pounds in one week.

GUEST POPULATION: This spa can accommodate 75 men and women. Guests range in age from 17 to 70. Eighty percent are women.

PACKAGES AND MINIMUM STAY: The recommended program is 7 days. A Sunday arrival is preferred by the health director, who meets with you upon your arrival. There is no minimum stay.

MEAL SERVICE: The dining room overlooks the ocean. There is a friendly hostess to seat you. Breakfast is served as a buffet; lunch and dinner are sit-down meals. A nice touch are the fresh flowers on the tables.

DRESS CODE: Casual attire is the norm here. Some guests dress in a slightly more formal manner for the evening meal.

ACCOMMODATIONS: Each guest room has 2 double beds, a private bath, cable TV, and a telephone. The decor is south Floridian, with rattan furniture and chintz print bedspreads and drapes. There is daily maid service. Laundry facilities are provided.

HOUSE RULES: There is absolutely no smoking or alcohol permitted on the premises.

PHYSICAL FACILITIES: This health resort has an exercise room, a Nautilus equipment room, two massage rooms, and a facial/beauty services room. The wet area includes a whirlpool and sauna, which are adjacent to the outdoor heated pool. At your front door is more than 20 miles of oceanfront beach for walking or jogging.

ACTIVITIES, TREATMENTS, AND PROGRAMS: Included in the 7-day program are personalized diet and nutritional guidance, organized beach walks, at least two exercise classes a day (yoga, pool exercises, or stretch-er-size), relaxation workshops, daily lectures on health and related topics, food preparation classes, and use of all spa facilities.

There are morning and afternoon exercise classes. In the morning, there is a health lecture or discussion with the medical director or a visiting speaker. In the afternoon, a food preparation class is offered. In the evening, the program may be a lecture or rap session on some aspect of behavior modification. Friday night is entertainment night.

OPTIONAL COSTS: For your convenience, massages, facials, hairstyling, manicures, and pedicures are available.

NICE TO KNOW: It certainly is nice to know that Gregory Haag, M.D., is on the staff full-time. There are two other doctors on staff part-time.

JUDY'S COMMENT: An excellent vegetarian program complete with dietary options, exercises and scores of lectures and seminars.

RESORT OF THE MOUNTAINS
1130 Morton Road
Morton, WA 98356
206-496-5885

The Resort is located on 320 acres of beautiful woodlands in the heart of the lower Cascade Mountains, near Mt. Rainier and Mt. St. Helens. Open year-round.

RATES: Affordable. No credit cards.

LOCATION AND TRANSPORTATION: The Resort is in the heart of Washington state's recreation area, about a two-hour drive from Portland, Seattle, and Tacoma. Transportation from the airports is available for a moderate charge.

EMPHASIS/PHILOSOPHY: ROM teaches the importance of preventive health care, using wholistic principles and stressing rest and relaxation in a natural setting. During your stay, you'll travel through seven colors of the rainbow from the red exercise day, to the orange meal-planning day, yellow day of mental studies, green day of healing, blue day of relaxation, and violet day of "intunement" and gratitude. On each day, the colors of the rainbow will be emphasized with foods, clothes, table settings, and classes.

DIET PROGRAMS: 800–1,000 calories per day. Well-balanced, portion-controlled meals, either vegetarian or nonvegetarian (milk, cheese, beef, and fish may be served). Menus feature organically grown fruits and vegetables, many from ROM's own gardens. No salt is used in preparation. A guest's individual diet is determined after an examination by a chiropractor/naturopath. Five pounds weight loss for the week is not unheard of, according to Lorraine Moffett, program director.

GUEST POPULATION: Coed. 50 guests.

PACKAGES AND MINIMUM STAYS: The basic programs are for one week. Nine months of the year a Tissue Cleansing and Bowel Management week is offered. During May, June, and July, the Woman Beautiful week is conducted three times.

MEAL SERVICE: Plate service is the rule of the day, with seconds available to those who want it.

DRESS CODE: Very casual—jogging outfits are fine. Bring along hiking shoes and warm sports clothes for all types of weather.

ACCOMMODATIONS: Guests may choose Tauscher Hall's sleeping rooms or Settler's Inn one-bedroom condominium units. There are twelve units in Settler's Inn, each with one bedroom, living room, fireplace, kitchen, bathroom and a huge deck overlooking Inspiration Pond.

HOUSE RULES: No smoking is allowed in any buildings and no alcohol is permitted.

PHYSICAL FACILITIES: Buildings at ROM include the Pioneer House, which houses offices; a natural foods store, a small clinic, spa areas, and the kitchen and dining hall; Settler's Inn Condominium, which has 12 one-bedroom units, a lecture room, a lounge, laundry facilities, a game room, a music room and the library; Tauscher Hall, a rustic structure for seminars, informal dining and exercising; the Chapel; The Pump House, with an 112-foot-deep, free flowing artesian well; the Machine Shed for the storage of equipment, such as bicycles, volleyballs, slant boards and trampolines; and the Teepee Shelter. Recreation facilities include 29 miles of hiking trails, a pond for summer swimming, badminton and croquet courts, and cross-country ski trails.

ACTIVITIES, TREATMENTS, AND PROGRAMS: Guests receive a physical examination upon arrival, which includes: iridology, sclerology, hair analysis, and neurological, digestive, respiratory, circulatory, and nutritional analyses. A diet and exercise program is tailored to your individual needs. Classes include aerobics, Jazzercise, yoga, reflexology, trampoline use, bicycling, and arts and crafts. Guests receive one massage, an individualized color-therapy class, and a personal nutrition session. There is daily hiking and weekly seminars on wholistic health. Programs include nutrition and cooking demonstrations, stress management, creative writing, and taped lectures.

A Day At Resort of the Mountains

7:00	Morning hike
8:00	Breakfast
9:00	Free time
10:00	Aerobic exercise
11:00	Swimming
12:00	Lunch
1:00	Rest and relax
2:00	Yoga
3:00	Massage
4:00	Free time
5:00	Dinner
7:00	Evening program

STAFF POPULATION: Dr. Karl Peterson and Dr. Russell Kolbo, both chiropractors and naturopathic physicians, run ROM's health services program and provide examinations and health care treatments. Other therapists work under their direction.

OPTIONAL COSTS: Additional massages, colonics, iridology, hair analysis, and other natural health care treatments are available. Purchases may be made at the gift shop and health food store. Tours are conducted to local points of interest.

NICE TO KNOW: One unique feature of this colorful spot is their hair analysis kit. Should you elect to have this done, you are asked to send in a lock of hair for chemical analysis a good month in advance of your arrival. If you don't buy the complete wholistic workup, there is a reduction in the rates. Guests may help with food preparation at the resort by working in the organic gardens or fishing in the trout-stocked lake. There are also chickens and goats on the property that provide eggs and milk. Wear your rose-colored glasses when you read their brochures; you'll need them to sift through the mountain of information.

JUDY'S COMMENT: Resort of the Mountains is an interesting rainbow of variety—more oriented toward preventive health than weight loss.

ROCKY MOUNTAIN WELLNESS SPA
P.O. Box 77, Steamboat Springs, CO 80477
Outside Colorado: 800-345-7770
Inside Colorado: 800-345-7771
Local: 303-879-7772

Located in one of Colorado's leading ski-resort areas, this spa is a wholistic resort facility which gets right down to the business of restoring health and happiness. Open year-round.

RATES: Moderate. Credit cards: MasterCard, Visa.

LOCATION: The spa is located one mile from Steamboat Springs. Its airport is serviced by a number of major airlines. The spa provides complimentary pickups.

EMPHASIS/PHILOSOPHY: According to spa founder/director Larry Allingham, "The goal of our program is to provide participants with a plan for their futures. This is more than just a place for a temporary fitness vacation, after which guests go home and forget what happened. When our guests leave here, they have their own personal program. They go home with a personal reference notebook compiled during their stay which gets them started down a road to fitness, health and happiness—total wellness."

DIET PROGRAM: The food here is vegetarian with no meat, wheat, dairy products, salt, sugar, caffeine, chocolate, or any food that tends to cause allergies. The menu is designed to detoxify your system. It consists of 65 percent complex carbohydrates including fruits, vegetables, and oat bran; 20 percent protein incorporating fish, soy beans, seeds, and sprouts; and 15 percent fat. This dietary regimen is to be followed only for the duration of the spa stay. After returning home, the formerly forbidden foods are reintroduced, one by one, to determine which ones affect you negatively. (An increased pulse rate is the indicator.) Once you know what to avoid, you continue with a more livable nutrition program. This is custom designed for you, using your favorite foods, before your departure. Weight loss at the spa averages 5–10 pounds.

GUEST POPULATION: According to Larry, "Guests come in all sizes and shapes." He estimates that 25 percent of the guests are couples. Groups are intentionally limited to 15 people to assure a maximum of individual attention. Coed.

MINIMUM STAY: As the program requires a certain amount of time and effort to be effective, the minimum stay is 5 nights. Extended stays are discounted up to 15 percent.

MEAL SERVICE: The food is a visual delight—much attention is given to color and layout. It makes you concentrate on what you have instead of what you do not have. Meals are served by waiters in the private dining room. Dinner is by candlelight, with soft music in the background.

DRESS CODE: Casual. Bring the appropriate togs for your favorite activity—skiing, horseback riding, or whatever.

ACCOMMODATIONS: Guests stay in luxurious guest rooms that are actually the bedrooms of condominium units. The common rooms of the condominiums are shared; two to six guests all have access to the kitchen, the centrally located living room with fireplace and a balcony with panoramic views. Each individual guest room has a queen-sized bed and private bath.

HOUSE RULES: No alcohol. No smoking.

PHYSICAL FACILITIES: The spa is located in a modern condominium complex, including indoor and outdoor swimming pools and Jacuzzis, two tennis courts, exercise rooms, a private dining room, and a meeting room. Both cross-country and downhill skiing are available. (The spa will provide cross-country skis.)

ACTIVITIES, TREATMENTS AND PROGRAMS: Included in the 7-night package are a 15-page computerized nutritional analysis of your typical daily menu; a mineral and vitamin analysis; nutritional counseling; individual wellness consultations; fitness and exercise classes; personal instruction in stress-release technique; use of all spa and resort facilities; three full-body massages; and seminars on stress and wellness.

STAFF POPULATION: Larry and Dorothy Allingham, married for 32 years, are the cofounders/directors. After having physical, emotional and financial problems, they decided to get back to the basics of living. They were so delighted about their new life-style that they decided to share what they had learned. Their vibrant personalities reflect their interest in and love of life. There is a full-time registered nurse on staff.

OPTIONAL COSTS: Local activities, such as downhill skiing and horseback riding, are extra.

SPECIAL PACKAGES: There are combination spa and ski programs as well as special programs to lower cholesterol, overcome hypoglycemia, and stop smoking. Call or write for details.

NICE TO KNOW: The spa gives you a complimentary T-shirt and cookbook.

Ever on the lookout for good skin and hair products, the spa uses several excellent products.

Steamboat Springs is one of the best places in the United States to go hot-air ballooning.

JUDY'S COMMENT: This is a program that focuses on wellness and rejuvenation, and gives you the rare opportunity to practice your schussing at the same time.

RUSSELL HOUSE OF KEY WEST
611 Truman Avenue
Key West, FL 33040
305-294-8787

A wholistic meals and juice-fasting program offered at a gingerbread-trimmed, turn-of-the-century mansion in historic old Key West. Open year-round.

RATES: Moderate. Credit Cards: American Express, MasterCard, Visa. Payment requested in advance.

LOCATION AND TRANSPORTATION: Most folks fly into Key West International from Miami on Air Florida (25 minutes) or PBA (50 minutes) and take a taxi to Russell House. Should you choose to drive from Miami, it takes approximately four hours to reach Key West.

EMPHASIS/PHILOSOPHY: Russell House offers health-seekers a juice fasting regimen based on a health theory established by the late nutritionist Paavo Airola. (The theory is based on juice fasting, not water fasting.) The program offers cleansing, education, rejuvenation, detoxification, and weight loss. Owner/director Enid Badler says: "It's a life-style we teach here. . . . We detoxify the body . . . we cleanse (it) of junk food, caffeine, tobacco, alcohol, refined flour, and white sugar. . . . Basically we're in the business of saving lives."

DIET PROGRAM: The liquid diet consists of freshly prepared raw fruit juices, herb teas, and potassium broth in the evening. The fast is broken by a meal of salads, yogurt, and tofu. Guests may drink all the natural spring water they desire. Most guests lose ten to fifteen pounds the first week. If not fasting, guests partake of wholesome vegetarian meals. A 550-calorie-per-day diet is recommended for weight loss. Menus are totally free of cholesterol, salt, sugar, and chemicals.

GUEST POPULATION: Coed. 50 guests. "Most folks come to lose weight, stop smoking, or maintain good health," according to Enid.

PACKAGES AND MINIMUM STAYS: One week is the minimum stay, Sunday to Sunday.

MEAL SERVICE: Guests share their meals three times a day, seated at outdoor tables on the patio. It's a social occasion!

DRESS CODE: Very casual; bring lightweight clothes for this climate. Russell House suggests you bring along walking shoes, bathing suits, and a shawl or jacket.

ACCOMMODATIONS: Rooms are in four buildings—Celebrity House, Club House, Cottage, or Girls' Dorm. Roommates can be provided at your request. No telephones are in rooms. Daily maid service is provided. Rates descend with location, with Celebrity House being most expensive.

HOUSE RULES: Drugs, alcohol, and caffeine are not allowed. Smoking is permitted on the outside porch only.

PHYSICAL FACILITIES: All facilities are coed and include a sauna, steamroom, large whirlpool, exercise equipment, and outdoor pool. Bicycles, a health food store, beauty salon, and boutique are also at Russell House. Public golf and tennis facilities are nearby, as are sailing, snorkeling, fishing, and sightseeing.

ACTIVITIES, TREATMENTS, AND PROGRAMS: Daily activities at Russell House include supervised juice fasting, weigh-in and blood pressure check, three miles of walking, and use of the sauna and whirlpool. Lectures are offered on wholistic health topics, nutrition, and behavior modification. Evening programs consist of talks on natural health, chiropractic, "sugar blues," and stress. A stop-smoking program is available to all guests at no extra charge. Massages and beauty treatments are available.

A Day at Russell House

7:00	Wake-up call
7:20	Warm-up stretches
7:30	Sunrise walk
8:30	Check in with nurse
9:00	Breakfast
9:30	Morning lecture (includes topics on nutrition and wellness)
11:00	Yoga
12:00	Private consultations with health director
1:00	Lunch

2:00   Afternoon activity such as fashion show or skin care class
3:00   Aquathenics
3:45   Happy hour—potassium cocktails
4:00   SES (smoking elimination seminars)
5:00   Dinner
7:00   Evening activity (includes a guest speaker or special event)
8:00   Sunset walk

OPTIONAL COSTS: Massages, facials, waxing, and other beauty services are extra, as are the services of a chiropracter, a hypnotist, a physician, and a licensed practitioner of colon irrigation.

JUDY'S COMMENT: If you want to try fasting and stop smoking, this may be the place! And remember, the only sure place to find sunshine and warmth in January is Key West.

SANS SOUCI WEIGHT CONTROL AND FITNESS RESORT
3745 Route 725
Bellbrook, OH 45305
513-848-4851
513-435-9778

Located on a beautiful 80-acre, wooded estate with a lake that adjoins a 600-acre park reserve. Open May through October.

RATES: Affordable. Credit cards: American Express, MasterCard, Visa.

LOCATION AND TRANSPORTATION: The spa is 27 miles from Dayton International Airport and 12 miles southeast of Dayton.

EMPHASIS/PHILOSOPHY: Emphasis is on individualized physical exercise combined with a sensible low-calorie nutritional regimen. Proper eating habits are taught within the framework of behavior modification in areas like stress management and assertiveness training.

DIET PROGRAM: You will enjoy a natural diet of 600–1,000 calories, high in fiber and potassium, moderate in protein and carbohydrates, low in salt and fat, and devoid of sugar or caffeine. Raw fruits

Courtesy of Sans Souci Weight Control and Fitness Resort

and vegetables plus dairy products are the main food source. Seafood is served perhaps twice a week, poultry once, and herbs are used as natural seasonings. Foods are presented in nouvelle cuisine style. For those who desire more rapid weight loss, a one-day juice fast is available with physician's approval. A typical menu would be: breakfast—low-calorie fruit such as strawberries or cantaloupe, egg white omelette with mushrooms and herbs, half slice of gluten toast, herb tea, and vitamin pill; lunch—gazpacho muesli, a delicious Swiss dish, or fruit plate with cottage cheese, herb tea, and vitamin pill; dinner—salad with garden fresh lettuce and different vegetables topped with cheese, baked potato shell, delicious homemade vegetable broth, juniper berries, and vitamin pill. Average weight loss during the week—7 or 8 pounds.

GUEST POPULATION: Coed. 7 guests. Guests have ranged from a slender model, who just wanted to keep in shape, to those needing to lose a substantial amount of weight. You'll find all ages, from 20 to 70 years old.

PACKAGES AND MINIMUM STAYS: Sans Souci offers a "short week," 5 days/5 nights, in on Sunday evening and out Friday afternoon. There is also a weekend package and a 1-day commuter.

MEAL SERVICE: All meals are served in Susanne's gracious dining room. Dinners are by candlelight.

DRESS CODE: Jogging outfits are perfect in this relaxed, intimate atmosphere.

ACCOMMODATIONS: Bedrooms are decorated in floral motifs. Each suite has its own separate dressing area and a whirlpool in each tub.

HOUSE RULES: Smoking is forbidden.

PHYSICAL FACILITIES: You will find a well-equipped beauty salon; exercise room; outdoor heated swimming pool; parcours with 18 exercise stations; and 80 acres of beautiful terrain, complete with meadows, woods, lake, and nature trails. Horseback riding is available.

ACTIVITIES, TREATMENTS, AND PROGRAMS: Susanne Kircher, registered nurse and owner, has put together the entire program, drawing from her years of experience as a fitness consultant to Olympic and national sport teams in her native Rumania. Susanne takes your physical history, weight and height, blood pressure, and body measurements when you arrive. She prepares your personal exercise as well as nutritional program, taking into consideration your likes and dislikes. One full-body massage is included. There is no fitness program on Saturday afternoons and Sundays.

A Day at Sans Souci

8:00	Program starts with a glass of lemon water
8:10	Outdoor stretching and breathing exercises
8:30	Breakfast
9:15	Supervised walking/jogging on the parcours—the European concept of a fitness circuit, with 18 exercise stations spaced over a 1.8-mile path
10:15	Snack of freshly pressed fruit juice
10:30	Swimnastics in the heated pool
12:00	Lunch
1:00	Rest and relaxation and scheduled program which may include nutrition education and motivation workshop, behavior modification in nutrition, or an hour of beauty suggestions; invited specialists come in to discuss various approaches on how to improve your well-being
3:00	Floor exercises to music
4:00	Snack of fresh pressed vegetable juice and bran wafer
4:30	Evening walk, enjoying the beauty of nature
5:00	Yoga class, learning proper breathing, stretching, relaxation, and positive thinking
6:00	Dinner by candlelight

7:00   Evening activities—group discussions on
       health and nutrition, TV, bridge, needlepoint,
       etc., or simply sharing ideas and chatting with
       other guests
10:00 Bedtime

OPTIONAL COSTS: Massages, facials, herbal wraps, loofah scrubs, manicures, hair care, and individual counseling sessions may be scheduled.

NICE TO KNOW: Sans Souci means "without worry." The retreat is located near the charming old town of Bellbrook, where one can walk and enjoy the ambience of Early American housing and living. For folks who live nearby, a commuter program is available. Every year, Susanne takes the Sans Souci program on the road. In 1988, it was a luxury cruise to the Virgin Islands. 1989 will find the program in Scotland, at an old castle that Champney's has refurbished as a modern luxury spa.

JUDY'S COMMENT: This individualized program combines the best of European and American traditions in a program that emphasizes both health and fitness.

SCOTT'S NATURAL HEALTH INSTITUTE
19160 Albion Road
Strongsville, OH 44136
216-238-6930

This is a fasting-only clinic located in an attractive farmhouse on three acres in suburban Cleveland. Open February through Thanksgiving.

RATES: Affordable. No credit cards.

LOCATION AND TRANSPORTATION: A fifteen-minute drive from Cleveland airport.

EMPHASIS/PHILOSOPHY: Scott's conducts a supervised fasting program with complete rest. D.J. Scott, D.M., D.C., director of Institute, says, "The purpose of the fast is primarily to allow the organism to reconstitute the enervated nervous system by rest.... To the extent that enervation is corrected, elimination is improved, and the

282   THE SPA BOOK

secretory and assimilative capacities are normalized . . . one is bene-
fitted by fasting."

DIET PROGRAM: Water fasting with raw fresh fruits and vegetables to break the fast. Following the water fast, freshly squeezed orange and vegetable juices are reintroduced, then whole raw fruits and
vegetables are added back into the diet. Diet can be individualized in
some cases to include eggs and milk products. No whole grains or
bread. Combinations are important (e.g., no proteins and carbohydrates at the same meal). Dr. Scott says the average weight loss is
"one pound a day but may be much more . . . for the very obese."

GUEST POPULATION: Coed. Nineteen guests, ranging from the
slightly overweight to the obese.

PACKAGES AND MINIMUM STAYS: A two-week program is the
minimum.

MEAL SERVICE: Buffet style for all meals.

DRESS CODE: Very casual.

ACCOMMODATIONS: There are no private rooms; two or three
guests share a room and bath. Linen is provided twice a week with
minimal maid service. Guests are responsible for keeping their own
rooms tidy.

HOUSE RULES: No smoking or alcohol is allowed in the clinic.
Guests must stay on the premises during the fasting program. All
guests must be ambulatory in order to attend.

PHYSICAL FACILITIES: Accommodations and dining facilities are
under one roof.

ACTIVITIES, TREATMENTS, AND PROGRAMS: The two-week
program begins with a supervised water fast and complete rest. Patients see Dr. Scott, a chiropractor, twice a day. A weekly blood study
is done. Tapes and books on natural hygienic care are available for
patients, as are a large number of blood and physiological tests.

NICE TO KNOW: It's a good idea to bring your own transistor
radio for entertainment. For the benefit of other guests, be sure you
don't forget earphones. No colonics are offered here. Mrs. Scott suggests you bring "light" magazines, easy to browse through; no heavy
reading here—literally!

JUDY'S COMMENT: Rest and reduce—but check with your own
M.D. before embarking on such a Spartan approach.

SHANGRI-LA HEALTH RESORT
P.O. Box 2328
Bonita Springs, FL 33923
813-992-3811

A natural hygiene institute set on eight attractively landscaped acres of tropical foliage with Japanese-style bridges overlooking a creek, which adds to the peaceful atmosphere. Open year-round.

RATES: Affordable. Credit Cards: MasterCard, Visa. Guests must pay in advance and the rates are the same for eaters and fasters. All treatments are extra.

LOCATION AND TRANSPORTATION: Shangri-La is in Southern Florida, 23 miles south of Fort Myers. Local bus or cab service is available from Fort Myers or Naples airports.

EMPHASIS/PHILOSOPHY: An educational institution, teaching one how to live an orderly and healthful life through fasting and vegetarianism.

DIET PROGRAM: Take your choice—supervised water fasting or a strict vegetarian diet. Meals consist of nuts, raw fruits and vegetables, seeds, and grains. No eggs or dairy products, no salt, no spices, no canned or frozen foods. Desserts and between-meal snacking are taboo. Food combinations are also regulated (i.e., no sweet fruit is served with acid fruit). Three steamed dinners and one hot soup are served per week. How much will you lose? According to Marti, the reservationist, "That's strictly individual (and dependent on how much you cheat), but people often lose up to ten pounds per week."

GUEST POPULATION: Coed. 100 guests. Attendees include health-conscious couples from the Midwest and East Coast along with young and old folks who have ailments that can be helped with proper nutrition.

PACKAGES AND MINIMUM STAYS: One week is the minimum stay, arrive any day. Some guests stay for months!

MEAL SERVICE: All meals are served buffet style. No room service.

DRESS CODE: Casual. Lightweight clothing is recommended in this Florida climate.

ACCOMMODATIONS: A variety of comfortable rooms in a wide range of prices is available in the main hotel and three motel annexes. Most of the rooms have air conditioning. There is also a women's dormitory that accommodates five guests. No telephones in rooms.

HOUSE RULES: Smoking and alcohol are positively not allowed in rooms or on the grounds. Offenders are asked to vacate the premises immediately.

PHYSICAL FACILITIES: Guests have unlimited use of the recreation hall, outdoor heated pool, solaria for men and women, badminton, shuffleboard, and tennis courts, paddle boats, exercise equipment, walking/jogging trails, jogging track, massage rooms, health food and bookstore, and laundry facilities. Beaches are nearby.

ACTIVITIES, TREATMENTS, AND PROGRAMS: The unstructured program includes natural hygiene lectures, fasting supervision, and use of all spa facilities. Daily activities include outdoor calisthenics, aquatic exercise, aerobic dancing, hiking, yoga, and movement rhythmics. Programs include sessions on self-awareness, meditation and relaxation, emotional poise, and stress management. The "learn by doing" nutrition instruction includes classes in fasting, sprouting, food combining, and food preparation.

A Day at Shangri-La

7:00	A trip to the beach for a morning hike
8:30	Breakfast
9:00	Aerobics
10:00	Massage
12:00	Lunch
1:00	Aquatics
2:00	Yoga
3:00	Sprouting demonstration
4:00	Free time
5:30	Dinner
7:00	Stress-management lecture

NICE TO KNOW: Rates are the same whether you choose to fast or dine on the vegetarian fare. Although they do not guarantee it, Shangri-La will try to match you up with a roommate if you so request. The city of Bonita Springs is named after the mineral springs on the property at Shangri-La, from which flows over a million and a half gallons of water every day. There's a no-tipping policy.

JUDY'S COMMENT: This retreat offers a sound natural health experience, with emphasis on teaching vegetarian habits to ensure or restore good health.

SIVANANDA ASHRAM YOGA CAMP
Eighth Avenue
Val Morin, Québec, Canada JOT 2RO
819-322-3226

A yoga retreat situated on 350 acres of wooded, rolling hills in the heart of the Laurentian Mountains. This is a sister facility to Sivananda Ashram Yoga Retreat listed below. Open year-round.

RATES: Affordable. No credit cards accepted. Prepayment for your stay is requested. All treatments are extra.

LOCATION AND TRANSPORTATION: The Camp is 45 minutes north of Montréal. Take a bus from downtown to Val Morin and a taxi to Sivananda Camp. Pickup from the airport can be arranged.

EMPHASIS/PHILOSOPHY: A wholistic approach is taken, employing yoga to teach the attainment of well-being through proper exercise, proper breathing, proper relaxation, proper diet, positive thinking, and meditation.

DIET PROGRAM: Strictly vegetarian meals are served, featuring fresh fruits, vegetables, seeds, nuts, and grains. No eggs are served, no meat, no caffeine, and there's limited use of dairy products. Juice and natural-water fasting clinics are scheduled regularly throughout the summer sessions. Winter guests should inquire about possible fasting supervision.

GUEST POPULATION: Coed. 300 guests.

PACKAGES AND MINIMUM STAYS: None. Arrive any day and leave any day.

MEAL SERVICE: Two family-style meals are served daily.

DRESS CODE: Casual's the byword. Bring your own meditation/exercise mat, towel, personal articles, and hiking shoes.

ACCOMMODATIONS: Simple rooms with private baths are offered in the two main residences. Many rooms are shared by two or three people. Camping in tents on the hillside is also available.

HOUSE RULES: No smoking, no alcohol, no drugs, no nonvegetarian food on premises; silence after 11:00 P.M. Attendance at meditations and asana (exercise class) is mandatory.

PHYSICAL FACILITIES: There is an outdoor pool, sauna, lake, hiking and skiing trails, a large open-air exercise platform, and spring water from underground springs. A health and yoga boutique is on the premises.

ACTIVITIES, TREATMENT, AND PROGRAMS: Daily classes include two meditation sessions, breathing exercises, asanas (yogic exercises), and deep relaxation. Programs include talks and discussions and a period of karma yoga (selfless service). Volleyball tournaments are often arranged, and an evening program of cultural events is offered on occasion.

A Day at Sivananda Camp

5:30	Rising bell
6:00	Meditation
7:30	Yoga (exercises and breathing relaxation)
10:00	Brunch
11:00–4:00	Free time
4:00	Yoga
6:00	Dinner
8:00	Meditation
10:30	Lights out

OPTIONAL COSTS: Massages and cross-country ski rental (downhillers, bring your own) are available.

NICE TO KNOW: Sivananda Camp was founded in 1962 by Swami Vishnu Devananda, disciple of Swami Sivananda, founder of the Divine Life Society. Devananda and his students chopped down trees, cleared the land, and established the camp at Val Morin. Families with children are welcome. The facility also offers a summer Kids' Camp and a teacher's training course.

JUDY'S COMMENT: If you're tuned in, this may be the place to get in touch with nature and yourself the yoga way.

SIVANANDA ASHRAM YOGA RETREAT
P.O. Box N7550
Nassau, Bahamas
809-326-2920

A rustic four-acre yoga ashram retreat facing the gentle Caribbean or tropical Paradise Island. This is a sister facility to Sivananda Ashram Yoga Camp listed above. Open year-round.

RATES: Affordable. No credit cards or even personal checks are accepted. Prepayment is requested for your stay.

LOCATION AND TRANSPORTATION: Fly into Nassau airport. Phone Sivananda Ashram when you arrive, and they'll send a boat to pick you up for the half-hour ride to Paradise Island, which is adjacent to Nassau.

EMPHASIS/PHILOSOPHY: The Sivananda Ashram describes itself as "the ideal place for a yoga vacation, class course lecture, or vegetarian meal. The Retreat ... provides a friendly and informal environment for guests who come to relax, enjoy, exercise, learn, and contact the peaceful center within themselves." Unlike the usual vacation, Sivananda claims to calm the senses rather than excite them.

DIET PROGRAM: Supervised fasting is available, using fresh tropical fruit juices and water. The retreat recommends no longer than a three-day fast for a first-timer. You break the fast by eating fresh raw vegetables only—two days for every day of juice fasting—before returning to regular food.

Strictly vegetarian meals are served featuring fresh fruits, vegetables, seeds, nuts, and grains. Lots of fresh coconut is used as well as herbs from the Retreat's garden. No fish, fowl, eggs, garlic, or onions are served. Sivananda will make no predictions as to weight loss "as every individual is different."

GUEST POPULATION: Coed. 140 guests. Most visitors come to relax, get fit, and learn about or increase their knowledge of yoga. Guests can increase self-discipline and join with others sharing similar interests.

PACKAGES AND MINIMUM STAYS: None. Come and go as you wish.

MEAL SERVICE: Two meals daily are served outside, family-style at an informal buffet table.

DRESS CODE: Very casual. Shorts and T-shirts will do fine. Sivananda says bring towels, toilet articles, exercise clothes, and a pair of sandals. If you intend to meditate, as most do, bring your own mat.

ACCOMMODATIONS: Lodgings range from semiprivate "Meditation Huts" overlooking the ocean to modern cabins clustered around an oriental-style footbridge and decorative pool to rustic bungalows nested amid palm groves. There are also airy dormitories in the main building, and tent space may be rented. Most rooms are shared by two to six people. No baths in the sleeping facilities. There are four bathhouses with showers and toilets on the property. Advance reservations are recommended to assure the specific room or type of accommodations you prefer.

HOUSE RULES: Attendance at both meditations and both daily yoga sessions is mandatory. Alcohol, tobacco, narcotics, and nudity are forbidden.

PHYSICAL FACILITIES: The colonial main building houses an exercise room, dorm-style sleeping quarters, lounges, and the kitchen. The other buildings consist of cabins, "Meditation Huts," and bungalows. There's an oceanfront beach, volleyball and tennis courts, snack bar, and boutique. Glass-bottom boat cruises are available nearby.

ACTIVITIES, TREATMENTS, AND PROGRAMS: You are expected to attend the two daily meditation and yoga sessions (including silent contemplation, chanting, and yoga exercises). Instruction is offered in proper exercise, breathing, relaxation, diet, positive thinking, and meditation. Recreational activities include tennis, volleyball, swimming, and a weekly talent show.

A Day at the Sivananda Ashram

5:30	Bell to rise
6:00–7:30	Meditation and chanting
8:00	Hatha yoga
10:00	Brunch
11:00–4:00	Free time
4:00	Hatha yoga
6:00	Dinner
8:00	Meditation
10:30	Lights out

NICE TO KNOW: The Retreat has a homelike family atmosphere. Guests are encouraged to "pitch in and lend a hand" in the kitchen, the garden or wherever you wish. The Retreat is part of the Sivananda Yoga Vedanta Centers International, a worldwide organization dedicated to spreading the principles of yoga as taught by Swami Sivananda, who died in 1963. Families with children are welcome, and children's rates are reduced according to age.

JUDY'S COMMENT: Good health and good karma are to be found on this tropical Caribbean island.

TURNWOOD ORGANIC GARDENS
Turnwood Star Route
Livingston Manor, NY 12758
914-439-5702

A no-frills, fasting-only retreat at a renovated farm in the valley of the Catskill Forest Preserve. Open May through October.

RATES: Affordable. MasterCard, Visa.

LOCATION AND TRANSPORTATION: Turnwood is 17 miles south of Binghamton, New York. From New York City airports, take a bus or limousine to Livingston Manor, then a cab to Turnwood.

EMPHASIS/PHILOSOPHY: To detoxify and regenerate the body according to wholistic principles.

DIET PROGRAM: Primarily fasting with water and/or juices. All juices are obtained from organically grown fruits and vegetables, using only natural fertilizers and insect control. The fast is broken two to three days before departure. Vegetables only are used to break the fast. Licorice root and herb teas are used to help break addictive habits (e.g., tobacco). No meat, fish, or eggs are ever served. What can you expect to lose? According to Rose Robbins, director of Turnwood, "Although everyone's metabolism is different, the average weight loss is 10 pounds for the week."

GUEST POPULATION: Coed. 15 guests.

PACKAGES AND MINIMUM STAYS: One week, with a five-day fast, is the minimum stay.

MEAL SERVICE: There's a family-style social hour to receive juices and break the fast.

DRESS CODE: The style here is casual, as might be expected.

ACCOMMODATIONS: Clean, comfortable, large sleeping rooms, each with two or three beds. A few private rooms are available. All bathrooms are shared.

HOUSE RULES: No smoking, alcohol, or nonprescription drugs are allowed in any of the facilities or on the grounds.

PHYSICAL FACILITIES: Extensive gardens, hiking trails, a nearby lake for swimming and boating, and lawn games are on hand. There are a lecture hall, formal meditation hall, and library with records and books on wholistic health practices.

ACTIVITIES, TREATMENTS, AND PROGRAMS: The main program centers around fasting, with optional classes in yoga, mild aerobics, sprouting and gardening, and lectures on food combining for optimum health. There are day trips, too, to a Zen monastery, craft shows, and antiques shops.

OPTIONAL COSTS: Extras include participation in boating and horseback riding and purchases of organic fruits and vegetables. Personal services, such as massage, reflexology, and chiropractic adjustment, are available on a per-session basis.

NICE TO KNOW: Garden tours and lectures are available. Turnwood is dedicated to the principles and practice of chemical-free farming, using the Biodynamic French Intensive method.

JUDY'S COMMENTS: For rapid, supervised weight reduction and detoxification. Turnwood might turn your life-style around.

VILLA VEGETARIANA HEALTH SPA
P.O. Box 1228
Cuernavaca, Morelos, Mexico
Telephone: Cuernavaca 13-10-44

This is a natural hygiene facility located on two acres of tropical foliage with fruit trees and organic vegetable gardens. Nestled in a valley and surrounded by mountains, the Villa has a magnificent view. Open year-round.

RATES: Affordable. No credit cards. Personal checks or traveler's checks are fine.

LOCATION AND TRANSPORTATION: One hour south of Mexico City; three miles from Cuernavaca. There are public buses or limousines from the airport.

EMPHASIS/PHILOSOPHY: Director Glen Hancock, M.D., and owner Marlene Stry say they will teach you "the natural hygienic way to lose weight and learn a life-style that is biologically correct, delicious, and economical."

DIET PROGRAM: Take your choice of supervised water fasting or a diet of low-cholesterol natural foods. Most food is eaten raw. The variety of fruits includes bananas, figs, guavas, grapefruits, papayas, mangoes, avocados, acerola beans, watermelons, coconuts, and maumees (a fruit that tastes like pumpkin pie). Fresh, organically grown fruits and vegetables are supplemented by bran, wheat germ, and granola. A typical breakfast consists of oatmeal with soy milk and fruit; lunch and dinner consist of an entree of vegetable soup (any combination of carrots, onions, potatoes, squash, and celery), raw vegetables with orange-avocado dressing, tortillas, tamales, or soya stew. According to Marlene Stry, "it is not uncommon for guests to lose five to ten pounds the first week."

GUEST POPULATION: Coed. 75 guests. Guests come from Mexico, the United States, and all over the world. Some come to rest and relax, some to lose weight, and some to join with other natural hygienists in learning more about healthy living.

PACKAGES AND MINIMUM STAYS: Short stays are permitted, but two weeks is recommended to give you time to learn new habits. One week is a typical stay; arrive any day.

MEAL SERVICE: All meals are served buffet style. Guests sit on the patio for breakfast and lunch and around big round tables in the Mexican-style dining room for dinner.

DRESS CODE: Casual. The Villa suggests you bring a lightweight raincoat and good walking shoes.

ACCOMMODATIONS: Spartan rooms, but all have private baths. Some have private solariums for nude sunbathing. No phones in rooms, but one is available at the main building.

HOUSE RULES: No smoking in public areas.

PHYSICAL FACILITIES: The Villa has a ceramic-tiled heated outdoor pool; a volleyball court; tennis courts; two racquetball courts; an outdoor walking/jogging track; an outdoor gym (with weightlifting equipment, slant boards, and chin-up bar); sauna; steam baths; private solariums; and minitrampolines. Swings and hammocks are scattered about the grounds for leisurely and stress-free relaxing.

ACTIVITIES, TREATMENTS, AND PROGRAMS: Activities include fitness classes (morning gymnastic exercises using poles and stools, aerobics, yoga, and eye-strengthening exercises); walking/jogging (through lovely gardens); and use of the pool and gym facilities. Classes in Spanish and organic gardening are also offered. Evening programs include round-table discussions and taped lectures by hygiene professionals. Frequent excursions into Cuernavaca are offered.

NICE TO KNOW: The weather at the Villa is quite temperate, averaging mid-eighties during the daytime and mid-fifties at night. Although Montezuma's Revenge is a common complaint among visitors to Mexico, it doesn't seem to be a problem here. Dr. Hancock attributes the lack of trouble to "proper food combining" and the pure spring water.

JUDY'S COMMENT;   Rejuvenate, reduce, reeducate, all at a place that has fresh flowers all year round.

THREE

MINERAL SPRINGS

6
WHERE WATER WORKS WONDERS

The wonders of water have bedazzled men and women all over the world since prehistoric times. Every primitive culture had its legends of miraculous water cures. American Indians tantalized European explorers with tales of a fountain of youth. Ancient Greek priests presided over temples of healing built near mineral springs. Devotees immersed themselves in the waters and engaged in fasting and massage. Like most other good Greek ideas, this one was adopted by the Romans, who built elaborate columned baths that included steam rooms. As Hippocratic medicine became established, its practitioners took over the bath franchises.

Bathing is an almost universal religious ritual; Moses and Mohammed admonished their followers to wash before praying. Orthodox Jewish women go to ritual baths after their monthly "unclean" periods. Christian baptism signifies spiritual purification.

When cares of state got too heavy for Peter the Great of seventeenth-century Russia, he sometimes took off for a quiet little town in the valley of the Ardennes Forest in Belgium. There, he enjoyed a natural mineral spring that had been frequented by European aristocrats as far back as the Roman Empire. The Czar was so convinced of its curative qualities that he erected a stone monument around the source and built an imposing casino nearby.

Peter's hideaway, the granddaddy of today's health resorts, was a town named Spa. The word quickly came to connote a retreat blessed with mineral springs.

These days, most Americans are far from any natural water source. Man-made Jacuzzis and hot tubs compensate for the uneven distribution of nature's bounty. In Europe and a few places in the United States, however, old-fashioned water towns are still going strong.

A mineral spring cannot be man-made; it just happens. Perhaps an erupting volcano discharges minerals or gases into underground waters. Rainwater or fluid from hot rocks deep in the earth might force its way to the surface through fissures or faults, carrying dissolved minerals with it, and presto—a mineral spring appears with health-giving properties.

Mineral water may come out soft, hard, hot, cold, aerated, sulfurized, or carbonated. Hot springs combine the well-known health benefits of heat with those of the minerals in the water, which act as catalysts in the healing process.

Your body can absorb these helpful minerals internally and externally. The rich fluids may be imbibed, inhaled as vapor, bathed in, or used as a douche. They can also be used to make mud packs for your skin. Some devotees like to alternate hot and cold water. Other just live for those moments when they can slip into a hot thermal bath—a balm for tense muscles and tired minds.

HYDROTHERAPY

What the ancients ascribed to miracles and spirits can now be explained scientifically. A Bavarian monk, Father Sebastian Kneipp, systematized the healing properties of water into the science of hydrotherapy. Father Kneipp preached that nature provides us with everything we need to be happy and healthy. He bathed in pure streams and, steeping himself in plant lore, learned how to extract aromatic essences.

Taken internally, mineral-rich water is believed to cut down inflammation of the digestive organs and the circulatory system and to have therapeutic effects on the nervous system and endocrine glands. The minerals, whether swallowed or absorbed through the skin, our most extensive tissue area, are supposed to correct chemical imbalances and deficiencies. Indeed, advocates claim good results in the treatment of a long list of ailments, including heart trouble, anemia, and diabetes.

TWO MINERAL SPRINGS CITIES

Hot Springs, Arkansas, is a watering-hole city in the European tradition. Being there is like being transported back in time to a more leisurely way of life.

Against the mountain backdrop and wide magnolia-shaded boulevards where horse-drawn carriages still roll, the streets are lined with rows of bathhouses and elegant hotels steeped in a tradition of service. The springs are the focal point of a variety of accommodations, from four-star, deluxe hotels to modest pensions. Some of the best hotels have their own bathhouses. The streets of the town are filled with visitors (no one seems to live there) strolling past the fancy shops replete with lovely things of now and yesterday, from bone china to oriental rugs.

Water is everywhere! You can fill your jug at a corner fountain or drink the hot bubbly stuff directly from the gushing spout. Winters are not severe enough to kill the lush foliage. Springtime is glorious, and summer is a riot of fragrant color, with floral displays all along the busiest streets.

The pace of life is slow. There's time for band concerts in the park at tea time and a stroll along the esplanade afterward. For diversion, there are the traditional gambling casinos and horse races. (Yes, even in the Bible Belt.)

And, of course, there are the baths—hot soaks in big tubs of 140° mineral water, piped in from the forty-seven nearby springs along the mountain slopes. You can gulp huge quantities of the pleasant-tasting fluid or inhale its vapors. All this and a $3 or $4 massage too!

If you've never been to a bathhouse before, try it. The procedure is fairly simple. At most bathing facilities, you follow a step-by-step process, and you're likely to be guided through the treatment by a personal attendant.

The routine at Bathhouse Row in Hot Springs is typical. Upon registering at the reception desk, you are asked to place your valuables (watch, jewelry, wallet, etc.) in a safety lockbox. You wear the key to the box on a rubber band around your wrist during the treatment. You are then escorted to a small dressing room, where you remove your clothes and don a sheet. Once you're ready, an attendant leads you to your private room (with piped-in music), where you are provided with towels and soap.

The full bath service lasts about one hour and forty minutes. This includes a hot tub treatment, a sitz bath (ten-minute limit), a vapor cabinet treatment (seven-minute limit), and a hot pack treatment (you lie down on a slant board for twenty minutes, wrapped in towels, while an attendant places hot packs on your achy spots). Your personal attendant brings you little cups of mineral water and will, on request, give you a loofah rub. The entire procedure costs less that $10!

After the thermal bath, many people take a twenty-minute massage (also under $10), for which you don't need to make an appointment in advance. Therapists are available during normal bathhouse hours, 7:00–11:30 A.M. and 1:30–3:00 P.M. Men and women go to separate massage areas and are treated, respectively, by masseurs and masseuses.

The thermal properties of the springs in this "valley of vapors" was legendary among the local Indians long before Hernando de Soto arrived. In 1804 President Jefferson sent a team of scientists to test these claims. In 1832 President Andrew Jackson signed legislation that made Hot Springs our first national park, its healing resources to be safeguarded for posterity. The area, with its mild climate, soon became a recreational mecca, drawing more than two million visitors yearly. The aged and infirm, accident victims, and just plain busy people seeking to wind down—all flocked to the Springs.

Hot Springs is the only watering place in the United States that is under federal regulation. More than seventy government-approved doctors dispense more than 200,000 thermal baths a year at nine hydrotherapy centers. Specialists from abroad come to study and do research.

The Arlington Resort Hotel and Spa, one of Hot Springs' grandes dames, was well known during the Roaring Twenties as a celebrity gathering place. In recent years a European-trained husband-and-wife team has revived its faded glory. The bathhouse is right in the hotel, so you can pad straight from your room (in a big, comfy terry robe and slippers provided by the hotel) to a private elevator that whisks to an unforgettable experience. The Arlington offers no regular diet program. However, there are full- and half-day "beauty" packages that do not include meals.

Saratoga Springs, New York, another internationally famous watering city twenty-two miles from the Albany airport, used to attract the eastern seaboard upper crust as a place to show off their diamonds and furs. Many people traveled there for the famous harness racing and casino, but the health-oriented went for the spouting geyser and springs. You don't have to choose between the two, of course. Take the waters during the day and be taken to the cleaners at night.

Saratoga Spa State Park is a 2,000-acre, year-round recreational preserve established in the 1930s to protect the springs. Its performing arts center is the summer home of the New York City Ballet and the Philadelphia Symphony Orchestra.

A ninety-minute watering session at the bathhouse in the park costs only $13. For this remarkable price, you lie down in a private room in a tub of the springs' naturally carbonated water. Millions of tiny bubbles sparkle over your body, and your skin takes on a pinkish invigorated tingle. Twenty minutes of this may not seem like nearly enough. But it's almost worth getting out of the tub to lie down on a table and receive a massage at the hands of a state-trained therapist. For a final touch, they wrap you in hot sheets. And then it's time to rest.

When your ninety minutes are up, you'll have plenty to do in the charming town of Saratoga Springs, a potpourri of Greek, Roman, Victorian, and Gothic architecture that alone may be worth the trip. Gideon Putnam Hotel, in the state park, is a short stroll from the baths. No diet program here—only the famous Gideon desserts. Go ahead and live it up, if you dare.

SLUICE AND REDUCE

As pleasant as Hot Springs and Saratoga Springs may be, they're not going to satisfy hard-core dieters. Mineral springs resorts that successfully combine weight reduction with water cures are rare on the North American continent, but I've turned up a few. They are described on pages 306-315.

NONDIET MINERAL SPRINGS

I must take you on a whirlwind tour of some western U.S. watering spots that don't as yet have resort facilities worthy of the name. These are towns where, if you want to take the baths, you normally check into a motel and go to a public bathhouse. Prices are bargain basement, and for a few extra dollars you can get such extras as heat treatments, mud baths, salt rubs, and inhalation therapy. Some of these places are drop-ins, where you can have a quick dip and sip, with or without massage and colonic treatments, and be on your way.

Each area has its own character, traditions, and lore. Calistoga, California, is the mud-bath capital of the world; the waters in Steamboat Springs, Colorado, ward off schizophrenia, according to one eager promoter. Since these places have no diet programs, they're not listed in the Directory section. But you can use the phone numbers on pages 300–303 to check on places to stay.

Let's start our tour at Thermopolis, Wyoming, two hours from Yellowstone National Park. Thermopolis, which also offers two state parks, claims to be the home of the world's largest hot spring. Big Spring pours forth 18 million gallons a day at a steady 135°. A free, year-round bathhouse in Hot Springs State Park contains both public Roman pools and private tubs in which you can set your own temperature. No accommodations are available in the parks, but there are several hotels in town.

Next we move southward to Colorado, which is literally sprinkled with mineral springs, most sporting only rustic accommodations. Our only stop is in Hot Sulphur Springs, 60 miles from the ski resort area of Winter Park. There we meet with Bob Ivie, who has a monopoly—his 17-room motel and bath cave. These hot springs were discovered in 1905 by the people who own the *Denver Post*. The bathhouse is a natural cave, complete with sweating walls and natural hot water springs, which you can see bubbling out of the ground. The bathing procedure goes like this: you shower before and afterward; take the water as hot as you can stand it; and then lie down for a short rest, which you'll need. Bath treatments cost $3 to $4, and you may stay as long as you want. These springs are reputed to aid arthritis and rheumatism.

There's a long list of mineral springs in New Mexico, but one stands out for its name—Truth or Consequences. That's right, the town changed its name from Hot Springs in 1950, when Ralph Edwards announced on his quiz show that he would sponsor an annual fiesta for any town that would take the show's name. True to his word, Edwards has adopted the town. You can say howdy to him each spring at the festival.

Truth or Consequences is in the middle of New Mexico, 150 miles north of Albuquerque, in an area noted for its healthful climate and mild winters (mornings are nippy, but daytime temperatures get up to 60°). It's a favorite perch for snowbirds and senior citizens. Bathhouses are public, and the community offers an array of wholistic practitioners as well as medical doctors. The hot springs average 100°, which may seem a bit tepid after some of the others sampled.

NONDIET MINERAL SPRINGS DIRECTORY

All the following areas have natural spring waters. When hotels are listed, it indicates that bathhouses are on the premises. No diet menus are available.

Arizona

BUCKHORN MINERAL WELLS
Box 3270
Mesa, Arizona 85205
602-832-1111

Mineral whirlpool baths, individual tubs, colonics, massages. Year-round. The San Francisco Giants have made the Buckhorn their health spa for 25 years.

Arkansas

HOT SPRINGS CHAMBER OF COMMERCE
800-643-1570 or
501-321-1700

All these hot springs and bathhouse facilities are regulated by the National Park Service:

THE MAJESTIC HOTEL-BATHS
Hot Springs National Park,
Arkansas 71901
501-624-3383

ARLINGTON HOTEL
Center Ave. and Fountain St.

Hot Springs National Park,
Arkansas 71901
501-623-7771

NATIONAL PARK SERVICE
Box 1860
Hot Springs, Arkansas 71902
501-624-3383

California

CALISTOGA CHAMBER OF COMMERCE
707-942-6333

DR. WILKINSON'S HOT SPRINGS
1507 Lincoln Avenue
Calistoga, California 94515
707-942-4102 or
707-942-6257

DESERT HOT SPRINGS CHAMBER OF COMMERCE
619-329-6403

Blessed with seemingly unlimited hot mineral water. Offers more hot
mineral springs than any other city in the United States. The Chamber of Commerce operates a tourist information center unequaled
elsewhere.

TWO BUNCH PALMS—RESORT AND SPA
67-25 Two Bunch Palms Trail
Desert Hot Springs, California 92240
619-329-8791

Colorado

STEAMBOAT SPRINGS CHAMBER OF COMMERCE
303-879-0880

COLORADO GEOLOGICAL DEPT. OF NATURAL
RESOURCES
1845 Sherman Street
Denver, Colorado 80203
303-866-2611

HOT SULPHUR SPRINGS BATHS
Hot Sulphur Springs, Colorado 80451
303-725-3306

New Mexico

TRUTH OR CONSEQUENCES CHAMBER OF COMMERCE
505-894-3536

New York

COBLESKILL CHAMBER OF COMMERCE
518-234-4691

For information on the Sharon Springs area.

SARATOGA SPRINGS CHAMBER OF COMMERCE
518-584-3255

GIDEON PUTNAM HOTEL
Saratoga Springs, New York 12866
518-584-3000

Virginia

THE HOMESTEAD
Hot Springs, Virginia 24445
703-839-5500

West Virginia

BERKELEY SPRINGS CHAMBER OF COMMERCE
304-258-2362

George Washington bathed here.

WHITE SULPHUR SPRINGS CHAMBER OF COMMERCE
304-536-2362

An area known in Indian times as a holy place and famous since 1778
for the springs' miraculous healing qualities.

GREENBRIAR HOTEL
White Sulphur Springs
West Virginia 24986
304-536-1110

Wyoming

THERMOPOLIS HOT SPRINGS CHAMBER OF COMMERCE
307-864-2636

Open year-round.

THE STATE BATH HOUSE
Thermopolis, Wyoming 82443
307-864-3848

Canada

BANFF NATIONAL PARK
Banff Lake Louise Chamber of Commerce
Box 1298
Banff, Alberta, Canada TOL-OCO
403-762-3777
403-762-4646

Mexico

MEXICAN GOVERNMENT TOURIST OFFICE
13 West 50th Street
New York, New York 10020

MEXICAN GOVERNMENT TOURIST OFFICE
John Hancock Center,
Suite 3612
Chicago, Illinois 60611

SPA MELIA SAN JOSÉ PURUA
San José Purua
(Michoacán)
Mexico

HOTEL BALNEARIO
San José Purua
(Michoacán)
Mexico

MUD CAPITAL OF THE WORLD

Finally, we return to Calistoga, California, the mud capital of the world located in the wine-rich Napa Valley, 70 miles north of San Francisco. The mud is mixed from volcanic ash and naturally hot mineral waters, both of which are abundant in the area. The result is a thick, warm, black oozing substance in which you lie for ten or fifteen minutes, followed by a shower, mineral bath or whirlpool, steam treatment, blanket wrap, and massage—the "works," as it's called at Dr. Wilkinson's Hot Springs, one of the many spa motels that also welcome day guests for treatments. According to Doc Wilkinson, the mud bath relaxes and cleanses your skin, drawing toxins out of your system by stimulating profuse perspiration. The penetrating heat seems especially helpful for arthritis and just plain sore muscles.

Dr. Wilkinson's mud treatments are part of a naturopathic approach. Colonic cleansing is offered, and a chiropractor and physical therapist are available. Other establishments in the area offer indoor and outdoor hot mineral pools, sulfur baths, corrective massage, reflexology, and, of course, the ubiquitous mud baths.

Calistoga is a charming little community that has retained its easily paced charm in spite of being the home of another old faithful geyser—which is only slightly less famous than the one at Yellowstone and is one of only three regularly erupting geysers in the world! Calistoga's version raises its spectacular plume at 40-minute intervals. The boiling water roars out of the ground at an unbelievable 350° and shoots up 60 feet or more.

The Calistoga spring water, "bottled from the geyser," is so pure and tastes so fine that it won two state fair gold medals. It has no artificial additives and absolutely no calories, and is great as a soft drink or mixer.

Our whirlwind tour has taken us to only a few of America's liquid treasures. There are thousands of other natural mineral springs out there, ready and waiting.

GET READY FOR THE WATERS

Here are a few final caveats regarding mineral springs. Despite the abundant evidence that mineral water is good for you, whether you drink it or bathe in it, don't expect too much. Not every claim is justified, not every program is successful, and not all facilities are adequate. So temper your expectations, be prepared for some minor discomforts and disappointments, and find out in advance exactly what the bathhouse of your choice has to offer.

First, many hotel/motel brochures claim that the mineral spring waters will alleviate serious ailments such as high blood pressure and liver trouble. Some places even claim the ability to cure various diseases and infirmities. There is little doubt that mineral water can serve as a beauty aid. A mineral water bath can help reduce the severity of some muscular problems, such as tension, spasms, arthritis, rheumatism, and bursitis. But beyond these benefits, which are sometimes either limited or temporary or both, results are uncertain. Hugh Crenshaw, assistant park manager at Hot Springs National Park, says the Park Service makes no claim that the baths will cure anything.

Second, unless you go to a resort hotel with mineral springs on the premises, don't expect to find luxurious accommodations. In Hot Springs, Arkansas, for example, you don't even get much privacy for dressing and undressing. The dressing room is doorless, and there are no mirrors to allow you to adjust your sheet discreetly. Ask a companion or another guest to check your coverage.

Third, the little cups of mineral water brought to you by your attendant add up. The result is that you drink lots of it during your treatment (at the same temperature as the water you soak in), and you may have good reason to use a nearby bathroom. Mineral waters can have a cathartic effect, so don't be surprised if you suddenly get the call.

Before closing our discussion of mineral springs, be alerted that Mexico is becoming increasingly popular as a vacation spot for Americans seeking the thermal spas once enjoyed by the Aztecs and Incas. There are more than 500 designated hot mineral pools in the country, most of which have been used by the Mexican people for thousands of years.

Mexican mineral springs are deservedly popular, but be forewarned of a few details. Communication in Mexico is difficult at best. If you are interested in locating the Mexican watering spots, try contacting the Mexican tourist bureau in your city (which will send you material on hot springs and nearby hotels), and call the editor of the travel department of your local newspaper. Also, purchase a good map of Mexico that shows all 32 Mexican states. In order to phone a Mexican city, you must know the name of the state that it's in. Be sure to do your homework because the watering spots in Mexico vary greatly in accessibility and quality of accommodations. Some are nothing more than rural mud holes while others offer resort hotels with thermal pools nearby or on the premises.

And now, if you're not too waterlogged, why not take the diet-and-mineral-spring plunge!

7
MINERAL SPRINGS: DIRECTORY

WHY, WHERE, AND HOW MUCH

All of the hotels and spas in this category depend on the restorative properties of the waters to be found there. All include a diet program as well.

Cost is based on a one-week stay, double occupancy, high-season rates, including tax and gratuities. Meals are included unless specifically stated otherwise:

> Affordable: up to $1,000
> Moderate: $1,000–$1,700
> Expensive: $1,700 and up

HOTEL ADLER
Sharon Springs, NY 13459
518-284-2285
Reservations: 718-494-8879

A hotel featuring kosher meals and sulfur waters of Sharon Springs. Located in the beautiful Mohawk Valley in the foothills of the Catskill Mountains. Open late May through late September.

RATES: Affordable. No credit cards. All treatments extra.

LOCATION AND TRANSPORTATION: The Adler is 40 miles west of Albany and 20 miles east of Cooperstown. Complimentary pickup from Sharon Springs bus terminal.

EMPHASIS/PHILOSOPHY: Rest, relaxation, and water work wonders! The Adler Hotel says, "Nowhere in the world is the water purer ... and it is here in abundance for those who suffer from arthritis, rheumatism, nervous disorders, and other dispositions."

DIET PROGRAM: Individualized weight-loss medically designed diets are available. Dietetic products are used. All meals are kosher. Meals feature fish and chicken, with fresh fruits and vegetables—and all the sulfur mineral water you want to drink!

GUEST POPULATION: Coed. 450 guests. Lots of Jewish senior citizens come to enjoy the waters, but according to Mr. Yarkony, "Gentiles are welcome!"

PACKAGES AND MINIMUM STAYS: Room rates are quoted on a weekly basis, and 20 percent discounts may be had in June and September. No checking in or out on Saturday. Guests also may sign on for a weekly package with all treatments included.

MEAL SERVICE: Three Glatt kosher meals are served daily (supervised by the Union of Orthodox Jewish Congregations). Table service.

DRESS CODE: Jackets are required for men at dinner. Women dress accordingly.

ACCOMMODATIONS: You'll find comfortable hotel rooms, all with telephone, some with color TV and air conditioning. There also are available rooms with fully equipped kitchens.

HOUSE RULES: No smoking on the Sabbath, from sundown Friday to sundown Saturday.

PHYSICAL FACILITIES: Sulfur baths are on the premises, and you can go directly from your room in robe and slippers to the baths. There is also a swimming pool, shuffleboard, Ping-Pong, and color TV room.

ACTIVITIES, TREATMENTS, AND PROGRAMS: Daily activities include exercise classes, services of a social director, synagogue services on premises, and entertainment and dancing nightly.

THE MOORS RESORT SPA
12–673 Reposo Way
Desert Hot Springs, CA 92240
619-329-7121

A quiet and secluded spa in the desert, with its own hot mineral water well. Open year-round.

RATES: Affordable. No credit cards. All treatments are extra.

LOCATION AND TRANSPORTATION: The Moors is nine miles from Palm Springs. The spa provides complimentary transportation from the bus station or airport.

EMPHASIS/PHILOSOPHY: The focus is on weight-control through fasting. The Spa says, "Let nature, the sun, the beautiful environment, and the healing waters help you feel like a new person."

DIET PROGRAM: Fasting is recommended for the first three days, with lemon water and herbal teas allowed. After that, you receive five servings of fruit and vegetable juices and vegetable broth per day. Mineral water, which comes from the ground at 180° and is cooled, is always available for drinking. On your last day, they serve you an apple, and you break your fast by eating fruits and salads at home. A 10-pound weekly weight loss is not uncommon.

GUEST POPULATION: Coed. 18 guests. Many people with arthritic, asthmatic, cardiac, digestive, and nervous conditions come here seeking improvement. Others just come for relaxation and rejuvenation.

PACKAGES AND MINIMUM STAYS: This little resort is quite informal. Come and go on your own schedule, but at least three days are needed to participate in the fast program.

MEAL SERVICE: Very informal, family-style meals.

DRESS CODE: Very casual; wear lightweight clothing in this climate, with a wrap for cool desert evenings.

ACCOMMODATIONS: The motel type rooms are comfortable and air conditioned, all with color TV and private baths. Some kitchen roomettes are available. Telephones are in the lobby.

HOUSE RULES: Anything goes.

PHYSICAL FACILITIES: There is a large, outdoor, heated swimming pool plus an indoor hot therapy pool. Equipment includes a well-equipped exercise room, Jacuzzi, and recreation room.

ACTIVITIES, TREATMENTS, AND PROGRAMS: Use of all spa facilities and hot-pool therapy are included in the room rate. Naturopathic and chiropractic doctors supervise fasting and may advise colonic irrigation.

OPTIONAL COSTS: Massages in your room are available for $25.

NICE TO KNOW: Bring along some good books—you'll have plenty of time to read, unless you go into Palm Springs, which is in view of The Moors and has a wealth of amusements, sports activities, and shopping.

JUDY'S COMMENT: A fasting retreat without a lot of rules or programs . . . and the curative water is drinking quality!

MURRIETA HOT SPRINGS RESORT AND HEALTH SPA
39405 Murrieta Hot Springs Road
Murrieta, CA 92362
Outside California: 800-322-4542
Inside California: 800-458-4393
714-677-7451

This historical mineral springs resort and spa is nestled in a valley between a mountain range and the desert. There are four active mineral springs and three outdoor mineral-water pools on the premises. Open year-round.

RATES: Affordable. Credit cards: Amercian Express, Diners Club, MasterCard, Visa.

LOCATION AND TRANSPORTATION: About one hour (60 miles) northeast of San Diego and two hours from Los Angeles. Courtesy transportation is available from Rancho, California, five miles from the resort and reachable by bus.

EMPHASIS/PHILOSOPHY: The Murrieta program promises that guests will learn how to combine exercise, nutrition, positive thought, rest, and relaxation to benefit their look, strength, flexibility, and endurance. The Fit'n'Trim program is for weight loss. It may be combined with either the Stress Management program or the Dynamic Relationships program.

DIET PROGRAM: The Proportional Diet is suggested for optimal weight lost. This vegetarian diet consists of 800 calories daily of raw and cooked fruits and vegetables, tofu, cottage cheese, sprouts, and beans. No eggs, fish, fowl, or red meat is served. An optional two-day juice fast is also offered. Several other diets are offered. Call for more information.

GUEST POPULATION: Coed. A maximum of 30 guests in the awareness programs. The resort accommodates over 500 guests.

PACKAGES AND MINIMUM STAYS: Participation in the Fit'n'Trim program requires a one-week stay—arrive by 3:00 Sunday, depart the following Sunday by 11:00. There are also four-week and six-week programs and weekend seminars.

MEAL SERVICE: There are two restaurants at Murrieta: the Spring Garden, which offers vegetarian dining for the health conscious; and Guenther's, which offers gourmet dining with an emphasis on fish, chicken, and extra-lean beef. Both restaurants open onto a Spanish-style garden patio. Dieters dine together at special tables. No room service.

DRESS CODE: Casual resort attire. Bring a sweater or jacket for evenings. The climate is considered "Mediterranean."

ACCOMMODATIONS: There are 240 rooms, ranging from cozy cottages to lodges with sitting areas and adjoining rooms. TVs and telephones are in all rooms. Weekly maid service.

HOUSE RULES: There are some nonsmoking areas.

PHYSICAL FACILITIES: The main lodge contains the front lobby, two restaurants, the Springs Gift Shop, Mr. G's Beer and Wine Bar, and the game room. The separate spa complex includes 20 mud baths (10 for men, 10 for women), 32 private mineral baths, exercise rooms, 25 massage rooms, a facial parlor and a manicure/pedicure room. The program complex adjoins the resort property and includes a classroom, individual massage rooms, and administrative offices.

Outdoor facilities include an Olympic-size mineral pool, a Roman whirlpool, and a small exercise pool. There is a small lake on the property as well as 14 newly resurfaced tennis courts, some lighted for night play. A resident tennis pro is available. Golf is nearby at Rancho California Country Club.

ACTIVITIES, TREATMENTS, AND PROGRAMS: On arrival, you are given an orientation tour of the facilities. Daily activities include Polarenergetics (a Western form of yoga), aerobics, exercise classes, and Aquaexercise. Treatments during your week on the "Fit'n'Trim" program include one daily natural mineral bath, one energy massage, and one Murrieta Mud Experience, which consists of a mud bath, a mineral bath, and a body wrap. Morning and afternoon lectures are offered on topics such as guidelines for diet and exercise, useful health information, stress management, relationships, the use of therapeutic massage, and self-awareness.

A Day at Murrietta Hot Springs

7:00	Morning walk
7:45	Breakfast
8:15	Polarenergetics
9:10	Aerobics
10:45	Morning class
12:15	Lunch

1:30 Toning class
2:45 Aquaexercise
4:00 Afternoon class
5:30 Dinner
7:00 Workshop

OPTIONAL COSTS: Extras include facials, massages, body work sessions (including energy-balancing, gravity-guidance and cellulite or lymph-cleansing), hair-care treatments, mineral baths, various types of body wraps, and tennis lessons. The Springs Gift Shop carries resort wear and sundries.

NICE TO KNOW: Murrieta Hot Springs has been well-known as a European-style spa since the early 1900s. For a long time, it was called "the Queen of the Spas." In the early 1980s, it was purchased by a communal based group, Alive Polarity. It was recently sold to a private owner, which has updated both the physical facilities and the program.

JUDY'S COMMENT: Murrieta has done a wonderful job of updating. They have an effective weight-loss program that is enhanced by the mineral-spring treatments.

RANCHO RIO CALIENTE
ADPO Postal 1-1187
Guadalajara, Jalisco, Mexico
Reservations Only: 818-796-5577

This British-run vegetarian spa is located in a magnificent valley alongside a natural hot mineral stream and across from a Mexican national forest. Open year-round.

RATES: Affordable. Credit cards are not accepted.

LOCATION: This spa is twenty miles from Guadalajara, near a small Indian village named La Primavera. The nearest airport is in Guadalajara. The one-hour taxi ride to the Rancho makes you wonder whether you've made the right choice. Just hang in there, for as soon as you see the gorgeous valley, you'll know you did!

EMPHASIS/PHILOSOPHY: This spa is very low key. If you are looking for Hilton-type amenities or Canyon Ranch–type activities, do not come here. Rancho Rio Caliente refers to itself as "a unique opportunity for self-care, restorative rest, weight goal achievement and relaxation." They consider good nutrition to be the most important factor contributing to good health. Water therapy plays a secondary role here.

DIET PROGRAM: The vegetarian diet features papaya as a cleansing agent. Many other tropical fruits and vegetables are also served, either raw or cooked. They include guava, jicama, malva, gauanbana, black and white zapote, mamey, lime and chirimoya. Grains, eggs and juices supplement the menu. Their breads are delicious. Purified water for drinking and kitchen use.

GUEST POPULATION: This coed spa accommodates 72 guests. Most guests come to unwind and put their health into proper perspective. An impressive 95 percent of the guests are repeaters. Many small groups make annual visits.

MEAL SERVICE: Meals are served buffet style. The dining room is as casual as the total atmosphere here.

DRESS CODE: Comfy, knock-around clothes are perfect. Bring sweatsuits or a sweater for early mornings and evenings.

ACCOMMODATIONS: There are many different types of accommodations available, ranging from single bedrooms to triple bedrooms. All have a private bath, fireplace, and electric blankets. There are no radios, TVs, or telephones in the rooms or in the common areas.

It is possible to contact a guest in case of an emergency by calling the California reservation number, which calls a Guadalajara answering service. They give the message to the cabdriver, who stops by every day, or, in case of extreme emergency, a special cab will be dispatched to the Rancho immediately.

HOUSE RULES: Children under eighteen are not permitted. Smoking is not allowed in the dining room and other public areas. Alcohol is not served. However, you may bring your own.

PHYSICAL FACILITIES: In addition to the sleeping facilities, dining room, kitchen, and office, there is one large common room for group activities. There are four swimming pools: 1 lap pool, 1 large general recreation pool, and 2 non-coed skinny-dipping pools. There is also a natural steam room.

ACTIVITIES, TREATMENTS AND PROGRAMS: There is no formal program here. The only schedule you'll need is this one:

Breakfast	8:30–10:00
Lunch	Noon–2:30
Dinner	6:00–8:00

All other activities are strictly up to the individual. Swimming, hiking, and horseback riding are favorites.

OPTIONAL COSTS: These treatments are available for an extra fee: massages, scalp massages, reflexology, acupuncture, herbal wraps, facials, manicures, and pedicures. Trips to Guadalajara and other local points of interest are also available.

NICE TO KNOW: Don't worry about drinking water, ice cubes, or washed fresh vegetables here. The Rancho purifies Spa water for drinking and kitchen use. Spa water is also pumped into the bathrooms. A unique touch: even the toilets flush hot!

JUDY'S COMMENT: A wonderful place for peace and quiet, restorative mineral baths, and slimming vegetarian cuisine—quite a combine!

SHARON SPRINGS HEALTH SPA
P.O. Box 288-A
Sharon Springs, NY 13459
518-284-2885

This country-home retreat is located in the rural setting of Sharon Springs, 1,200 feet above sea level, and is known for its sulfur and magnesium mineral waters. The area is marked with old historic Indian trails immortalized in Drums Along the Mohawk. Open May 31 to Labor Day.

RATES: Affordable. No credit cards are accepted.

LOCATION AND TRANSPORTATION: Sharon Springs is 185 miles northwest of New York City. Fly to New York City, Albany, or Utica and take Greyhound or Amtrak to Sharon Springs.

EMPHASIS/PHILOSOPHY: DeLores Schneider, founder/director, with a degree in nutritional counseling, has created a wholistic program geared for "rest, relaxation, slenderizing, and detoxification the natural way."

DIET PROGRAM: Calorie count: 600–1,500 per day. Juice or water fasting is available. No white flour, sugar, or salt is used. This vegetarian program includes fresh fruits and vegetables, eggs and dairy products, wheatgrass, sprout salads, and whole grains. You can expect to lose 5 to 10 pounds weekly, they say.

GUEST POPULATION: Coed. 18 guests. Guests are young and young-at-heart and vary in size and shape. Most folks come for weight loss or just plain R & R. Many guests come from nearby Albany and historic Cooperstown.

PACKAGES AND MINIMUM STAYS: Two days is the minimum stay, but packages include a Mid-Week (Monday to Friday), Mini-Week (Thursday to Sunday), and Weekend (Friday to Sunday). There are also weekly and monthly rates.

MEAL SERVICE: Informal; most meals are table service.

DRESS CODE: Jeans or jogging outfits are perfect in this casual setting.

ACCOMMODATIONS: The rooms are all newly decorated—each one differently. The walls are covered with sheets that match the bedding. Each room is named for the linen design, such as Crystal Dreams. No private baths or air conditioning. Television and phones are available in the lobby.

HOUSE RULES: No smoking is allowed in the buildings.

PHYSICAL FACILITIES: Even though Sharon Springs is not a physical fitness center, you'll find sauna, whirlpool, massage room, exercise room with mini-rebounders, slant boards, backswings (like gravity boots), and weight equipment. Nearby are the famed mineral springs, nature trails, and tennis courts.

ACTIVITIES, TREATMENTS, AND PROGRAMS: There are numerous exercise classes offered daily: aerobics, yoga, and dancercize. Swimmers are provided transportation to Glimmerglass Park for a dip in Lake Otsego. Evening programs offer a variety of topics: positive mental attitude, nutrition, money management, and iridology. There are also workshops on shiatsu, reflexology, and personal growth.

OPTIONAL COSTS: Optionals include massages (shiatsu and reflexology), herbal wrap, sulfur and mud baths, facials, saliva tests (individualized analysis of your body's chemical and vitamin needs), reflexology, iridology, and Reiki therapy, a Japanese form of "hands-on" healing through energy transference to afflicted areas. Horseback riding is available nearby. A new treatment offered here is the non-surgical face-lift, which utilizes low-frequency electrical waves to strengthen muscles and increase their tone and to improve blood circulation to the skin.

NICE TO KNOW: During the "Golden Age of Spas," 1870–1900, Sharon Springs was world-famous and the mineral waters prize-winning for curative effects. The Sharon Springs area abounds with history, from Indian lore to its own health-giving mineral springs and sulfur baths. DeLores has been in the health-related field for twenty years. She imports mud and salts from the Dead Sea for use in body toning and baths. The Sharon Springs Public Bath Houses are but a stone's throw away. Spa guests are encouraged to take the waters daily.

JUDY'S COMMENT: This could be a good invitation into the world of wholistic health as well as an exciting trip to an historic miner-springs town.

FOUR

MEDICAL WEIGHT-CONTROL CENTERS

8
NO-NONSENSE DIETING

Obesity is a disease. In fact, in the United States, it's the greatest health hazard of our time. Though illnesses associated with under-nourishment, such as rickets and scurvy, have virtually disappeared, they have been replaced by disorders connected with overeating: hypertension, diabetes, angina, and cardiovascular disease.

Heart disease has always been considered the domain of males. This is no longer true. According to the National Center for Health Statistics, reported chronic heart disease is now more common in women than it is in men. In 1986 there were over 12 million women whose chronic heart disease was reported, compared to less than 11 million men.

Several factors that have contributed to the rise of heart disease among women are the use of birth control pills, the increased number of female smokers, and the increased stress put upon women holding jobs outside the home.

The one constant factor, that has always and will always contribute to heart disease, is overweight. In fact, significant overweight makes your chance of contracting heart disease two-and-a-half times greater than if your weight were normal.

Most of us know when we weigh too much. Your ever-expanding waistline tells the story. If you have any doubt, consult the medical charts to find out the ideal or desirable weight for your sex, height, and build. Most doctors would call you clinically obese if you're 10 percent heavier than these norms.

Regardless of what's desirable or ideal (and that can be partly in the eye of the beholder), the hard fact is that 32 percent of men and 63 percent of women are at least 10 percent above the desirable weight for their height and build; and 16 percent of men and 24 percent of women are 20 percent above, according to the National Center for Health Statistics.

So, when your doctor warns you to take that weight off, but you can't control the urge to duck exercise and sneak snacks, the solution may be a medically supervised residential weight-control center.

WHO GOES AND WHY

A trip to a medical weight-control center is different from your usual pampered spa trek. This is a no-nonsense, hard-core, lose-weight-or-else business. The centers offer full-time supervised medical programs to help you reduce. Most of the facilities will insist on a complete medical checkup by their own medical staff before you're admitted.

So the guests are patients and the diets are prescriptions? It's not as grim as it sounds. The fact is, a lot of people check into medical weight-control centers time after time not only because their doctors advise it but because these establishments offer much the same magical benefits as other health retreats: a home away from home in a stress-free environment. And don't discount that sublime feeling you get when the scale shows that you've achieved your objective and taken control of yourself.

Many of the guests are victims of the yo-yo syndrome—gaining and losing over and over again. The problem is essentially the same whether they have ten pounds to lose or a hundred. Whatever your goal, peer group pressure can prod you to meet the challenge of the daily weigh-in.

Not all the clients of these centers are fatties. While the four weight-control centers, in Durham, North Carolina, specialize in treating obesity, the three Pritikin programs in California, Pennsylvania, and Florida cater to a more diverse clientele. There, you'll meet people with degenerative diseases—coronary conditions, diabetes, high blood pressure, hypertension—which may or may not be accompanied by a serious weight problem. You'll also find people who are neither fat nor ill but simply interested in learning a new life-style.

Thus, medical weight-control centers serve a multitude of people and problems. Guests come in all shapes and sizes. There aren't any wheelchair cases, though—you must be self-sufficient and able to get around on your own two feet.

In fact, getting around on your feet is a big part of the treatment. Walk, walk, walk is the heart of the exercise program at almost all of these centers. Of course, you don't have to go to one of these establishments to reap the undeniable benefits of putting one foot in front of the other. Covert Bailey, author of *Fit or Fat*, says, "If I were grossly fat, I would give up whatever was necessary—job, housework, whatever—and walk three to four hours per day."

Fine, if you can do it, but I think it takes a lot more time and discipline than most of us can muster. It is far easier to go to a residential weight-control center where medical supervision will help you establish a healthy diet and exercise regimen for you to follow the rest of your life.

HOW LONG AND HOW MUCH?

At most medical weight-control centers, you can count on a 4-week stay. The folks who run these places figure that's the least time it will take, in most cases, to stabilize your weight and begin to effect lasting changes in your habits and attitudes. A couple of Pritikin clinics now offer a 13-day option, but they prefer that you stay the full 26 days. Another short program is available at St. Helena in Napa Valley, California, where 12-day packages are scheduled at periodic intervals. But if you have to lose dozens of pounds, think in terms of several months.

Being away from your job or family responsibilities for a month or more may seem impossible and totally self-indulgent at first. But if your health—your most precious possession—is at stake, think again. You may return to your ordinary routines more vital and recharged. If it is literally a matter of survival, or longer life, what could be more important? I have known women with young children who were so determined to lose forty, fifty, or sixty pounds that they arranged for proxy parents to stay with their kids for as long as it took.

Four weeks away from home does not come cheap, as you can imagine. Costs range from a rock-bottom $1,550 to $6,000 and up. Don't forget that a hefty chunk of the tab goes for the required medical workups. However, you often have the option of returning within a year for a readmittance exam at little or no additional charge.

If you think you can't afford it check at your place of work and you may be pleasantly surprised. Some enlightened companies will underwrite your trip to a weight-control center, realizing that the dividend for them will be a more productive worker. Your health insurance program might cover all or part of the cost.

A VIEW OF FAT CITY

Durham, North Carolina, is a beautiful place surrounded by mountains and rolling hills. The climate is mild year-round, allowing 365 days for walking off those fat cells. In the center of the city is the beautiful campus of Duke University.

What distinguishes Durham from many pretty college towns is that it has four separate weight-control centers within its city limits. There are Dr. Kempner's Clinic and Rice House and the Duke Diet and Fitness Center, both using Duke's Medical Center; Structure House; and the relatively inexpensive Stuelke Thin for Life clinic.

Most people come for at least six weeks, register at one of the weight-control centers, and settle in. Sweatsuits are the outfit of the day; you will see all colors and styles being worn about town as the walking prescription is carried out. There's a variety of reasonably priced hotels, motels, and rooming houses. One of the most popular spots looks like a transplanted Florida resort: a large swimming pool surrounded by two- and four-story motel-like structures. A three-room apartment averages $475 a month.

All of Durham caters to the needs of reducers. Imagine an entire supportive city geared to help you lose weight! Feel free to eat out. All the big hotels (the Hilton, Imperial 400, Radisson, and Washington Duke) offer salt-free, sugar-free, low-fat menus that list calorie count and fat content.

Each center has a different dietary approach. Dr. Kempner's Rice Diet (true to its name) consists of not much more than rice for the first month. Later, when weight loss is progressing nicely, fruit, vegetables, fish, poultry, and lean meats are added. Men and women from 16 to 60 have lost hundreds of pounds on this regimen. The before-and-after pictures are startling. But it's not an overnight, wave-a-magic-wand affair. Stays of up to a year may be necessary to achieve such dramatic results.

The other three programs at Durham offer more balanced diets of approximately 700 calories daily. (See the Directory in Chapter 9 for specifics.) The success rate at all four facilities is "unbelievably good," according to my sources.

PRITIKINIZING THE NATION

Lovely, leggy Shirley MacLaine is still in superb shape after more than twenty-five years in show business—and that's despite her admitted weakness for foods of all kinds. Shirley is one of those yo-yos whose weight can fluctuate wildly. She long ago became a Pritikin follower to maintain herself at a lithe 118 to 120 pounds.

The Pritikin diet is based on complex carbohydrates—whole grains, vegetables, and no salt, fat, or sugar. Unlike conventional diets that cut down on starch, Pritikin claims that carbohydrates are the dieter's friend, not enemy, because they quicken the metabolism and give the body the energy it needs for aerobic activity.

The diet was developed by Nathan Pritikin, a self-made man with no formal medical training. In 1957 doctors told him he had a dangerous narrowing of the coronary arteries. With his self-designed diet, plus jogging, he lowered his blood cholesterol level by two-thirds. The result was a complete cure with no medication! And that was the beginning of what is today a multimillion-dollar business.

Hundreds of pilgrims with coronary problems, high blood pressure, hypertension, and other ailments, as well as the severely obese and those merely seeking an ounce of prevention, flock to the Pritikin meccas. These true believers have an almost religious fervor. The food may not be rich, but most of the disciples are. The 26-day program costs upward of $6,000.

The Pritikin diet is effective for those who are highly motivated—usually their doctors have told them to "take it off or else!" Detractors insist that it's unrealistic, monastic, and hard to integrate into daily life. It's one thing to follow the ascetic Pritikin routine in the totally controlled environment of a Pritikin retreat; it's another thing to do it at home or when out for a business lunch or social dinner. You almost need a full-time caretaker to tend to your meals. Since no medication is given, you must stick to the diet religiously, and the need for constant support causes many Pritikinites to return regularly to the "nest" for reinforcement.

The Pritikin Longevity Center at Santa Monica, California, is the original home of Pritikinism. The 26-day program is based on a 13-day rollover. Every 13 days a new group of initiates arrives for the indocrination cocktail party: Perrier with lime in champagne glasses. The table is beautifully set with exquisite chafing dishes of hot tamales, vegetable-filled tortillas, and other delicious ethnic dishes—all made with a buckwheat base. You'd never guess that health food could be so elegant!

Pritikinites wear their name tags everywhere, even to bed. You'll feel lost without yours. With it, you can hardly get lost. The tag has the Center's phone number imprinted, with quarters attached in case you're "off campus" and your willpower fails or you suddenly feel ill. Tags are color-keyed to your fitness level and list your pulse rate, medical information, and the specific program you're on.

The first few days are hectic. You'll have a complete physical, a treadmill evaluation, and blood stress tests. The tests themselves can be stressful, indeed. You're asked to sign a release freeing the institution from responsibility in case you suffer an injury during a test.

It would be nice if these exams could be completed the first day, but don't count on it. They don't rush you through this individualized program. And your assigned doctor is available any time you want to talk to him or her.

Your medical test results will determine your exercise program. There are five or six different exercise levels, each geared at the fitness of the participant. Mornings may find you doing some warm-up stretches, running on the treadmill for half an hour, or doing some furious pedaling on an Exercycle. The goal is to work up to your maximum heartbeat, within safe limits. You'll learn to take your own pulse and to press a neck artery to monitor your heart rate.

You're supposed to walk twice a day, and in Santa Monica that's no sweat. The beach and shopping malls are full of sweatsuits of all sizes, shapes, colors, and styles. Everyone talks about his or her health problem. By the end of the first week, every client is an expert. You never saw so many authorities in one place in your life! A lot of the comradely conversation revolves around the diet. On weekends local color is added, as the townspeople head for the beach and fill the air with rainbow-hued Frisbees and kites.

Cooking classes are a featured attraction of the Pritikin learn-by-doing philosophy. Despite the presence of lots of single men, however, the classes are intended to teach women a new way to cook for their husbands. Yes, in the Pritikin world, wives are their husbands' keepers. If that's not understood between spouses, the whole thing may be a waste of time and money.

The day is chock-full of things to do. When you've had your fill of lectures on such topics as "Obesity," "Why I Am a Chocoholic," "Judging Food Portions," "How to Select Foods," and "The Addictive Personality," you can take a field trip to a local grocery or health food store to get field experience. In fact, there's so much to do that you have to rise by 6:00 A.M. to get it all in. A friend of mine was kept so busy that during her entire 26 days, she couldn't find time to fit in a manicure.

You'll leave Pritikin equipped with gourmet recipes and fortified for a new, healthier way of life. You'll be asked to have your cholesterol checked every three months by your regular doctor. The door will be open for you to come back for a weekend or a 13-day session, and you will be urged to join a support group once you're back home.

TIPS AND CAVEATS

Medical weight-control centers differ. Some are based on behavior-modification principles, some aren't. Settings, costs, programs, and philosophies vary greatly. For these reasons, it is very important to investigate every center as thoroughly as you can. Set your goals in advance (making sure they are realistic) and find the program that best fits them. Watch out for quirks, oddities, and specializations that might not suit your needs.

In picking a medical weight-control facility, inquire carefully, armed with the following Directory as a guide, into the question of how large a part reeducation plays. For any systematic weight-loss program to be effective, you must have a clear idea of how your body works. Dieting and exercise programs are combined with cooking classes and even therapy sessions at some weight-control centers. That's why so many attendees come out sounding like walking medical dictionaries.

Don't expect to lose as much weight at Pritikin centers as at some of the others. Not everyone is there to lose weight, and the same food is served to dieter and nondieter alike; it's up to you to monitor your caloric intake. One woman I know returned from a 26-day stay with an 8-pound loss to show for it—and that's not far from the norm. Men can expect to lose twice as much as women, who are born with more of those fatty cells. On the other hand, Structure House, one of the Durham clinics, claims that losses of 15 to 30 pounds per month are common.

The Pritikin emphasis is not on straight weight loss. You might lose less on their complex-carbohydrate-vegetarian diet than on a high-protein one, but you will be indoctrinated with a total approach to changing your life.

When considering a visit to a medical weight-control center, be sure to get all the facts in advance. For instance, at Dr. Kempner's you must stay with the program until you reach your "normal" weight and have other health problems under control. If you wish to be treated, you must sign a form agreeing to these conditions. One potential problem in this regard is Dr. Kempner's recommended weights, which are unusually low and do not take into account your age or skeletal structure. Theoretically, your stay could be much longer than anticipated.

And remember, some diets may not be suitable for you, either for medical or personal reasons.

One general warning: Most medical weight-control centers try to get you off medication while you're still in the program, so you must be cautious when you get home. If you fail to adhere rigidly to the prescribed regimen, you might not be able to remain medication-free. Be honest with yourself, and consult with your own physician before and after participating in a weight-control program.

9
MEDICAL WEIGHT-CONTROL CENTERS: DIRECTORY

WHY, WHERE, AND HOW MUCH

These centers, some of which do not like being referred to as "spas," because of their medical orientation, address obesity and related diseases seriously, although most will accept guests with only a few pounds to lose. Generally, they stress reeducation and life-style change. Most require a medical examination before beginning the program.

Cost is based on one week's expense, including meals. However, many of these centers require longer programs, often up to four weeks, so total expenses can mount. Best Buys are indicated by an asterisk.

> Affordable: up to $1,000
> Moderate: $1,000–$1,700
> Expensive: $1,700 and up

DUKE UNIVERSITY DIET AND FITNESS CENTER
804 W. Trinity Avenue
Durham, NC 27701
919-684-6331

Using medical and clinical/behavioral approaches to weight control, the Center is part of Duke University Medical Center's Department of Community and Family Medicine.

RATES: Affordable. Housing is not included in the rates, however. Credit cards: American Express, MasterCard, and Visa.

LOCATION AND TRANSPORTATION: Many airlines serve Raleigh/Durham airport, which is only 20 minutes from the Center in the city of Durham. This is the verdant Piedmont region of the state, which has a moderate climate and a rich cultural history.

EMPHASIS/PHILOSOPHY: The Center takes a multidisciplinary approach to weight control, combining recent findings in the fields of medicine, behavior modification, dietetics, and education. "Weight loss is not our only concern; we want our patients to learn new habits that will enable them to continue dieting and maintaining their weight loss after leaving the clinic," says Dr. Michael Hamilton, director of the program.

DIET PROGRAM: 700–750 calories per day. Well-balanced meals contain no sugar, no salt, and low fat. Dietetic products are used. Breakfast and lunch are served buffet style, portion-controlled by food servers; dinner is table service. "Absolutely normal food," says one satisfied customer. At each meal there is a choice of many items, and chicken is available every evening for dinner.

GUEST POPULATION: Coed. The Center usually has 40–100 guests in residence.

PACKAGES AND MINIMUM STAYS: The basic program is 4 weeks, but there also is a 2-week Executive Program. New patients enter on Monday morning.

DRESS CODE: Dress is casual at all times.

ACCOMMODATIONS: Guests are expected to provide their own housing from a wide selection of hotels and motels in Durham. A list will be sent to you on request, or you can find housing when you arrive. Innkeepers in Durham are used to accommodating Center visitors.

HOUSE RULES: The required medical examination is given at Duke University Medical Center. Smoking is allowed only in lounge areas.

PHYSICAL FACILITIES: The program is housed in an attractive building, providing under one roof extensive medical, nutritional, and fitness evaluations; workshops and seminars; dining facilities; and exercise facilities, including a large gym and indoor pool. Beauty salons, boutiques, golf courses, and the like are to be found locally.

ACTIVITIES, TREATMENTS, AND PROGRAMS: The program consists of four components. (1) *Medical.* Each participant receives a detailed health assessment, based on medical history, physical examination, and lab tests. Other medical services include counseling on preventive health and planning for medical needs after returning home. (2) *Behavioral*. Through group discussions, workshops, and seminars, participants become aware of their eating and exercise patterns in relation to personality traits and life-style. This component emphasizes the importance of long-term commitment to change. (3) *Nutrition*. The goal of this component is to help the participant develop healthier eating patterns. All meals are taken at the Center, and good eating habits are reinforced through lectures and seminars. (4) *Fitness*. Exercise increases weight loss, provides the individual with positive activity, reduces feelings of hunger, and is an excellent way to reduce tension and stress, says the Center. Thus, special efforts are made to provide each participant with exercise opportunities that meet their special needs, both at the Center and at home later.

A Day at the Duke Diet and Fitness Center

7:30	Morning walk
8:00	Breakfast and voluntary check-in with a member of the medical, nutrition, or fitness staff
9:00	Floor aerobics
10:00	Seminar
11:00	Seminar
12:00	Lunch
1:00	Pool aerobics
2:00	Swimming
3:00–5:00	Workshops, demonstrations of low-cal food shopping and cooking, etc.
5:00	Dinner

On weekends, only meals and swimming activities are provided.

JUDY'S COMMENT: The program here is serious-minded and scientifically sound. It's not a quick fix, but rather a realistic attempt to help individuals make a new beginning in the interest of personal health and well-being. Of course, basic change is difficult, and it's ultimately up to you. But how nice to know that there's a facility such as the Duke Diet and Fitness Center where you can find a sensible, safe, and supportive program for positive change.

GREEN MOUNTAIN AT FOX RUN
P.O. Box 164, Fox Lane
Ludlow, VT 05149
802-228-8885

An Aspen-type lodge nestled in the beautiful Green Mountains of

MEDICAL WEIGHT-CONTROL CENTERS   329

Vermont and surrounded by 20 wooded acres overlooking a nine-hole golf course. Open year-round. Women only.

RATES: Moderate. Credit cards: MasterCard, Visa.

LOCATION AND TRANSPORTATION: The spa is 230 miles from New York City (4½ hours by car). Lebanon, New Hampshire, and Rutland, Vermont, are the nearest airports. Bus service is available from New York, Boston, or Montreal. At Ludlow or Rutland bus station, Green Mountain provides courtesy pickup and return on opening and closing days of sessions. Green Mountain is located 1½ miles from the town of Ludlow.

EMPHASIS/PHILOSOPHY: Here you'll find a no-nonsense, serious approach to becoming the woman you want to be by changing your attitude toward food, health, and your life-style itself. This is an educational facility, and the emphasis is on knowledge, instruction, and behavior modification. You will burn off fat cells by means of exercise in combination with a diet you can live with and attitudinal changes. Green Mountain takes an educational approach for long-term management of weight loss and obesity. The emphasis here is on inches lost, not pounds.

DIET PROGRAM: 1,000–2,000 calories per day in well-balanced meals with low salt, low fat, and no sugar. No foods are excluded, and they serve foods you usually eat at home or at a restaurant. Portion-controlled menus could include such items as a salad plate, a pita sandwich, cottage cheese and fruit, and moussaka. Chef Gilbert Dillon whips up other delicacies such as shrimp and scallop scampi, green onion quiche, turkey divan, and silver dollar pancakes (with syrup?).

GUEST POPULATION: Women only. 45–55 guests, ages eighteen and over. According to the admissions office, "Our guests come from all over the world with varied professions . . . everything from doctors and lawyers to teachers and students (lots of students here in the summer). "A cosmopolitan crowd. Why do most women come to Green Mountain? Directors Thelma and Alan Wayler tell us, "It is the last resort . . . for weight control . . . because they are too fat and they have tried it all; everything from ear staples [remember that one?] to intestinal bypass surgery have passed through these doors."

PACKAGES AND MINIMAL STAYS: The minimum stay is 2 weeks, but savings are to be had on the 4-week program. Sessions begin on specific Sundays and close on Saturdays.

ACCOMMODATIONS: All the lodge rooms have a mountain view. Simply gorgeous! There are dormitory-type rooms with double beds and modern bathrooms. Roommates can be arranged.

HOUSE RULES: No smoking in the dining room or public areas. Daily participation is required for a walk/jog and exercise class.

PHYSICAL FACILITIES: Green Mountain does not consider itself a spa in the traditional sense. Therefore, it does not have a beauty salon or the usual array of pampering treatment facilities. You will find an outdoor pool, two jogging tracks, a golf course, three exercise rooms, two saunas, and outdoor tennis courts.

ACTIVITIES, TREATMENTS, AND PROGRAMS: The program at Green Mountain is quite structured. Activity programs account for 60 to 70 percent of the day's schedule and, besides exercising, include walking/jogging, stationary biking, and soft aerobics. Musculoskeletal activities include body conditioning, rhythmical exercise, flexibility, light weight training, yoga, cross-country skiing in winter, tennis in summer, and more. Every one of the dieters, be she 10 pounds or 100 pounds overweight, spends most of her day exercising. Programs also include lectures on nutrition and stress management.

Once a week the ladies get together in small groups to mull over their feelings about being overweight. "We're getting these women to identify their eating and behavioral problems and then come up with their own self-modification techniques for repatterning eating and activity," says Thelma Wayler. "Lifelong weight control is simply a head thing, not a belly thing . . . the women develop techniques for controlling problem behavior around food. Some techniques include leaving food behind, removing the top slice of bread from a sandwich, delay tactics, and so on. Successful weight loss demands a commitment to changing your life style."

"Repatterning" starts upon acceptance, when Thelma mails each guest an eating questionnaire that becomes an actual graph of their eating behavior while at Green Mountain. Evening activities might include cooking classes or awareness workshops. Some people read, go to the movies in town, or talk. "The talk is good," says one happy Green Mountaineer.

NICE TO KNOW: Tuition fees at Green Mountain may be tax-deductible under the heading of "Health Institute Fees," as 30 percent of the clientele are physician referred. Should you not want beef or be a lacto-ovo vegetarian, your preferences can be accommodated. Having a car will help you see the countryside and go antiquing. You're allowed to come and go on the property as you please.

JUDY'S COMMENT: Spectacular weight-loss statistics have been compiled at Green Mountain. Theirs is a serious and effective program conducted in beautiful surroundings by certified professionals for the person who truly needs and wants to change her life-style.

HILTON HEAD HEALTH INSTITUTE
P.O. Box 7138
The Cottages in the Shipyard Plantation
Hilton Head Island, SC 29938
803-785-7292

This weight-control program is based on a beautiful resort island in the Atlantic in the heart of South Carolina's low country. A 542-acre forest preserve is nearby. Open year-round except for two weeks at Christmas.

RATES: Moderate. No credit cards accepted.

LOCATION AND TRANSPORTATION: The facility is located on Hilton Head Island, one of the "Golden Isles" off the coast of South Carolina. The Institute is 45 miles north of Savannah. Historic Charleston lies a modest distance to the north. Limousine service is available to and from Savannah airport for a fee, and airline service may be found directly into Hilton Head Island.

EMPHASIS/PHILOSOPHY: According to the Institute, "Behavior modification, nutritional education, and supervised physical activity are combined to achieve permanent weight control." Dr. Peter Miller, a clinical psychologist, designed the diet program, after observing patients for many years, "to help the dieter lose weight safely and permanently." He believes that overweight people do not necessarily eat more than their slimmer counterparts but rather suffer from "metabolic suppression," that is, they do not burn off calories as efficiently. Dr. Miller says that by altering their diet, outlook, and eating habits dieters can eat normally without weight gain due to metabolic inefficiency. The program is geared toward long-term education rather than spa-style temporary change.

DIET PROGRAM: The basic diet is 800 calories per day, going up to 1,100 calories during the third week of the four-week program. The diet, developed by Dr. Miller, is well balanced, featuring moderate protein, moderate carbohydrates, low fat, low sodium, and restricted cholesterol. Dietetic products are used. The emphasis is on complex carbohydrates, including fruits, vegetables, potatoes, cereal, and bread. Dr. Miller believes that complex carbohydrates fuel the metabolism, causing it to function at a higher level, thus burning off more calories. Meals, most of which are served sit-down style, are served four times a day. There are occasional buffet breakfasts and lunches, with servers present to control portion size. A typical day's menu might consist of sugarless cereals and milk, grapefruit, and tea for breakfast; cottage cheese on lettuce with strawberries and melon for lunch; baked chicken, baked potato, green vegetables, and strawberries with yogurt for dinner; and a midevening "metabo-meal" of cinnamon toast and tea.

GUEST POPULATION: Coed. 40 guests. People who come range from those needing to lose 10–20 pounds to the severely obese.

PACKAGES AND MINIMUM STAYS: There are two programs: the 26-day Weight-Control Program and the 12-day Executive Health Program. Both begin on specific Sundays throughout the year, with checkout on Saturday at any time.

DRESS CODE: Informal and casual are the watchwords.

ACCOMMODATIONS: Guests reside in lovely shared villas, with private bedrooms and bath. (Private villas are available at additional cost.) The Institute proper is an easy walk from the villas or cottages. No room service.

HOUSE RULES: No smoking is allowed.

PHYSICAL FACILITIES: The Institute houses the dining room, lounge, and lecture/seminar rooms. Guests have access to all of the amenities of Shipyard Plantation: swimming pool, whirlpool, sauna, exercise facilities, an equipment room, racquetball courts, golf club, miles of bicycling and walking trails, and 12 miles of sandy beach along Hilton Head Island's shoreline. Tennis courts are nearby.

ACTIVITIES, TREATMENTS, AND PROGRAMS: A medical exam is given upon arrival and monitoring occurs throughout the program. Each patient helps design a personal exercise regimen, which may include walking, stretching, calisthenics, and aerobics (classes offered daily). Jogging, bicycling, swimming, tennis, and golf are also encouraged. Programs include lectures and discussions on relaxation techniques, family support, and how to manage stress, deal with food cravings, control binge eating, and deal with social occasions and eating at restaurants. Basic nutrition classes cover topics such as portion control and cooking with herbs. Individual consultation and a stop-smoking program are available to patients.

A Day at the Institute

8:00	Breakfast
8:30	Walk
9:00	Health seminar
10:00	Aerobic exercise
11:00	Break
11:45	Calisthenics or weights
12:30	Lunch

1:00	Walk
1:30–5:00	Activity of choice; optional exercise classes
5:00	Health seminar
6:00	Dinner
6:30	Walk
7:00	Free time

STAFF POPULATION: The director, Peter M. Miller, Ph.D., is a clinical psychologist and a professor at the University of South Carolina. He is author of the book *The Hilton Head Metabolism Diet* and editor-in-chief of the professional journal *Addictive Behaviors.* There are two consulting physicians. Other professionals in health education, physical fitness, and nutrition are on the staff.

NICE TO KNOW: Both the 26-day and 12-day programs are offered once a month and begin on the same date. Their purpose is to teach healthier life-style patterns and reduce the risk of cardiovascular disease. The programs focus on physical activity, nutritional planning, health education, behavior modification, and stress management.

JUDY'S COMMENT: Clinical psychology is here turned to practical advantage for those who wish to lose weight and keep it off through changed life-style. You'll find a realistic program within a lovely vacation setting.

PRITIKIN LONGEVITY CENTER
975 E. Lincoln Highway
Downingtown, PA 19335
Telephone: Outside Pennsylvania: 800-344-3243
In Pennsylvania: 800-344-8243
215-873-0123

The Pritikin program is a separate and complete facility located within the framework of the Tabas Resort Hotel in Downingtown, Pennsylvania. The setting is in the hills of a semirural Pennsylvania Dutch community. Open year-round. Other centers are located in California and Florida (see following).

RATES: Expensive. Guests are asked to prepay their entire stay upon arrival. Credit cards: MasterCard, Visa.

LOCATION AND TRANSPORTATION: The Center is 30 miles from Philadelphia. Limousine service is available from the Philadelphia airport for a fee.

EMPHASIS/PHILOSOPHY: The Pritikin program is a health and nutrition program, the goal of which, according to the Center, is to "help you get healthy and stay healthy the rest of your life." The Pritikin program deals not only with degenerative diseases but also places special emphasis on weight loss. According to the late Nathan Pritikin, founder of the Center, weight loss not only helps control many diseases but it can actually prevent many of them from occurring.

DIET PROGRAM: At this Pritikin Center you eat five times per day, including foods such as fresh fruits and vegetables, potatoes, pasta, corn on the cob, bean soup, and whole grain bread. Chicken, turkey, or fish are served twice a week. No fats, salt, sugar, oils, whole milk products, processed foods, caffeine, or salt or sugar substitutes are used in preparation. Women consume 1,000 calories per day, men 1,200. The diet is made up of 75 to 80 percent complex carbohydrates; 10 percent natural fat (the average American diet is 40 percent fat); 50 grams of dietary fiber; and 3½ ounces of animal protein. Pritikin discourages the use of vitamins and tobacco. Projected weekly weight loss for women is 5–8 pounds; for men, 8–10 pounds.

GUEST POPULATION: About 40 guests. The Center is coed; men and women of all ages, many with heart disease, diabetes, hypertension, others with weight-control problems, and still others simply wishing to reduce.

PACKAGES AND MINIMUM STAYS: A 13-day program and a 26-day program, with both groups arriving the same Sunday for evening dinner and an orientation program. The 13-day program is aimed at those with controlled hypertension, mild overweight, claudication (limping), and diabetes (if on oral medication). The 26-day program is for those with advanced conditions such as heart disease, obesity, uncontrolled hypertension, or insulin-treated diabetes. People without serious illnesses can participate in whichever program they desire. Departure is on Saturday afternoon.

MEAL SERVICE: Daytime snacks and meals are served buffet style while the sit-down dinner is served by waiters and waitresses. Food consumption begins with cereal at 7:15, followed by snack break at 10:00, lunch at 12:00, snack break at 3:00, and dinner at 5:45. Your caloric intake level is determined by a physician. Starches and fruits are portion-controlled by servers in the buffet line, but raw greens and vegetables are unlimited.

DRESS CODE: Casual at all times.

ACCOMMODATIONS: Pritikin guests stay in their own wing of the Tabas Resort Hotel. All accommodations are modern, with private bath, cable TV, and daily maid service. Some two-room suites are available, which have a refrigerator (all the easier to cheat), serving bar, desk, and sofa bed.

HOUSE RULES: No smoking is allowed in the Center.

PHYSICAL FACILITIES: Pritikin guests have access to indoor and outdoor pools, saunas, tennis courts, and a golf course—all hotel owned and operated. The Center itself houses a large carpeted gym with treadmills, exercise bicycles, weight machines, rowing machines, and a walking/jogging track.

ACTIVITIES, TREATMENTS, AND PROGRAMS: Medical services include complete medical history, cardiovascular exam, initial lab blood tests analysis, exercise treadmill exams to evaluate cardiovascular fitness, skinfold test, and daily blood pressure test. Upon completion of the thirteenth day of the program, one of the two fulltime physicians will summarize your progress and discuss your cardiovascular profile with you. Exercise activities include track walking, treadmilling, exercycling, rowing, weight training, jogging, and aerobics (all individually supervised and geared to your level of fitness). An at-home exercise program is prescribed for each person before departure.

The 40 hours of educational programming during your stay include instruction in nutrition, food shopping, meal preparation, stress reduction, relaxation; study groups on low back pain; foot care and blood test results; lectures, movies, slide presentations, displays, and question and answer sessions daily, as well as sessions with one's spouse or companion, who is encouraged to learn about the program.

A Day at Pritikin Longevity Center

6:45	Wake-up/slow stretching exercises
7:30–9:30	Breakfast: cereal, banana, and herb tea
8:00	Lecture: Exercise and Your Heart
9:10	Exercise class: treadmill workout
9:30–11:30	Morning snacks: fresh fruit and vegetables
10:30	Doctor's appointment
11:00	Cooking class: Pritikin brunch
11:30–2:30	Lunch: soup, vegetables, Pritikin pizza
1:00	Lecture: Composition of Foods
2:00	Exercise class: Straighten Up! back and posture exercises
2:30–4:30	Afternoon snacks: baked potato, bowl of soup
3:00	Lecture: Stress and the Modern Jungle
4:00	Weight-loss discussion group

5:00   Walk or jog outdoors
6:00–7:15 Dinner: salad, main entree, fruit for des-
          sert
7:30   Entertainment

STAFF POPULATION: The professional, full-time staff includes two physicians, two nutritionists, and six exercise instructors.

NICE TO KNOW: Pritikin Longevity Centers suggest you pack casually for your stay, as most guests wear warm-up suits, shorts and jeans, and running shoes. Some prefer to dress up a bit more in the evenings. Besides the regular newsletters and mailings from the Center, Pritikin will put alumni from a specific region in touch with one another so they can build a support group for each other once they're back home. Robert Pritikin, owner and son of the founder, often drops in for a visit, so don't be surprised if he turns up for dinner one night.

JUDY'S COMMENT: The many health success stories boasted by Pritikin graduates are testaments to the effectiveness of the program. Still, it takes a lot of grit to avoid backsliding into the fat-rich American diet we've grown up with. Upon returning home, do check with your own medical doctor, and don't be too hasty in throwing your medication down the drain.

PRITIKIN LONGEVITY CENTER
OF CALIFORNIA
1910 Ocean Front Walk
Santa Monica, CA 90405
Outside California: 800-421-9911
In California: 800-421-0981
215-450-5433

A medically supervised program housed in a former beachfront resort on the shore of the Pacific. Open year-round.

RATES: Expensive. Guests are asked to prepay their entire stay upon arrival. No credit cards.

LOCATION AND TRANSPORTATION: The Center is right on the ocean in Santa Monica, 15 miles from downtown L.A. and 6 miles southeast of Los Angeles International Airport. With prior notification, someone from the Center will meet you at the airport.

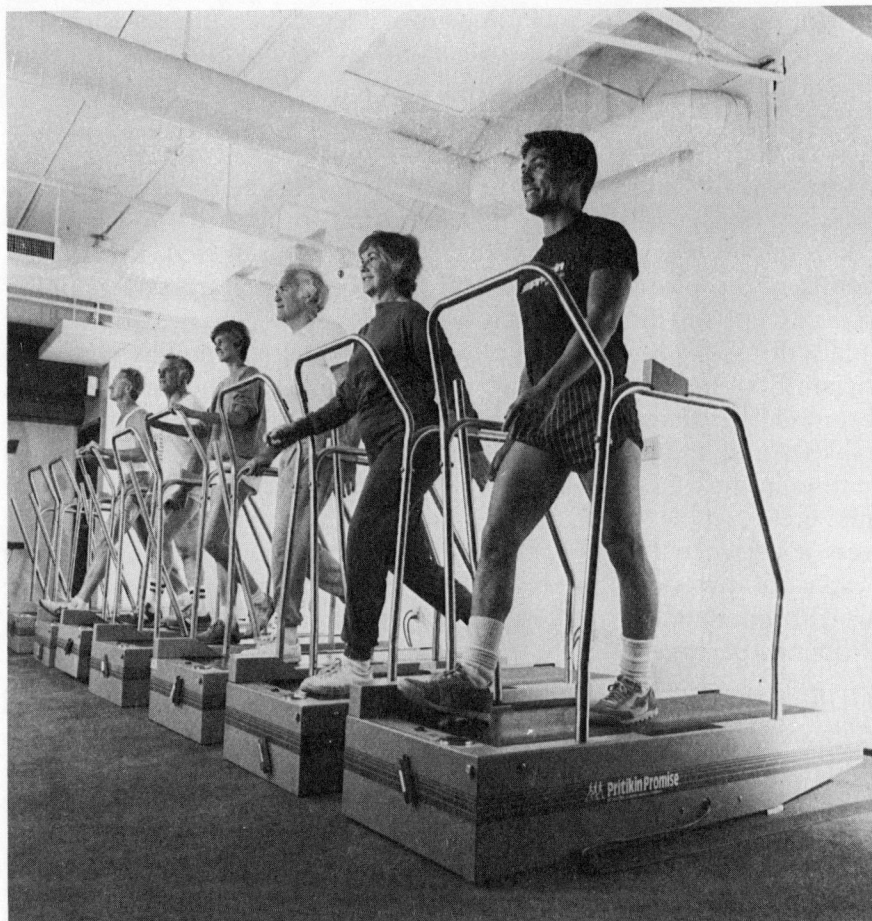

Courtesy of Pritikin Longevity Center of California

EMPHASIS/PHILOSOPHY: The Pritikin Centers cater to people who suffer from angina, hypertension, adult-onset diabetes, and other diseases as well as from overweight. The Pritikin program concentrates on two elements: basic restructuring of a way-of-life diet and development of an ongoing exercise and nutrition program. The patient's daily regimen must be a combination of the two. Nathan Pritikin, founder of the Centers and author of the bestseller *The Pritikin Program for Diet and Exercise*, calls the program "the most significant breakthrough in man's age-old quest for rejuvenation . . . there is no pill, no injection, no drug, no powder, no yoga, no potion, no other process that produces the revitalization effects achieved by [the program]."

DIET PROGRAM: The aim of the diet is to lower blood cholesterol levels; it includes six small meals per day, consisting of 80 percent complex carbohydrates including vegetables, fruits, and starches such as whole grain cereals, brown rice, and pasta. The diet also contains 10 percent natural fat. (The American Heart Association recommends fat intake be kept below 35 percent although the average American diet contains 40 percent.) The remaining 15 percent is protein. Small portions of fish and poultry are served two or three times a week. No fats, salt, sugar, oils, whole milk products, processed food (such as white flour), caffeine, salt, or sugar substitutes are used. Pritikin discourages the use of vitamins and tobacco. Meals are served buffet style except for dinner, which is a sit-down meal served by waiters and waitresses. One of three calorie levels is determined by your physician. Starches and fruits are portion-controlled, the control being exercised by servers stationed at the buffet table. Greens and vegetables are unlimited. There is a commercial toaster located at a food station in the dining area. Always available to guests are whole wheat pita bread, whole wheat matzo, and Japanese rice crackers (which are very good when warmed). Herbal teas and lemons for making lemon water are always at hand. There is no room service. The average weight reduction for men is 3 to 4 pounds per week; for women 2 to 3 pounds per week.

GUEST POPULATION: Coed. 80–130 guests. Many come to seek reversals of serious health problems but some merely wish to improve and prolong their health. One delighted Pritikinite was happy to have Hume Cronyn and Jessica Tandy as dinnermates. Shirley MacLaine and John Travolta are also devotees of the Pritikin diet plan.

PACKAGES AND MINIMUM STAYS: There is a 13-day program and a 26-day program. The 26-day program is particularly structured for those with advanced health conditions, such as heart disease, insulin-dependent diabetes, or obesity. The 13-day program is primarily for people with early hypertension, mild weight problems, mild diabetes (on oral medication), or those who simply want a solid education in Pritikinized living.

DRESS CODE: Casual. Bring comfortable walking shoes, exercise outfits, and a few sports costumes for dinner and shopping trips.

ACCOMMODATIONS: "A totally Pritikinized environment" describes the Center, which is housed in a 1920-era hotel with 120 guest rooms. Each of the small but attractive rooms has a private bath, color TV, direct-dial phone, and daily maid service. The Center is a self-contained, controlled environment where all facilities are located under one roof.

HOUSE RULES: None, but smoking is discouraged.

PHYSICAL FACILITIES: The Center houses an 800-square-foot gym illuminated by natural sunlight, with 60 motorized treadmills and exercise bikes. There are laundry facilities and a fitness boutique. You'll find miles of beach for walking or jogging. Tennis courts, bowling, and golf courses are nearby.

ACTIVITIES, TREATMENTS, AND PROGRAMS: Medical treatment at the center consists of an initial medical examination and history (including a complete physical, blood chemistry workup, and a treadmill tolerance test using an electocardiogram); daily blood pressure checks; twice-weekly doctor appointments; weekly blood tests; and a second treadmill test before departure. The exercise program consists of one mandatory hour-long exercise class per day with people at similar endurance levels (warm-up stretch and toning, two laps around the gym, and 30 minutes on the treadmill). Walks or runs on the beach, depending on your level of fitness, are encouraged. Optional classes include aerobics, yoga, race walking, back exercises, and use of the weight training equipment in the gym. An "at home" exercise program is prescribed for each person before departure.

The Pritikin Education Program includes physician-taught classes for people with the same medical problems; forty hours of lectures on nutrition and health (such as classes on heart disease, consequences of obesity, long-term effects of exercise, practical guidelines to weight loss, food purchasing and preparation); and group counseling on how to stop smoking, control compulsive overeating, manage stress, cut down on alcohol; as well as sessions with one's spouse or companion who is encouraged to learn the Pritikin life-style. To encourage patients to continue the program, Pritikin publishes a free monthly newsletter, maintains a toll-free hot line for backsliders, and encourages alumni to form small support groups in their hometowns. Leisure time activities include classes in meditation, art, sculpture, and frequent bus trips to a nearby shopping mall.

STAFF POPULATION: There are 43 professional staff members, including 10 physicians.

NICE TO KNOW: The program schedule for the week terminates at noon on Saturday, leaving the patient on his or her own to explore or exercise for a day and a half. The names of restaurants in the area serving Pritikin diet meals are made available to guests wishing to dine out on the weekends. Since well-fitting shoes are essential for the exercise program, an osteopath comes to the Center to custom fit shoes for you, supplying lifts, heel cups, etc. Special reduced rates are available to spouses and companions undergoing the program with their mates.

JUDY'S COMMENT: This Spartan diet/exercise program represents a severe change in one's life-style. It's a rigid discipline, but the rewards can be great for sufferers of cardiovascular and other diseases. "Pritikinizing the nation" is quite a business.

PRITIKIN LONGEVITY CENTER OF FLORIDA
5875 Collins Avenue
Miami Beach, FL 33140
800-327-4914
305-756-5353

The Pritikin Center of Florida is a medically supervised, live-in program on the shore of the Atlantic Ocean. Open year-round.

RATES: Expensive. No credit cards. Payment in full is expected upon arrival.

LOCATION AND TRANSPORTATION: Limousine service is available from Miami airport for a charge.

EMPHASIS/PHILOSOPHY: A comprehensive diet and exercise program aimed at controlling and preventing disease. The Pritikin Center says, "Underlying our program are scores of recognized medical studies, which show that populations on high-fat cholesterol diets tend to die early of heart, vascular, and other degenerative diseases. Similar health problems are rare in those populations that eat a natural diet such as the one recommended by the Longevity Center." The principles they follow are enumerated in *The Pritikin Program for Diet and Exercise*, written by Nathan Pritikin, founder of this Center and others in California and Pennsylvania.

DIET PROGRAM: Aimed at lowering blood cholesterol levels, the diet program consists of six meals per day. It includes vegetables; fruits; starches such as whole grain cereals, pasta, and brown rice; and small portions of fish and fowl. Starches and fruits are portion-controlled while greens and vegetables are unlimited. The component breakdown of the diet is 80 percent complex carbohydrates, 10 percent natural fat, and 10 percent protein. No fats, salt, sugars, oils, whole milk products, processed foods, caffeine, salt, or sugar substitutes are used in preparation. A physician determines your proper calorie level. Some dishes included in the diet are homemade lasagna, Chinese vegetables and chicken, salmon loaf, stuffed peppers, eggplant cannelloni, spaghetti, and an ever-present fresh-vegetable salad bar. Five of the meals are served buffet style, but dinner is a sit-down affair served by waiters and waitresses. A dozen or so tables with white tablecloths and floral centerpieces, each seating six, are scattered about the oceanfront dining room. The average weight reduction in four weeks is 13 pounds for men and 10 pounds for women.

GUEST POPULATION: Coed. 90 patients. Guests come in all

shapes, sizes, and stages of physical health. One diverse group included a teenager with diabetes, several thirtyish matrons with weight problems, and several men and women over sixty-five who sought to reverse the debilitating effects of heart disease.

PACKAGES AND MINIMUM STAYS: There is a 13-day program available for people with early hypertension, mild weight problems, type II diabetes (oral medication), or those who simply wish a firm foundation in Pritikin living. The 26-day program is for those with advanced health conditions such as heart disease, high blood pressure, and severe weight problems.

DRESS CODE: Casual clothing, exercise garb, beachwear, and proper walking shoes are recommended.

ACCOMMODATIONS: Guests are housed in a comfortable oceanfront hotel, some rooms have an ocean view. All rooms have a private bath plus all the amenities one would expect.

HOUSE RULES: None, although smoking is discouraged.

PHYSICAL FACILITIES: The hotel contains a complete Pritikin gymnasium with treadmills, Exercycles, rowing machines, and weight-training equipment. There is a large oceanfront swimming pool. At the ocean, you'll find a mile-long, hard-packed sand strip on the beach for walking and jogging. Golf and tennis facilities are nearby.

ACTIVITIES, TREATMENTS, AND PROGRAMS: Medical services include a complete medical history, a cardiovascular examination, an initial laboratory blood analysis, exercise treadmill examinations to evaluate cardiovascular fitness, a skin fold test, and daily blood pressure checks. Upon completion of your program, your assigned physician will summarize your progress and discuss your cardiovascular risk profile with you. Exercise activities include treadmilling, cycling, weight training, and walking or jogging on the beach. Activities are all individually supervised. Programs include instructions in food shopping, meal preparation, study groups on low-back pain, lectures on medical topics, movies, slide presentations on nutrition topics, displays, and question and answer sessions daily.

STAFF POPULATION: Physician and trained counselors administer the medical program on an around-the-clock basis.

NICE TO KNOW: Special reduced rates are available to spouses or companions undergoing the program with their mates.

JUDY'S COMMENT: The Pritikin Centers offer a valuable learning experience that may "turn your health around," although one must remain very self-motivated to continue the program at home. Get healthy and enjoy the Florida surf and sun in a luxury setting—a great combo.

THE RICE DIET
Kempner Clinic
P.O. Box 3099
Duke University Medical Center
Durham, NC 27710
919-684-3418

This well-known diet program was developed by Walter Kempner, M.D. It is now used for the treatment of severe obesity. The program centers in Durham, North Carolina, home of Duke University, and uses Duke's medical facilities. Open year-round.

RATE: Moderate. No credit cards.

LOCATION AND TRANSPORTATION: Fly into Raleigh-Durham airport, which is only 20 minutes from Duke University.

EMPHASIS/PHILOSOPHY: In the 1940s the rice diet was developed for treatment of renal insufficiency and severe hypertensive cardiovascular disease. It was later modified as a treatment for diabetes. More recently, it was adapted for the treatment of severe obesity. White rice was found to satisfy the requirements for a low-calorie, low-salt, low-protein, low-fat, virtually cholesterol-free diet. This program is strictly geared to weight loss; it is not a behavioral-modification approach.

DIET PROGRAM: The initial diet for most patients consists of five raw fruits a day (apples, oranges, bananas, mixed fruit, half grapefruit) and two bowls of white rice (one for lunch, one for dinner). Dr. Kempner believes salt is our main enemy. No diet drinks are allowed because of the sodium content. Permissible drinks are decaffeinated coffee and tea, water, and their own lemonade.

Once your sodium count is down, usually after four weeks, a special tomato sauce for the rice is substituted for two of the daily fruits. Here is the recipe: Drop tomatoes in boiling water for five minutes. Drain, peel, and chop coarsely. Put into pot with green pepper and scallions or onions. Use over rice.

The next stage of the diet substitutes two vegetables at lunch and two at dinner for the rice. There is no fruit at this stage. Vegetables are cooked until limp (Southern style) and include carrots, broccoli, brussels sprouts, collards, butternut squash, yellow squash, baked onions, zucchini, and tomato sauce. A baked potato is considered a vegetable and may be substituted for two vegetables.

The final stage of the diet consists of protein three times a week (chicken or fish) and a small tossed salad. This stage is Dr. Kempner's way of preparing his patients for the outside world. It should be mentioned here that if a patient's sodium count goes back up, the patient is back to the regimen of phase one—rice and raw fruits. Meals are served at tables by waitresses, and selections are made from the menu. Fresh lemon slices are always on the table along with ZeroCal, a sugar substitute. A multivitamin is taken daily. Mealtimes are the only time the program participants are all together. The average weight loss is 20–25 pounds per month.

GUEST POPULATION: Coed. About 150 patients. This program is for the seriously obese person. The Kempner Clinic does not like to be thought of as a "spa."

PACKAGES AND MINIMUM STAYS: There is no minimum stay required. But people with 200 or 300 pounds to lose will often stay a year or a year and a half. Others who may have only 60 pounds to lose will stay perhaps three months. In any event, you "should be prepared to stay without interruption until you have reached a normal weight level" according to the following chart:

DR. KEMPNER'S WEIGHT CHART

Women Height	Weight Should Be Below (Pounds, Fully Dressed)	Men Height	Weight Should Be Below (Pounds, Fully Dressed)
4'11"	91	5'2"	110
5'	94	5'3"	115
5'1"	97	5'4"	120
5'2"	100	5'5"	125
5'3"	104	5'6"	130
5'4"	108	5'7"	135
5'5"	112	5'8"	140
5'6"	117	5'9"	145
5'7"	122	5'10"	150
5'8"	127	5'11"	155
5'9"	132	6'	160
5'10"	137	6'1"	165
5'11"	142	6'2"	170
6'	147	6'3"	175
		6'4"	180
		6'5"	185

DRESS CODE: None.

344   THE SPA BOOK

ACCOMMODATIONS: While on the treatment program, patients obtain accommodations in a motel, private home, or apartment in the Durham area.

HOUSE RULES: A three- to five-day medical examination is required for all before entering the program. No smoking is allowed in Rice House.

ACTIVITIES, TREATMENTS, AND PROGRAMS: The initial medical examination is done at Duke University Medical Center. All meals and daily weigh-in and blood-pressure checks are held at Rice House, a satellite facility. A urine specimen is taken twice weekly, which reveals the sodium count and whether or not the patient has adhered to the diet regimen. Exercise prescriptions are individualized and vary with the age and sex of the patient, the history of any known disabilities, and the results of a ten-flight exercise test. Daily walking is encouraged to the point of maximum tolerance in terms of comfort. Three to five hours daily of required walking is not unheard of—it's more the norm. One North Shore matron reported that her walking prescription was six miles a day. In addition to the walking, most patients join the local "Y" for additional exercise workouts such as pool class and calisthenics. There is a meeting for new patients once a month at the Rice House. The speaker is a formerly-fat alum.

STAFF POPULATION: Dr. Kempner and his associates are personally on hand for daily rounds at the Rice House. This is the time to broach any questions you might have, so make the most of it!

READMISSION PROCEDURE: Patients are encouraged to return from time to time for reevaluation and perhaps further treatment. If a patient returns to the program, initial medical-exam costs usually are lower because some tests need not be repeated.

NICE TO KNOW: One young female patient observed that in the beginning time hung heavy on her hands but it was easy to meet people at meals and make friends. Young people often gather at night spots where the college crowd hangs out for dancing, and the older group may get together and play cards and chat. All patients have the opportunity to participate in the University programs, which are plentiful. Your first three days at Durham are set aside for medical examinations and tests. During these days you can eat what you want and do what you want. Some clients rent a car and take in the sights before beginning the rigors of the program.

JUDY'S COMMENT: This is an effective program of diet and exercise, however unconventional. It should be noted that Dr. Kempner's weight charts are based on one weight for every height and do not take into account age or bone structure. His recommended weights are among the lowest I've ever seen.

It is rumored that Elvis Presley once hummed and strummed here at Dr. Kempner's and a known fact that Buddy Hackett has been in attendance.

ST. HELENA HOSPITAL AND HEALTH CENTER
Deer Park, CA 94576
800-358-9195
In California: 800-862-7575
707-963-3611

A 12-day clinical/behavioral approach to weight management, located in a separate building used for all St. Helena's health programs. Open year-round.

RATES: Expensive. Credit cards: MasterCard, Visa.

LOCATION AND TRANSPORTATION: St. Helena is 70 miles north of San Francisco in the Napa Valley, smack dab in the middle of wine country. Courtesy transportation is provided from the airport with prior arrangements.

EMPHASIS/PHILOSOPHY: This is a learn-by-doing program run by a multidisciplinary team (physicians, counselors, nutritionists, and exercise physiologists). The goal of the program, according to St. Helena Hospital, is "To help you change your eating and exercise habits and to help you learn how you can reduce tension and fatigue while changing those habits." They'll also help you plan a realistic, long-term program for self-management.

DIET PROGRAM: The weight-management program allows 750 calories per day on a portion-controlled, ovo-lacto (eggs and milk) vegetarian diet. Your first day is a 350-calorie day of primarily fruits and juices. No fish, poultry, beef, or sugar are used; clients are educated in calorie control of these foods when they return home. The diet uses low salt and NutraSweet. A typical day's menu consists of fruit, eggs, toast, nonfat milk, and bran for breakfast; Waldorf salad, Western stew, cauliflower, and cherry tomatoes for dinner (the midday meal); and split pea soup, salad plate with cottage cheese dip and broccoli, carrots, and strawberry gelatin with banana for dessert. All meals are served table service in the Center's dining room. According to one of the patient counselors, most patients lose 7 to 10 pounds during their 12-day stay.

GUEST POPULATION: Coed. About 20 patients. You must be over 18. Patients range from those with only 15 to 20 pounds to lose to the seriously obese. Spouses and companions are encouraged to join the program at reduced rates as it's most beneficial that both partners be involved and supportive.

PACKAGES AND MINIMUM STAYS: The weight-management program is 12 days. St. Helena has nine additional programs—smoking cessation, alcohol recovery, pain rehabilitation, and so on. Weekend retreats are also conducted. Arrive Sunday between noon and 2 P.M., depart Friday at 10:30 A.M.

DRESS CODE: Dress is casual.

ACCOMMODATIONS: Modern hotel-style rooms and program facilities are housed in a separate four-story wing of St. Helena community hospital. All activities, except medical examinations, are held in this area.

HOUSE RULES: No smoking allowed in buildings. Medical clearance by a staff physician is required.

PHYSICAL FACILITIES: Facilities include an outdoor pool, sauna, Jacuzzi, gymnasium, badminton court, pickleball (similar to paddleball) court, a teaching kitchen, hillside trails for walking/jogging, and a beauty shop.

ACTIVITIES, TREATMENTS, AND PROGRAMS: Medical procedures include initial review of your medical history, treadmill stress test by a cardiologist, consultation with dietician, and an individual personality assessment including personalized psychological report and daily blood pressure check if needed. Treatments include hydrotherapy and massage sessions. Daily activities include a three-mile walk, gymnastic exercise classes, and pool exercises (including water volleyball). The program includes training in relaxation exercises for stress management, biofeedback, classes on food selection and preparation, and a weight-management lecture and film series. An individualized exercise program and meal planning guide are developed for each patient to take home.

A Day at St. Helena

7:00	Three-mile walk (easy, moderate, or hard)
8:30	Breakfast
9:30	Gymnastic exercises
10:30	Pool exercise (including water volleyball)
12:00	Dinner
1:00	Lecture
3:00	Individual counseling

6:00 Supper
7:00 Lecture
8:00 Recreation (board games, group games, tour of facility)

STAFF POPULATION: A full complement of physicians, counselors, nutritionists, and exercise physiologists are on hand to serve your needs.

NICE TO KNOW: For those of you who want to stop smoking while losing weight, St. Helena can help you. Of course, the stop smoking course in conjunction with the weight-management program is not as intense as the smoking-cessation course offered by itself. The director of the kick-the-nicotine-habit programs says that in the combination program "we'll provide (1) printed material to support nonsmoking behavior; (2) meetings with an individual stop-smoking counselor on a daily basis if needed; and (3) optional chest X-rays, blood workup, and evaluation at extra cost to you." The physical fitness program is the same for both the weight-management and smoking-cessation programs.

JUDY'S COMMENT: St. Helena offers an effective behavioral base for healthy folks seeking a realistic long-term program for weight self-management. You'll also receive a real rate break for spouses, who can play an important role in reaching your goals.

* STRUCTURE HOUSE
3017 Pickett Road
Durham, NC 27705
919-688-7379

A beautiful new colonial building is the heart of the Structure House program, a clinical and psychological outpatient program for weight loss. Open year-round.

RATES: Affordable. Credit cards: MasterCard and Visa.

LOCATION AND TRANSPORTATION: Structure House is in Durham, North Carolina. Take a taxi from Raleigh-Durham airport. Some clients rent a car to use for evening or weekend touring.

EMPHASIS/PHILOSOPHY: Structure House offers an intensive program of behavioral counseling with reinforcement from a supportive atmosphere. The goals include teaching patients how to replace

Courtesy of Structure House

bad habits with constructive ones as well as learning to adapt to the world of eating reality. The staff attacks problems such as depression, anxiety, and low self-esteem that often result from excessive weight.

DIET PROGRAM: You'll receive 700 calories per day. Well-balanced, portion-controlled diet contains no salt, no sugar, and low fat. Meals consist of raw and cooked fruits and vegetables, eggs, dairy products, grains, fish, chicken, and beef. A typical day's menu might include scrambled eggs for breakfast, soup and a grilled cheese sandwich for lunch, and salad, pepper steak, and Brussels sprouts for dinner. Dietetic products are used. Menu modifications are made for vegetarians and those with special needs. All meals are served in a special dining room at Structure House.

GUEST POPULATION: Coed. 100–125 persons. The late actor James Coco and comedian Buddy Hackett are two show folks who have attended the program at Structure House.

PACKAGES AND MINIMUM STAYS: The minimum is two weeks, but a four-week stay is recommended. Sunday is check-in and check-out day.

DRESS CODE: Casual attire is acceptable at all times.

ACCOMMODATIONS: Structure House is the center for dining, exercising, and individual and group therapy. Patients may reside either at Structure House on-campus or in-town apartments. Each of the on-campus apartments has one or two bedrooms, is handsomely furnished and has a telephone, washer/dryer, color TV with HBO, linens, storage area, and weekly maid service. The in-town apartments have one bedroom (some with twin beds) but are two miles from Structure House, which may necessitate car rental. In both facilities, all utilities are included in the monthly cost. Other lodging arrangements can also be made.

HOUSE RULES: No smoking is allowed.

PHYSICAL FACILITIES: You'll find an indoor pool, exercise rooms, jogging track, and Nautilus equipment on the premises. Tennis, racquetball, golf, and "Y" facilities are nearby. (Many clients augment their exercise and walking regimen by joining the "Y.")

ACTIVITIES, TREATMENTS, AND PROGRAMS: A medical evaluation and exercise orientation are done on your first full day at Structure House. The nurse and exercise director help you chart an individual fitness regimen based on your age, weight, and state of health. The exercise program consists of a brisk daily walk, jogging, swimming, bicycling, aerobic and conditioning classes, restaurant and nutrient workshops, a calorie-portion self-test, and group discussions on depression/assertiveness, food and life processes, and the benefits of exercise. Individual exercising is encouraged during free time.

Here are some of the activities and services you may experience during your stay at Structure House:

PSYCHOLOGICAL TREATMENT

Consultation with Dr. Musante
  Psychological evaluation
  Behavior-modification training
  Group and individual psychotherapy
  Weight-control groups with Dr. Musante
  Assertiveness-training sessions
  Life-style change sessions
  Stress-management workshops
  Instruction in understanding:
    Depression
    Body image
    Environmental control
    Life and time management
    Alcohol and drugs

DIETARY REEDUCATION

Workshops and Demonstrations
  Nutrition

Misinformation
Calories and portions
Menu planning
Structured eating
Restaurant dining
Cooking
Weight loss and plateaus
Weight maintenance

EXERCISE TRAINING

Fitness testing
Individualized conditioning program
Supervised aerobic walk/jog
Monitored nonaerobic exercise
Instruction in stationary bike, weight training, trampoline, aerobic swim
Exercise classes
Water exercise

Workshops and Demonstrations:
    Benefits of exercise
    Exercise misconceptions
    Muscle-specific exercise
    Fitness and safety
    Aerobic exercise

HEALTH EDUCATION

    Evaluation of medical records
    Blood pressure monitoring
    Instruction in self-glucose monitoring
    Lab test, physical exams, and exercise stress tests
    Appointments with specialists as needed
    Instruction in cardiac risk-prevention and wellness

STAFF POPULATION: The founder and director of this program, Gerard J. Musante, Ph.D., is a clinical psychologist. Staff includes consulting physicians, psychotherapists, psychiatric social workers, a dietician, and registered nurses.

*BEST BUY AND WHY: This program is a "Best Buy" because:
    • The entire program at Structure House is geared to behavioral adaptation at home.
    • Rates are most affordable.

NICE TO KNOW: Although Structure House does not take responsibility for finding you a roommate, there is an in-house bulletin board where you can post messages to other participants. People seem to have good luck trying this approach.

JUDY'S COMMENT: A practical, take-home approach to reducing that will help you keep it off!

STUELKE INSTITUTE— THIN FOR LIFE
P.O. Box 2894
Durham, NC 27705
919-683-5547

A program for the treatment of obesity run by the founder, Dr. Richard G. Stuelke, M.D., a nationally known authority on addictive problems such as overeating. Open year-round.

RATES: Affordable. Credit cards: American Express, MasterCard, Visa.

LOCATION AND TRANSPORTATION: Located in downtown Durham, North Carolina. Limousine service is available from Raleigh-Durham airport for a fee.

EMPHASIS/PHILOSOPHY: Richard G. Stuelke, founder of the clinic, believes that obesity is the result of an addictive eating disorder, a chronic disease that requires lifelong treatment. The purpose of the clinic is threefold: (1) to involve the patient in the 12-step program of Overeaters Anonymous (both during one's stay and after returning home), (2) to use Rational Emotive Therapy counseling to train one to deal with one's feelings by ways other than eating, and (3) to place the participant on a weight-reducing diet.

DIET PROGRAM: The Institute uses Siegfried Heyden's 700-calorie-per-day "Working Man's Diet." The well-balanced portion-controlled diet features high-protein and low-carbohydrate foods. No salt is used. There are no breads and no desserts; dietetic products are used. Patients plan their menus one week ahead. Daily dinner choices include broiled chicken, broiled beef patty, or the special for the day. Patients average a 6 to 8 pound loss the first week and 2 to 5 pounds weekly thereafter.

GUEST POPULATION: Coed. 30 patients. The Institute will treat anyone with an overweight problem, from those with a few pounds to shed to the massively obese. They also treat bulimics—a first.

PACKAGES AND MINIMUM STAYS: There is no minimum, but the Institute prefers you stay until you reach your desired weight, which usually takes four to eight weeks. The weekly program runs Monday through Sunday, but a patient can enter any weekday.

DRESS CODE: Very casual.

ACCOMMODATIONS: The Thin for Life Institute conducts its program at the Imperial 400 motel in Durham and suggests that participants reside there. However, guests are free to stay at the Radisson Inn nearby or find other accommodations.

PHYSICAL FACILITIES: The Imperial 400 has an outdoor pool, exercise rooms, and a beauty salon.

ACTIVITIES, TREATMENTS, AND PROGRAMS: Medical supervision and testing includes medical history, laboratory tests (blood work, chemistries, urinalysis, electrocardiogram, and psychological testing), daily check-in and medical consultation. The exercise program includes daily one-hour sessions of walking, aerobics, and water aerobics. Patients are encouraged to join the local "Y." Morning lectures are held three times weekly on such topics as diabetes and dealing with high blood pressure. Group therapy sessions on the problems of food addiction are held twice a week. Patients attend evening meetings of Overeaters Anonymous.

A Day at the Institute

8:00	Breakfast
9:00	Group therapy
10:30	Aerobics
12:00	Lunch
1:00	Water aerobics
3:00	Daily walk
5:30	Dinner
7:30	Overeaters Anonymous meetings

STAFF POPULATION: Dr. Stuelke is the resident physician, assisted by a full-time nurse and a psychologist.

NICE TO KNOW: The Institute uses Rational Emotive Therapy, based on the work of Dr. Albert Ellis, in helping people overcome overeating behavior. Ellis believes one must do away with the notion of absolute rules and "shoulds" in one's thinking. For further information on the therapy, talk with Dr. Stuelke before checking in.

JUDY'S COMMENTS: The diet is sound and effective, but the responsibility for success is yours—and that's how it "should" be.

UNIVERSITY HEALTH CENTER AT PALM-AIRE
2501 Palm-Aire Drive North
Pompano Beach, FL 33069
800-327-4960
305-972-3300

This center has a wellness program that combines good nutrition, exercise, and stress reduction. The University Health Center and The Spa at Palm-Aire (see "Resort Spas") are both located on the magnificent grounds of the Palm-Aire Resort. They share some facilities. Open year-round.

RATES: Expensive. Credit cards: American Express, Diners Club, MasterCard, Visa.

LOCATION AND TRANSPORTATION: The Center is 30 minutes north of Fort Lauderdale/Hollywood International and 1 hour north of Miami International Airport and West Palm Beach. No airport service is provided, but taxis are readily available.

EMPHASIS/PHILOSOPHY: The University Health Center at Palm-Aire is a personalized wellness program, developed by a physician from Tufts University, to evaluate, educate, and motivate positive behavior. The program focuses on weight control, exercise, and life-style changes. It provides the participant with the tools to develop an improved, energetic, healthier life-style. The program consists of weight management, personalized eating plan, nutrition information, individual and group exercise programs. Relaxation methods to relieve stress and tension, techniques for improving life-style, personal counseling, group seminars, evaluation, and follow-up are included.

DIET PROGRAM: You will ingest approximately 800 calories per day if you are a woman, 1,000 if a man. During the first week of the plan, you receive an individualized menu for calorie control to achieve your ideal body weight. Nutritionists explain how to shop for, prepare, and serve healthy food once you return home. Your menu during the weeks you attend are based on your medical tests, background, need for weight loss, etc. Calorie counts are on the menus.

GUEST POPULATION: Coed. About 80 guests are in the wellness program, broken down to include approximately 30 men and 10 to 15 couples.

PACKAGES AND MINIMUM STAYS: The program requires a minimum stay of 13 days and 14 nights.

MEAL SERVICE: Both informal and formal/casual restaurants are available. A hot-lunch buffet is available as well as elegant sit-down meals for evenings. Because there is a full-service hotel adjacent to the spa, all types of meals are served and the restaurants are open to the public. Hostess seating is provided, and fresh flowers and elegant china grace the tables.

DRESS CODE: Informal to formal. A spa wardrobe is provided, but many people bring additional exercise clothing, leotards, and tights. Many guests are very informal, but some like to get dressed up to go to the restaurants in the evening. Jacket and tie are not required. Jogging outfits are acceptable for lunch and breakfast. Bring your bathing suit!

ACCOMMODATIONS: Guests stay in luxurious, designer-coordinated rooms, which are frequently redecorated. Telephones, TVs, private baths, air conditioning, and daily maid service are provided. Spa and wellness guests are housed together in a separate wing from other hotel patrons and condo owners.

HOUSE RULES: No smoking is permitted in the spa and in other designated areas. The separate hotel, however, houses non-spa guests, so smoking as well as alcohol are permitted.

PHYSICAL FACILITIES: Accommodations are at the beautiful Palm-Aire Hotel in a separate section for spa and wellness program guests. A full-service beauty shop is on the premises, as are three boutiques selling everything from evening to active wear and a sundry shop for small supplies. There are separate men's and women's spa facilities, but a coed gym is available. Some people say this place has the best and most extensive water program in the country. You'll find a golf course, 3 racquetball courts, 37 tennis courts, separate men's and women's pools plus a coed pool, 12 facial rooms, 9 herbal-wrap rooms for women, and 23 massage rooms. Additionally, there is a jogging track, plunge pools, 8 Jacuzzis, and a sauna. This place combines weight control with the total spa experience!

ACTIVITIES, TREATMENTS, AND PROGRAMS: Upon arrival, medical and blood tests are done. Further tests determine what your individual exercise plan will be and what your diet program will consist of. The full exercise package is tailored to your level of ability and needs: low, intermediate, or advanced. Daily activities include the following: choice of four exercise classes, aromatherapy, herbal wrap, whirlpool, massage, and a facial. Massages are half-hour and aroma therapy is one hour long. When you leave, a health and exercise plan (including your own videotape) individualized to your continuing good health habits, is provided.

A Day at the University Health Center

7:30–8:15	Walk/jog
8:30–9:00	Breakfast
9:00–10:00	Nutrition group session
10:00–10:50	Exercise circuit class
11:00–11:30	Personal service
11:45–12:45	Life-style group session
1:00–1:45	Lunch
2:00–4:00	Exercise and personal service options:
	Exercise classes
	Tennis
	Golf
	Swimming
	Personal services (massage, sauna, whirlpool, etc.)
4:00–6:00	Individual sessions (30 minutes)
	Nutrition
	Life-style
	Exercise
	Personal services
6:30–7:30	Dinner
8:00–9:00	Evening activities:
	Lecture
	Seminar
	Discussions
	Movies
	Field trips

STAFF POPULATION: There is a full-time physician on staff, a full-time registered nurse, a dietician and a life-style counselor.

NICE TO KNOW: This is a personalized wellness program that strives to give you new knowledge and behavioral guidelines for life. Thus, the attention is paid to positive behavior and life-style adaptations rather than just losing a "few pounds." Evaluation and follow-up on participants helps to keep motivation high. Each class is small, with no more than 10–12 participants. Spouse or companion involvement is encouraged to help the participant maintain his or her new way of life. Other Palm-Aire activities, such as tennis or golf, are available for those companions who do not wish to participate in the wellness program; meals can be taken with the wellness participant.

JUDY'S COMMENT: The University Health Center is an unusual mix of spa fun and pampering and serious weight-loss attention. If you can afford it, go for it!

356 THE SPA BOOK

THE WHITAKER WELLNESS INSTITUTE
21112 Pacific Coast Highway
Huntington Beach, CA 92648
714-851-1550

A 12-day, medically supervised, residential program located on the grounds of a retirement community, two miles from the Pacific.

RATES: Expensive. No credit cards.

LOCATION AND TRANSPORTATION: The Institute is 45 miles south of Los Angeles and 20 minutes from Long Beach airport. Limousine service is available from there and from LAX for a charge.

EMPHASIS/PHILOSOPHY: This residential program is for sufferers of degenerative conditions such as heart disease, diabetes, and high blood pressure. Obesity and its attendant problems also respond well to the diet and exercise program. "This structured environment is geared to produce the maximum beneficial changes in the shortest amount of time through diet and exercise," says Julian M. Whitaker, M.D., founder and director of the Institute.

DIET PROGRAM: This diet is based on the Pritikin diet, with the addition of vitamin supplements. Calories are not counted on the diet that has the following components: 73 to 80 percent complex carbohydrates (vegetables, fruits, and starchy foods such as whole grain cereals, brown rice, and pasta); 12 percent protein; 6 to 12 percent natural fat; and 2 to 5 percent natural sugars. (The typical American diet consists of 40 percent fat although the American Heart Association recommends that fat intake be kept below 35 percent.) No added fats, salt, sugar, whole milk products, or processed foods (white flour) are used. No caffeine, salt, or artificial sweeteners are used. Vitamin supplements are taken with meals. Patients typically lose 8 to 10 pounds a month on the program. All meals are sit-down, served occasions.

GUEST POPULATION: As noted, this program is geared primarily to those patients with specific medical problems. It accommodates 11 patients plus spouses or companions, for a total of 22 people. Spouses and companions receive special rate consideration.

PACKAGES AND MINIMUM STAYS: The basic program is 12 days; arrive Sunday afternoon, begin on Monday, and check out at noon the following Friday. The actual program is conducted Mondays through Fridays with weekends free. There is also a 5-day program and a 1-day assessment for those pressed for time.

DRESS CODE: Casual.

ACCOMMODATIONS: The Institute is a self-contained environment with accommodations, exercise facilities, dining room, and clinic all under the same roof. All guest rooms contain a private bath.

HOUSE RULES: No smoking.

PHYSICAL FACILITIES: These include an exercise room with stationary bicycles, electric treadmills, rebounders, and miles of walking/jogging trails.

ACTIVITIES, TREATMENTS, AND PROGRAMS: Medical procedures include a complete physical examination with emphasis on the cardiovascular system, blood chemistry evaluation, daily weigh-in and blood pressure check, weekly monitoring of blood chemistries, consultations twice weekly with a physician, and all nutritional supplements. The Monday-through-Friday exercise program consists of walking/jogging, minitrampoline exercises, and aerobic exercise classes. Individual exercise programs are prescribed by a physician and are reevaluated every few days as tolerance is increased. Each guest uses an oxygen mask daily for half an hour to reduce the effects of atherosclerosis.

Daily programs consist of lectures on such health-related topics as protein myths and the cholesterol controversy (the recommended amount of fat in the American diet). Lectures by nutritionists are held three times weekly, covering such topics as food preparation (no cooking demonstrations), how to shop for food, and how to read food labels intelligently. After-dinner lectures by guest speakers and movies are held nightly, but your weekends are free of scheduled activities.

A Day at the Institute

8:00	Weigh-in, blood-pressure check
8:30	Breakfast
9:30	Lecture
10:30	Aerobic exercises
12:00	Lunch
1:00	Oxygen therapy
2:00	Food-preparation lecture
4:30	Biofeedback; stress-reduction techniques
5:30	Dinner
7:00	Movie

STAFF POPULATION: The Institute is run by Julian M. Whitaker, M.D., a former surgeon and staff physician at the Pritikin Longevity Center in California.

NICE TO KNOW: Dr. Whitaker predicts that those participating in the 12-day program will experience a 10 to 30 percent lowering of blood cholesterol level, a significant drop in blood pressure, and a significant improvement in angina and diabetes with reduction or cessation of medication (where warranted). Dr. Whitaker's book, *Reversing Heart Disease* (Warner Books, 1985), emphasizes the treatment of cardiac problems without surgery.

JUDY'S COMMENT: Not an original diet approach, but an effective program in lowering blood cholesterol and improving cardiovascular health.

FIVE

LIFE-STYLE MODIFICATION

10
TAKING HOME
THE SPA SPIRIT

Back home again! You're pounds lighter and inches smaller. You're recharged, revitalized, and all those other wonderful "Rs" I promised you at the beginning of this book.

Now what? Reality! One week, you're in the never-never land of Jacuzzis, strawberry facials, exercise machines, and mind-expansion moods beside a quiet mountain stream. The next week, the oven needs cleaning and the children beckon and the boss has a dozen projects for you.

It's not surprising that people get results at spas and other health havens. After all, they have nothing to think about but reducing and relaxing. There are ready-made diet and exercise programs to help them, a supportive staff, and fellow fleshfighters to cheer them on.

The real test comes when you leave that sheltered scene. You're probably not able to hire a full-time beautician, fitness director, and dietician. But it's really not expertise that you need in order to extend the health-seeking experience to your everyday life. It's your attitude—and fortitude.

A healthy mind and body are the prizes we all hope to capture at a health establishment. But you'll lose those benefits if you revert to your old habits and frame of mind. Pounds and inches can creep back fast. A new, healthier life-style is the answer!

A week or a month at a health farm can be more than a sharp break from your everyday routines or a desperate shortcut to quick weight loss. It can be the start of a long-term fitness program. It can also help you zero in on attitudes that have prevented you from becoming the robust, attractive person you could be. Your true goal should be to come away with a carry-over regimen that helps you attain—and maintain—a healthier way of life. Then, your trip will become the smartest investment you ever made!

THE TRUTH IS HARD TO SWALLOW

Let's face it: dieting is no picnic. As movie star Arlene Dahl has said, "The feeling of hunger is indispensable to a successful diet." And you're probably going to have to live with that feeling for quite a while.

Furthermore, if you're like most people, you won't keep the weight off for long without some special tricks. According to Dr. Gabe Mirkin, author of *Getting Thin*, the chances of keeping lost weight off for a year are only one in ten. After 5 years, the odds drop to one in twenty.

Why are so few of us successful in maintaining weight loss? Because we literally have to fight our bodies. For one thing, Dr. Mirkin says, when we cut our caloric intake, our metabolic rate slows down. It's the body's way of defending itself against starvation, but it also makes it harder to burn up calories. What's more, according to Dr. William Bennett and Joel Gurin, authors of *The Dieter's Dilemma*, your body has a sort of inner thermostat that keeps gravitating back toward a set amount of fat.

But you can fool your body and reset that inner thermostat. A brisk half-hour walk or run each day can hype your metabolism so that you'll burn calories faster the rest of the day. Aerobic exercise is the other side of your double-barreled attack on fat. The simple truth is that you'll lose weight only when you work off more calories than you consume.

To lose weight, eat less and exercise more. To maintain your weight, eat just a smidgen more, but exercise accordingly. That's especially true as you get older, when your metabolism slows down and you have to work all the harder to burn up calories.

As we've seen, different people have different metabolic rates. Fat people and older people burn up their food more slowly than do young, skinny types. Fortunately, however, your rate is not carved in stone. Moderate aerobic exercise thrice weekly, will serve to increase your metabolic rate and make dieting more effective.

In fact, proper aerobic exercise can cut your dieting time in half. Here's how it works—if you cut out 300 calories a day, you'll normally lose one pound in about ten days. Now, suppose you cut your daily caloric intake by 300 and burn up an additional 300 calories through exercise. Result—you'll lose that pound in five days instead of ten, and feel better while you do it.

FITTING IN A FITNESS ROUTINE

The best exercise program for you is the one you will fulfill every day, that you find pleasant or at least tolerable, and that fits your lifestyle. Scheduling regular exercise time is as important as picking the right kind of exercise, and timing can be more challenging. It may take some experimentation before you settle on a system that doesn't disrupt your life.

If you are the exercise-alone type and can afford to invest in equipment, you might want to order an Exercycle, Lifecycle, or tread-mill through your local sporting goods store. If you're a social exer-ciser, join a health club that's not too far away or too expensive. You might even consider taking classes at your local park district.

What's the best time of day to exercise? Experts disagree. Some say midday when your body is performing at its peak—fully awake and not yet fatigued. Many people follow through most faithfully in the early morning. On the other hand, evening exercise can release the day's tensions. Do what feels best for you.

CREATE YOUR OWN HEALTH ENVIRONMENT
AT HOME OR AWAY

Each time I go to a health resort, a transformation takes place. I arrive weary and worn out. When I leave, fellow guests comment that my eyes are bright and I have a bounce to my step and a glow of happi-ness, energy, and well-being.

That glow can last. It need not fade, since you can create your own fitness experiences at home and even when you're on the road. Traveling need not interfere with an exercise regimen; in fact it's even more important to keep up your program if you're dining out a lot, as most of us do when we're away from home.

Wherever I go, I pack my jump rope, jogging shoes, shorts, sweatpants, ankle weights, and a sports bra—I'm always set! My hus-band and I have walked the parks of Washington, D.C., the palace grounds of Tokyo, and the beaches of Bali. Six o'clock in the morning is a magic time to be up and active while most of the world sleeps. And be advised, there are few better ways to get acquainted with a foreign city than an early morning run through its streets.

MODERATION, BALANCE, HARMONY, AND JOY

Losing weight and keeping it off is a more active process than many of us care to admit. It's an ongoing daily struggle, like wrestling with an inner devil. But you can win—and what a wonderful sense of power that gives you. You can feel deliciously smug when your stom-ach has shrunk and you are literally not capable of eating the huge portions you ate before.

What you do every day, not counting your occasional binges and backsliding or even your health escapes, determines your physical, mental, and spiritual state. Your health is in your own hands. And, please, no extremes. The Duchess of Windsor was wrong when she said, "You can never be too rich or too thin." As we all know, being too thin is a sign of illness. Anything taken to an extreme is un-healthy.

The ancient Greeks spoke of moderation as the Golden Mean,

and it's a good motto for modern health-pilgrims. Eat moderately, exercise moderately, and you'll be well on the road to good health and beauty.

If you learn to monitor and balance your food intake and exercise output, you won't have to bother counting calories. Just gauge your daily activity level: "I did a lot today—I can have a little more for dinner"; or, "I've been sitting all day—better go light on lunch."

Fasting once a week is ideal for weight maintenance and cleansing, but it's difficult to do when you're responsible for serving meals to a household. If you live alone or if your spouse goes away on business, you might wish to set aside a special day just for you. Drink herbal tea, Hauser's or Dr. Jensen's Vegetable Broth, fresh lemon and water, and fruit juices. (Low-cal sodas are all right, but check the sodium content.) Alternate hot with cold liquids to stave off boredom. Retire early—away from the refrigerator—equipped with those books you've been meaning to catch up on, and treat yourself to a dry-brush massage and an herbal bath. Light a scented candle and turn on soft music. Sink in and let your tense, aching muscles unwind. That deep relaxation is your reward for a day well spent.

Where does harmony come in? It's the feeling you get when you're in tune with nature and yourself, when you've balanced your life with equal parts of movement, relaxation, and proper nutrition. You've achieved harmony when you look in your mirror and like the person who looks back, when you feel in every pore and nerve ending that it's joyful to be alive!

APPENDIX

POSH SPAS

WOMEN-ONLY SPAS

An asterisk indicates that the facility has occasional men-only or coed sessions.

FASTING SPAS

SPAS WITH FULL-TIME STAFF M.D.

Most Medical Weight-Control Centers

GEOGRAPHICAL
INDEXES

OUTSIDE THE U.S.

GENERAL INDEX

Best Buys are in caps.

B = Beauty Spa
M = Medical Weight-Control Center
MS = Mineral Springs
N = Natural Health Retreat
R = Resort Spa
S = Structured Spa

YOUR COMMENTS

Suggestions, information, and ideas are very welcome in the interest of keeping this book current and useful. We especially appreciate hearing from those of you who have visited spas and can provide data based on personal experience. Address the author in care of Spa Resource Ltd., Box 456, Glencoe, IL 60022.

NOTES:

To enter the sweepstakes, please fill in the information below and return it to:

THE SPA BOOK SWEEPSTAKES
The Putnam Publishing Group
Department SPA
200 Madison Avenue
New York, NY 10016

No purchase necessary. Void where prohibited by law. For complete rules, see below.

Name_____

Address_____

City/State_____Zip_____

Phone (   )_____

          Area code

Mail this entry form no later than March 20, 1989. A plain 3″ by 5″ piece of paper with the requested information may be used in lieu of the official entry form.

- -

WINNER WILL RECEIVE: A five-day and four-night stay at The Norwich Inn and Spa (not including personal expenses). Transportation will be provided to and from the Inn. *No purchase necessary.*

- -

OFFICIAL RULES

1. On an official entry form or plain 3″ by 5″ piece of paper, hand-print your name, address, and telephone number, and mail your entry in a hand-addressed envelope (#10 size) to THE SPA BOOK SWEEPSTAKES, The Putnam Publishing Group, Department SPA, 200 Madison Avenue, New York, NY 10016. No mechanical reproductions of entries are permitted.

2. Enter as often as you wish, but each entry must be mailed separately. The winner will be determined on April 1, 1989, in a random drawing from among all entries. The winner will be notified by mail.

3. This sweepstakes is open to all U.S. and Canadian (excluding Quebec) residents 18 years of age or older. If a resident of Canada is selected in the drawing, he or she will be required to answer correctly a skill question to claim the prize. Void where prohibited. Employees (and their families) of The Putnam Publishing Group, MCA, their respective affiliates, retailers, distributors, and advertising, promotion, and production agencies are not eligible.

4. Taxes, if any, are the sole responsibility of the prize-winner. Winner will be required to sign and return a liability/promotional release within 14 days of notification. Names and likenesses of the winner and companion may be used for promotional purposes.

5. Travel and accommodations are subject to space and departure availability. Reservations, once made, are *final* and may not be rescheduled thereafter. Certain travel restrictions may apply, including specific blackout dates during peak travel periods. All travel must be completed by April 30, 1990. No substitution of prizes is permitted. Prizes are nontransferrable.

6. For the name of the prize-winner, send a self-addressed, stamped envelope to: THE SPA SWEEPSTAKES, The Putnam Publishing Group, Department SPA, 200 Madison Avenue, New York, NY 10016.